CANCER CHEMOTHERAPY:
A Guide for Practice

SUSAN HOLMES

Second Edition

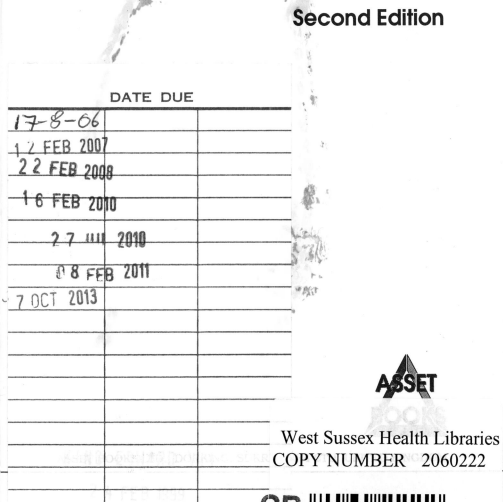

DATE DUE

17-8-06	
1 2 FEB 2007	
2 2 FEB 2008	
1 6 FEB 2010	
2 7 JUL 2010	
0 8 FEB 2011	
7 OCT 2013	

ASSET

GAYLORD   PRINTED IN USA

CR

Asset Books Ltd
1 Paper Mews, 330 High Street,
Dorking, Surrey RH4 2TU

First published in 1988 by Austen Cornish Ltd in association with
the Lisa Sainsbury Foundation

This edition published in 1997 by Asset Books Ltd

A catalogue record for this book is available from the British Library.

ISBN 1 9001 79 11 3

Some illustrations prepared by Simon Ward

Printed and bound in Great Britain by Hobbs the Printer Ltd

CONTENTS

PREFACE

The aim of this book is to provide the fundamental principles underlying the use of cancer chemotherapy in the treatment for malignant disease. It must be recognised, however, that not all cancer centres or units will follow exactly the same policy with regard to chemotherapeutic techniques. For this reason readers are advised to check on local policy with regard to the procedures employed.

Throughout this book the female gender has been used to refer to nurses, and other health care practitioners, of both sexes and the male gender to describe the patient, unless specific examples require otherwise.

Neither the Publishers nor the Author wish to offend or in any other way discriminate against either male health care professionals or female patients but have chosen to use this convention so as to avoid the cumbersome use of gender whenever a nurse or patient is discussed. This system has been chosen since, at present, the majority of health care workers in the UK, particularly nurses, are women.

Susan Holmes
Leatherhead, Surrey
July 1997

INTRODUCTION

The use of chemicals to kill cells (ie. that are cytotoxic) is a comparatively recent form of cancer treatment and so is subject to continuous change and development as new and more effective drugs and methods of administration are introduced, all with the same aim - to cure cancer. The advantage of cytotoxic drugs over other methods of treatment, such as surgery or radiotherapy, is their ability to destroy malignant cells throughout the body and not just at the site of the primary tumour. The disadvantage is that such drugs are relatively non-selective as they cannot discriminate between malignant and non-malignant cells so that they often damage normal tissues as well as tumour cells. The extent of such damage depends on a variety of different factors, amongst which are the dose, time, and route of administration and the ability of normal tissues to repair cellular damage more rapidly and more effectively than cancer cells. Much of the skill of the cancer chemotherapist comes from a knowledge of the effects of cytotoxic drugs on normal tissues and the ways in which the harmful, toxic effects can be ameliorated.

Future developments, such as the use of monoclonal antibodies and/or photodynamic therapy, may mean that cytotoxic agents can be 'targeted' directly at malignant cells or activated at the site of the tumour. At present, however, this is not the case and side-effects are an almost inevitable consequence of such treatment. These can be difficult for the patient to tolerate and there is much truth in belief that, in some cases at least, the treatment is worse than the disease itself.

Chemotherapy is used to treat a significant proportion of cancer patients. It may be the primary form of treatment or be used as an adjunct to surgery or radiotherapy and be used with either curative or palliative intent.

Patients undergoing chemotherapy are often very vulnerable since it may be employed as an initial treatment, immediately following diagnosis, or as the last in a long line of debilitating treatments. As a result, many fears and anxieties may affect not only the patient but also his family and friends. Skilled care is, therefore, required. This cannot be successfully achieved unless the carers themselves understand the principles underlying this method of treatment.

CHAPTER 1   THE PAST AND THE FUTURE

Although cancer is often thought of as a 'modern disease' it clearly dates back to prehistoric times. The earliest evidence of cancer comes from ancient Egyptian and Greek civilisations (Shimkin, 1977); indeed, malignant disease was documented in Egyptian mummies over 5000 years ago (Pack and Ariel, 1968). There is also evidence of early treatments for both benign and malignant tumours. There is, for example, description of the use of metallic salts (eg. zinc, silver, copper, lead) in attempts to treat malignancy (Pack and Ariel, 1968) and Cline and Haskell (1980) report that effective therapy is a comparatively recent development; it was not until 1865 that Lissauer reported the benefits of potassium arsenite in treating leukaemia and 1878 when Cutler and Bradford reported a return to a normal white cell count in 'leucocythaemia'. Arsenic remained the accepted treatment for chronic myeloid leukaemia (CML) falling into disuse only after the discovery of X-irradiation (Zubrod, 1979). Even today, heavy metals (eg. platinum) are the mainstay of treatment for many solid tumours.

In 1946, Haddow and Sexton reported the antitumour effects of urethane, demonstrating its benefits in treating CML in both animals and man (Paterson et al, 1946); others used it successfully to treat multiple myeloma (Alwell, 1947; Loge and Rundles, 1949). At the same time, drug research expanded to include hormonal agents and effective and reliable treatment for carcinoma of the prostate and breast was reported (Huggins and Hodges, 1941; Haddow et al, 1944) thus laying the foundations of current treatments of, for example, some tumours of the breast and prostate.

The years between 1940 and 1955 were the most exciting in terms of drug development although many of the drugs identified originated from research directed towards rather different objectives. For example, nitrogen mustard originated with chemical warfare, methotrexate from the study of folic acid metabolism and actinomycin-D from tuberculosis research (Zubrod, 1979). From such work, it became clear that drugs could be used to cause regression of human cancers. The foundations of a deliberate search for anticancer drugs were laid and extensive drug development programmes were established in both the UK and the United States.

The next three decades saw rapid developments. The increased resources made available for drug development, combined with an increased interest in the chemotherapeutic approach to cancer treatment, led to the discovery of several important drugs (eg. vinca alkaloids, procarbazine) although, again, interest was aroused from outside cancer research. For example, the periwinkle (*vinca roseus*), believed to induce hypoglycaemia (Noble, 1961), was a traditional folk remedy for diabetes. However, in 1955, animal studies showed that not only did periwinkle extracts cause hypoglycaemia but also leucopoenia (Beer, 1955) leading, in turn, to the isolation of vinblastine (Noble, 1961). A variety of alkaloids were then identified, the most important being vincristine and vinblastine (Neuss et al, 1959) and, more recently, vindesine and vinorelbine. This stimulated the search for other plant-based cytotoxic substances and extracts of thousands of plants have been screened for anticancer activity resulting, for example, in the identification of taxanes, isolated from the Pacific yew (Wani et al, 1971), and precursors of paclitaxel (the active agent) from other yew species, (eg. the European yew) (Dennis and Greene, 1988).

Studies in other areas continued to contribute to the development of anticancer drugs. For example, studies into monoamine oxidase inhibitors lead to discovery of procarbazine (Zeller et al, 1963) while cytosine arabinoside was derived from interest in the biological activities of sponges (Cohen, 1963). Asparaginase was isolated from *Escherichia coli* laying the foundation for the use of enzymes in cancer therapy. 'Traditional' antibiotic research led to identification of the antitumour antibiotics (eg. Arcamone et al, 1968; Tan et al, 1965) and cisplatin was discovered during studies of electric fields and bacteria (Rosenberg et al, 1965). Unusually, fluorouracil came directly from biochemical research (Rutman et al, 1954) when it was predicted that the fluorinated derivatives of uracil would be effective antitumour agents (Heidelberger et al, 1957). Such drugs were quickly entered into screening programmes.

MILESTONES IN THE TREATMENT OF METASTATIC DISEASE

Although, during the '50s and '60s, thirty or more new drugs were discovered and evaluated, other developments occurred and, after early experimentation with combinations of drugs, it was possible to consider the control or cure of metastatic disease. For example, early attempts at treating metastatic choriocarcinoma (Li et al, 1956) and Burkitt's lymphoma (Oettgen et al, 1963a; 1963b) were extremely successful; use of intermittent doses of single agents thus raised the hope that cure could be achieved in other tumours. However, despite continuing development and evaluation of new drugs, success was limited.

Until this time, despite the considerable success of combination therapy in treating bacterial infections, drug combinations were rarely used in cancer therapy. Of particular importance was the work of Frei et al (1965) demonstrating that a combination of methotrexate and 6-mercaptopurine produced a greater percentage of complete remission in leukaemia-B than did either drug when given alone and that of Selawry and Frei (1964) revealing that prednisone and vincristine, given together, were remarkably active in inducing remission. From such work, the concept that drugs with differing toxicities, could be combined to enhance tumour cell kill with less damage to normal cells, particularly bone marrow, emerged (Zubrod, 1979). This enabled increased attempts at cure while minimising deleterious toxicity, providing the basis of many of the drug combinations used today, and resulted in long-term remission, more effective prevention of drug resistance and increasingly tolerable side-effects at maximal doses (eg. Krakoff, 1977; Murinson, 1981).

Another innovative approach was that of adjuvant therapy based on recognition that, despite surgery and/or radiation, many cancers recur, probably due to undetected metastases (Ch. 5). Farber et al (1960) were amongst the first to recognise that drugs, combined with surgery or radiotherapy, might be useful in controlling metastatic disease and preventing recurrence by eradicating any remaining malignant cells wherever they occurred (Ch. 5). Research was then directed towards the use of adjuvant therapy and Simpson-Herren et al (1974) provided excellent reasons why this should be effective since metastatic deposits are generally 'younger' than the primary tumour and have a larger growth fraction which, in theory at least, makes them more susceptible to complete eradication.

The use of chemotherapy primarily evolved from a need to treat disseminated disease. Adjuvant therapy has proved to be highly successful in treating certain tumours (eg. Wilm's tumour, osteosarcoma, Ewing's sarcoma and non-seminomatous testicular cancer).

Despite such successes, the goal remains that of identifying drugs which will, when administered after localised treatment, eradicate any remaining malignant cells, wherever they are deposited. Investigation of this approach to treatment continues.

FUTURE PERSPECTIVES

There is little doubt that, historically, the search for effective drugs capable of curing cancer has often seemed impossible and it is interesting to note that many such discoveries have been a by-product of other areas of research. It is fortunate that the researchers had the foresight to recognise that their work might have potential in other fields, such as cancer chemotherapy.

However, the continuing search for new drugs, and new methods of administering existing agents, holds hope for the future. In the meantime, the role of drugs continues to evolve. In general, however, although advances continue to be made, the greatest of these have not been in the discovery of large numbers of new cytotoxic agents but rather in the design of improved regimens for the concurrent use of two or more drugs, or new methods of administration designed to prevent or minimise toxicity. At the same time the use of adjuvant chemotherapy has increased as knowledge about the initiation and growth of tumours is gained.

Many areas of enquiry into the clinical uses of cytotoxic agents remain. For example, the testing of new drugs continues and many are administered to cancer patients in clinical trials directed towards identifying the optimal dose, timing, route of administration and toxic side-effects; other studies then follow to determine which tumours are most responsive to which drug (Ch. 17). The efficacy of such drugs, in combination with either other drugs or other methods of treatment (eg. surgery, radiotherapy or biotherapy), is evaluated the aim being to assess and measure the effect of that drug on the survival of patients with particular tumours. At the same time, the 'old' drugs are being used in new and innovative ways. For example, both autologous bone marrow transplantation and colony stimulating factors may be used as adjuncts to chemotherapy allowing use of doses of drugs, previously not thought to be possible (Ch. 9).

There is mounting evidence that the use of recombinant haemo-poietic growth factors can mitigate the bone marrow toxicity of anti-cancer therapy (Kaufman and Chabner, 1996). Both granulocyte colony-stimulating factor (G-CSF) and granulocyte-macrophage colony-stimulating factor (GM-CSF) have been shown to be capable of reducing the incidence of infectious complications and the require-ment for hospitalisation during chemotherapy (Petros and Peters, 1996) (Ch. 9). Erythropoietin has been used to reduce anaemia (eg. Abels, 1992) although further work is clearly required to understand its kinetics and to clarify its role as an adjunctive therapy (Petros and Peters, 1996). New agents are being sought; research into the most appropriate use of such agents is continuing.

However, one major problem remains with most of the currently available antineoplastic drugs, that of a lack of specificity. Thus, although they can destroy malignant cells, such drugs continue to inflict damage on normal cell populations. This limits their clinical usefulness. Thus considerable research is directed towards ways of overcoming such problems although, to date, many are still in the developmental stages and it may be some time before they will be of any true benefit to the patient.

One such development is that of photodynamic therapy which differs from conventional treatment as the drugs, once given, need to be activated by light (usually from a laser) thus, by directing light specifically at the tumour, some degree of selectivity can be obtained (Moan and Berg, 1992). To date, this approach has been based on the use of natural pigments (primarily porphyrins) which are known to be selective for tumours and which are also phototoxic (Wainwright and Phoenix, 1995). When exposed to light, such pigments become electronically excited leading to the formation of free radicals and cytotoxicity within the cells (Amato, 1993). Thus, depending on the location of the photosensitiser, various parts of the cell may be damaged (eg. DNA and RNA) (Wainwright and Phoenix, 1995).

Further developments will focus on the use of biological response modifiers (Table 1.1) which modify the biological response to the presence of tumour cells (Mihich and Fefer, 1983). If such effects can be harnessed, making it possible to modulate the immune system to destroy malignant cells, biotherapy is likely to become a prominent treatment for cancer (Hood and Abernathy, 1991). One of the most promising of such approaches is that of drug targeting. Improved understanding of the biological processes involved in cancer cell proliferation, combined with technological advances permitting manipulation of nucleic acids and proteins, has enabled significant research in this area.

Substances such as monoclonal antibodies, antisense oligo-nucleotides, expressed genes and peptidomimetics have been studied (Table 1.2). However, although the concept of targeting a specific molecule in treating cancer is a simple one there are still many limitations in practice.

Table 1.1   Biological response modifiers

Agent	Mode(s) of action
Lymphokines (eg. interleukin-2, interferon-γ)	Immunomodulation.
Tumour necrosis factor	Direct cytotoxic or cytostatic effects.
Interferon or interferon inducers	Immunomodulation; direct cytotoxic or cyto-static effects.
Non-specific immunomodulating agents (eg. bacille Calmette-Guérin, *Corynebacterium parvum*	Immunomodulation.
Adoptive immunotherapy	Immunomodulation.
Active specific immunisation with tumour cells	Immunomodulation.
Growth factors (G-CSF, GM-CSF, erythropoietin)	Other biological effects (eg. bone marrow stimulation).

The production of monoclonal antibodies holds great promise for the development of treatments specific for a variety of cancers (Hood and Abernathy, 1991) permitting highly-specific antibodies to selected antigens to be produced from a single immortalised cell of the immune system (ie. monoclonal antibodies). Monoclonal antibodies, directed against growth factor receptors and other cell surface antigens, have undergone extensive testing in cancer (Waldman, 1991). They may prove valuable in cancer therapy as they can be linked to cytotoxic agents (eg. radioactive isotopes, toxins or drugs) and directed at tumour cells where they may facilitate preferential entry (Moldawer and Murray, 1988). There are, however, problems with this approach as it is possible that linking an antibody to a drug alters its ability to 'recognise' cancer cells; normal cells may also be affected. Although clinical trials have shown some efficacy for most tumours most responses are, to date, short-lived (Clark, 1996).

Another new and promising approach to the targeting of treatment centres on the isolation and characterisation of the genes responsible for the transformation of cells. Gene therapy relies on *'insertion of new genetic material into cells and its expression in those cells to alter their biological behaviour with intended therapeutic benefit'* (Clark, 1996). The intention is to provide affected cells with normal functional genes or to suppress the function of mutated genes. However, although this is a valid approach, and is being actively pursued in treating inherited genetic disorders, there are difficulties in achieving this due to the need to introduce such genes into the vast majority of malignant cells.

Table 1.2   Molecular targets of targeted therapies (Clark, 1996)

Potential agents	Targets
Antisense oligonucleotides	RNA, DNA, intracellular proteins.
Gene therapy	Neoplastic cells, immune cells (to stimulate mediator cells), normal cells (to stimulate synthesis of specific proteins).
Ribozymes	RNA, DNA.
Monoclonal antibodies	Intracellular proteins, growth factor receptors, cell surface antigens.
Peptidomimetics and altered peptides	Growth factor receptors, cell surface antigens, intracellular and extracellular proteins (eg. enzymes).

Other hurdles yet to be overcome include the inefficiency of gene transfer into cells and the problem of maintaining continued expression of such genes in affected cells over time (Clark, 1996). As a result, the current approach to gene therapy is directed towards making cells more immunogenic so as to activate host-mediated killing of malignant cells (Russell et al, 1991). Such research, combined with the ever-increasing understanding of both cell biology and cancer, opens up many new areas for future development. Knowledge has now reached the point at which it is realistic to consider manipulating molecular systems to achieve a specific therapeutic effect (Clark, 1996).

Antisense oligonucleotides are synthesised to have a nucleotide sequence complementary to DNA or RNA (Clark, 1996). When such therapy is directed towards mRNA (p17), binding of the oligonucleotide to a specific sequence inhibits synthesis of the particular protein encoded by that mRNA thus blocking its function (Clark, 1996). Other intracellular molecules, such as DNA or specific protein sequences, may also be targeted. Research using this approach is ongoing and both Phase I and Phase II clinical trials are in progress.

Although malignant disease has been long been recognised it was not until about forty years ago that progress began to be made in identifying appropriate drug therapy. It was initially thought that drugs were ineffective against cancer. Twenty years ago only embryonic and haematological tumours were believed to be treatable

Past and future

by antineoplastic drugs. Today, however, the use of combination therapy and adjuvant approaches have enabled considerable success in the treatment of widespread malignancy. A better understanding of cancer, combined with such improvements in therapy, have led to improved survival. There is, however, a long way to go.

There is little doubt that the ideal drug for treating cancer would be one that is capable of reaching and destroying every part of a tumour and eliminating even the most slowly dividing cells and that has few, if any, acute or chronic side-effects. Future developments will, undoubtedly, focus on this area.

REFERENCES

Abels RI, 1992, Use of recombinant human erythropoietin in the treatment of anemia in patients who have cancer, Seminars in Oncology **19**(Suppl 8), 29-35.

Alwell N, 1947, Urethane and stilbamadine in multiple myeloma: report on two cases, Lancet ii, 388-99.

Amato I, 1993, Hope for a magic bullet that moves at the speed of light, Science **262**, 32-3.

Arcamone F, Francesci G, Orezzi P, 1968, The structure of daunomycin, Tetrahedron Letters 3349.

Beer CT, 1955, The leucopoenic action of extracts of *vinca rosea*, Annual Reviews of the British Empire Cancer Campaign **33**, 487-8.

Clark JW, 1996, Targeted therapy. In: Chabner BA, Longo DL (Editors), Cancer Chemotherapy and Biotherapy: Principles and Practice (Second edition), Lippincott-Raven, Philadelphia.

Cline M, Haskell C, 1980, Cancer Chemotherapy, WB Saunders Co., Philadelphia.

Cohen SS, 1963, Sponges, cancer chemotherapy and cellular aging, Perspectives in Biological Medicine **6**, 215-27.

Dennis J-N, Greene AE, 1988, A highly efficient approach to natural Taxol, Journal of the American Chemical Society **110**, 5917-9.

Farber S, D'Angio G, Evans A, et al, 1960, Clinical studies of actinomycin-D with special reference to Wilm's tumor in children, Annals of the New York Academy of Science **89**, 421-5.

Frei E, Freireich EJ, 1965, Progress and perspectives in the chemotherapy of acute leukemia, Advances in Chemotherapy **2**, 269-98.

Haddow A, Watkinson JM, Paterson E, 1944, Influence of synthetic oestrogens upon advanced malignant disease, British Medical Journal **2**, 393-8.

Haddow A, Sexton WA, 1946, Influence of carbamic esters (urethanes) on experimental animal tumours, Nature **157**, 500-3.

Heidelberger C, Chaudhuri NK, Danneberg P, et al, 1957, Fluorinated pyrimidines, a new class of tumor-inhibitory compounds, Nature **179**, 663-6.

Hood LE, Abernathy E, 1991, Biologic response modifiers. In: Baird SB, McCorkle R, Grant M (Editors), Cancer Nursing: A Comprehensive Textbook, WB Saunders Co., Philadelphia.

Huggins C, Hodges CV, 1941, Studies on prostatic cancer. 1. The effect of castration, of oestrogen and of androgen injection on serum phosphatases in metastatic carcinoma of the prostate, Cancer Research **1**, 293-7.

Kaufman D, Chabner BA, 1996, Clinical strategies for cancer treatment: the role of drugs. In: Chabner BA, Longo DL (Editors), Cancer Chemotherapy and Biotherapy: Principles and Practice (Second edition), Lippincott-Raven, Philadelphia.

Krakoff IH, 1977, Systemic cancer treatment: cancer chemotherapy. In: Horton J, Hill GJ (Editors), Clinical Oncology, WB Saunders Co., Philadelphia.

Li MC, Hertz R, Spencer DB, 1956, Effect of methotrexate upon choriocarcinoma and chorioadenoma, Proceedings of the Society of Experimental Biological Medicine **93**, 361-6.

Loge JP, Rundles RW, 1949, Urethane (ethyl carbamate) therapy in multiple myeloma, Blood **4**, 201-16.

Mihich E, Fefer A, 1983, Biological Response Modifiers, Subcommittee Report, Monograph No. 63, National Cancer Institute, Bethesda.

Moan J, Berg K, 1992, Photochemotherapy of cancer: experimental research. Yearly review, Photochemistry and Photobiology **55**, 931-43.

Moldawer N, Murray JL, 1988, The clinical uses of monoclonal antibodies in cancer research, Cancer Nursing **8**, 207-13.

Murinson DS, 1981, Clinical pharmacology. In: Rosenthal SN, Bennett JM (Editors), Practical Cancer Chemotherapy, Medical Examination, Garden City, New York.

Neuss N, Gorman M, Svoboda GH, et al, 1959, Vinca alkaloids III. Characterisation of leucoserine and vincaleukoblastine, new alkaloids from *vinca rosea Linn*, Journal of the American Chemical Society **81**, 4754-5.

Noble RL, 1961, Symposium on vincaleukoblastine (VLB), Canadian Cancer Conference **4**, 333-8.

Oettgen HF, Clifford P, Burkitt D, 1963a, Malignant lymphoma involving the jaw in African children - treatment with alkylating agents and actinomycin-D, Cancer Chemotherapy Reports **28**, 25-34.

Oettgen H, Burkitt D, Burchenal J, 1963b, Malignant lymphoma involving the jaw in African children - treatment with methotrexate, Cancer **16**, 616-23.

11

Pack GT, Ariel JM, 1968, The history of cancer therapy. In: American Chemical Society (Editors), Cancer Management: A Special Graduate Course on Cancer, JB Lippincott Co., Philadelphia.

Paterson E, ApThomas I, Haddow A, et al, 1946, Leukaemia treated with urethane compared with deep x-ray therapy, Lancet i, 677-83.

Petros WP, Peters, WP, 1996, Colony-stimulating factors. In: Chabner BA, Longo DL (Editors), Cancer Chemotherapy and Biotherapy: Principles and Practice (Second edition), Lippincott-Raven, Philadelphia.

Rosenberg B, Van Camp L, Krigas T, 1965, Inhibition of cell division in *escherichia coli* by electrolysis. Products from a platinum electrode, Nature **205**, 698-9.

Russell SJ, Eccles SA, Flemming C, et al, 1991, Decreased tumorigenicity of a transplantable rat sarcoma following transfer and expression of an IL-2 cDNA, International Journal of Cancer **47**, 244-6.

Rutman RS, Cantarow A, Pashkis KE, 1954, Studies in 2-acetylaminofluorene carcinogenesis III. The utilisation of uracil-2-C by preneoplastic rat liver and rat hepatoma, Cancer Research **14**, 119-34.

Selawry OS, Frei E, 1964, Prolongation of remission in acute lymphocytic leukemia by alteration in dose schedule and route of administration of methotrexate, Clinical Research **12**, 231 (Abstr).

Shimkin MB, 1977, Contrary to nature, Department of Education and Welfare publication (NIH), US DHEW, Public Health Service, Washington DC.

Simpson-Herren L, Sanford AM, Holmquist JP, 1974, Cell population kinetics of transplanted and metastatic Lewis lung cancer, Cell and Tissue Kinetics **7**, 349-61.

Tan C, Tasaka H, DiMarco A, 1965, Clinical studies of daunomycin, Proceedings of the American Association for Cancer Research **6**, 64-5.

Waldman T, 1991, Monoclonal antibodies in diagnosis and therapy, Science **252**, 1657-62.

Wani MC, Taylor HL, Wall ME, et al, 1971, Plant antitumour agents: VI. The isolation and structure of Taxol, a novel antileukaemic and antitumour agent from *Taxus brevifolia*, Journal of the American Chemical Society **93**, 2325-7.

Zeller P, Gutmann H, Hegedus B, et al, 1963, Methylhydrazine derivatives, a new class of cytotoxic agents, Experientia **19**, 129-34.

Zubrod CG, 1979, Historic milestones in curative chemotherapy, Seminars in Oncology **6**, 490-505.

CHAPTER 2   CELL BIOLOGY

Although a complete review of cell biology is inappropriate here, a basic knowledge is essential if the ways in which cancer chemotherapy affects cellular function is to be appreciated and its beneficial and deleterious effects understood.

What is cancer?

It is firstly necessary to recognise that cancer is a collective term that describes a group of diseases sharing the common feature of uncontrolled and unregulated cell growth that leads to invasion of surrounding tissues and spread (metastasis) to parts of the body distant from their site of origin (King, 1996).

The process of carcinogenesis is complex and can be described in terms of three stages. The initiation and promotion stages are those which lead to the development of a cancer from a normal cell; progression describes the additional changes occurring after cancer has formed and includes both invasion and metastasis (Figure 2.1).

Figure 2.1   Stages of carcinogenesis

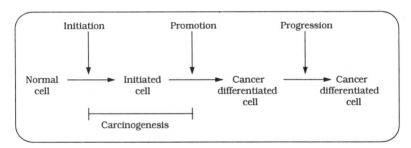

It thus becomes clear that, although the typical clinical presentation is as either a mass (tumour) or as disseminated disease, such growth has originated from changes affecting a single cell. 'Something' has affected that cell causing it to express two traits: unregulated growth and loss of function.

The pattern of growth and the nature of cell function are genetically regulated in both normal and malignant cells. Alteration of the specific genes regulating growth and function is, however, a significant aspect of carcinogenesis; such transformed genes are

13

known collectively as *oncogenes*. The gene present in normal cells is known as a *proto-oncogene* so as to distinguish it from the altered gene in cancer cells. Factors stimulating change in a proto-oncogene may be the result of a variety of different processes including exposure to environmental or chemical carcinogens, viruses or radiation; incomplete or altered genes may also be inherited.

Just as there are genes capable of being transformed and initiating cancer, so there are others that have the ability to regulate growth and inhibit carcinogenesis. The loss of these *repressor genes* may also result in uncontrolled growth. Although they are sometimes described as *antioncogenes* it can be seen that repressor genes do not always act to counteract the effect of oncogenes. In fact, the two types of gene act synergistically in that oncogenes gain a function due to mutation while repressors lose a function (King, 1996). This inter-action thus explains the changes in both growth and loss of function.

However, although the starting point of cancer development is the mutation of genetic material, its continued progression is not straightforward. It is not usually the initial transformed cell that is so characteristic of cancer; indeed cancer may not be seen until many generations have been produced by the affected cell.

This quiescence, during which the traits of cancer are not expressed, is known as the *latent period* and suggests that events other than the initial genetic transformation are necessary for the full development of cancer. It is this second stage that causes initiated cells to start the unregulated proliferation characteristic of cancer, which is described as promotion. Once a cell is transformed, by exposure to a carcinogenic insult, and has lost its ability to differentiate, it may continue to divide *ad infinitum* limited only by the available blood supply and, hence, the availability of nutrients, and possibly by the host's ability to mount an immunological defence (Pratt et al, 1994).

Control of intracellular processes

All cellular functions are controlled by deoxyribonucleic acid (DNA), a nucleic acid present in the nucleus of the cell (Table 2.1). DNA is a self-replicating 'template' for the chromosomes, the 'carriers' of the genetic material (the genes). Each molecule of DNA consists of many thousands of subunits, called nucleotides, each of which is made up of three further subunits - a phosphate group, a pentose (five carbon

Table 2.1   **Functions of deoxyribonucleic acid (DNA)**

Control of all the biochemical processes of the cell
Promotion and maintenance of cellular function
Promotion and maintenance of cellular reproduction
i.e.   Transfer of genetic information
        Cell reproduction
        Synthesis of proteins, enzymes and hormones

sugar) and a nitrogen-containing base. There are four types of nucleotide, which differ only in the kind of nitrogenous base they contain. The pyrimidines are cytosine and thymine and the purines - adenine and guanine. These are arranged in a chain-like pattern; the sugar and phosphate groups form alternate links in the chain and the nitrogenous bases are attached to the sugars at right angles to the chain (Figure 2.2).

Figure 2.2   **Formation of a single chain of DNA**

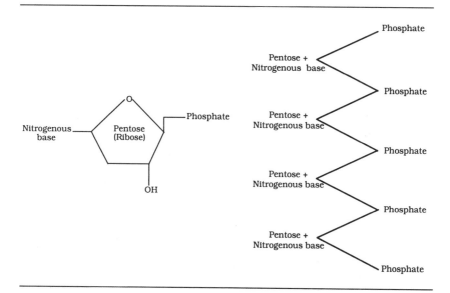

The DNA molecule consists of two such chains which are twisted together to form a double helix (Figure 2.3); opposing spirals are held together by hydrogen bonds that link the nitrogenous bases projecting into the spaces between the strands. This bonding occurs only between specific bases and is determined by their particular molecular configuration. Thus adenine binds with thymine and guanine with cytosine binding the chains together. Since each base can bind with only one of the four possible bases on the opposing chain it is possible to identify the sequence of the bases of one chain by knowing the sequence of the other. It is the sequence of bases of the DNA making up the chromosomes that carries the genetic code and determines the structure and function of the cell.

Figure 2.3   **Formation of the DNA double helix**

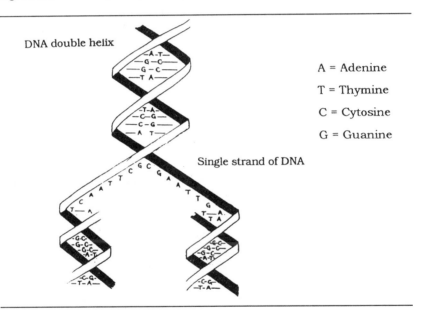

Thus, during DNA synthesis, the nucleus must not only double its DNA content but, if genetic conformity is to be maintained, also produce DNA identical to that already present. This is achieved by separation of the strands and, since each base can pair with only the same type of base from which it was separated, each chain then acts as a 'template' ensuring that genetic information is passed from parent to daughter cells. The important functions of DNA in this regard are, therefore:

    a.   Replication - to provide new DNA for cellular proliferation.

    b.   Transcription through which the genetic information contained in the chromosomes is passed to RNA and, subsequently, 'translated' into essential proteins.

Although RNA is synthesised from a single strand of DNA its structure differs. RNA contains the same purine bases (guanine and adenine) but only one of the pyrimidines (cytosine). The thymine of DNA is replaced by uracil. Since the genetic information contained in the single strand of RNA, is derived from DNA it is dictated by base-pairing rules similar to those responsible for the double-stranded DNA; the difference is that the adenine of DNA pairs with uracil during RNA synthesis. RNA is central to protein synthesis.

The RNA synthesised in the nucleus as an exact copy of a single strand of DNA, is known as messenger RNA (mRNA) and acts as a template for protein synthesis. The genetic information it contains dictates the specific amino acid sequence of individual proteins.

Some RNA (ribosomal RNA (rRNA)) plays a structural role in the cells when it contributes to the formation of the ribosomes and assists in protein synthesis by those ribosomes. The third major form of RNA, transfer RNA (tRNA), is specifically associated with individual amino acids each of which has its own tRNA.

THE CELL CYCLE

An awareness of the mechanisms and rate of cellular change provides the basis for understanding of both the actions and side-effects of chemotherapeutic agents. Such knowledge is used when developing treatment regimes and scheduling drug administration so as to maximise therapeutic effectiveness and minimise toxicity. As chemo-therapeutic agents act primarily against actively dividing cells, it is essential that the cell cycle is understood.

The cell cycle and its importance

The cell cycle (Figure 2.4) describes a sequence of steps through which both normal and malignant cells replicate. This is a continuous process in which, under normal circumstances, cells are in dynamic equilibrium with those in prolonged rest and is described as the interval between the mid-point of mitosis in a cell and the mid-point of subsequent mitosis in one or both daughter cells (Baserga, 1971).

The cycle comprises four stages during which a series of discrete activities takes place resulting in the emergence of two identical new cells. During G_1, the phase following cell division, synthesis of both

RNA and protein occurs preparing the cell for DNA synthesis. The end of the G_1 phase is defined by the onset of the S (synthetic) phase when DNA is synthesised and the amount of DNA is doubled.

Normal and malignant cells differ in the amount of time they spend in the S phase which may last between 10 and 30 hours (Brown, 1987). Many anticancer drugs act by causing irreparable disruption to the organisation of DNA during synthesis; this ultimately causes cell death.

Figure 2.4   The cell cycle

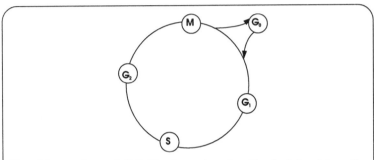

M = Mitotic phase. Cell divides to produce two identical daughter cells.

G_0 = Resting phase. Cell is quiescent. All cell functions continue but cell is unable to divide.

G_1 = Post-mitotic gap. A pre-synthetic phase in which the enzymes needed for DNA synthesis are produced.

S = DNA synthesis takes place in preparation for cell division.

G_2 = Pre-mitotic gap during which specialised proteins and RNA are synthesised in preparation for cell division.

After DNA synthesis is complete, the cell enters a second resting phase (G_2) when preparation for cell division occurs; further synthesis of RNA and protein takes place and the mitotic spindle is formed; G_2 lasts between 1 and 12 hours. During mitosis (M) the chromosomes, formed during DNA synthesis, separate to form two identical daughter cells each of which contains the same number and type of chromosomes as the parent cell.

Mitosis (cell division)

The mitotic phase of the cell cycle is, in turn, divided into four stages that take place at the time of cell division (Figure 2.5).

Figure 2.5   The stages of mitosis

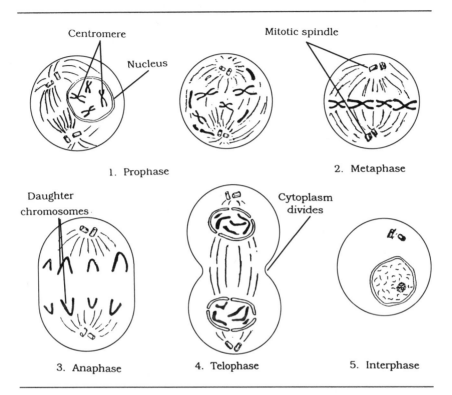

1. Prophase

2. Metaphase

3. Anaphase

4. Telophase

5. Interphase

1. *The Prophase* when the chromosomes first become visible as long thin filaments which become progressively shorter and thicken. Each chromosome has already split to form two chromatids (daughter chromosomes) held together by a specialised structure known as the centromere.

2. *The Metaphase* when the nuclear membrane disappears and the mitotic spindle forms between opposite poles of the cell. The chromosomes arrange themselves at the middle of the cell lying across the spindle and attached to it by the centromere thus forming the equatorial plate.

3. *The Anaphase.* During this stage the chromatids separate moving to opposite poles of the spindle.

4. *The Telophase* when the chromosomes elongate, a new nuclear membrane forms and the spindle disappears. The cytoplasm then divides (cytokinesis).

The formation of the spindle, separation of the chromosomes and cell division take about 1 hour. The period of the cell cycle between successive mitoses is described as the *Interphase*.

At completion of the M phase, cells re-enter the cell cycle at G_1 to undergo further maturation or enter the resting phase, G_0, to await recruitment into the growth fraction.

The cells comprising any given tissue may be in any stage of the cycle. In addition, some cells that have the ability to divide may not be actively dividing; such cells are said to be in the G_0 phase and are regarded to be temporarily removed from the cycle. They may be stimulated to move into G_0 and enter the active cycle. The time required for completion of the cycle (i.e. the time between mitoses) is called the cell cycle time (Tc) or the generation time and varies not only between cells in individual tissues but also between normal and malignant cells. In most dividing cells the S, G_2 and M phases are of relatively constant duration; variations in the length of the cycle usually occur in G_1. It is believed that the duration of G_1 is, somehow, related to the proliferative activity of a tissue since, when this is high, G_1 is short and, when activity is low, G_1 tends to be prolonged. Indeed, Prescott and Flexer (1982) suggested that G_1 arrest is defective in malignant cells. It is not, however, clear what stimulates even normal cells to leave G_1 and begin DNA synthesis.

TUMOUR GROWTH

A basic knowledge of tumour cell kinetics is helpful in developing understanding of the rationale underlying the schedules and regimes employed in cancer therapy.

Non-neoplastic growth, in all tissues, shares one common feature which is that increased cell proliferation ceases once the stimulus to growth is removed. In contrast, the proliferation of neoplastic cells appears autonomous and occurs regardless of the needs of the host (ie. it is not demand-led) (Woolf, 1986).

Normal cells are subject to internal and external inhibitory signals that are lost during the process of carcinogenesis. Thus, although proliferation in normal tissues ceases once cells come into contact with adjacent cells, such contact inhibition is lost in malignant cells although the mechanism through which this occurs is unclear (King, 1996). There are two basic possibilities: firstly, there may be a failure of some inhibiting mechanism(s) which normally inhibits excessive cell proliferation or, secondly, abnormal growth may be due to an

20

abnormal response to normal growth factors so that growth continues irrespective of the needs of the host. At same time, it appears that malignant cells also depend on fewer exogenous growth factors depending instead on the production of polypeptide growth factors by the tumour itself that stimulate its growth (Woolf, 1986).

Growth in all tissues involves three different cell populations (Baserga, 1971): the growth fraction, the clonogenic fraction and the end (non-clonogenic) cells (Figure 2.6). The growth fraction represents those cells which are actively dividing (cycling cells). The clonogenic cells are those which, although quiescent (G_0), are capable of dividing if given an appropriate stimulus.

Figure 2.6   Functional 'compartments' within tumours

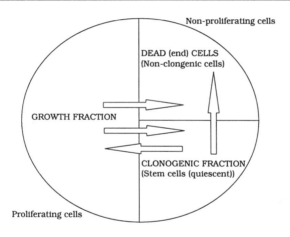

Tumours contain different cell compartments that are classified according to whether that compartment is proliferating or non-proliferating. The inter-relationships between these compartments are shown in this diagram.

Cycling and resting cells can be further subdivided into stem cells and non-stem cells (Hill and Baserga, 1975; Hill, 1978). Stem cells replenish the stem cell pool that is drawn on to maintain the continued survival and integrity of individual cell populations; non-stem cells differentiate and enter the maturing groups of cells. As long as stem cells remain within the G_0 population damaged cells can be replaced. End (or non-clonogenic) cells are differentiated cells which are viable and complete their life cycle without dividing again.

21

Cell biology

Although the growth fraction may be very large (>70%) or very small (<10%) (Calman et al, 1980) it is difficult to estimate with any accuracy. Clonogenic cells may be recruited to maintain growth if, for example, the growth fraction is reduced by effective therapy. Thus, one of the major aims of anticancer therapy is to increase the number of non-clonogenic cells present in a tumour and reduce the potential for growth (Figure 2.7). Clearly, a tumour with a large growth fraction, and a large reserve of clonogenic cells, is likely to increase in size more rapidly than one with a lower growth fraction and smaller reserves. Growth is dependent on the balance between the number of cells produced and the number that die, while the rate of growth depends on the cell cycle time.

Figure 2.7   **The relationship between the cell cycle and the functional compartments of a tumour**

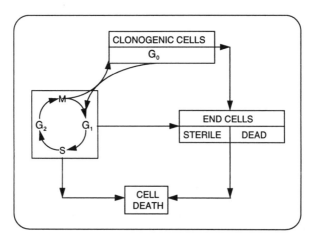

Antineoplastic drugs affect both normal and malignant cells by disrupting cellular activity during one or more phases of the cell cycle. Although both normal and malignant cells die as a result of irreparable damage caused by chemotherapy, normal cells are better able to repair minor damage. This difference between cell populations is exploited when treating cancer.

The fraction of the tumour cell population in active division at any time varies with the type of malignancy and the stage of its history. Most tumours have a relatively high growth fraction when young and small and a relatively low growth fraction when the tumour is large (Hancock and Bradshaw, 1981). This is because, as tumour size

22

increases, the doubling time (Td) increases (Carter et al, 1977), an effect known as Gompertzian growth (Figure 2.8). This believed to be due to an increase in the number of resting (clonogenic) cells (Hancock and Bradshaw, 1981), although this may vary between different types of tumour.

Figure 2.8   Gompertzian growth

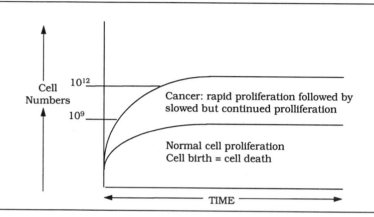

The above discussion assumes that all tumour cells remain within a tumour continuing to produce future generations of cancer cells (Figure 2.9). However, research suggests that large numbers of cells are rapidly lost from the total tumour cell population. For example, exfoliation may result in a loss of cells from the surface of the tumour (eg. GI tumours), cells may migrate from the periphery of the tumour into the blood or lymphatic system from where they may 'seed' elsewhere causing metastasis, the decreased vascularity of large tumours may lead to local anoxia and focal necrosis in some solid tumours and, since tumour growth is abnormal, many of the developing cells are either not viable or are unable to divide. Finally, tumour cells may be overcome by the immune system.

This 'cell loss factor' may account for some 50-90% of all the cells produced by an individual tumour. Although this seems remarkably high it should be remembered that cell division is normally controlled so that the function of the tissue/organ is maintained and, in adults, although cell loss is replaced, no additional cells are produced and tissue size remains constant (ie. zero growth occurs). Thus, since it appears that cell division within a tumour occurs at an apparently normal rate, cell loss is reduced and the tumour continues to increase in size. However growth may also be reduced as the size of a tumour increases since nutrient availability may be decreased as the blood supply is outgrown (Henshaw, 1981)

Figure 2.9   The balance between cell gain and cell loss

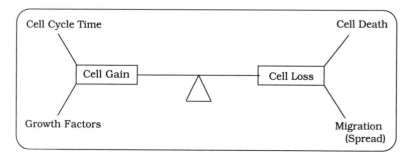

IMPLICATIONS FOR CANCER CHEMOTHERAPY

Central to the problem of curing cancer is an understanding of the ways in which normal and cancer cells differ (Jarman, 1989). It is known that cancer is essentially a problem of abnormal cell growth, due to a variety of causes, all of which interact with the DNA in normal cells transforming them so that normal control mechanisms no longer function. The end result is that cancer cells reproduce uncontrollably, invade surrounding tissues and, eventually, spread to form metastases at sites distant from the primary tumour (Jarman, 1989). It is these effects that make cancer so difficult to treat.

Tumours, like all other tissues, comprise a mixture of dividing and non-dividing cells. Current drug treatment is directed towards controlling abnormal cell growth and reducing the number of actively dividing cells. Although antineoplastic agents differ from one another in a variety of ways (Ch. 4) they also share major characteristics. Firstly, since all dividing cells must synthesise DNA during their life cycle, they act by interfering with DNA synthesis and/or replication. They are, therefore, most effective in destroying cells that are either preparing for, or actively involved in, cell division. Thus tumours with a high growth fraction and a short generation time (Tc) are those which are most sensitive to chemotherapy whereas those comprising cells with a long Tc or a small growth fraction are often resistant to such treatment. Thus chemotherapy is generally most effective against rapidly growing, small tumours.

Cell biology

Most currently available antineoplastic drugs appear to work through interactions affecting the enzymes, or their substrates, involved in either the synthesis or function of DNA or by disrupting the DNA molecule itself. An undesirable consequence of such interactions is that those normal tissues undergoing rapid proliferation are also subject to damage; it is the effects on normal tissues that are described as the side-effects of chemotherapy.

Tumour growth characteristics are amongst those which determine the choice of antineoplastic agent used against that tumour; they are explored further in Chapter 3.

REFERENCES

Baserga R, 1971, The Cell Cycle and Cancer, Marcel Dekker Inc., New York.

Brown J, 1987, Chemotherapy. In: Groenwald SL, Frogge MH, Goodman M, Yarbro CH (Editors), Cancer Nursing: Principles and Practice (Second edition), Jones and Bartlett Publishers, Boston.

Calman KC, Smyth JF, Tattersall MNH, 1980, Basic Principles of Cancer Chemotherapy, The Macmillan Press Ltd., London.

Carter SK, Babowski MT, Hellman K, 1977, Chemotherapy of Cancer, John Wiley and Sons, New York.

Hancock BW, Bradshaw JD, 1981, Lecture Notes on Clinical Oncology, Blackwell Scientific Publications, Oxford.

Henshaw EC, 1981, Introduction. In: Rosenthal SN, Bennet JM (Editors), Practical Cancer Chemotherapy, Medical Examination Publishing Co., New York.

Hill BT, Baserga R, 1975, The cell cycle and its significance for cancer treatments, Cancer Treatment Reviews **2**, 159-75.

Hill BT, 1978, Cancer Chemotherapy: the relevance of certain concepts of cell cycle kinetics, Biochemica et Biophysica Acta **516**, 389-417.

Jarman M, 1989, The development of anti-cancer drugs, Chemistry in Britain **25**, 51-4.

King RJB, 1996, Cancer Biology, Addison-Wesley Longman Ltd., Edinburgh.

Pratt WB, Ruddon RW, Ensminger WD, et al, 1994, The Anticancer Drugs (Second edition), Oxford University Press, New York and Oxford.

Prescott DM, Flexer AS, 1982, Cancer: The Misguided Cell, Sinauer Associates Inc., Publishers, Massachusetts.

Woolf N, 1986, Cell, Tissue and Disease. The Basis of Pathology (Second edition), Ballière Tindall, London.

CHAPTER 3   FACTORS AFFECTING THE USE OF CHEMOTHERAPEUTIC DRUGS

It is difficult for any discussion of the factors affecting the use of chemotherapeutic agents to cover all aspects of this complex subject. The preceding chapter has described the way in which cells grow and divide as well as the basis of tumour growth and how it can be used in determining effective therapeutic approaches. This chapter focuses only on the major factors involved in the clinical use of cancer chemotherapy.

DETERMINANTS OF DRUG RESPONSE

The responsiveness of tumours to drugs depends on various factors related to the tumour, the pharmacology, timing and combination of drugs employed and factors related to the patient himself.

Tumour-related factors

Depending on the type of cancer, the time taken for the production of a clinically detectable mass may be months or even years (Ch. 2). Once growth commences, this may be very rapid or, for some tumours, very slow; it may be limited by the availability of nutrients, particularly in solid tumours.

Small tumours depend on diffusion for the provision of oxygen and other nutrients (Folkman, 1990) and, because of this, a steady state may be reached in which newly generated cells are balanced by older dying cells (Pratt et al, 1994). Tumours may remain dormant for some time, perhaps for years. A tumour must be at least 1cm in diameter, when it contains 5×10^9 cells, before it can be clinically detected.

Tumours will grow to about 1mm in diameter in the absence of new blood vessels (angiogenesis); additional growth requires the production of angiogenic growth factors by cancer cells (King, 1996). These induce the growth of capillaries into the tumour from surrounding normal tissues (Folkman, 1990). Once this occurs, new growth is initiated that may continue until the host dies unless this is prevented by effective therapy. As growth continues, nutrients (eg. fat, amino acids, carbohydrate, vitamins and minerals) are consumed rapidly leading to one of the most common signs of progressive

26

malignant disease, weight loss (see Ch. 12).

If any drug is to be effective in treating a particular tumour it must be present in an appropriate concentration at its site of action; an adequate blood supply is, therefore, essential. Even the most sensitive of tumour cells cannot be destroyed unless exposure to the drug can be ensured. This can be difficult to achieve, particularly in solid tumours that have two types of blood vessel: those created from the host's capillary network and those derived from the pre-existing vasculature to the tissue of origin (Pratt et al, 1994). The effect is that some areas of a tumour are well vascularised while others are not; cells in the latter areas will be less affected by drugs (King, 1996). This makes it difficult to predict how solid tumours, particularly those with a poorly vascularised and necrotic core, will respond to anticancer therapy.

As tumour growth continues, and the number of cells increases, the growth rate changes as previously described (p20-24). In brief, during the initial development, tumour growth is slow; this is described as the lag phase. This is followed by a period of rapid growth, known as the logarithmic growth phase (log phase), during which there are repeated doublings of the cell number. The growth curve shown in Figure 2.8 is a visual depiction of tumour growth. As cell numbers and, therefore, tumour size increase the doubling time also increases and becomes prolonged (the plateau phase). Thus, as time passes, the doubling time lengthens and the growth rate decreases. This may be due to a smaller growth fraction, a change in the length of the cell cycle or an increased rate of cell loss. Tumour growth characteristics, at least in part, determine the choice of therapeutic agent employed.

Although cytotoxic drugs are most effective during the log phase (Skeel, 1995) the major implication of these factors is that the selection of a drug(s) for treating individual tumours should probably differ for large and small tumours. A small, rapidly growing tumour will have a high growth fraction and a high viable cell population consisting of those cells in active division as well as resting (G_0) cells which have the potential to divide on appropriate stimulation. Thus drugs that are effective against rapidly dividing cells should be prescribed. An advanced tumour, in which tumour volume is high but the growth fraction is low, is more likely to respond to phase non-specific drugs regardless of cell division.

However, when the total malignant cell population can be reduced

27

by other means (eg. surgery or radiotherapy) chemotherapy may be more effective since a greater fraction of the remaining cells is likely to be in the logarithmic phase of growth. Such 'debulking' may also stimulate the remaining cells to enter the proliferative, drug-sensitive phase increasing their susceptibility to chemotherapy. Secondly, metastases may, initially at least, have a growth fraction and doubling time resembling those of the early stages of growth of the primary tumour; they may, therefore, be more susceptible to anti-cancer drugs if they are treated early in their development (Pratt et al, 1994). As a result, chemotherapy is frequently initiated soon after surgery or radiotherapy rather than waiting for metastases to be clinically identified.

The cell cycle and cytotoxic therapy

Since the target of cytotoxic therapy is the malignant cell itself the cell cycle has many therapeutic implications; the stages of the cycle are central to the action of antineoplastic agents. In general, actively dividing cells are those most sensitive to attack by most of the commonly used chemotherapeutic drugs.

The early studies of the effects of X-ray therapy showed that there were changes in the sensitivity to treatment as the cycle progressed. Most cells were found to be particularly sensitive to irradiation during the G_2 phase and during mitosis when the amount of DNA present is doubled; they were less sensitive during G_1. This suggested that a similar variation in sensitivity may occur when using other cytotoxic drugs. However, results were equivocal although it was found that most cytotoxic drugs fall into one of three main categories. Depending on their mechanism of action antineoplastic agents may affect both proliferating and resting cells (non-specific agents), proliferating cells only (cycle specific) or only a specific portion of the proliferative pool (phase specific) (Figure 3.1).

Some workers (eg. Knopf et al, 1984) refer to a broad class of chemotherapeutic agents called *cell cycle specific agents* which, although damaging to both proliferating and resting cells, tend to be most effective against actively dividing cells. Thus resting cells will not be significantly affected by cycle specific drugs.

For the sake of clarity, and because the distinction is relative rather than absolute, drugs are classified as either cell cycle phase specific or cell cycle phase non-specific.

Cell cycle phase specific drugs kill proliferating cells only in a specific phase of the cell cycle. For example, the vinca alkaloids (mitotic spindle poisons) are lethal to cells in the M phase, while cytosine arabinoside is specific to the S phase when it inhibits DNA synthesis.

Figure 3.1   Examples of phase specific agents

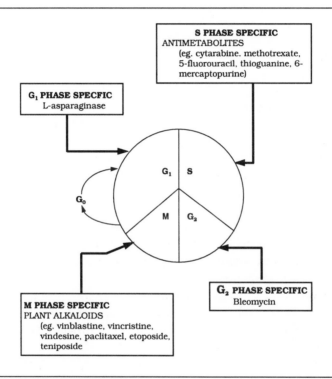

Because phase specific agents are active not only on cells in active cycle but also in a specific phase of the cycle, they are most effective against those cells that are rapidly dividing. An important consideration for the use of phase specific drugs is the fact that only a certain percentage of the cells in any given tumour are in active replication at any time.

Phase non-specific agents destroy the cell by interrupting or destroying cellular functions that are not limited to a particular phase of the cell cycle.

Cell cycle phase non-specific agents act independently of the stage of the cell cycle. They may affect cells in all phases of the cycle; resting cells are as vulnerable to cytotoxic effects as dividing cells. They are often effective against tumours with low proliferative activity (Knopf et al, 1984). Cisplatin, chlorambucil and daunorubicin are examples of phase non-specific drugs.

Resting (G_0) cells, may be particularly resistant to chemotherapy due to their lack of activity and their ability to repair cellular damage whilst resting. However, phase non-specific drugs, such as the nitrosoureas, appear to be effective whether cancer cells are in cycle or are resting (Skeel, 1995).

Cell kill hypothesis

The cell kill hypothesis describes the theoretical ability of anti-neoplastic drugs to kill cancer and suggests that drugs kill cancer cells on the basis of first order kinetics (i.e. a certain drug dosage will kill a constant *percentage* of cells rather than a constant *number* of cells). Thus repeated doses of drug(s) are required to reduce the number of cells and, in theory at least, the number of cells remaining after therapy is dependent on the results of prior therapy, the time between repeated doses and the doubling time of the tumour.

This, as will be shown, is a simplified approach and it is now known that cells can mutate over time causing resistance to treatment. Furthermore, patients with similar tumours may differ in their response to the same treatment (Goodman, 1988). The cell kill hypothesis cannot, therefore, provide an accurate prediction of the response to chemotherapy. This is discussed further throughout this chapter.

PLANNING OF CHEMOTHERAPEUTIC REGIMENS

A number of theoretical constructs are used to guide the way in which treatment is planned. Regimes for the maximum tumour cell kill can be designed when the cell cycle specificity of antineoplastic agents is known. The principles of synchronisation and recruitment may then be employed.

Synchrony

The fact that the cells making up a tumour may be in various stages of the cell cycle can have significant effects on treatment. For example, if a phase specific drug was used in treatment only some of the tumour cells would be in the appropriate phase of the cycle. Thus the concept of phase specificity may have marked therapeutic implications.

One way in which the benefits of such treatment could be enhanced, and cell kill maximised, would be to block the cell cycle and bring all dividing cells to the same phase at the same time following this with treatment with an appropriate drug. Alternatively, all dividing cells may be destroyed by use of appropriate therapeutic agents so that resting cells are 'recruited' into the cycle and treated with another cytotoxic agent (Hancock and Bradshaw, 1981).

Synchronisation refers to the process through which the percentage of tumour cells in specific phases of the cycle is increased so that they are vulnerable to agents which act in that phase (Hill, 1978). This can be achieved using *cytostatic* agents - which block the cell cycle - or *cytotoxic* agents that will kill cells in a specific sensitive phase. For example, the cytostatic properties of cytosine arabinoside will cause cells to arrest at the boundary of the G_1 and S phases thus 'trapping' an increased proportion of cells and rendering them vulnerable to agents specific for the S phase (Hill, 1978). Both experimental and clinical studies have demonstrated the efficacy of this approach in treating many forms of malignant disease (Pratt et al, 1994).

Recruitment

The term 'recruitment' refers to the transformation of resting cells (G_0) into dividing cells. It may occur as a consequence of the cellular destruction arising from chemotherapy which may stimulate recruitment of resting cells into active cycle thus helping to maintain the tumour cell population. Thus, as long as stem cells remain within the resting cell population, damaged cells can be replaced.

Selective toxicity

True selective toxicity towards cancer cells remains an elusive goal in cancer chemotherapy although there is some evidence that most of the chemotherapeutic agents in common use have a greater toxicity for malignant than for normal cells (Pratt et al, 1994). Furthermore, it is believed that there are differences in the ability of normal and cancer cells to repair treatment-induced damage. For example, Cline and Haskell (1980) suggested that synthesis of major intracellular components, including DNA and RNA, is more easily disrupted in

31

cancer cells than in normal cells. In general, however, normal cells can repair partial damage whereas cancer cells cannot; neither normal nor malignant cells can repair total damage. It is important to realise, however, that any such differences between normal and malignant cells may be slight.

The side-effects of cytotoxic drugs will be most acute in those normal tissues that are actively and rapidly proliferating, such as the bone marrow, hair follicles and GI mucosa. It is the development of toxicity in these sensitive tissues that limits the usefulness of such drugs. Nonetheless, despite similarities in their rate of replication, normal and cancer cells are not always equally vulnerable so that the principles of selective toxicity can still be employed provided that treatment is carefully planned. It is clear, however, that the margin of safety is often very narrow.

Pharmacological factors

Cytotoxic therapy may be affected by both the pharmacokinetic and pharmacodynamic properties of the drug concerned since it is the interrelationship between these factors that determines the balance between drug concentration and its therapeutic and toxic effects.

A detailed discussion of pharmacology is outside the scope of this book but, in brief, pharmacokinetics determines the plasma/tissue concentration of a drug and depends on its absorption, distribution, metabolism and excretion whereas pharmacodynamics concerns the pharmacological and toxicological effects produced by that concentration (Brodie and Harrison, 1986). Thus the efficacy of anti-cancer drugs may be affected by a variety of pharmacological factors.

For example, any factor that alters the concentration of a drug at its site of action, or which affects the period of time during which it is available for activity at the biological receptor, must be taken into account. It is, therefore, necessary to consider the route of administration, drug absorption, distribution, biotransformation and excretion.

Route of Administration

Chemotherapy may be administered through multiple routes. This is largely dictated by the characteristics of individual drugs and the desire to optimise drug availability.

Although, in theory at least, drugs may be administered orally or parenterally or instilled locally into a body cavity, the possible route is, in practice, dictated by the stability, solubility and sclerosant (vesicant) properties of the drug concerned (Ch. 8). Thus, for example, some drugs cannot be given orally as they are unstable in the GI tract; others cannot be given parenterally because there is no suitable vehicle for solubilisation. However, careful selection of an appropriate route of administration may improve the anti-neoplastic effect by enabling a high concentration of the drug to reach the tumour.

The most common routes used are the oral and intravenous routes. The oral route is used for drugs that are well-absorbed and which do not irritate the gastrointestinal tract. Oral administration, however, carries various disadvantages since, when GI function is impaired (as is common in cancer/cancer therapy), absorption may be disrupted and an effective drug concentration may not be achieved. Alternatively, the patient may fail to take the drug or fail to take it at the correct time. Although non-compliance is not a common problem in clinical oncology individuals receiving oral drugs that cause nausea (eg. cyclophosphamide or procarbazine) may well be non-compliant (Barofsky, 1984).

Although cytotoxic drugs can be administered subcutaneously, intramuscularly or intravenously, the intravenous route is preferred since the drug is instilled directly into the bloodstream and, by means of continuous infusion, it is possible to ensure a constant drug concentration for a defined period. Furthermore, the drug may remain in the circulation for periods varying from a few minutes to several days, depending on the drug involved. While this is advantageous in enabling the drug to reach metastatic deposits at sites far distant from the primary tumour it also increases the risk of toxicity since, while in the circulation, the drug is carried to all body tissues which are, inevitably, exposed to its cytotoxic effects.

The subcutaneous and intramuscular routes are of limited value because many antineoplastic agents are irritating to the tissues.

Other possible methods of administration seek to cross the blood-brain barrier, localise the drugs in a selected area of the body, minimise systemic side-effects or maximise therapeutic effectiveness. These include instillation into a body cavity (intracavity), intra-arterial administration or topical application all of which represent attempts to use chemotherapy as a localised therapy by confining its activity to a specific body site and minimising the generalised toxicity accompanying systemic treatment.

Factors affecting the use of chemotherapy

Intra-arterial administration was investigated as long ago as 1923 (Segall, 1923) when ligation of the hepatic artery, and interruption of the blood flow, were shown to be successful in achieving local tumour control. However, it was not until 1950 that Klopp et al suggested that regional chemotherapy may have a role in treating malignant disease. After a fortunate accident, in which a patient was inadvertently given nitrogen mustard through the brachial artery, it was noted that, although an intense local reaction occurred, there were few systemic effects. Attempts were then made to treat a number of different tumours by injecting nitrogen mustard directly into the main artery supplying those tumours; significant regression was noted.

Thus, Klopp et al (1950) suggested that intra-arterial injection could lead to improved treatment of malignant disease. Since then other studies have shown that intra-arterial infusion may be successful when patients have large amounts of localised disease, such as that of the head or neck or widespread metastatic disease of the pelvis (Collins, 1984; Levin et al, 1989).

This approach appears to have several advantages in that high local drug concentrations may be achieved in the tissues supplied by a single artery and, provided a tumour is localised in an area fed by that artery, should result in intensive cytotoxic action within the tumour. At the same time, the concentration of the drug elsewhere in the body is reduced thus minimising systemic toxicity and reducing the incidence of side-effects.

For such treatment to be used to its best advantage a drug that is either completely absorbed by the tumour on its first passage through its capillary bed or which is very rapidly metabolised should be used (Priestman, 1980). Unless this is the case, the active drug will remain in the circulation causing systemic toxic effects. Since few such drugs exist, attempts to prevent this have centred on the vascularisation of the area to be treated or on temporary occlusion of the bone marrow so as to protect the stem cell population.

An alternative approach has involved the use of a drug, such as methotrexate, which can be rendered harmless by administration of an antagonist, such as folinic acid (Guy, 1991; Pratt et al, 1994). Patients with hepatoma provide good examples of those who have responded well to continuous intra-arterial infusion when 5-fluorouracil (5-FU) is injected directly into the hepatic artery (Chabner and Longo, 1996).

34

Intracavity administration (the introduction of drugs directly into a body cavity) provides another means of achieving a high local concentration and minimising systemic effects. This may, for example, involve injection into the pleural or peritoneal cavity and is particularly useful when it is known that a drug given intravenously does not readily penetrate that cavity (Priestman, 1980) or when used as an adjunctive therapy.

This approach is most commonly used to control malignant effusions but may be used to treat well-localised tumours. Intraperitoneal treatment is being used more frequently, especially in ovarian cancer where metastatic seeding of the peritoneum is common (p102). Drugs used in this way include cisplatin, doxorubicin and 5-FU (Markman et al, 1984) and paclitaxel (Chabner and Longo, 1996).

The blood-brain barrier consists of tight junctions between the endothelial cells of cerebral capillaries, choroid plexuses and arachnoid villi and acts to 'protect' the brain from exposure to toxic substances. Although lipid-soluble drugs can readily cross the blood-brain barrier, water-soluble substances (eg. most cytotoxic agents) have little access to the brain; thus the central nervous system acts as a 'sanctuary' for neoplastic cells (Rahr, 1984). Thus, in attempts to reach tumour deposits, cytotoxic agents must be given intrathecally (ie. injected directly into the subarachnoid space) (Brodie and Harrison, 1986). Cytotoxic drugs used in this way include methotrexate and cytosine arabinoside (Chabner and Longo, 1996).

A few cytotoxic drugs (eg. 5-FU and methotrexate) have been incorporated into creams and/or ointments suitable for topical application. Since absorption through this means is limited this approach is only suitable for extremely superficial lesions (Calman et al, 1980; Priestman, 1980).

Drug distribution

Drug distribution and transport may significantly influence the effects of chemotherapy. Following absorption, drugs may be bound to serum albumin or other blood components prior to entering the various body compartments (Cline and Haskell, 1980). Thus changes in the serum protein concentration, combined with concurrent administration of a number of drugs, may influence both the binding to serum transport proteins and the proportion of the free drug in the bloodstream. Since hypoalbuminaemia is common in malignant disease (Holmes and Dickerson, 1987) this can significantly affect the distribution of cytotoxic drugs. Similarly binding of one drug can be influenced by the presence of a second since they may 'compete' for the same binding sites thus reducing the amount of both drugs that can be bound and increasing the quantity of the free drug in the circulation.

One of the possible consequences of an increased circulating level of a drug is an increase in its action and an associated increase in toxicity. Alternatively, an increase serum drug concentration may increase the rate of elimination through renal filtration or hepatic diffusion thus shortening the serum half life ($t_{1/2}$) of the drug and reducing its therapeutic effect.

As most antineoplastic drugs exert their effects through inter-actions with intracellular target molecules the ability of a drug, or its active metabolite(s), to reach cancer cells is of major importance. Alterations in serum protein concentration may, therefore, have significant effects on treatment by causing a redistribution of the drug from the circulation into the rest of the body (Calman et al, 1980) enhancing pharmacological and toxic effects and increasing the rate of glomerular filtration.

Conversely, some drugs may be excluded from certain areas because of other factors affecting distribution, such as the blood supply of the tumour or the fat solubility of the drug (von Ardenne and van Ardenne, 1975).

Biotransformation

Clearly the distribution of a drug can affect its efficacy; its metabolism is another important factor. Cytotoxic drugs may under-go a wide range of metabolic transformations including oxidation, reduction, hydrolysis or conjugation. Since some are inactive when administered biotransformation is essential to convert the drug to its active form. Other reactions convert the drug to a more lipid soluble form to facilitate excretion.

Most such transformations occur in the liver where the micro-somal enzymes catalyse the necessary reactions (Figure 3.2). Bio-transformation is of clinical importance and an understanding of the metabolism of cytotoxic drugs is essential if they are to be used effectively. For example, cyclophosphamide is not effective as an anti-neoplastic agent until hepatic biotransformation has taken place converting it to a potent alkylating agent.

Figure 3.2   **Schematic representation of drug metabolism**

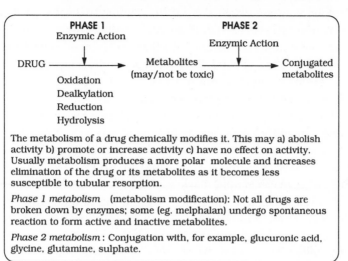

PHASE 1
Enzymic Action

PHASE 2
Enzymic Action

DRUG ⟶ Metabolites ⟶ Conjugated
Oxidation   (may/not be toxic)   metabolites
Dealkylation
Reduction
Hydrolysis

The metabolism of a drug chemically modifies it. This may a) abolish activity b) promote or increase activity c) have no effect on activity. Usually metabolism produces a more polar molecule and increases elimination of the drug or its metabolites as it becomes less susceptible to tubular resorption.

Phase 1 metabolism (metabolism modification): Not all drugs are broken down by enzymes; some (eg. melphalan) undergo spontaneous reaction to form active and inactive metabolites.

Phase 2 metabolism : Conjugation with, for example, glucuronic acid, glycine, glutamine, sulphate.

Excretion

The most common routes of excretion of cytotoxic drugs are through the kidneys and the liver; the function of these organs is, therefore, critical to successful treatment and, particularly, the reduction of toxic effects since impaired clearance may give rise to increased toxicity.

For example, drugs that are excreted through the kidneys (eg. cisplatin) may cause toxicity when renal function is impaired. Conversely, it is not unusual for successful chemotherapy to result in the release of significant amounts of uric acid, from the breakdown of cancer cells, so that uric acid nephropathy may reduce renal function reducing the clearance of drugs normally excreted in this way. Alternatively, some drugs (eg. methotrexate), when given in high doses, may precipitate in the renal tubules so that high renal blood flow and effective glomerular filtration are essential if clearance is to be achieved (Calman et al, 1980).

Obstruction of the biliary tract may necessitate major modifications of drug dosage if excessive toxicity is to be prevented.

The anthracycline antibiotics (eg. adriamycin, daunorubicin) and the vinca alkaloids, particularly vincristine, are primarily excreted by this route so that their toxicity to the bone marrow and peripheral nerves may be increased when liver function is abnormal (van den Berg et al, 1982; Brenner et al, 1984).

Drug interactions

Interactions between drugs are not uncommon; cancer chemotherapy is no exception (Hancock and Bradshaw, 1981). One drug may either inhibit or potentiate the action of other drugs thus modifying their therapeutic or toxic effects. Such consequences may arise not only between antineoplastic agents but also between cytotoxic agents and any other drugs the patient is receiving. Since Calabresi and Parks (1980) found that hospitalised patients often receive nine or more drugs concurrently, and many are also self-prescribing over-the-counter medications, such interactions are not unlikely.

Drug interactions may occur due to accelerated or inhibited metabolism (Calabresi and Parks, 1980) and, in this context, two main mechanisms are involved: enzyme inhibition and enzyme induction (Calman et al, 1980).

Enzyme inhibition results when one drug inhibits the enzymes concerned with the biotransformation of a second drug, an effect known as competitive inhibition. Competitive inhibition occurs when many substrates (in this case drugs) compete for the same enzymes and may bind irreversibly with those enzymes; their metabolites may also be effective inhibitors. Drugs known to produce such effects include atropine, morphine and cocaine, which are not uncommonly administered to cancer patients.

One such interaction, which produces significant effects and markedly augments toxicity, is that between allopurinol and 6-mercaptopurine (6-MP) (Cline and Haskell, 1980; Hancock and Bradshaw, 1981). Allopurinol exerts profound inhibitory effects on some of the hepatic drug metabolising enzymes, notably xanthine oxidase, significantly disrupting 6-MP metabolism to the extent that, if these drugs are to be used in combination, the dose of 6-MP must be reduced by 70-75% (Calabresi and Parks, 1980; Barton-Burke et al, 1991).

Enzyme induction. The activity of drug metabolising enzymes can be increased by administration of some drugs and by exposure to certain environmental chemicals; such inducers of enzyme activity are not necessarily substrates for affected enzymes. Furthermore, chronic administration of a drug may stimulate its own metabolism as well as that of other drugs so that interactions may occur between any drugs that are administered simultaneously. Examples of drugs

38

that may cause such effects include chlorpromazine, steroids, phenytoin and phenylbutazone. The metabolism of other drugs given concurrently is accelerated and their therapeutic efficacy is reduced.

A number of other interactive effects have been reported. Some are easily observed (eg. drug precipitation in IV tubing) but others are less easily identified. For this reason, it is important that those prescribing or administering drugs are aware of potential drug inter-actions since such effects may have significant clinical consequences. For example, nitrogen mustard and many of its derivatives are highly reactive chemical compounds; chemical reactions between mixtures of drugs are not unlikely. This may result in inactivation of one or more of the drugs present.

Drug absorption may also be affected when gastric emptying is modified by, for example, antiemetic therapy (Ch. 11) (Hancock and Bradshaw, 1981) or by the concurrent administration of drugs that suppress the GI microbial flora (eg. antibiotics).

Timing of chemotherapy administration

Many biological processes are more active at certain times of the day causing changes in drug metabolism and elimination. This appears to result from variations in the metabolism and proliferation of normal cells which are, in turn, dependant on the circadian rhythm of hormone and growth factor release to which tumour cells are less sensitive (Pratt et al, 1994); this may have a profound effect on the therapeutic index (King, 1996). Animal studies have shown that giving drugs at specific times of the day may generate greater levels of cell kill and reduced toxicity than when they are given haphazardly (Hrusheshky, 1985). Extrapolation to man has produced promising results in clinical trials (Caussanel et al, 1990). Although the influence of natural rhythms is only beginning to be understood it seems that they may be important considerations when attempting to design maximally effective therapeutic regimens.

Patient-related factors

Several of the factors influencing the response to chemotherapy are intrinsic to the host rather than to the tumour. One of the most important of these is the general status of the patient and their ability to withstand the toxic effects of chemotherapeutic agents. Since all such agents have at least some side-effects this must clearly be taken into account in planning treatment for individual patients.

Although the impact of such effects can be minimised the risk of toxic effects may limit the use of some drugs, particularly in the debilitated or elderly patient in whom tolerance to cytotoxic therapy is likely to be poor (Pratt et al, 1994).

The patient's immune status is another important determinant of the response to therapy. This is particularly true of that related to cell-mediated immunity (CMI), that is the effects mediated by T-lymphocytes and activated macrophages. Studies have clearly shown a reduced responsiveness to anticancer drugs when CMI is decreased (Pratt et al, 1994).

Immunocompetence, particularly as it affects a tumour, may also be affected by haemodynamic factors thus reducing the availability of immune cells (eg. antitumour antibodies) or polypeptides (eg. tumour necrosis factor) within the tumour itself and limiting their ability to 'attack'. A variety of physiological factors may contribute to this impaired delivery of immune cells to a tumour. These include: the heterogeneous blood supply, an elevation of interstitial pressure, fluid effusion from the tumour periphery and the large diffusion distances associated with a large tumour mass (Jain, 1989).

DRUG RESISTANCE

The development of resistance to antineoplastic agents is a common problem in cancer therapy. The first dose of an anticancer drug may be extremely effective but effectiveness may decrease with successive doses until, eventually, no effect is observed. Clearly such effects may severely limit the success of therapy.

Such resistance may be primary (natural or intrinsic) or acquired and represents the combined characteristics of a specific drug, a particular tumour, and a specific host whereby the drug is ineffective in controlling the tumour without excessive toxicity to that host (Skeel, 1995).

The initial unresponsiveness of a tumour to a given drug is described as natural or intrinsic resistance and may result from various factors. For example, transport of the drug to the tumour may be inhibited by the poor vascularity of large tumours (pharmacological resistance); slow growing tumours may have a low growth fraction and so be less susceptible to antineoplastic agents and, finally, it is suggested that some tumours may mutate spontaneously thus causing resistance to specific drugs and that large tumours possess greater numbers of resistant mutations

40

(Goldie and Coldman, 1979). Thus some cells within a tumour may initially be resistant to a drug; as time passes this resistance will become increasingly evident as those cells that are sensitive to the drug diminish. As a result only a certain proportion of tumour cells will receive adequate treatment.

Acquired (secondary) resistance may also account for the failure of treatment (Woolley and Tew, 1988). It occurs at the cellular level after the drug has been administered and is generally considered to be the most common reason for the failure of drug therapy with initially sensitive tumour (Skipper and Schabel, 1978: Pratt et al, 1994).

Although this is an area of ongoing research, a number of possible causes have been identified. It seems that, when cells acquire the property of drug resistance, they undergo a heritable change in genetic composition which is then passed on to successive generations. This may occur in two ways:

1. The cell may undergo a mutation which interferes with its ability to interact with the drug directly or to carry out some function necessary for drug effect.

2. The cell may undergo gene amplification when the gene coding for a particular protein is multiplied. Affected cells can then synthesise more of that protein and are then able to survive in the presence of drug concentrations that would normally be lethal   (Pratt et al, 1994).

In addition, it seems that alterations in the permeability of cell membranes may inhibit the transport of the drug in the cell (Curt et al, 1984; Trent, 1989) while changes in enzyme activity may influence the activation or inactivation of drugs and resistant mutagens may develop. It has been suggested that the resistance exhibited by some cancer cells may be similar to that which bacteria exhibit towards antibiotics so that similar approaches can be adopted to overcome it (Cline and Haskell, 1980).

Thus large initial doses, combinations of drugs, alternating combinations of drugs and the earliest possible treatment may be employed in attempts to overcome resistance.

The above discussion shows that there are four categories of drug resistance:

- Kinetic
- Biochemical
- Pharmacological
- Non-selective

Factors affecting the use of chemotherapy

Cell kinetics and resistance

Drug resistance based on cell population kinetics relates to the growth fraction of the tumour and the cycle or phase specificity of the drug(s) involved and the implications of these factors on the responsiveness to specific agents; the schedule of drug administration is also important.

Of particular importance is the fact that many tumours are in a plateau growth phase, with only a small growth fraction which, as previously shown, renders many cells insensitive to antineoplastic agents, particularly the antimetabolites (Skeel, 1995). Resistance due to kinetic effects may be overcome by some of the approaches used below:

- Reduction of tumour bulk using other treatment methods (eg. surgery or radiotherapy)
- Use of drug combinations which include the use of both cell cycle phase specific and phase non-specific agents so as to increase the cytotoxic effect by use of drugs depending on different biochemical pathways including drugs which affect resting (G_0) cell populations
- Scheduling of drugs to enhance synchrony and increase cell kill.

Biochemical causes of resistance

A variety of biochemical factors can contribute to the development of drug resistance. For example, changes in enzyme activity may lead to a failure to convert a drug into its active form, impair its metabolism or interfere with the ability of a tumour to inactivate the drug. Furthermore, as has been observed, spontaneous genetic mutations occur in all cell populations giving rise to traits that can then be passed to successive generations. Kartner and Ling (1989). suggest that such mutations occur in somewhere between one in 10^5 and one in 10^8 cells; despite their rarity, such cells may have a significant impact on the response cancer chemotherapy. It is suggested that all clinically detectable tumours contain some drug resistant cells (Goldie and Coldman, 1979) so that, although remission may be achieved initially due to destruction of drug sensitive cells, tumour growth continues as the remaining resistant cells continue to divide and, ultimately, dominate the tumour population (Figure 3.3). This may also explain why curability of a small tumour cannot always be ensured despite treatment or why significant variation in response can be seen in identically treated patients, with diseases of the same primary site and similar histological features (Schackney, 1985).

Figure 3.3   **Diagrammatic representation of the concept of drug resistance** (based on Kartner and Ling, 1989)

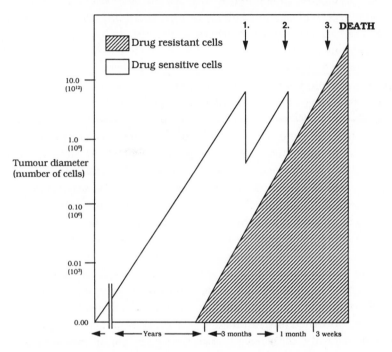

1. First course of chemotherapy (CT) successfully decreases tumour bulk by killing the majority of drug-sensitive cells. It does not, however, affect drug-resistant cells which continue to grow exponentially.

2. Second course of CT again decreases the drug sensitive population but has no effect on drug-resistant cells now present in larger numbers.

3. Final course of CT has no apparent effect. Tumour growth continues leading, ultimately, to death.

Laboratory evidence suggests that, in malignant cells, exposure to a single cytotoxic drug can lead to resistance to multiple agents. This is particularly true of many of the agents derived from natural products (eg. adriamycin, vinblastine) (Trent, 1989). One of the major causes of multidrug resistance (MDR) is believed to be a large glycoprotein (p-glycoprotein) found on the cell surface. Cancer cells showing such resistance have been shown to possess very high

43

numbers of these cell surface proteins while cells which are sensitive to chemotherapeutic agents have very few, if any (Trent, 1989). It is clear that p-glycoprotein is over-produced as a result of gene amplification (see below) (Kartner et al, 1985). It is believed that p-glycoprotein acts as a pump at the cell surface which enables drugs to enter the cell but then quickly pumps them out again thus leaving cells undamaged by chemotherapy (Kartner and Ling, 1989). p-glycoprotein is also present on the surface of some normal cells, particularly those known to be resistant to anticancer drugs (eg. liver, kidney, adrenal glands) while cells that are highly chemosensitive (eg. blood cells) have almost no p-glycoprotein (Trent 1989).

Additional mechanisms of drug resistance have been described. These include: gene amplification, development of alternative metabolic pathways that permit cell survival, and antineoplastic alterations which increase genetic instability and mutation rate (Schackney, 1985). Thus, if a drug acts as to inhibit an enzyme within the cell then over-production of that enzyme may permit survival even in the presence of cytotoxic drug concentrations.

Resistance to several antineoplastic agents has been shown to arise in this way. For example, Trent et al (1984) have shown that gene amplification may cause resistance to methotrexate following prolonged exposure to low doses (2-5mg weekly for three years). Methotrexate no longer inhibits intracellular production of the enzyme concerned (dihydrofolate reductase) (Shimke, 1984). Similarly Goldstein et al (1989) have shown that gene amplification results in enhanced production of p-glycoprotein finding the highest levels of the amplified gene in chemoresistant tumours, such as those of the colon, kidneys, liver, adrenal cortex and non-small cell tumours of the lung. Other tumours possessing the amplified gene include phaeochromocytoma, islet cell tumours of the pancreas, carcinoid tumours and chronic myelogenous leukaemia in blast crisis (Goldstein et al, 1989).

Pharmacological resistance

True pharmacological resistance results when the transport of cytotoxic agents is impaired. For example, as described, many drugs do not cross the blood-brain barrier so that the central nervous system provides a 'sanctuary' for malignant cells. However, apparent resistance to cytotoxic therapy can, as described, be the result of poor or erratic absorption, increased catabolism or excretion of the drug or drug-drug interactions, all of which may reduce the blood levels of the drug. Strictly speaking, however, such effects are not the result of true resistance but rather reflect the outcome of inadequate blood levels. Since such factors may not be recognised by the clinician it may appear that the tumour is resistant to the drug(s) employed (Skeel, 1995).

Non-selectivity and resistance

This does not truly provide an explanation for drug resistance. Instead it provides a recognition that for most tumours, and most drugs, the reason for both resistance and selectivity are not yet fully understood. Research continues since increasing understanding of the actions of chemotherapy at the cellular level is essential and holds the key to successful treatment of malignant disease. In the meantime attempts to overcome it continue. For example, the earliest possible institution of chemotherapy may minimise the development of resistant clones thus increasing curability. Combination chemotherapy may be more effective than single agents while minimising toxicity; this approach provides for a broader range of coverage of new or resistant cell lines (DeVita, 1985). Increasing understanding can only lead to improvements in therapy.

REFERENCES

Barofsky I, 1984, Therapeutic compliance and the cancer patient, Health Education **10**, 43-56.

Barton-Burke M, Wilkes GM, Berg D, et al, 1991, Cancer Chemotherapy: A Nursing Process Approach, Jones and Bartlett Publishers, Boston.

Brenner DE, Wiernik PH, Wesley M, et al, 1984, Acute doxorubicin toxicity: relationship to pretreatment liver function, response and pharmacokinetics in patients with acute nonlymphocytic leukemia, Cancer **53**, 1042-8.

Brodie MJ, Harrison I, 1986, Practical Prescribing, Churchill Livingstone, Edinburgh.

Calabresi P, Parks RE, 1980, Chemotherapy of neoplastic diseases In: Goodman Gilman AG, Goodman LS, Gilman A (Editors), Goodman and Gilman's The Pharmacological Basis of Therapeutics (Sixth edition) Macmillan Publishing Co. Inc., New York.

Calman KC, Smythe JF, Tattersall MNH, 1980, Basic Principles of Cancer Chemotherapy, The MacMillan Press Ltd, London

Caussanel JP, Levin S, Brienza JL, et al, 1990, Phase 1 trial of a 5 day continuous venous infusion of oxaliplatin at circadian-rhythm-modulated rate compared with constant rate, Journal of the National Cancer Institute **82**, 1046-50.

Chabner BA, Longo DL, 1996, Cancer Chemotherapy and Biotherapy: Principles and Practice (Second edition), Lippincott-Raven, Philadelphia

Cline M, Haskell C, 1980, Cancer Chemotherapy, WB Saunders Co., Philadelphia.

Collins J, 1984, Pharmacologic rationale for regional drug delivery, Journal of Clinical Oncology **2**, 498-504

Curt GA, Clendeninn NH, Chabner BA, 1984, Drug resistance in cancer, Cancer Treatment Reports **68**, 87-99.

DeVita VT, 1985, Principles of Chemotherapy. In: DeVita VT Hellman S, Rosenberg SA (Editors), Cancer: Principles and Practice of Oncology, JB Lippincott Co., Philadelphia.

Folkman J, 1990, What is the evidence that tumours are angiogenesis dependent? Journal of the National Cancer Institute **82**, 4-6.

Goldie JH, Coldman AJ, 1979, A mathematical model for relating the drug sensitivity of tumours to their spontaneous mutation rates, Cancer Treatment Reports **63**, 1727-33.

Goldstein LJ, Galaski A, Fojo M, et al, 1989, Expression of a multidrug resistance gene in human cancers Journal of the National Cancer Institute **81**(2), 116-24.

Goodman MH, 1988, Concepts of hormonal manipulation in the treatment of cancer, Oncology Nursing Forum **15**(5), 639-47.

Guy JL, 1991, Medical oncology - the agents. In: Baird SB, McCorkle R, Grant M (Editors), Cancer Nursing: A Comprehensive Textbook, WB Saunders Co., Philadelphia.

Hancock BW, Bradshaw JD, 1981, Lecture Notes on Clinical Oncology, Blackwell Scientific Publications, Oxford.

Hansten PD, 1985, Drug Interactions: Clinical Significance of Drug-Drug Interactions (Fifth edition), Lea and Febiger, Philadelphia.

Hill BT, 1978, Cancer chemotherapy: The relevance of certain concepts of cell cycle kinetics, Biochemica et Biophysica Acta **516**, 389-417.

Holmes S, Dickerson JWT, 1987, Malignant disease: nutritional implications of disease and treatment, Cancer and Metastasis Reviews **6**, 357-81.

Hrushesky WJM, 1985, Circadian timing of cancer chemotherapy, Science **228**, 73-5.

Jain RK, 1989, Delivery of novel therapeutic agents in tumors: physiological barriers and strategies, Journal of the National Cancer Institute **81**, 570-86.

Jarman M, 1989, The development of anticancer drugs, Chemistry in Britain **25**, 51-4.

Kartner N, Ling V, 1989, Multidrug resistance in cancer, Scientific American **260**, 26-33.

Kartner ND, Evernden-Porelle G, Bradley G, et al, 1985, Detection of p-glycoprotein in multidrug resistant cell lines by monoclonal antibodies, Nature **316**, 820-3.

King RJB, 1996, Cancer Biology, Addison-Wesley Longman Ltd., Edinburgh.

Klopp CT, Alford TC, Bateman MO, et al, 1950, Fractionated intra-arterial cancer chemotherapy with methyl-bis-amine hydrochloride: a preliminary report, Annals of Surgery **132**, 811-32.

Knopf MKT, Fischer DS, Welch-McCaffery D, 1984, Cancer Chemotherapy: Treatment and Care (Second edition), GK Hall Medical Publishers, Boston.

Levin V, Sheline G, Gutin P, 1989, Neoplasms in the central nervous system. In: DeVita VT, Hellman S, Rosenberg SA (Editors), Cancer: Principles and Practice of Oncology (Third edition), JB Lippincott Co., Philadelphia.

Markman M, Howell SB Lucas WE, et al, 1984, Combination intra-peritoneal chemotherapy with cisplatin, cytarabine and doxorubicin for refractory ovarian carcinoma and, other malignancies primarily confined to the peritoneal cavity, Journal of Clinical Oncology **2**, 1321-6.

Pratt WB, Ruddon RW, Ensminger WD, et al. 1994, The Anticancer Drugs (Second edition), Oxford University Press, New York and Oxford.

Priestman TJ, 1980, Cancer Chemotherapy: An Introduction, Farmitalia Carlo Erba Ltd., Barnet, Herts.

Rahr V, 1985, Giving intrathecal drugs, American Journal of Nursing **85**, 829-31.

Schackney SE, 1985, Cell kinetics and cancer chemotherapy. In: Calabresi P, Schein PS, Rosenberg SA (Editors), Medical Oncology: Basic Principles and Clinical Management of Cancer, Macmillan Press, New York.

Segall HN 1923, An experimental anatomic investigation of the blood and bile channels in the liver, Surgery, Gynecology and Obstetrics, Little, Brown and Co., Boston.

Shimke RT, 1984, Gene amplification, drug resistance and cancer, Cancer Research **44**, 1735-42.

Skeel RT, 1995, Biologic and pharmacologic basis of cancer chemotherapy. In: Skeel RT, Lachant NA (Editors), Handbook of Cancer Chemotherapy (Fourth edition) Little, Brown and Co., Boston

Skipper HE, Schabel FM, 1978, Experimental therapeutics and kinetics: selection and overgrowth of specifically and permanently drug-resistant tumour cells, Seminars in Haematology **5**, 207-10.

Taylor JR, Halpin KM, 1977, Effect of sodium salicylate and indomethacin on methotrexate-serum albumin binding, Archives of Dermatology **113**, 588-91.

Trent JM, Buick RN, Olson S, Horns RC, Schimke RT, 1984, Cytologic evidence for gene amplification in methotrexate-resistant cells obtained from a patient with ovarian carcinoma, Journal of Clinical Oncology **2**, 8-15.

Trent JM, 1989, Mechanisms of drug resistance in human cancer. In: Proceedings, Advances in Clinical Oncology, (March), Snowbird, Utah.

van den Berg HW, Desai ZR, Wison R, et al, 1982, The pharmacokinetics of vincristine in man: reduced drug clearance associated with raised serum alkaline phosphatase and dose limiting elimination, Cancer Chemotherapy and Pharmacology **8**, 215-22.

von Ardenne VM, von Ardenne A, 1975, Pharmacokinetic aspects of tumour tissue impairment by cancerostatics, Arzeimittel-Forschung **25**, 863-70 (English Abstract).

Wooley PV, Tew KD, 1988, Mechanisms of Drug Resistance in Neoplastic Cells, Academic Press, New York.

CHAPTER 4   CHEMOTHERAPEUTIC DRUGS

Since the chemical structure and the physiological and biochemical actions of cancer chemotherapeutic agents differ significantly such drugs exert their effects in a variety of ways. There are, however, similarities between certain of the drugs that enables them to be classified according to the mechanisms through which they exert their antineoplastic effects.

There are, currently, 4 main groups of chemotherapeutic agents (Table 4.1), together with a group of miscellaneous drugs that includes a variety of agents with unique antineoplastic effects. Hormones and hormone antagonists may also be used to inhibit tumour growth.

Within each group drugs vary with regard to their specific antineoplastic action and in their toxic effects. Such differences may be significant in treating individual tumours since a tumour that is resistant to one drug may be sensitive to another even within the same general classification; similarly the toxic effects may show marked variation. Despite this an understanding of the general classification of chemotherapeutic agents, in terms of their mode of action, methods of administration, common toxicities and side-effects, will help in planning appropriate patient care.

ALKYLATING AGENTS

The alkylating agents are a diverse group of chemical compounds which are highly reactive and function by interacting with intracellular DNA and preventing replication. More specifically, by substituting an alkyl groups for the hydrogen atoms present in cellular molecules, alkylating agents cause both single and double strand breaks and cross-linking of the strands of DNA. As a result the DNA strands are unable to separate, an action necessary for the replication of genetic material, thus causing either inhibition or inaccurate replication and leads to mutation or cell death (Chabner and Myers, 1985).

Such effects, on both normal and malignant cells, are similar to those resulting from exposure to ionising radiation (see Holmes, 1996) so that alkylating agents are often described as radiomimetic agents.

Table 4.1   Classification of chemotherapeutic drugs

Alkylating agents	Highly reactive compounds that cause cross-linking and abnormal base pairing of DNA so that transcription and replication cannot occur. Synthesis of DNA and other cellular components continues leading to cellular imbalance and eventually to cell death. eg. cyclophosphamide.
Antimetabolites	Structural analogues of intracellular metabolites required during replication. Act by competing with, or substituting for, metabolites or by binding to them so that dysfunction results. Generally cell cycle phase specific, the exception being 5-fluorouracil. eg. methotrexate and cytosine arabinoside.
Antitumour antibiotics	Derived from microorganisms, these drugs inhibit synthesis of both DNA and RNA; they also have some antimicrobial effects. Usually cell cycle phase non-specific. eg. bleomycin, adriamycin.
Plant products	These drugs are derived from a variety of plants and plant extracts. They include the vinca alkaloids, taxanes and podophyllum derivatives as well as other topoisomerase inhibitors. Known as 'spindle poisons' both vinca alkaloids (eg. vinblastine and vincristine) and taxanes (eg. paclitaxel) function by inhibiting mitosis although their mechanisms of action are different (see text). Podophyllotoxins are topoisomerase II inhibitors (eg. etoposide, teniposide).
Hormones and hormone antagonists	Hormones are not themselves cytotoxic but, since the growth and development of some tumours depend, in part at least, on a specific hormonal environment alterations in that environment may influence their growth. This may be achieved using hormones or hormone antagonists. For example, antagonistic steroids may inhibit growth while 'blocking' hormone receptors may deprive cells of a growth stimulant. Oestrogens, anti-oestrogens, androgens and progestogens have all been used in anticancer therapy.
Miscellaneous agents	A wide variety of drugs may be employed all of which exhibit cytotoxic effects. Examples include: cisplatin, L-asparaginase and pro-carbazine.

Although there are marked differences in the pharmacological activity and clinical uses of the alkylating agents, as a group they are considered to be cell cycle phase non-specific as they interact with a variety of intracellular components including preformed DNA, RNA and other proteins (Skeel, 1995). They, therefore, exert effects throughout the cycle but tend to be more effective against rapidly dividing cells perhaps because such cells have less time to repair damage caused in G_1 before they enter the sensitive S phase (Chabner and Myers, 1985). Because alkylating agents are also active against resting (G_0) cells, they may be used to 'debulk' a tumour causing resting cells to be recruited into active cycle when they will be vulnerable to cell cycle phase specific agents.

The alkylating agents have been proven effective against Hodgkin's disease and other lymphomas, multiple myeloma and breast cancer. They are, however, associated with a number of side-effects due to their effects on rapidly dividing cells, particularly the gastrointestinal, haemapoietic and reproductive cells. Nausea and vomiting are common, particularly when drugs are given intravenously. The haematological effect is primarily leucopoenia which reaches its nadir in 7-14 days and recovers in approximately 30 days; cumulative myelosuppression follows repeated administration (see Ch. 9).

Nitrosoureas are a subgroup of the alkylating agents which, unlike most cytotoxic drugs, are fat-soluble and can readily cross the blood-brain barrier. Although they are alkylating agents, the nitrosoureas are often classified separately as they have additional mechanisms of action and toxicity. They undergo extensive biotransformation which leads to a variety of biological effects that include alkylation, carbamoylation and inhibition of DNA repair; they also appear to exert other damaging effects on both dividing and non-dividing cells.

Although their ability to cross the blood-brain barrier is clearly beneficial in treating meningeal and other brain tumours, they cause significant, but delayed, bone marrow depression, often occurring 4-6 weeks after administration (Skeel, 1995) (Ch. 9). Nitrosoureas are unique among the alkylating agents since, in addition to their lipid solubility, they are non cross-resistant. Common alkylating agents include: mechlorethamine, ifosfamide, melphalan, lomustine, cyclophosphamide, carmustine, thiotepa, streptozocin, dacarbazine.

ANTIMETABOLITES

Antimetabolites are structural analogues of normal, intracellular metabolites essential for cell function and replication and so are used to disrupt cellular metabolism. They may inflict damage by one of three main mechanisms (Haskell, 1985):

1. By substituting for a metabolite which is normally incorporated into a key molecule thus making that molecule function abnormally.

2. By competing with a normal metabolite for the catalytic site of a major enzyme.

3. By competing with a normal metabolite which acts at the regulatory site of an enzyme to control the catalytic rate of that enzyme.

Thus, because they are mistaken by the cell for the normal metabolite, antimetabolites will either inhibit the critical enzymes

51

involved in nucleic acid (DNA and RNA) synthesis or become incorporated into the nucleic acids themselves, disrupting cellular function and transcription of genetic material. The end result is that DNA synthesis is prevented and cell death results (Skeel, 1995). They are cell cycle specific agents.

As most antimetabolite cytotoxicity occurs during the synthetic (S) phase these agents are most effective when used against rapidly dividing cell populations; they are, therefore, more active against fast-growing tumours than those which grow more slowly.

Antimetabolites in common use include folic acid antagonists (such as methotrexate and trimetrexate), purine antagonists (eg. 6-mercaptopurine), pyrimidine antagonists (eg. cytosine arabinoside) and fluoropyrimidines (eg. 5-fluorouracil and 6-thioguanine).

Bone marrow suppression, which reaches its nadir 1-2 weeks after administration and causes severe leucopoenia, is a common side-effect; anaemia and thrombocytopoenia are less severe. Gastro-intestinal (GI) symptoms, such as nausea and vomiting and diarr-hoea, are also common due to the effects on the GI mucosa.

There are, in addition, two important side-effects that occur with specific antimetabolites - methotrexate, 6-mercaptopurine (6-MP) and 6-thioguanine (6-TG). Folic acid analogues, such as methotrexate, inhibit the enzyme dihydrofolate reductase which is crucial to replication and to DNA synthesis in all cells, normal and malignant. Thus methotrexate can be lethal if given without an antidote. Leucovorin, a reduced form of folic acid is, therefore, given 24-36 hours after initiation of therapy. This competes with methotrexate for entry into the cells and also bypasses the inhibition of DNA synthesis allowing cell function and replication to continue. The purine antagonists, 6-MP and 6-TG, may cause hepatic damage. This is particularly important in those receiving cancer chemotherapy as many antineoplastic drugs are excreted through the liver.

ANTITUMOUR ANTIBIOTICS

The antitumour antibiotics are natural products isolated from micro-organisms, most notably the *Streptomyces* species (Knopf et al, 1984). Although they have both cytotoxic and antimicrobial activity the former limits their antimicrobial value while proving valuable in treating a wide range of cancers (Skeel, 1995). They act primarily by binding to DNA inhibiting its synthesis and replication (Chabner and Myers, 1985); they also disrupt synthesis of RNA. As a group they are active in all phases of the cell cycle and so are classified as cell cycle non-specific. For example, bleomycin causes single and double strand breaks in DNA while the anthracycline antibiotics (eg. dauno-mycin, doxorubicin) prevent DNA from acting as a template for synthesis of both RNA and DNA, a process known as intercalation (Chabner and Myers, 1985); they also cause oxidative-reductive reactions and interact directly with cell membranes altering their function. Mitomycin has similar effects but also acts as an alkylator.

The major side-effects of the antitumour antibiotics are similar to those of the alkylating agents. The majority cause myelosuppression, especially leucopoenia and thrombocytopoenia. Alopecia and GI mucositis are common. Some of these drugs, however, have unique side-effects. For example, bleomycin may cause pneumonitis leading to pulmonary fibrosis while doxorubicin and daunorubicin may, uniquely, cause a dose-related cardiotoxicity; hepatic, renal and clotting dysfunction may be associated with mithramycin therapy. In addition, severe tissue necrosis and sloughing may occur when all these drugs (other than bleomycin and plicamycin) are extravasated.

Antitumour antibiotics in common use include bleomycin, mitomycin, daunorubicin, epirubicin, actinomycin-D, plicamycin, doxorubicin, mitoxantrone and mithramycin

PLANT PRODUCTS

The search for new antineoplastic agents led to the screening of many plants and plant extracts resulting in the identification of a number of antineoplastic agents. These include the vinca alkaloids, taxanes and podophyllum derivatives and other topoisomerase II inhibitors.

Vinca alkaloids

Vinca alkaloids are amongst the most useful cytotoxic agents. They are naturally occurring substances that were isolated from the pink periwinkle, *vinca roseus* (now known as *cantharanthus roseus*) over 30 years ago thus supporting the traditional belief that periwinkles possessed 'miraculous' healing powers (Crossland, 1980). Their use in the treatment of diabetes led to screening to identify the cause of their hypoglycaemic activity; this turned out to be of little importance when compared to their cytotoxic properties (Johnson et al, 1967; Johnson, 1968). Their major antineoplastic effects are exerted during the metaphase of the mitotic process when they cause mitotic arrest by binding to the microtubular proteins essential for formation of the

Classification of antineoplastic agents

mitotic spindle (see p18-20); the cell, unable to divide, dies. They are, therefore, often known as 'spindle poisons'.

Vinca alkaloids are also capable of many other biochemical and biological activities including: disruption of RNA, DNA and protein synthesis, inhibition of purine biosynthesis, and inhibition of glycolysis amongst others (Rowinsky and Donehower, 1996). This multiplicity of actions means that they are difficult to classify but, as their activity is primarily due to their ability to disrupt mitosis, they are generally regarded as cell cycle phase specific.

Despite their chemical similarity these drugs exhibit a spectrum of efficacy and toxicity; all are vesicants (Ch. 8) so that administration through a central line is recommended (p93 *et seq*). Neurotoxicity, manifested by constipation, urinary retention and, rarely, joint pain, may occur. Peripheral neuritis/neuropathy, characterised by parasthesiae and hyperasthesiae, is common. This typically cumulative and its severity is related to both the total dose delivered and the duration of treatment (Rowinsky and Donehower, 1996). GI toxicity (nausea and vomiting) may arise; constipation is common and often due to autonomic dysfunction. Haematological effects differ between the agents (Table 4.2). Vinca alkaloids in current use are vincristine, vinblastine, vindesine and vinorelbine.

Table 4.2   Haematological effects of vinca alkaloids

Vincristine	Mild-moderate anaemia, leucopoenia and thrombocytopoenia
Vinblastine	Leucopoenia is the principal toxicity; nadir occurs 4-10 days after treatment and recovery occurs within 7-10 days. Thrombocytopoenia and recovery are less common.
Vindesine	Neutropoenia is the most common toxicity with the nadir neutrophil count occurring in about 7 days and recovery within 14 days of treatment. Thrombocytopoenia is less common.
Vinorelbine	Neutropoenia is a dose-limiting toxicity of vinorelbine. The neutrophil count nadirs within 7-10 days of treatment; recovery is usually complete within 7-14 days. Mild to moderate anaemia is common while clinically significant thrombocytopoenia is rare.

Taxanes

The taxanes are an important new class of antineoplastic agent which, like vinca alkaloids, exert their effects on the microtubules. Their mechanism of action, however, differs. Taxanes were discovered as part of a National Cancer Institute programme, in which

54

thousands of plants were screened for anticancer activity, and were isolated from the bark of the Pacific yew (Wani et al, 1971). Later work found that a precursor of paclitaxel (the active agent) existed in other yew species (eg. the European yew (*Taxus baccata*)); this is likely to produce sufficient quantities to meet the commercial demand (Dennis and Greene, 1988).

Taxanes display a high affinity for binding to microtubules and inhibit cellular proliferation inducing a sustained mitotic block at the metaphase-anaphase boundary (Jordan et al, 1993). Both paclitaxel, and its semisynthetic analogue, docetaxel, have been shown to be effective in a range of tumours which are generally refractory to conventional therapies (eg. advanced breast cancer, chemotherapy-resistant ovarian cancer and head and neck tumours (Rowinsky et al, 1992). Myelosuppression, particularly neutropoenia, is the principal toxicity of both agents yet, despite their structural similarity, the type and frequency of non-haematological side-effects differs (Table 4.3).

Podophyllotoxins

Etoposide and teniposide, semisynthetic podophyllotoxins derived from the root of the mayapple plant (*podophyllum peltatum*) are examples of the topoisomerase II (Top2) inhibitors. Such drugs form a complex with Top2, an enzyme necessary for the complete replication of DNA. This interaction results in DNA strand breakage and causes the arrest of cells in the late S and early G_2 phases of the cell cycle (Skeel, 1995). Other drugs in this class include aminoacridines, such as amsacrine, and ellipticines. Certain antibiotics (eg. doxorubicin, daunorubicin and epirubicin) also function as Top2 inhibitors.

Toxicities associated with etoposide and teniposide, when given at conventional doses, include myelosuppression which, although it may be dose-limiting, is not cumulative. Nausea and vomiting may occur together with alopecia. Both drugs may, in rare cases, cause hypotension. Acute hypersensitivity reactions have been reported and are generally more common with teniposide than etoposide (Weiss, 1992). When given at high doses, etoposide is associated with mucositis and hepatotoxicity both of which may be dose-limiting (Pommier et al, 1996).

The most important toxicity associated with the aminoacridines is a dose-dependent myelosuppression; moderate to severe leuco-poenia, thrombocytopoenia and anaemia occur in virtually all patients treated with such drugs. Nausea, vomiting, phlebitis and

55

hepatotoxicity may also be encountered (Pommier et al, 1996) and a low incidence of cardiotoxicity has been reported (Weiss et al, 1996).

Table 4.3   **Effects of paclitaxel and docetaxel**

PACLITAXEL	
Hypersensitivity reactions (25-30% of patients)	Include dyspnoea with bronchospasm, urticaria and hypotension within 10 minutes (usually within 2-3 minutes of first or second dose).
Myelosuppression	Neutropoenia 8-10 days after treatment with complete recovery within 15-21 days of therapy. Severe anaemia or thrombocytopoenia are rare.
Cardiotoxicity	Cardiac arrythmias and transient asymptomatic brady-cardia affect about 20% of patients although their importance is not known. More important brady-arrythmias may affect very small numbers of patients. Rarely myocardial infarction, cardiac ischaemia and ventricular tachycardia may arise.
Neurotoxicity	Sensory neuropathy with 'glove and stocking' distribution 24-72hrs after treatment. Transient myalgia 2-5 days after treatment at doses >170mg/m^2.
Mucositis	Most commonly associated with 96hr infusions and/or patients with leukaemia.
Alopecia	Primarily affects the scalp but all body hair may be lost with cumulative therapy.

DOCETAXEL	
Hypersensitivity reactions (≈ 25% patients)	Similar to those associated with paclitaxel resolving within 15 minutes of cessation of treatment. May be reduced by appropriate pre-medication.
Myelosuppression	Neutropoenia 9 days after treatment with recovery within 15-21 days. Effects on platelets and red blood cells are rare.
Cumulative fluid retention syndrome	Characterised by oedema, weight gain, pleural effusions and/or ascites at cumulative doses >400mg/m^2. Resolves slowly after treatment ceases.
Cutaneous effects	50-75% patients develop skin reactions typically characterised by erythematous pruritic maculo-papular rash of forearms/hands. Superficial desquamation of hands/feet; discoloured, ridged and brittle finger nails. Alopecia.
Neurotoxicity	Mild-moderate peripheral neurotoxicity in about 40% patients typically causing parasthesiae and numbness; peripheral motor dysfunction may cause weakness of the extremities.
Miscellaneous	Asthenia (58-67% patients). Stomatitis, mild nausea, vomiting and diarrhoea may occur; severe GI toxicity is rare.

Ellipticines are primarily used in treating the bone metastases associated with breast cancer; a high incidence of haemolytic and allergic reactions have been reported (Sternberg et al 1985). Other toxicities include nephrotoxicity which is the most severe adverse effect (Pommier et al, 1996); xerostomia may also be dose-limiting.

MISCELLANEOUS DRUGS

A variety of antineoplastic drugs exist which, since their mechanisms of action differ from those described, cannot be listed in any of the above categories. Many have unique cytotoxic activity and may be used in active treatment or in a research setting. They include drugs such as procarbazine, dacarbazine, cisplatin and L-asparaginase.

Procarbazine: This drug is a weak inhibitor of monoamine oxidase and undergoes significant biotransformation before exerting cytotoxic effects by interference with a variety of biochemical processes. The precise mechanism(s) through which this occurs are uncertain although its metabolites are known to disrupt DNA, RNA and protein with the cell. Since many food and drug interactions are possible, special precautions may be needed during such therapy although the clinical significance of such effects is thought to be low (Skeel, 1995).

Dacarbazine: The exact mechanism through which dacarbazine exerts its antineoplastic effects remains unknown although it is clear that biotransformation is necessary. It acts as both an antimetabolite and, following biotransformation, an alkylating agent. The vast majority of patients receiving dacarbazine will experience moderate to severe nausea and vomiting and, at high doses ($>1200mg/m^2$), severe but short-lived watery diarrhoea. Myelosuppression is a common causing mild to moderate thrombocytopoenia and leucopoenia. Less frequently, a flu-like syndrome, comprising fever, myalgias and malaise, may occur and last for several days.

L-asparaginase: Asparagine is a non-essential amino acid required by tumour cells for their growth and development. The enzymes needed to synthesise this amino acid, present in many normal tissues, are lacking in certain tumour cells, particularly those arising from T-lymphocytes (Chabner and Myers, 1985). Such cells derive asparagine from the circulating pool of amino acids. L-asparaginase hydrolyses asparagine into its constituent parts (aspartic acid and ammonia) and rapidly deplete the body pool and depriving malignant cells of the asparagine they need thus causing cell death; resistance to treatment may arise through an increase in the L-asparagine synthetase activity in tumour cells (Haskell and Canellos, 1969).

Approximately two thirds of those receiving L-asparaginase experience nausea, vomiting and chills as an immediate reaction. Such effects can be minimised by the use of antiemetics, anti-histamines or, in severe cases, corticosteroids. Other toxic effects result from the inhibition of protein synthesis including hypo-albuminaemia, a decrease in clotting factors and a reduced serum insulin leading to hyperglycaemia. Haemostatic abnormalities are common and most frequently lead to thrombosis although haemorrhage may also arise probably due to a decreased availability of the vitamin-K dependent clotting factors (Chabner and Loo, 1996). However, its use is limited as many normal tissues are also sensitive to L-asparaginase. The only current use is in the treatment of acute lymphoblastic leukaemia. It is usually considered to be cell cycle phase non-specific although it may also block some cells in the G_1 or S phase (Hill and Baserga, 1975).

HORMONALLY-ACTIVE AGENTS

Since hormones are not themselves cytotoxic use of hormones or hormonally-active agents cannot truly be described as cancer chemo-therapy. However, since the growth and development of some tumours (eg. breast, thyroid, prostate and uterine cancers) depends, at least in part, on their existing in a specific hormonal environment, alterations in that environment may influence their growth.

The action of hormones is dependent on the presence of specific receptors in the cell that bind to hormones transferring them to the nucleus where they facilitate synthesis of mRNA (Ch. 2) and, ultimately, the synthesis of protein and cell division. Antitumour effects can, therefore, be achieved by:

- Preventing hormone production
- Blocking the hormone receptors with competing agents
- Substituting chemically similar agents for the active agent.

This may be achieved by pharmacological or surgical means.

Hormones commonly used in cancer therapy include oestrogens (eg. diethylstilboestrol, oestradiol), androgens (such as testosterone), progestational agents (eg. medroxyprogesterone acetate (Provera, Farlutal, Depo-Provera)), megestrol acetate (Depostat) and hydroxy-progesterone caproate (Delalutin)). Corticosteroids (eg. prednisone, prednisolone, dexamethasone and hydrocortisone) are also useful in treating certain neoplasms (Table 4.4).

Table 4.4   Hormones and hormone antagonists

Agent	Possible effects
Oestrogens	Suppress testosterone production (through the hypothalamus) in males. In females, alter the response of breast cancer cells to prolactin.
Progestational agents	Demonstrate a wide range of antagonistic effects against oestrogens, androgens and gonadotrophins. Appear to act directly at the level of the malignant cell receptor to promote differentiation.
Androgens	May exert antineoplastic effects by inducing alterations in pituitary function or by direct effects on neoplastic cells.
Corticosteroids	Cause lysis of lymphoid tumours. May recruit malignant cells from the G_0 phase of the cell cycle into active division rendering them vulnerable to damage by cell cycle specific chemotherapy.
Anti-oestrogens (eg. Tamoxifen)	Block peripheral functions of oestrogen on target tissues. Also thought to decrease plasma prolactin concentration.
Anti-adrenal agents (eg. aminoglutethimide)	Cause 'chemical adrenalectomy' blocking adrenal production of steroids thus reducing levels of glucocorticoids, mineralocorticoids and oestrogen. Inhibit peripheral aromatisation of androgens to form oestrogens.
Anti-androgens	Inhibit androgen uptake or inhibit nuclear binding of androgen in target tissues or both.

Anti-oestrogens (such as Tamoxifen), anti-androgens (Flutamide) and anti-adrenal agents (eg. aminoglutethimide) are not hormonal but, instead, act to significantly alter the hormonal environment of those cancer cells that retain hormone dependency; they are useful adjuncts to other forms of cancer therapy.

The side-effects of hormonal therapy are directly related to the normal action of the hormones concerned and usually represent an accentuation of their effects. Thus, for example, the sexual hormones may cause fluid retention, changes in libido and changes in secondary sexual characteristics (eg. hirsuitism and deepening of the voice). The corticosteroids may lead to side-effects such as hypertension, fluid retention, hyperglycaemia, emotional instability and osteoporosis; muscle weakness, peptic ulceration and the development of Cushingoid features; increased susceptibility to infection and masking of pyrexia may also occur.

The side-effects of the hormone antagonists are similar to the effects of deficiencies of their natural hormone counterparts. Thus, for example, anti-oestrogens will cause hot flushes and nausea and

Classification of antineoplastic agents

vomiting while anti-adrenal agents will suppress adrenal function. Overall, however, hormonal treatments are usually well-tolerated.

In some cases, however, malignant cells do not retain the hormone dependency of their tissue of origin and so lack the receptor for that hormone. In this situation, manipulation of the hormonal environment will not affect tumour growth. Such patients would be treated with an alternative anticancer therapy.

REFERENCES

Chabner BA, Myers CE, 1985, Clinical pharmacology of cancer chemotherapy. In: DeVita VT, Hellman S, Rosenberg SA (Editors), Cancer: Principles and Practice of Oncology, JB Lippincott Co., Philadelphia.

Chabner BA, Loo TI, 1996, Enzyme therapy: L-asparaginase. In: Chabner BA, Longo DL (Editors), Cancer Chemotherapy and Biotherapy: Principles and Practice (Second edition), Lippincott-Raven, Philadelphia.

Crossland J, 1980, Lewis's Pharmacology (Fifth edition), Churchill Livingstone, Edinburgh.

Dennis J-N, Greene AE, 1988, A highly efficient approach to natural Taxol, Journal of the American Chemical Society 110, 5917-9.

Haskell C. 1985, Cancer Treatment (Second edition), WB Saunders Co., Philadelphia.

Haskell CM, Cannellos GP, 1969, L-asparaginase resistance in human leukaemia-asparagine synthetase, Biochemical Pharmacology 18, 2578-81.

Hill BT, Baserga R, 1975, The cell cycle and its significance for cancer treatments, Cancer Treatment Reviews 2, 159-75.

Holmes S, 1996, Radiotherapy: A Guide for Practice, Asset Books, Leatherhead.

Johnson IS, Armstrong JG, Gorman M, et al, 1967, The vinca alkaloids: a new class of oncolytic agents, Cancer Research 23(1), 1390-3.

Johnson IS, 1968, Historical background of vinca alkaloid research and areas of future interest, Cancer Chemotherapy Reports 52, 455-7.

Jordan MA, Tose RJ, Thrower D, et al, 1993, Mechanisms of mitotic block and inhibition of cell proliferation by Taxol at low concentrations, Proceedings of the National Academy of Science (USA) 90, 9552-6.

Knopf MKT, Fischer DA, Welch-McCaffery D, 1984, Cancer Chemotherapy: Treatment and Care (Second edition), GK Hall Medical Publishers, Boston.

Pommier Y, Fesen MR, Goldwasser F, 1996, Topoisomerase II inhibitors: the epidophyllotoxins, m-AMSA, and the ellipticine derivatives. In: Chabner BA, Longo DL (Editors), Cancer Chemotherapy and Biotherapy: Principles and Practice (Second edition), Lippincott-Raven, Philadelphia.

Rowinsky EK, Donehower RC, 1996, Antimicrotubule agents. In: Chabner BA, Longo DL (Editors), Cancer Chemotherapy and Biotherapy: Principles and Practice (Second edition), Lippincott-Raven, Philadelphia.

Rowinsky EK, Donehower RC, 1991, The clinical pharmacology and use of antimicrotubule agents in cancer chemotherapeutics, Pharmacological Therapeutics, **52**, 35-84.

Rowinsky EK, Onetto N, Canetta RM, et al, 1992, Taxol: the prototypic taxane, an important new class of antitumour agents, Seminars in Oncology **19**, 646-2.

Skeel RT, 1995, Antineoplastic drugs and biologic response modifiers: classification, use and toxicity of clinically useful agents. In: Skeel RT, Lachant NA (Editors), Handbook of Cancer Chemotherapy (Fourth edition), Little, Brown and Co., Boston.

Sternberg CN, Yagoda A, Casper E, et al, 1985, Phase II trial of elliptinum in advanced renal cell carcinoma and carcinoma of the breast, Anticancer Research **5**, 415-7.

Wani MC, Taylor HL, Wall ME, et al, 1971, Plant antitumour agents: VI. The isolation and structure of Taxol, a novel antileukaemic and antitumour agent from *Taxus brevifolia*, Journal of the American Chemical Society **93**, 2325-7.

Weiss RB, 1992, Hypersensitivity reactions, Seminars in Oncology **19**, 458-77.

Weiss RB, Grillo-Lopez AJ, Marsoni S, 1996 Amsacrine-associated cardiotoxicity: an analysis of 82 cases, Journal of Clinical Oncology **4**, 918-20.

CHAPTER 5 CHEMOTHERAPY AS A TREATMENT FOR CANCER

As chemotherapy is the only major systemic treatment for malignant disease it is a vital part of treatment for many patients. Its systemic nature is the principle characteristic that distinguishes chemotherapy from surgery or radiotherapy the therapeutic effects of which are confined to the anatomical site to which they are applied. This means that chemotherapy is indicated when the disease is widespread or when metastasis is suspected and may be used in conjunction with localised treatment.

There is a large variety of clinically useful agents (Ch. 4) so that, when treatment is selected for individual patients, the indications must be carefully considered. This includes understanding of the natural history and/or behaviour of the particular tumour, together with an awareness of the extent and rate of progress of the disease and previous treatment received by that patient (Cline and Haskell, 1980). For each type of cancer a number of prognostic factors can be identified. These include the age and sex of affected patients, as well as the tumour histology which may influence both the response to therapy and overall survival. Such information is important not only to individual patients but also when comparing the results obtained using different methods of treatment (eg. in clinical trials (Ch. 17)).

STAGING OF THE DISEASE
Clearly histological/pathological confirmation of the diagnosis is needed before any form of anticancer therapy is instigated. Once the diagnosis is confirmed the physician must be certain that this is consistent with the clinical findings. If this is not the case additional information must be sought.

Rarely, in less than 1% of all patients, antineoplastic therapy is undertaken before the diagnosis has been confirmed (Skeel, 1995) although this is only carried out when withholding immediate treatment would increase morbidity or mortality or when benign disease is considered unlikely. Examples include an acute condition, such as spinal cord compression or diagnosis of a cerebral tumour. In general, however, since chemotherapeutic drugs are themselves

62

potentially toxic and/or carcinogenic, and carry a narrow margin of safety, such treatment is not instigated without a histopathological diagnosis of malignancy. Thus the following guidelines are followed when treating a patient with malignant disease:

- Chemotherapeutic agents are used only when the diagnosis has been confirmed
- The response to treatment is carefully monitored
- Chemotherapy is not used unless the facilities available are adequate and enable monitoring of the potential toxicity of the agent to the patient's normal tissues.

(Cline and Haskell, 1980)

In the past, chemotherapy was employed only when surgery or radiotherapy were ineffective or when the disease was 'advanced' at the time of diagnosis. In other words, chemotherapy was, in most cases, used only as a 'last resort' or as a palliative treatment. As knowledge has accumulated, and malignant growth and tumour cell kinetics are increasingly understood, the value of chemotherapy has been recognised. Drug therapy is now the most widely used alternative to surgery (King, 1996). However, the response to such therapy is, as has been shown, dependent on a variety of both tumour- and host-related factors (Ch. 3). The extent of the disease is also important in determining the type of therapy to be employed.

Attempts to define the size of the tumour and the sites of metastases are known as *'staging'*; diagnostic tests designed to evaluate the spread of the disease are known as *'staging procedures'*. Most tumours have a natural history from which the expected pattern of progression and metastasis can be predicted so that a variety of classification systems have been identified and can be described as shown below:

- *Clinical staging* relying only on clinical measurements and methods to identify the size and spread of the tumour.
- *Post-Surgical staging* in which clinical findings, noted at the time of surgery, are used to improve diagnostic sensitivity.
- *Pathological staging* when tissue removed for biopsy, or during surgery, is subjected to histopathological study.
- Further investigations (eg. computerised axial tomography (CAT scans)), radiological procedures or monitoring of biological tumour markers (eg. alphafetoprotein or carcinoembryonic antigen) may add useful information.

Chemotherapy as treatment for cancer

The *TNM System*, an internationally recognised clinical staging procedure, is that most commonly used to characterise the degree of growth and spread of solid tumours (King, 1996). This is useful not only in establishing the extent of disease but also in improving communication about both the degree of spread and evaluation of the response of individual tumours to specific treatments. It is dependent on the three criteria:

1. Tumour size.
2. Spread to the lymph Nodes.
3. Metastasis to distant sites.

Each parameter is further evaluated with numerical subscripts (Table 5.1). Pathological data may also be added (pTNM). Tumours are further classified into stages: *Stage 1* reflects local disease that has not progressed outside its original site, *Stage II* - regional disease and *Stage III* metastatic disease; *Stage IV* growth is widespread.

The staging of individual tumours is, however, subject to some variation thus, although internationally agreed staging systems are useful, their benefits depend on the care with which staging investigations are carried out. Tumours may also be graded using histological criteria such as the number of mitosis, irregularities of the cell nucleus and 'architectural' resemblance to the tissue from which it is derived. Low grade tumours closely resemble the tissue from which they originate while a high grade tumour has changed significantly and only marginally resembles its tissue of origin. Both stage and grade are important as they provide information about different parameters of cancer and can be used to predict its likely course; they may, however, incompletely, reflect tumour bulk.

GOALS OF TREATMENT

The goal of cancer therapy is a major factor in selecting any therapeutic method. Possible goals include cure, disease control with prolonged survival or palliation directed towards symptom relief and maintaining or improving the quality of life but with no hope of cure (Table 5.2). Whenever treatment with chemotherapeutic agents is considered the goal of that treatment must be clarified. When cure, or improved survival, is likely acute toxic effects are more acceptable than if the goal is palliation. However, when survival is prolonged or cure achieved, the risk of chronic or delayed toxicity gains in importance, particularly when there are two equally effective methods of treatment.

64

Table 5.1   The general principles of the TNM system

CLINICAL CLASSIFICATION
Designated cTNM; based on evidence acquired prior to treatment (eg. from physical examination, imaging, endoscopy, etc.).

T   - PRIMARY TUMOUR
     T_x -   Primary tumour cannot be assessed
     T_0 -   No evidence of primary tumour
     T_{is} -   Carcinoma *in situ*
T_1, T_2, T_3, T_4, Increasing size and/or local extent of primary tumour.

N   - REGIONAL LYMPH NODES
     N_x -   Regional lymph nodes cannot be assessed
     N_0 -   No regional lymph node metastasis
N_1, N_2, N_3, Increasing involvement of regional lymph nodes.

M   - DISTANT METASTASES
     M_x -   Presence of distant metastasis cannot be assessed
     M_0 -   No distant metastasis
     M_1 -   Distant metastasis may be further specified according to the site of metastasis

PATHOLOGICAL CLASSIFICATION
pT - PRIMARY TUMOUR
     pT_x -   Primary tumour cannot be assessed histologically
     pT_0 -   No histological evidence of primary tumour
     pT_{is} -   Carcinoma *in situ*
pT_1, pT_2, pT_3, pT_4, Increasing extent of the primary tumour histologically.

pN - REGIONAL LYMPH NODES
     pN_x -   Regional lymph nodes cannot be assessed histologically
     pN_0 -   No regional lymph node metastasis histologically
pN_1, pN_2, pN_3, Increasing involvement of regional lymph nodes histologically.

pM - DISTANT METASTASES
     pM_x -   Presence of distant metastasis cannot be assessed microscopically
     pM_0 -   No distant metastasis microscopically
     pM_1 -   Distant metastasis microscopically. Can be further classified dependent on the site of metastasis.

These stages may be applied to all tumours. Further definition may be applied to specific tumours (eg. breast, lung, bladder).

Table 5.2   **Goals of cancer chemotherapy** (based on Cella, 1995)

	Cure	Disease control with extension of life	Palliative
Purpose	Eradication of disease.	Extending life.	Control of distressing symptoms and improving the quality of life.
Trade-off	Acceptance of acute side-effects; long-term effects of greater concern.	Acceptance of some acute effects in exchange for extension of life; some concern for the quality of the 'added time'.	Acute side-effects are not acceptable even in the interests of symptom control.
Treatment	Aggressive therapy is acceptable; minimal intervention in those believed to be cured.	Treat only when value of therapy outweighs side-effects.	Treat when cost of not treating causes greater distress and reduces quality of life.
Challenges	Establish willingness to tolerate therapy and accept side-effects in quest for cure.	Estimate cost-benefit to patients - consider time involved, likely extent of symptom relief and incidence of side-effects.	Establish benefits of treatment c.f. toxicity and incidence of side-effects.

Curative treatment: The primary objective of curative treatment is to eradicate the disease so that neither it nor its treatment will markedly affect the expected life span. If this is achieved it can be said that the patient is cured of cancer. However, when discussing cancer, the concept of cure is a difficult one since disappearance of all clinically detectable disease does not, of necessity, indicate that cure has been achieved; individual micrometastases, containing up to 10^8 malignant cells, may still be present (Priestman, 1980). The term for this situation, when there is no evidence of disease although the patient is not necessarily free of cancer, is *complete remission*.

The term *5-year disease-free survival* is also commonly used since metastasis or recurrence is most likely within the first five years of diagnosis/treatment. As a result, there is a tendency to equate 5-year survival with cure (Priestman, 1980). However, although this is appropriate for some tumours, for others this may be too long or too short. For example, for tumours with a large growth fraction and a rapid mitotic rate, a 1-2 year disease-free period after treatment may represent cure; for others, those with a slow mitotic rate, a disease-free period of 15-20 years may be required. Indeed, in some cancers, (eg. breast) disease-free survival in excess of 15 years is not a guarantee of cure. This highlights the difficulty associated with the use of the term 'cure' in describing the results of any cancer therapy so that, in most clinical trials, results are reported in terms of periods of disease-free survival rather than in terms of cure. Perhaps the best definition of cure remains that given below:

'We may speak of a cure of a disease when there remains a group of disease-free survivors, probably a decade or two after treatment, whose annual death rate from all causes is similar to that of a normal population group of the same age and sex distribution'.
(Easson and Russell, 1968)

When the extent of disease is such that it is believed to exceed the ability of chemotherapy to eradicate it the goals of treatment become those of disease control, prolongation of life and maintenance of its quality. The degree of success achieved depends on various factors including the chemosensitivity of the tumour, the extent/stage of the disease and the physiological and psychological status of the patient.

Palliative treatment: The relief of distressing symptoms in patients with otherwise untreatable disease is an important aspect of care. Some may reach this stage after a protracted period of treatment, others may present at a stage when neither cure nor control is possible. The emphasis on symptom relief means that the method of treatment is significantly different since the objectives of care are such that acute side-effects are not tolerated although the risk of delayed or chronic toxicity is not usually a major concern (Ch. 15).

SELECTION OF TREATMENT

Although chemotherapy can be curative for many types of cancer many solid tumours are extremely difficult to treat (Table 5.3). Some of the reasons for this have been described in the previous chapter. In some cases chemotherapy is used alone or as an adjunct to other therapies. Even when the goal is control or palliation rather than cure, chemotherapy may result in worthwhile remission or prolong life and maintain quality of life. The situations in which chemo-therapy can be used may be summarised as shown below:

1. Conditions which are known to be completely curable by chemotherapy.
2. Conditions in which chemotherapy, although not curative, will produce a longer remission than is possible with other

methods of treatment.

3. Conditions in which chemotherapy provides an additional, or alternative, method of treatment.

4. Other conditions.

In most other cases of malignant disease chemotherapy, although it has no established value, may, in otherwise intractable cases, result in remission or improve the quality of life.

Table 5.3   Response of specific tumours to cancer chemotherapy
(Brager and Yasko, 1984; Grahame Smith and Aronson, 1984)

HIGHLY RESPONSIVE (Treatment often curative)
Burkitt's lymphoma
Choriocarcinoma
Hodgkin's lymphoma
Rhabdomyosarcoma
Wilm's tumour (children).

RESPONSIVE (>50% effective; responders have prolonged life expectancy, some are cured)
Acute lymphoblastic leukaemia
Ewing's sarcoma
Histiocytic lymphoma
Non-Hodgkin's lymphoma
Retinoblastoma
Testicular carcinoma

MODERATELY RESPONSIVE (effectiveness 20-50%; clinical remission is common; survival may be increased)
Acute adult leukaemias
Carcinoma of breast and prostate
Endometrial carcinoma
Multiple myeloma
Oat cell carcinoma of lung/undifferentiated carcinoma
Ovarian carcinoma

PARTLY RESPONSIVE (Little prolongation of life but regression may be achieved)
Carcinoma of adrenocortex
Head and neck tumours
Islet cell carcinoma (pancreas)

MINIMALLY RESPONSIVE (Effectiveness <20%)
Bladder carcinoma
Carcinoid tumours
Carcinoma liver/bile ducts
Colorectal carcinoma
Melanoma
Neuroblastoma
Renal carcinoma
Pancreatic adenocarcinoma

In most other cases of malignant disease chemotherapy, although it has no established value, may, in otherwise intractable cases, result in remission or improve the quality of life.

Although the primary role of cancer chemotherapy is as a treatment for systemic metastatic malignant disease, it may also be used to treat tumours that have not spread but which are not adequately controlled by surgery or radiotherapy or when a tumour is not amenable to surgical removal. It may be used alone, or in conjunction with radiation, so as to decrease tumour size before surgical intervention is attempted. Antineoplastic drugs may be used as an adjunct to surgery or radiotherapy to eliminate clinically undetectable micrometastases.

Regardless of the patient's condition, or the purpose of treatment, certain general principles can be applied to the use of chemotherapy. These, in turn, are based on the cell cycle (see Ch. 2).

1. The faster the cell cycle the more likely is chemotherapy to 'catch' cells in a sensitive phase.

2. The greater the number of cells in synchrony in the cell cycle the greater the effects of a 'pulse' of chemotherapy. The lower the number of cells the greater the need for prolonged therapy.

3. The larger the tumour the less responsive it is likely to be. There are two reasons for this. Firstly, many cells tend to be in the G_0 phase of the cycle when they are relatively unresponsive to chemotherapy. Secondly, large tumours tend to be poorly vascularised so that penetration of the drug through the tumour may be poor and insufficient to enable adequate concentrations of the drug to reach tumour cells for a period long enough to result in its destruction. This can, at times, be overcome by giving larger doses thus increasing the risk of systemic toxicity.

4. As many chemotherapeutic agents affect only those cells in a particular phase of the cell cycle they kill a proportion of tumour cells rather than a fixed number (Ch. 4). Thus there may be considerable variability in the responses between individual cell types and it is difficult to destroy all tumour cells. Due to the proportionality of cell kill chemotherapy can reduce tumour bulk and lead to clinical remission but does not always eradicate the tumour. If cells are not eradicated, remission may be short-lived as cell

division continues ultimately resulting in relapse. Similar effects may result from drug resistance (see p40-45).

5. The sensitivity of the malignancy to the chosen agents is also considered.

These then are the major tumour factors that influence the selection of chemotherapeutic agents in treating individual tumours. Other factors to be considered include the patient's age, present physical condition, past medical history (such as cardiac, pulmonary, renal or hepatic disease), current renal and hepatic function, bone marrow status, nutritional status, psychological condition and previous treatment. Such assessment is essential. For example, renal and hepatic function must be evaluated due to their importance in both the metabolism and excretion of drugs. Thus clinical findings may necessitate changes in the treatment plan both in terms of drug selection and dosage and also in terms of the care required.

EVALUATION OF THE RESPONSE TO CHEMOTHERAPY (Table 5.4)

Clearly, when administering a potentially toxic treatment, its effects must be monitored and the response evaluated. This can be achieved using a combination of parameters designed to establish:

a. Objective changes in tumour size or release of tumour products.

b. Subjective changes in the patient's condition.

c. Survival.

Objective Response

Objective parameters are measured before treatment commences thus providing a baseline against which effectiveness can be evaluated. Parameters used include: hepatic function, as measured by liver function tests or liver scan; enlarged lymph nodes, which can be palpated and compared with previous findings, or changes in tumour size or tumour product.

However, it is not always possible to measure changes in tumour size, so that the products of a tumour (eg. hormones, antigens or antibodies) may be measurable and, therefore, provide an objective assessment of tumour response. Examples include human chorionic gonadotrophin (HCG), produced in choriocarcinoma and testicular malignancy (Skeel and Ganz, 1995), and carcinoembryonic antigen (CEA) in some GI or breast cancers.

Table 5.4   Evaluation of the response to treatment

Relies on three essential parameters:
   a. Tumour size
   b. Duration of remission achieved
   c. Duration of survival from start of therapy

Defined in terms of five standard definitions

1. *Complete remission (CR)*: disappearance of all signs and symptoms of disease for a period of at least 4 weeks.

2. *Partial remission (PR)*: shrinkage of tumour to <50% of initial size for at least 4 weeks. Based on the sum of the products of the greater or lesser diameters of all measured lesions combined with absence of any new lesions during therapy. No progression of existing lesions.

3. *Progressive disease (PD)*: Increase in tumour size (25% or more) or the emergence of new lesions during treatment

4. *No change (NC) or stable disease (SD)*: Neither partial response nor progressive disease.

5. *Failure:* Any new lesion or >25% increase in tumour size.

Other objective parameters include:
   Pulmonary lesions (x-rays)
   Liver involvement (scans, LFTs)
   Enlarged lymph nodes (palpation, lymphangiogram)
   Restaging may be used to establish the current extent of the disease.

Subjective parameters
   Even when there is no objective response the patient may feel better. This may represent improvement from the patient's perspective.

In some cases, the response to therapy is assessed by restaging. This involves re-establishing the clinical extent of disease at the completion of treatment or on relapse. Physical examination and radiography are repeated and particular attention is paid to studies that were positive at diagnosis so as to clarify the true position. Restaging does not, however, mean that a patient who enters remission reverts to a lesser stage; the stage at the time of diagnosis characterises the disease throughout even when there is no clinical evidence of the disease following treatment.

Other objective features may arise but may not be so easy to quantify (eg. neurological changes secondary to a brain tumour).

However, it should be remembered that, although response indicates sensitivity to therapy, it does not necessarily equate with survival (Green et al, 1983); the duration of remission provides a better index.

Subjective information

Subjective information is also valuable and is of often of equal if not greater importance to the patient. If the patient feels worse after treatment he may not feel it worthwhile. However, if such subjective changes are short-term, lasting only for the period of treatment, and the treatment carries a likelihood of cure or control, most patients will agree this is worth the cost. In other words, a temporary reduction in the state of health and general well-being may be acceptable if it results in subsequent long-term improvement.

Assessment of performance status has been used to provide information about the effect of cancer and its treatment on individual patients. It is believed to provide an independent measure of the level of activity of which the patient is capable. One such measure in common use - the WHO Performance Scale (WHO, 1979) (Table 5.5) - can aid in individualising therapy suggesting whether or not a patient will benefit from specific therapy. Such scales can provide an objective measure of changes in the patient's physiological status before, during and after treatment.

Table 5.5   The WHO Performance Scale (WHO, 1979)

Grade	Definition
0	Able to carry out normal activities without restriction.
1	Restricted in physically strenuous activity but ambulatory; able to carry out light work.
2	Ambulatory; capable of self-care but unable to carry out light work. Bed/chair-bound <50% of waking hours.
3	Capable of only limited self-care. Bed/chair-bound >50% of waking hours.
4	Completely disabled. Cannot carry out any self-care. Totally confined to bed/chair.

This data, taken together, provides a complete 'picture' of the patient and can be used to guide decisions regarding treatment (ie. should chemotherapy be continued, modified or abandoned?).

Survival

The goal of all cancer therapies is primarily that of enabling all affected patients to live as long as they would have done had they not developed the disease (Skeel, 1995). Only when this has been achieved can it be claimed that the patient has been cured of cancer. The limitations of this parameter are clear since it would only be possible to evaluate the effects of specific treatments after patients had survived a normal life span. Thus, to evaluate specific treatments, a cohort of patients is followed for a defined period of time and their survival compared with comparable, but non cancer-bearing, individuals. In general, even in those patients developing treatment-related complications, survival is likely to be longer than if treatment had not been given but shorter than it would have been had the individual not developed cancer (Skeel, 1995).

When cure is not achieved

For those in whom cure is not possible, or when attempts at cure have failed, there are may be long periods during which treatment is directed towards disease control. It is for this reason that cancer is often described as a chronic disease. In such cases the goal is that of enabling the patient to live longer and more comfortably than he would if treatment were not given. Awareness of such factors is important to both physician and patient since the former must recommend treatment and the latter must accept or reject it.

When aiming for cure or control is inappropriate the possibility of palliative care and treatment must be considered. Chemotherapy may be effective in relieving pain, in preventing bleeding or compression or obstruction of vital organs (see Ch. 15).

THE TREATMENT PLAN

Most successful forms of treatment with cytotoxic agents rely on the use of intermittent intensive chemotherapy which enables large doses of drugs to be given over relatively short periods of time with intervals for the recovery of normal tissues between treatments. The theory of this approach is that a large fraction of tumour cells will be destroyed with each successive exposure to chemotherapy at the expense of transient and reversible toxicity to normal tissues.

Combination chemotherapy

The most common approach to chemotherapy is the administration of combinations of cytotoxic agents since this has been found to be significantly superior to single drug therapy in treating a number of tumours (Scofield et al, 1991). Furthermore a combination of drugs may optimise tumour destruction whilst minimising toxic effects.

Because, as has been observed, chemotherapeutic agents are associated with a variety of toxic effects of varying severity and duration, drugs can be selected for use according to their individual pattern of toxicity. Thus drugs with different modes of action, and minimal overlapping toxicity, can be selected to achieve therapeutically synergistic effects. For example, drugs which are myelosuppressive can be combined with those which are marrow-sparing or which differ in terms of the time of onset or recovery time of their myelosuppression. Similarly, drugs which are nephrotoxic, and are excreted through the kidneys, can be combined with others that are not nephrotoxic or which are excreted by another route.

Combination chemotherapy may also circumvent, at least in part, the problem of drug resistance (King, 1996). Tumours comprise a heterogeneous population in which drug resistance arises through a variety of different mechanisms (Ch. 3) so that the sensitivity of tumour cells is variable. Even within a single tumour, some cells will be resistant to one drug, others will respond to a different drug while still others will be insensitive to all chemotherapeutic agents. Combination therapy optimises the chances of destroying cells within a tumour by employing at least one drug to which they are sensitive.

Adjuvant chemotherapy

Adjuvant chemotherapy involves the use of anticancer drugs following treatment with surgery or radiotherapy the objective being to eliminate any remaining metastatic deposits reducing the chance of a subsequent relapse (Curt and Chabner, 1987). It is administered, for example, in treating patients with breast cancer when it is given immediately after surgery when the tumour burden is low.

Neo-adjuvant therapy is a newer concept when chemotherapy is used to reduce the size of a tumour prior to surgery or radiotherapy when it may lessen the need for mutilative surgery or increase the likelihood of a favourable response to radiotherapy. Used in this way chemotherapy serves a useful 'debulking' role whilst also helping to control metastasis (Calvert and McElwain, 1988). It is particularly appealing in those with advanced disease when it may enhance local or regional control and overall survival by promoting regression of macroscopic disease prior to local treatment; it also provides early treatment of the micrometastases.

High-dose chemotherapy

On occasions, high doses of chemotherapeutic agents are given in the hope that this will destroy a correspondingly high proportion of the tumour. Such regimes always produce life-threatening granulocytopoenia and leucopoenia or both of at least a week's duration (Neidhart, 1995). Such treatment involves administration of drugs whose major toxic effects are exerted at the bone marrow since the marrow can be removed prior to the therapy and reinfused once treatment is completed (see Ch. 9).

Second-line therapy

First-line therapy is that which is used during the initial treatment of malignant disease and involves use of those drugs known to be effective against the tumour; as a result, it is likely to be effective in producing cure or remission. If the tumour recurs, probably as a result of drug resistance, second-line drugs may be employed. Such drugs are those known to have less activity against the tumour but a response or second remission may still be possible In some cases, third- and even fourth-line therapy may be available.

REFERENCES

Brager BL, Yasko J, 1984, Care of the Client receiving Chemotherapy, Reston Publishing Company Inc., Reston, Virginia.

Calvert H, McElwain TJ, 1988, The role of chemotherapy. In: Pritchard, P (Editor), Oncology for Nurses and Health Care Professionals (Second edition), Volume 1, Pathology, Diagnosis and Treatment, Harper and Row, Beaconsfield.

Cella DF, 1995, Using quality of life and cost-utility assessments in cancer treatment decisions. In: Skeel RT, Lachant RA (Editors), Handbook of Cancer Chemotherapy (Fourth edition), Little, Brown and Co., Boston.

Cline M, Haskell C, 1980, Cancer Chemotherapy, WB Saunders Co., Philadelphia.

Curt GA, Chabner BA, 1987, Medical oncology: decade of discovery, Archives of Internal Medicine **73**, 881-95.

Easson EC, Russell MH, 1968, The curability of cancer in various sites, Pitman Medical, London.

Grahame Smith DG, Aronson JK, 1984, Oxford Textbook of Clinical Pharmacology and Drug Therapy, Oxford University Press Inc., Oxford.

Green JA, Macbeth FR, Williams CJ, et al, 1983, Medical Oncology, Blackwell Scientific Publications, Oxford.

Haskell CM, 1985, Principles of cancer chemotherapy. In: Haskell CM (Editor),

Cancer Treatment (Second edition), WB Saunders Co., Philadelphia.

King RJB, 1996, Cancer Biology, Addison-Wesley Longman Ltd., Edinburgh.

Neidhart JA, 1995, High dose chemotherapy and the role of progressive cell and cytokine support. In: Skeel RT, Lachant RA, (Editors), Handbook of Cancer Chemotherapy (Fourth edition), Little, Brown and Co., Boston.

Priestman TJ, 1980, Cancer chemotherapy - an introduction, Farmitalia Carlo Erba Ltd., Barnet, Herts.

Scofield RP, Liebman MC, Popkin JD, 1991, Multimodal therapy, In: Baird SB, McCorkle R, Grant M (Editors), Cancer Nursing: A Comprehensive Textbook, WB Saunders Co., Philadelphia.

Skeel RT, Lachant RA (Editors) 1995, Handbook of Cancer Chemotherapy (Fourth edition), Little, Brown and Co., Boston.

Skeel RT and Ganz PA, 1995, Systematic assessment of the patient with cancer and long-term medical complications of treatment. In: Skeel RT, Lachant RA (Editors), Handbook of Cancer Chemotherapy (Fourth edition), Little, Brown and Co., Boston.

World Health Organisation, 1979, Handbook for Reporting Results of Cancer Treatment, WHO Publications Number 46, WHO, Geneva.

CHAPTER 6 PREPARATION AND ADMINISTRATION OF CHEMOTHERAPY

Chemotherapy is employed as both an attempt to cure or control malignant disease or as a palliative therapy to alleviate distressing symptoms and improve the quality of life. Therapeutic regimes may also be designed to develop or evaluate more effective or safer methods of administration, such as investigation of new drug combinations, or attempts to promote optimal absorption, maximal contact with the tumour or reduction of adverse effects (ie. clinical trials) (Ch. 17).

It is, therefore, important that the rationale, aims and goals of all treatment regimes are fully understood and it is essential that instructions given for the preparation and administration of *all* drugs are closely followed. If this is not so, pharmacological action may be impaired and complications, which are not only unnecessary but may also be uncomfortable and dangerous, may occur. Drugs must, therefore, be prepared and administered *only* by those who are both knowledgeable about, and technically competent to administer them.

Like any drug, anticancer agents may be administered intra-venously, via a central or peripheral vein, applied topically or given orally, subcutaneously, intramuscularly or into a body cavity. Alternatively, they may be delivered directly to a tumour by means of an intra-arterial infusion, or into pericardial, peritoneal or pleural effusions. The route of administration is determined by the physician and based on an assessment of both the patient and the drug(s) concerned. Regardless of the route of administration considerable care is required in preparing the drugs prior to administration.

THE DOSE OF CHEMOTHERAPEUTIC AGENTS

The required dose of most chemotherapeutic drugs is calculated for individual patients and is based on the body surface area (Cline and Haskell, 1980). This is calculated, from the patient's height and weight using the formula shown in Table 6.1 thus stressing the need for accurate recording of height and weight which, because their importance is not always recognised, are often measured carelessly and inaccurately (Ch. 12).

Table 6.1   Calculation of body surface area (Cline and Haskell, 1980)

$$M^2 = W^{0.425} \times H^{0.725} \times 0.007184$$

Where M^2 = surface area in square metres
         H = height in centimetres
         W = weight in kilograms

The exact dose for each patient is then established by applying the recommended drug dosage per m^2 of the body surface area although it may be modified as a result of patient-related factors (eg. prior or concurrent radiotherapy, bone marrow suppression or general condition). A safe and effective dose range has thus been established for most anticancer drugs so that, although the prescription for each patient is subject to some degree of variation, most will fall within an average range. Doses falling significantly outside this range should be questioned and, if necessary, recalculated.

Clearly a dose falling below that which is clinically necessary will result in ineffective treatment; a dose exceeding that required may lead to life-threatening complications. For this reason, 'double checking' during drug preparation is essential; when necessary the physician should be asked to clarify any discrepancies.

PREPARATION AND HANDLING OF CHEMOTHERAPEUTIC AGENTS

Many cytotoxic agents are carcinogenic, mutagenic or teratogenic (eg. Barry and Booher, 1985); the local irritant properties of some such agents are also well-established (Ch. 8). Such drugs may, therefore, pose hazards to those who handle them routinely and health care workers may be at risk of adverse effects.

Although the level of exposure during preparation, administration and disposal is much lower than that received by the patient(s), the effects may be cumulative (Sotaniemi et al, 1983). Exposure may occur through inhalation, absorption through skin or mucous membranes, through needle stick injury during either preparation and handling of drugs or exposure to body fluids. Rarely, ingestion of contaminated food or drink may be a contributory factor.

There are many potential hazards of exposure to cytotoxic agents. The literature reports that various symptoms, such as eye, membrane and skin irritation, facial flushing, dizziness, nausea, headaches and alopecia, may be experienced by those failing to use safe handling procedures (Ladik et al, 1980; Neal et al, 1983).

Some studies (eg. Waksvic et al, 1981; Hirst et al, 1984) have shown increased mutagenic activity in the urine and chromosomal damage in those handling such drugs the frequency of which was directly related to the total period of exposure. However, when drugs were mixed in a closed-faced, vertical laminar flow hood no increase in mutagenic activity was found (Nguyen et al, 1982). As a result, concern about handling these agents has received considerable attention (eg. Hoffman, 1980; Hirst et al, 1984) and many studies have attempted to both identify and quantify the risk of exposure to those involved in preparing and administering such drugs (eg. Falck et al, 1979; Staiano et al, 1981; Waksvic et al, 1981). To date, results have been equivocal and the health risks associated with anticancer drugs are not entirely clear. However, since there is a possibility that there may be some risks for those involved, a variety of guidelines have been proposed to minimise direct contact with both drugs and equipment during preparation, administration and disposal (eg. Knowles and Virden, 1980; Davis, 1981; Zimmerman et al, 1981).

An awareness of the possibility of chemotherapy-associated risks should mean that practical safety measures are a consistent part of daily practice since, until the risks are clarified, it is clearly wise to take measures to reduce exposure. Indeed, evidence suggests that, if appropriate safety measures are employed, potential hazards can be minimised (Barton-Burke et al, 1990). Detailed guidance on this subject was published by the Department of Health (DoH, 1988).

Applying such measures requires that all those involved are informed of the risk and that local guidelines are available for the safe preparation and administration of anticancer drugs. Although current guidelines are subject to local variation they are designed to ensure:

1. Accuracy of the dose administered.
2. Sterility of parenteral agents.
3. Safety of those preparing and administering cytotoxic drugs.
4. Correct/safe disposal of chemotherapy waste.

In some units all chemotherapeutic drugs are prepared in the pharmacy and, in others, under a laminar airflow cabinet (British Standard (BS) 5726) thus ensuring that contaminated air is filtered so that aerosol contamination cannot occur. Others feel that, as research is inconclusive, such expense is not justified and local rules exist to reduce air-borne exposure. In some units, preparation takes place in a suitable side-room on the wards or in outpatient clinics.

Such a room must be free from draughts and should not be used for any other purpose while drugs are being prepared. Advice is available from the Health and Safety Inspectorate.

All those preparing and administering chemotherapy should wear masks and thick latex surgical gloves (over non-absorbent sleeve protectors), particularly when ampoules containing powders are being handled and the negative pressure technique for handling vials is not employed (Bergemann, 1983). Gloves should be discarded immediately if they are punctured and should be changed routinely after 30 minutes of drug preparation or administration. A closed-fronted gown with tightly fitting cuffs is recommended although a plastic apron may be worn. Safety glasses (BS 2092) should be worn. Strict aseptic technique should be observed at all times and all steps should be taken to control drippage and prevent aerosol production.

A. Ampoules
a. Ensure all fluid/powder is cleared from the top or neck of the ampoule.
b. Swab the neck of the ampoule with 70% isopropyl alcohol allowing this to 'air dry'.
c. Place a dampened cotton wool ball or gauze pad around the neck of the ampoule before breaking it off with a sharp, snapping motion, pulling it up and away from the body to prevent fluid from splashing.
d. Tilt the ampoule slightly, insert the needle tip into the fluid ensuring that it does not touch the side or neck of the ampoule.
e. Pull back on the plunger of the syringe and withdraw the required volume of fluid.
f. Remove the needle, replace it with either a clean needle of the appropriate size or a syringe cap.
g. If a syringe cap is used ensure that the syringe is clearly labelled and that a second label carries the words *'Caution: Cancer Chemotherapeutic Agent'*.

B. Multi-dose vials/solutions requiring reconstitution
a. Swab the top of the vial with 70% isopropyl alcohol and allow to 'air dry'.
b. Use a venting needle with a hydrophobic filter to avoid spraying (aerosol) and spillage when the needle is with-

drawn. Alternatively, withdraw an equivalent volume of air before introducing fluids into the vial.

c. Attach an 18-21G needle to a syringe of the appropriate size and, with the bevel of the needle facing up and away, insert this, at an angle of 45°, into the rubber closure of the vial until the bevel is half-covered. Turn the needle and syringe perpendicular (90° angle) to the rubber closure and insert into the vial.

d. Keep the needle in the vial, invert and withdraw the required amount of fluid, adjust the fluid level in the syringe so that no fluid is present in the syringe hub or needle.

e. Place a cotton wool ball, dampened with alcohol, around the needle and the top of the vial during withdrawal of the needle.

f. When it is necessary to eject air bubbles from a filled syringe a dampened cotton wool ball or gauze pad should be placed at the tip of the needle.

g. A new sterile needle should be used for administration. Alternatively the syringe may be capped and the syringe labelled as previously described. At all times, care should be taken to avoid self-inoculation (needle stick injury).

DISPOSAL

Careful disposal of all waste products (needle, syringes, vials, swabs, gloves etc.) is required; needles should be recapped and needle and syringe combinations disposed of intact. Waste must be placed in a leak and puncture-proof container that is clearly labelled 'Cancer Chemotherapy Waste'. The container must be sealed and incinerated. Unused drugs should be treated toxic chemical waste and disposed of by incineration; most manufacturers recommend a temperature of 1000°C. This is not easily achieved using hospital incinerators (Scott, 1989); where there is doubt that the appropriate temperature can be reached, unopened drugs should be returned to the manufacturer, carefully packed and labelled 'Cytotoxics for destruction'. Units sending drugs off-site for incineration must label these as special waste (DoH, 1988). Although the DoH (1988) states that small amounts of drugs can be discarded into the sewage system, as long as they are flushed with copious amounts of water, hospitals should check with their local water authorities to ensure that they have no objections to this procedure. Since body fluids are known to contain high concentrations of cytotoxic drugs excreta must be regarded as contaminated.

When a laminar airflow cabinet has been used the interior should be cleaned using 70% isopropyl alcohol once drug preparation is completed. Gloves should not be removed until this has been carried out. Hands should be washed after gloves are removed. Linen and gowns should be placed in a sealed laundry bag and clearly labelled.

MANAGEMENT OF ACUTE EXPOSURE OR SPILLAGE

Gloves or outer garments that are overtly contaminated must be removed at once. Hands must be washed immediately as some cytotoxic agents can penetrate gloves (Knowles and Virden, 1980). In cases where there is skin contact with an anticancer drug, the affected area should be washed thoroughly with soap and cool water and medical attention sought as soon as possible. If a cytotoxic drug enters the eye this should be flushed with copious amounts of water and medical attention sought immediately.

Accidental spillage on to a work surface or floor must be cleared immediately. Those involved should wear protective clothing; two pairs of gloves are recommended. If there is visible powder spillage, a mask is mandatory. The drug should be wiped up using a damp cloth or disposable towel and placed in a polythene bag, sealed and placed in a second bag. This should be clearly labelled stating the contents and marked 'Contaminated'. Affected surfaces must be washed with copious amounts of water and dried carefully; washing materials should be disposed of as previously described.

ADMINISTRATION OF CHEMOTHERAPY

Although all first level practitioners are regarded competent to administer drugs and to take responsibility for so doing, the complexity of cancer treatment means that chemotherapy is generally given only by those who have received specialised training. Though the process of training varies between institutions, based on local policies, educational programmes must be comprehensive and include both theoretical knowledge and clinical skills.

Those giving chemotherapy must not only understand the pathophysiology of cancer but also the pharmacology of antineoplastic drugs, the principles underlying safe handling, preparation and administration, and the assessment, diagnosis and management of potential complications and side-effects of treatment. Such knowledge must be supported by clinical skills relating to intravenous therapy (eg. selecting the site, venepuncture and cannulation), techniques of administration and management of venous access devices as well as the more complex techniques, such as intracavity, regional and intrathecal therapy, arterial lines and internal/external infusion pumps (Lind and Bush, 1987).

Because the field of cancer chemotherapy is constantly changing, provision should also be made for ongoing education and training so as to promote high quality care and ensure patient safety.

Safety during administration

Protective clothing should be worn during drug administration as previously described. Air bubbles should be removed from the syringe only when sterile cotton wool/gauze, dampened with alcohol, is placed at the needle tip. The needle should be changed prior to administration. Great care must be taken when priming intravenous giving sets. The distal tip cover should be removed; priming should be performed into a sterile alcohol-dampened sponge/pad that is disposed of in the usual way. Neither giving sets nor syringes should be primed into a sink or open receptacle. Hands should be washed thoroughly after gloves are removed. The intact needle and syringe, gloves and other waste products are disposed of after administration.

Women who are pregnant (particularly in the first trimester) or breast feeding should not be expected to prepare or deliver chemotherapy since there is considerable evidence to show that cytotoxic drugs may increase the risk of spontaneous abortion and foetal abnormalities (eg. Selevan et al, 1985; Rogers and Emmett, 1987). However, it is believed that, if procedures for safe handling are followed, the potential for exposure will be minimised. It is essential that female staff are provided with adequate information to enable them to make an informed decision. Sanctions should not be applied to those who prefer not to administer such agents.

PREPARATION FOR ADMINISTRATION

Those who are involved with the administration of chemotherapy must be sure that they clearly understand the purpose of treatment, the type of drug to be given and the route through which it is to be administered. Each drug must be carefully assessed not only in terms of its pharmacological effects, both therapeutic and toxic, but also with regard to its implications for care. This requires consideration of factors related to the drug itself, the individual patient and appropriate clinical guidelines (Table 6.2).

Table 6.2   Guidelines for the administration of chemotherapy

1. Ensure that informed consent has been obtained.	9. If unable to insert cannula/start infusion after 2 attempts seek help.
2. Check the drug pharmacology - mechanism of action, usual dosage, route of administration, acute and long-term side-effects and route of excretion.	10. Treat all drugs as potential vesicants unless information to the contrary is available; take care to avoid drug infiltration into the tissues.
3. Review relevant laboratory data ensuring that all parameters are within normal limits.	11. Do not mix drugs together when giving combination chemotherapy. Flush cannula with normal saline between drugs and following completion.
4. Double check prescription and question anything unusual. Check height and weight, calculate required dosage.	12. Have emergency equipment (drugs and an extravasation kit) readily available.
5. Administer any prescribed pre-medications.	13. Listen to the patient particularly with regard to unusual sensations, etc. (extravasation).
6. Prepare drugs according to instructions adhering to local safety procedures.	14. Dispose of equipment according to local policies, procedures and guidelines.
7. At bedside, check that the right drug is to be given to the right patient in the correct dose at the right time.	15. Observe patient carefully for signs of an adverse reaction.
8. Give drugs according to local procedures using aseptic technique.	16. Document drug administration in the patient's notes.

Drug-related factors

The date and time of administration must be ascertained and other medication(s) to be given in conjunction with, or following, chemotherapy identified (eg. antiemetics, sedatives). Written informed consent should be obtained, particularly when the patient is participating in a clinical trial or research study (see Ch. 16 and 17).

Patient-related factors

The general condition must be assessed to ensure that there are no contraindications to chemotherapy administration. The most recent

84

haematological results (full blood count, particularly white blood cells and platelets) should be reviewed as bone marrow depression may be dose-limiting; bone marrow function must be assessed before chemotherapy is given and before periodic pulses of myelosuppressive drugs (Table 6.3). Previous exposure to radiation can increase bone marrow toxicity. Severe myelosuppression may necessitate adjustments to the dose or temporary withholding of therapy to allow bone marrow recovery. Guidelines for such action include a white cell count below $4 \times 10^9/l$ and/or a platelet count below $100 \times 10^9/l$.

Table 6.3   **Examples of myelosuppressive drugs**

	Degree of suppression	Nadir	Comments
Alkylating agents			
Melphalan	Moderate-severe	Unpredictable	Effects cumulative; may be dose-limiting.
Chlorambucil	Moderate	21-28 days	Potentiated by radiotherapy and other cytotoxic drugs.
Cyclophosphamide	Moderate	14 days	Potentiated by allopurinol; reduced risk of thrombocytopoenia. Effects cumulative.
Nitrosoureas			
Lomustine	Severe	21-28 days	Effects cumulative; may be dose-limiting.
Plant products			
Vinblastine	Moderate	10 days - may be delayed	Thrombocytopoenia rare.
Vindesine	Moderate	10 days	Most likely to cause leucopoenia.
Etoposide	Moderate-severe	14 days	Effects cumulative; may be dose-limiting.
Antimetabolites			
Methotrexate	Moderate	10 days	Effect dose-related; side-effects reduced by folinic acid 'rescue'. Effects are dose-related.
5-fluorouracil	Moderate-severe	10-14 days	Effects are cumulative.
6-mercaptopurine	Moderate	10-14 days	
Antitumour antibiotics			
Doxorubicin	Severe	10-14 days	Myelosuppression may be dose-limiting.
Mitomycin-C	Moderate	21-28 days	Myelosuppression may be delayed; particularly affects platelets; effects cumulative.
Miscellaneous			
Carboplatin	Moderate-severe	14 days	Effects may be dose-limiting.
Cisplatin	Mild-moderate	14 days	Effects may be dose-limiting.

Renal function must also be evaluated since many chemo-therapeutic drugs are dependent on renal function and integrity for their metabolism and/or excretion or for excretion of the cellular breakdown products released by destruction of malignant cells (Cline and Haskell, 1980). Similarly, since the liver is involved in the biotransformation and metabolism of many chemotherapeutic agents, malfunction may increase the risk of toxicity or influence the therapeutic effects. Thus evidence of organ dysfunction may affect either the pharmacodynamics or pharmacokinetics of the drug (Ch. 3); a reduction in dose or delay in treatment may necessary. Renal and hepatic function must, therefore, be monitored closely.

Similarly, the patient's psychological status and level of anxiety should be assessed and reassurance provided as required. Care must be taken to ensure that the patient fully understands the rationale underlying his treatment and the procedures to be undertaken. He should be informed of the risk of side-effects and the need to monitor both bone marrow and renal function. Similarly, he should be informed of the risk of toxic effects, the likely symptoms and the need to inform staff of their occurrence. This means that consideration must be given to those interventions that can be planned to reduce the risk of side-effects and to the actions that may be appropriate to minimise the severity of both side-effects or the toxic consequences.

ROUTES AND METHODS OF CHEMOTHERAPY ADMINISTRATION

There are two fundamental methods of administering antineoplastic drugs: systemic and regional. Systemic therapy is designed to destroy tumour cells in both the primary tumour and distant metastases. The goal is to provide a concentration of the drug(s) sufficient to achieve an appropriate therapeutic (cytotoxic) effect without causing excessive toxicity to normal cells and tissues. Such therapy may be given orally, subcutaneously, intramuscularly or intravenously.

Regional therapy represents an attempt to localise the effects of chemotherapy by delivering drugs directly into the blood vessel supplying a tumour or to the cavity in which a tumour is situated (Galassi et al, 1996).

Oral administration

Despite the fact that oral agents are easier to administer than those requiring parenteral administration they are no less toxic. Similarly, although administration is usually straightforward, it is important to ensure that the patient is aware of the current dose and scheduling.

The importance of compliance with the prescribed regime must be stressed particularly when the patient has poor social support and/or the regime causes nausea (eg. cyclophosphamide, procarbazine) since such patients are more likely to be non-compliant (Barofsky, 1984). The patient and/or his family must be given clear, written instructions containing the name(s) of all his medications, the required dose and the time at which these should be taken.

Intramuscular and subcutaneous administration

Few chemotherapeutic drugs can be given by either of these routes due to the risk of tissue damage (particularly from vesicant or caustic agents), incomplete absorption, bleeding and discomfort. Drugs that may be given in this way include some hormonal agents, methotrexate. L-asparaginase, bleomycin, cytosine arabinoside and cyclophosphamide. Both continuous and intermittent chemotherapy, relying on agents that do not irritate the tissues (eg. cytosine arabinoside, bleomycin), may be achieved using ambulatory infusion pumps (p90) (Sticklin et al, 1989).

When giving drugs by either of these routes, the smallest possible needle, that will allow passage of the solution, must be selected; the needle should be changed after the solution has been withdrawn from the ampoule or vial and a suitable site for administration, with adequate muscle and/or subcutaneous tissue, chosen. Sites of administration should be rotated if the medication is given frequently so as to prevent tissue irritation and development of induration and/or fibrosis (Tipton, 1995).

Intravenous (IV) administration

Most anticancer agents are administered intravenously, primarily because absorption is more reliable than when drugs are given either intramuscularly or subcutaneously and therapeutic drug blood levels are quickly achieved. In addition, many drugs must be administered into a vein in which rapid dilution by blood can occur. This helps to prevent irritation to the vein and surrounding soft tissue. It may also reduce the need for repeated injections (Table 6.4). The intravenous route is always used for administration of vesicant drugs.

Drugs may be given:

1. By bolus administration.
2. Through an existing intravenous line.

Table 6.4   Advantages and disadvantages of the intravenous route
(Pritchard and David, 1988)

Advantages	Disadvantages
Therapeutic effects are achieved immediately as drug is delivered rapidly to site of action.	Cannot remove drug once it has been given; may increase toxicity or risk of hypersensitivity reactions.
Dose can be calculated precisely as drug is totally absorbed.	Inadequate control of administration may cause speed shock.
Avoids the pain that may be associated with intramuscular or subcutaneous administration.	Risk of microbial contamination, irritation of the vein, drug interactions or incompatibilities.
Used for drugs that cannot be given by any other route (eg. due to irritation to or instability in GI tract).	

3. As a short-term infusion.
4. As a continuous infusion over several hours or days.

The method selected is often dictated by the vesicant properties of the drug(s) involved (Ch. 8), their potential to cause venous irritation (phlebitis) and the demands of a particular treatment protocol. Other factors which are considered include the likelihood of immediate or longer-term complications (eg. allergic reactions, hyper/hypotension).

Most drugs are given as bolus injections having first flushed the vein to ensure both its patency and integrity. The decision to give drugs through an existing IV infusion is largely dependent on whether the patient requires that infusion for some other purpose (eg. hydration or antibiotic therapy). The 'direct push' approach is preferred for vesicant drugs as it permits precise control and prevents the drug 'backing-up' into the IV tubing. It is often believed that it is desirable for vesicants to be injected into an existing infusion through a Y-connector since infusing the drug while the IV fluid is flowing freely ensures continual dilution and minimises irritation to the vein. Using this approach, the site can be observed during the infusion and monitored for possible extravasation (Ch. 8). Either method is safe provided the vein is flushed with 20-30ml of saline between the administration of each agent to ensure complete delivery and to prevent the mixing of incompatible agents.

Short-term infusion is useful for drugs that require dilution and administration over a longer period of time. It is usually reserved for drugs that cause untoward symptoms or complications when given

88

as a bolus (eg. hypotension, perivenous irritation and/or discomfort, acute nausea and vomiting). Examples of drugs given in this way include etoposide, teniposide, cyclophosphamide and carmustine. Vesicants are rarely given in this way, except through a central venous device (Tipton, 1995) as the IV site may not be constantly observed and extravasation may, therefore, go unnoticed.

Continuous infusion is used to administer chemotherapy over a prolonged period, typically 24-96 hours. This may overcome cyto-kinetic resistance, enhance tumour response and minimise toxicity (Goodman, 1991). It is believed that prolonged exposure of tumour cells to anticancer drugs may increase intracellular levels of the drugs due to enhancement of cellular transport mechanisms (Carlson and Sikic, 1983). Continuous infusion also helps to prevent the peak plasma levels associated with bolus administration thus reducing toxicity (Brenner et al, 1984). Such infusions can be given both in hospital and at home using portable ambulatory infusion pumps or implanted pumps (Tipton, 1995). Vesicants may be administered by this means but only through a central venous line.

Since the intravenous route provides direct access to the systemic circulation certain important points must be considered (eg. the risk of infection). Strict asepsis must be maintained during both preparation and administration of drugs. Thorough hand-washing is the single most important preventive measure in the transmission of infection. Soaps containing hexachlorophene are effective in reducing staphylococci and iodine-based compounds (eg. povidone iodine) in protecting against gram negative organisms and fungi (Graze, 1980).

The skin overlying the selected area should be thoroughly cleansed using a defatting agent (eg. alcohol, acetone) followed by an iodine-based antiseptic; the area should be allowed to dry and should not be touched prior to insertion of the intravenous cannula.

Selection of a suitable site. Careful selection of an appropriate vein is essential, particularly because of the need for repeated vene-puncture. Factors affecting selection include the expected duration of the infusion and the volume/type of solution to be given. Extremities with impaired venous circulation or lymphatic drainage, or in which axillary nodes have been resected, should be avoided while sclerosed, thrombosed or phlebitic veins are inappropriate (Galassi et al, 1996).

Drugs which are not vesicants can be administered through the metacarpal veins on the distal surface of the hand or through the basilic and cephalic veins of the forearm (Figure 6.1). Small lumen veins should not be used both to decrease the risk of damage due to friction and because of the reduced ability to dilute drugs/solutions.

Figure 6.1   Basilic and cephalic veins in the area marked are those most suitable for administration of vesicant drugs

Vein selection should begin distally and proceed proximally in order to avoid extravasation at the site(s) of recent venepuncture; venepuncture sites should be alternated throughout the course of treatment. In general, the antecubital fossa is best avoided as the large amount of subcutaneous tissue may increase the extent of tissue damage. Furthermore, if venous fibrosis occurs, drawing blood from that vein could be difficult and will, in any case, render smaller veins, distal to the obstruction useless due to poor drainage.

To minimise the risk of thrombophlebitis and infection it is essential that aseptic techniques are followed scrupulously when inserting the needle and during intravenous line manipulation and drug administration. Vigorous hand-washing should always precede venepuncture and gloves should be worn.

Prior to insertion, a tourniquet should be applied above the selected site and the skin thoroughly cleansed as previously described. The needle should then be inserted into the vein and, once a back-flow has been observed, the tourniquet removed and the solution instilled at the prescribed rate. When an intravenous infusion is to be established, the needle should be firmly secured, using hypoallergenic tape (Figure 6.2).

The risk of haemorrhage in patients who are thrombocytopoenic (Ch. 9), means that sustained pressure should be applied to the insertion site once the needle is removed.

Figure 6.2   A suggested method for securing an intravenous cannula

1. Place first strip of adhesive tape under the cannula 'sticky side up'   2. Fold the ends over as shown and stick to the skin

3. Using a second strip of adhesive (sticky side down) overlapping slightly so as to stick to the skin

Selection of the cannula. The type of cannula selected for use during administration of chemotherapy depends largely on the length of the infusion. A 19- or 21G needle may permit a more rapid infusion and so minimise the effects of potentially irritating substances on the vein; care must, however, be taken to avoid 'speed shock' manifested by a flushed face, headache, tightness of the chest and congestion. Smaller gauge needles (eg. 22- or 23G) may, however, be easier to insert, be less painful, cause less mechanical phlebitis and produce less scar tissue (Tipton, 1995). A 23G 'butterfly' needle is often used for ease of insertion and minimal vein irritation, particularly in the outpatient setting; larger cannulae are used for longer infusions or administration of large volumes of fluid.

Venous access devices

Since most cancer chemotherapy is delivered through the intravenous route, a variety of venous access devices has been developed so as to avoid repeated and progressively more difficult venepuncture and permit easy and safe, long-term access to the venous circulation. Using such devices it is possible to ease the discomfort of repeated venepuncture and to allow outpatient treatment for many who would otherwise require hospitalisation.

Permanent venous access devices can be considered in two main categories: external (tunnelled) catheters and subcutaneously implanted ports.

Tunnelled catheters

External catheters are typically made of siliconised rubber (Silastic) and inserted into the central venous circulation and then tunnelled some distance in the subcutaneous tissue from the insertion site before exiting the body (Figure 6.3).

Figure 6.3   **Insertion of a central venous catheter**

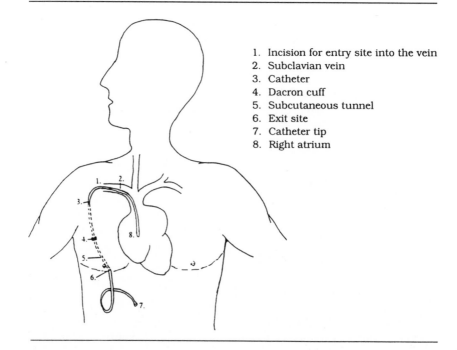

1. Incision for entry site into the vein
2. Subclavian vein
3. Catheter
4. Dacron cuff
5. Subcutaneous tunnel
6. Exit site
7. Catheter tip
8. Right atrium

Such catheters are usually threaded through the cephalic vein and into the superior vena cava (SVC) or, more commonly, through the SVC into the right atrium. When the cephalic vein is not suitable, the right internal jugular or the common facial vein may be used. The catheter is inserted, using fluouroscopy, under strict asepsis.

A two inch incision is made in the deltopectoral groove below the acromium of the right clavicle and the cephalic vein isolated. A subcutaneous tunnel is created, using long forceps, exiting at an area between the nipple and sternum. The catheter is then drawn through the tunnel, inserted into the vein and positioned in the lower SVC at the entrance to the right atrium (Bjeletich and Hickman, 1980). A suture is placed around the vein and the incision closed. The exit site, at the lower end of the tunnel, is also sutured. A small, Dacron cuff, 30cm from the catheter hub, plugs the tunnel in the subcutaneous tissues where it initiates fibrosis and reduces the risk of descending infection from the exit site (Cox, 1985).

The incidence of catheter-related infection can be reduced still further by the addition of a subcutaneous cuff constructed of a biodegradable collagen matrix impregnated with bactericidal silver (Maki et al, 1988). After insertion, subcutaneous tissue will grow into the matrix which both anchors the catheter and creates a barrier against invasion by extrinsic organisms on the skin; the presence of silver augments the mechanical barrier and exerts bactericidal effects. Heparinised saline is injected into the line and the line capped before it is looped and taped securely against the body to prevent tugging or twisting at the exit site; it must not be allowed to hang loose. Three or four sutures will mark the exit site and can usually be removed after 7-10 days.

The exit site is usually redressed on alternate days unless the dressing becomes soiled or wet. The site is cleaned, often using povidone iodine solution; a sterile non-adhesive dressing is applied, attached by means of hypoallergenic tape. The suture around the catheter remains in place for at least 21 days to promote dense fibrosis. The entry site is also dressed until the sutures are removed and the wound has healed.

When the catheter is not needed for infusion it should be flushed with heparinised saline (500iu heparin per 5ml saline). Units vary with regard to the frequency with which this is carried out; local procedures must be followed. However, unless an IV infusion is in progress, the line should always be heparinised after drugs have been given. The line should also be flushed with normal saline between different infusions. These procedures must be carried out under aseptic conditions while wearing sterile gloves.

Damage can occur if a central line is used improperly, usually resulting from accidental severing of the tubing with scissors or from the use of clamps with 'teeth' or prongs. However, provided that damage is not within 4cm of the chest wall, this can be repaired (Cox, 1985); catheter repair kits are available. The line should be always be clamped, using rubber-covered clamps, before the cap is removed. This will help to prevent bleeding and reduce the risk of air or infection entering the catheter.

Infection, clotting or severing are the most common complications (Bjeletich and Hickman, 1980; Williams, 1985). Clotting usually results from inadequate irrigation or heparinisation. Two approaches may be adopted, under medical supervision, to clear the line. Either heparinised saline or urokinase may be injected into the catheter which is then clamped and left for 15-20 minutes. Attempts are then made to irrigate the line; this should take only 3 or 4 attempts. The procedure may be repeated but, if unsuccessful, it may be necessary to remove the line (Cox, 1985).

Local or systemic infection is most likely when the patient is neutropoenic. When infection is suspected blood samples should be taken from both the catheter and an uncatheterised vein and sent for culture. A broad spectrum antibiotic is then administered until the infection is identified when a specific drug may be prescribed. If only one culture is positive it is usually possible to treat the infection successfully without removing the catheter; if repeated blood cultures are positive the catheter must be removed.

Although catheter removal is relatively easy, it may create considerable anxiety for the patient who may require premedication (eg. diazepam) prior to removal. The exit site is cleaned and the catheter wrapped around the hand and firmly and steadily pulled, stretching the line with constant pressure; jerking may break the line. The pressure is maintained until the fibrous tissue surrounding the Dacron cuff loosens and the line breaks free. Once the line is released, constant firm pressure will bring the line through the exit site. As the cephalic vein closes after the catheter is removed there should be no bleeding at the insertion site. There may, however, be some bleeding at the exit site due to passage of the cuff. Occasionally the cuff may remain attached to the tissue although the line pulls through; provided the cuff is not infected this is of little concern and need not be removed. If it is necessary to remove the cuff for cosmetic reasons this is easily achieved under local anaesthesia.

Central venous catheters are available as single lumen, double lumen and triple lumen designs; the needs of the patient are taken into account when selecting the most appropriate for use in specific situations.

The patient, and his family, should be taught to look after his central line. Although most are apprehensive at first they can, with careful guidance, be taught to change the dressing and heparinise the line. Involving the family is beneficial as it includes them in the patient's care and can help to ease family tensions (Cox, 1985). Similarly, the relatives can take care of the line if the patient is unwell. Such preparation is particularly important when a child is involved as the parents are often required to look after the catheter.

There is no reason why a patient cannot be discharged from hospital and resume a normal life once such a line has been inserted. Bathing, and even swimming, can safely be enjoyed provided that the catheter is firmly secured to the chest wall and covered with a water-proof dressing.

Although tunnelled catheters have clear advantages there are some distinct disadvantages; they are expensive, require exit site care and frequent flushing and, for some patients, may lead to concern over body image; long-term central venous catheters may also provide continuous reminders of the disease (Thompson et al, 1989).

Implantable venous access devices

Subcutaneous implantable ports are silastic catheters that connect to a plastic or titanium housing implanted in the subcutaneous tissues. The housing contains a self-sealing silicone septum which may be used to administer systemic fluids or drugs or for blood sampling (Figure 6.4). An arterial port, placed for regional drug therapy, should be used only for that therapy (see p99-100).

A special Huber point needle (opening on the side) must be used to avoid damage to the septum. Both right-angled and 'butterfly' Huber needles are available for use in establishing an intravenous infusion through the port; the thick silicone septum holds the needle in place.

The implanted catheters are inserted into the same locations and by the same techniques as external catheters and are then tunnelled for a short distance to a subcutaneous pocket created for the port.

Preparation and administration of chemotherapy

The patency of the line is maintained using 3-6ml of heparinised saline which is instilled after drug and fluid administration and on a routine, intermittent basis.

Figure 6.4 **Diagrammatic representation of an implantable venous access device**

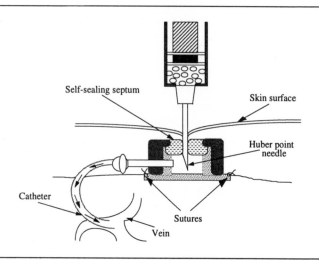

This method has several advantages. Since the port is entirely under the skin no dressing is required once the incision has healed. Body image is likely to remain intact as there is only a small bump to remind the patient of its presence. The patient is free of the responsibility for heparinisation as this is usually carried out in the outpatient clinic once a month or following use of the port for administration of drugs or fluids. Arterial catheters are heparinised once a week or after medication/fluids; more frequent heparinisation is required due to the greater pressure in the arterial system. The importance of regular attendance for heparinisation must be stressed since the risk of clotting and/or infection of the line remains.

Peripherally-inserted central catheters, of small gauge, may be used in patients requiring short-term therapy. These are placed non-surgically, through the cephalic or basilic veins, and threaded into the superior vena cava following which an external hub or an implantable subcutaneous port may be attached (Winters et al, 1990).

Care and management during intravenous chemotherapy

The techniques required for the general management of intravenous infusions are outside the scope of this book; however, those points relevant to the administration of cancer chemotherapy will be discussed. For example, since some drugs are extremely caustic (vesicant), causing local necrosis if infiltrated (extravasated) into the tissues (Ch. 8), careful observation of the IV site is essential. The area proximal to the infusion must always be observed as leakage may occur elsewhere. Complaints of burning or pain during drug administration may indicate infiltration. However, since slow leakage of fluid may not be noticed during infusion, the patient must be advised of the signs and symptoms of extravasation and asked to inform staff if this occurs later. Some vesicants have specific anti-dotes which should be applied if infiltration occurs; others require steroid therapy and the application of hot or cold compresses to reduce spread of the drug (p141).

Although administration of some drugs (eg. etoposide, bleomycin) is associated with the risk of anaphylaxis (p132-6) any drug may provoke an idiosyncratic response in sensitised individuals. Thus emergency equipment and drugs (eg. adrenaline) must be available. 'Test doses' may be given if there is identified potential for an allergic response. This must be explained to the patient who is often very anxious; reassurance and supportive care are essential.

Normal saline is used to 'flush' or irrigate the IV cannula between individual drugs when giving combination chemotherapy (Pritchard and David, 1988). This ensures complete delivery of the drug and also provides a means of checking that the cannula has not been displaced during drug administration; a final flush of normal saline is given at the end of drug administration by restarting the infusion or changing the syringe.

Some drugs are administered in a large volume of fluid over a defined time period as this will maintain a constant blood level; it may also decrease the pain associated with the infusion. The required flow rate must be calculated once the infusion has been established. This is achieved using the formula shown in Table 6.5.

Use of the formula enables the rate of infusion to be calculated accurately. Most currently available giving sets have an average of 15 drops per minute. Some, however, have a smaller needle so that the formula must be modified to take this into account when calculating the required drip rate for individual infusions.

Table 6.5   Calculating the required flow rate for an intravenous infusion

---

$$\frac{\text{Volume of fluid (ml)} \times 15}{\text{Time (hours)} \times 60} = \text{drops per minute (DPM)}$$

in which:

Volume (ml)	=	number of millilitres in the infusion
Time	=	number of hours of the infusion
15	=	number of drops per millilitre
60	=	conversion from hours to minutes

A variety of factors may cause alterations in the flow rate through individual infusions. These include the following:

1. The type of equipment involved.
2. The height of the infusion bottle in relation to the patient.
3. Dysfunction of the flow control device or clamp which may cause unintentional opening and increase the rate. Similarly, the clamp may affect the flexibility of the tubing through general 'wear and tear'.
4. Obstruction of the venting needle or airway tubing, needle or cannula may reduce the flow.
5. Since it is more difficult to 'push' thicker fluids through the tubing the flow rate is inversely proportional to the viscosity of the fluid (ie. as viscosity increases the rate decreases). Viscosity is affected by the ambient temperature increasing as temperature decreases.
6. Alterations in the patient's vascular pressure may change resistance to the infusion affecting the flow rate.

Infusion pumps are often used to facilitate the administration of intravenous fluids; chemotherapy is no exception. They are essential in intra-arterial therapy when drugs are given against arterial pressure. Infusion pumps help in administration by controlling the gravity flow or by peristaltic action exerting positive pressure on the tubing. The majority are electrically controlled; the flow is regulated by means of a timer preset to the required rate. A photo-sensitive sensor registers each time a drop of fluid crosses the beam of light. Many also have alarm devices which indicate when the pump cannot maintain the rate set for whatever reason (eg. infiltration, an empty bottle, air in the tubing or occlusion of the line). Thus they permit chemotherapy administration to be controlled with precision.

Compact battery-operated pumps enable patients to receive continuous chemotherapy on an outpatient basis or in their own homes; they allow the patient greater mobility since the pump can be carried in a shoulder bag or pocket or attached to a belt. Although they are battery-operated their mechanism of action is as previously described. Totally implantable infusion pumps are also available; these are discussed further on page 100.

REGIONAL DRUG ADMINISTRATION

The inability to achieve an appropriate concentration of a drug at a tumour site without undue toxicity to normal tissues is a recognised problem of systemic chemotherapy. Regional therapy represents an attempt to enhance the concentration of the drug in a tumour while lowering systemic drug exposure (Keizer and Pinedo, 1985). Since this approach also increases the contact time between the drug and tumour cells it also increases the likelihood of effective therapy. Drugs which are most effective include those which are either completely absorbed by the tumour on their first passage through the capillary bed or which are very rapidly metabolised. The site of delivery should have a low exchange rate so that systemic absorption is minimised (Collins, 1984). Such therapy may be administered intra-arterially, intraperitoneally, intraventricularly and intrathecally.

Intra-arterial administration

Hepatic artery infusion is the most commonly used form of intra-arterial administration and may significantly improve the quality of the patient's life. Several drugs may be administered in this way, including methotrexate, mitomycin-C, bleomycin, 5-fluorouracil, etoposide, cisplatin and cytosine arabinoside.

An arterial catheter is inserted and connected to either an implanted port or a pump. Catheter insertion is an aseptic procedure carried out in conjunction with angiography which is used to assess the vascular supply and locate the major artery. One of two types of placement may be used: surgical or percutaneous. However, since this primarily a palliative procedure, percutaneous catheters are often preferred. This has disadvantages as it may be necessary to re-insert the catheter before each course of treatment; surgically placed catheters may remain in place for extended periods. Patients may receive their treatment during a short hospital stay or may go home with an infusion pump for long-term administration; on occasions an infusion pump may be surgically implanted during catheter insertion.

The period required for rehabilitation depends on the location of the tumour, the method of insertion and whether or not an infusion pump has been implanted. Possible complications include failure of the pump, kinking, leaking or breaking of the catheter; haemorrhage and infection may also occur (Garvey and Manganarro, 1982). It is also important to remember that intra-arterial therapy does not protect the patient against systemic effects although their incidence may be reduced.

Care of the patient receiving intra-arterial therapy

Intra-arterial chemotherapy requires highly skilled care which is dependent on whether a percutaneous or surgical placement is required. Percutaneous insertion may be carried out under sedation and local anaesthesia; surgical placement requires a general anaesthetic. In either case, pre-operative teaching, support and reassurance are essential. Prior to insertion the equipment required should be explained to the patient who should be encouraged to examine, touch and question its function. This provides the opportunity to assess both the level of anxiety and the ability to handle the equipment. The level of understanding of the treatment must also be evaluated. He is likely to be extremely anxious and in need of considerable support. Listening to the patient will be helpful in planning appropriate interventions. Teaching about the equipment and drug side-effects will be crucial if the patient is to be discharged with a portable infusion pump.

In the immediate post-operative period the nurse should accept responsibility for the patient's care; teaching should be recommenced on the second or third post-operative day when his condition has physically improved. Since the catheter is threaded into an artery the insertion site must be observed for signs of bleeding or swelling; similarly the circulation of the distal extremity should be monitored. Evidence of infection should be assessed. The pump apparatus must be regularly examined as malfunction may result in serious complications (eg. air embolism or a reduction in the dose of the drug reaching the tumour).

When surgical placement is undertaken an infusion pump may also be implanted. This is usually positioned in a pocket fashioned from the subcutaneous layers of the abdominal wall; the cannula extends through the pump into the relevant artery so that no part of the pump or cannula are located externally. This is not a common procedure and an ambulatory infusion pump is usually used to ensure that drug administration is accurately controlled. This enables continuous administration and can maximise the effect on the tumour and reduce the severity and duration of side-effects. Furthermore, it permits the patient to be ambulatory throughout his treatment (see page 105).

Intracavity administration

On occasions the effectiveness of chemotherapy is decreased when anatomical or physiological barriers reduce the contact between drugs and tumour cells. One such is the blood-brain barrier; others include the pleura and the peritoneum so that injection directly into these cavities is particularly useful when it is known that a drug given intravenously does not readily penetrate into that cavity.

The goal of such treatment is to achieve effective destruction of malignant cells by increasing the contact of cytotoxic drugs with such cells while reducing undesirable side-effects. Clearly, normal cells present in the cavity are also exposed to the drugs and so may be affected by their cytotoxic effects although these are normally less severe than when drugs are given systemically. This approach, therefore, represents an attempt to use chemotherapy as a localised treatment. Chemotherapy may also be used to treat recurrent malignant effusions. Effusions may significantly compromise the patient's ability to live a 'normal' life and markedly reduce its quality.

When chemotherapy is administered into the pleural cavity any fluid present is removed before the drug is instilled. This may be achieved by simple chest aspiration or, alternatively, by thoracotomy and continuous suction drainage. Once all fluid has been removed the drug, appropriately diluted, is instilled into the cavity. Following this the patient should be repositioned every 10 minutes to maximise distribution of the drug throughout the cavity. Drugs used in this way include 5-FU, bleomycin and nitrogen mustard. This procedure is often used to achieve sclerotic changes in the pleural lining and to prevent fluid re-entering the cavity.

Premedication and antiemetic therapy may be necessary prior to the procedure and the patient may require considerable support and reassurance. Following administration, analgesics and antipyretic agents (eg. aspirin) may be needed since significant pleural pain may follow pleuradesis (Moores, 1991).

Preparation and administration of chemotherapy

Intraperitoneal chemotherapy is most often used for locally recurrent ovarian cancer. It bears many similarities to the techniques used in peritoneal dialysis. Insertion of the catheter, clearly a sterile procedure, is carried out under local anaesthesia. A Tenckhoff catheter is inserted into the peritoneal cavity, through an incision just below the umbilicus, and threaded through a subcutaneous tunnel to an exit site some 5-10cm from the incision. This tunnel, together with a Dacron cuff, which holds the catheter in place, and the Luer lock on the catheter, interact to reduce the risk of infection entering the cavity. Daily dialysis, using heparinised solutions, is then carried out until healing is complete, usually after 7-10 days. Alternatively, the catheter may be attached to an implanted port. The catheter may then be used for administration of chemotherapy. When a single dose of intraperitoneal chemotherapy is given this is usually instilled after abdominal paracentesis.

The drug is mixed in 1 litre of dialysate and administered over about 20 minutes. The patient changes position frequently to enhance fluid distribution. The drug is either drained or allowed to remain in the peritoneal cavity from where it is absorbed (Swenson and Iricksson, 1986; Zook-Enck, 1990). A possible complication of this technique is fibrous in-growth around the catheter or port which prevents drainage. This affects about 30% of all patients (Markman et al, 1984) and occurs whether or not the catheter is irrigated. Although it may cause temporary discomfort, due to abdominal distension, this poses no long-term difficulty as the dialysate is gradually absorbed.

Strict asepsis is essential when caring for the catheter or the entry and exit site. Close observation must be maintained and the patient monitored for the signs and symptoms of infection as well as those of chemotherapy-induced side-effects. The procedure itself may be uncomfortable, and the chemotherapy may cause local irritation. The patient should be helped to be as comfortable as possible; medication and other symptom control measures should be employed.

Intrathecal or intraventricular administration

Since most chemotherapeutic drugs cannot cross the blood-brain barrier the central nervous system (CNS) provides a 'sanctuary' in which cancer cells are protected from their cytotoxic effects (Cline and Haskell, 1980). Thus, in an attempt to reach tumour deposits within the CNS, cytotoxic drugs may be injected directly into the subarachnoid space.

Intrathecal administration depends on performance of a lumbar puncture which may cause marked anxiety and result in severe or uncomfortable headaches. However, although this approach is quick and easy, its main disadvantage is that a drug may reach only the epidural or subdural space.

An intraventricular device, such as an Ommaya or Rickam reservoir, can be used to overcome this problem (Figure 6.5). These are similar to implantable venous access devices comprising a reservoir with a catheter attached; they are surgically placed under the scalp with the catheter extending into the ventricle (Goodman, 1991).

Figure 6.5   Diagrammatic   representation   of   an   Ommaya reservoir

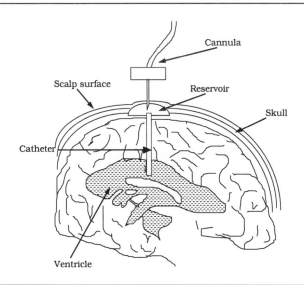

Before accessing, the scalp is shaved if necessary and cleaned using an antiseptic solution, such as povidone-iodine; the reservoir should be primed by depressing it several times. The reservoir is accessed using a 25G scalp needle; cerebrospinal fluid (CSF) is gently aspirated and the drug injected slowly over 5-10 minutes followed by preservative-free saline or CSF. Once the needle is removed, the reservoir is again depressed several times to facilitate dispersal of the

Preparation and administration of chemotherapy

drug. Such devices require no routine maintenance although the patient and his family should be taught to care for the reservoir by avoiding trauma to the area and keeping a small area free of hair so that chemotherapy can be administered easily.

Care during intrathecal or intraventricular therapy

As previously stated, intrathecal administration requires that a lumbar puncture be performed. This involves the introduction of a needle into the lumbar subarachnoid space below the termination of the spinal cord. It is passed through the intervertebral space between either the third and fourth or fourth and fifth lumbar vertebrae. The patient should be positioned so as to maximise separation of the vertebrae. This is normally a lateral horizontal position with the back on the edge of the bed or examination table. The knees should be drawn up towards the chest and the head/trunk flexed to widen the intervertebral spaces; this may be described as the 'foetal position'. Ideally, the patient is supported behind the neck and the knees.

Strict asepsis is essential to prevent the introduction of infection into the spinal canal. The procedure is usually carried out under local anaesthesia which is administered at the site selected for needle insertion; if this is not given at the midline it may come into contact with one of the dorsal nerve roots causing pain to 'shoot' down one leg. This can be alleviated immediately by moving the needle. Affected patient will require reassurance that no permanent damage has occurred since this is an acutely uncomfortable experience.

During the procedure the patient's vital signs must be closely observed since respiratory arrest can occur if the medulla is compressed. On completion, the patient is advised to lie flat for at least 4hrs to reduce the occurrence of headaches which are likely after the withdrawal of spinal fluid or the administration of chemotherapy. A headache is usually relieved by remaining flat, applying an ice-pack and administration of an analgesic (eg. aspirin). An increased fluid intake may also be beneficial.

The patient should be closely observed for the occurrence of side-effects associated with both the procedure and the specific drug administered since systemic effects may occur even though drugs are given by the intrathecal route. If signs of an increase in intracranial pressure are noted (Table 6.6) the patient's level of consciousness, pulse, respirations, blood pressure and pupil reactions must be recorded every 30 minutes for the first two hours and then every

104

hour for the next 12 hours. It is essential that the nurse is constantly aware of the patient's condition. Physician's are reliant on nurses for accurate reporting since this will enable appropriate care to be rapidly initiated.

TABLE 6.6   Neurological signs and symptoms indicating raised intracranial pressure

---

Alterations in mental status - restlessness, irritability, confusion
Altered level of consciousness
Elevation of blood pressure
Gradual lowering of pulse and respiratory rate
Motor and sensory changes
Headache
Nausea - with/without projectile vomiting

NB.   Diagnosis is clinically difficult until signs and symptoms are overt.

Patient care differs little when drugs are administered through an Ommaya or Rickam reservoir. However, following insertion, a pressure dressing should be maintained over the wound for the first 24 hours after which a sterile dressing should be applied until the wound has healed. The risk of infection and blockage of the cannula are important considerations.

Continuous ambulatory chemotherapy

Until comparatively recently, chemotherapy was always administered according to intermittent schedules requiring admission as an in-patient or day case. The increasing trend towards the use of ambulatory chemotherapy, given as continuous infusion, has dramatically altered cancer treatment, particularly but not exclusively, for patients with breast cancer, multiple myeloma and colorectal disease, and has enabled increasing numbers to receive their treatment at home (Smith et al, 1995; Cunningham et al, 1997).

This approach has a number of advantages for both the treatment itself and for patients. For example, some cytotoxic drugs, particularly those with relatively short half lives (eg. bleomycin, doxorubicin), have been found to be more effective when given continuously as this ensures that effective drug concentrations are present in/around the cells when they replicate (Garvey, 1987). This is particularly important in the treatment of solid tumours which have been found to be more responsive to continuous exposure due to the prolonged length of the cell cycle. For patients, this approach to treatment has been shown to increase independence and sense of control over their lives (Schulmeister, 1992). This has, in turn, been shown to encourage a more positive attitude towards treatment and to enable the family to become involved and provide a greater level of support; it also allows patients to receive their therapy at home thus reducing the costs of such treatment.

There are, of course, disadvantages of home administration of chemotherapy. For example, professional support is less easily obtained should problems arise and it must be recognised that all patients are able or willing to manage their therapy at home (Woollons, 1996). Changes in perceived body image, associated with long-term central venous access catheterisation (Thompson et al, 1989), may be exacerbated by being connected to an infusion pump for several days or weeks at a time (Schulmeister, 1992). Such factors also provide a continuous reminder of the presence of the disease.

REFERENCES

Barofsky I, 1984, Therapeutic compliance and the cancer patient, Health Education **10**, 43-55.

Barry LK, Booher RB, 1985, Promoting the responsible handling of antineoplastic agents in the community, Oncology Nursing Forum **12**(5) 41-6.

Barton-Burke M, Wilkes GM, Berg D, et al, 1990, Cancer Chemotherapy: A Nursing Process Approach, Jones and Bartlett Publishers, Boston.

Bergemann DA, 1983, Handling antineoplastic agents, American Journal of Intravenous Therapy and Clinical Nutrition **10**, 13-7.

Bjeletich J, Hickman RO, 1980, The Hickman indwelling catheter, American Journal of Nursing **80**, 60-5.

Brenner DE, Grosh WW, Noone R, et al, 1984, Human plasma pharmacokinetics of doxorubicin: comparison of bolus and infusional administration, Cancer Treatment Symposia **5**, 77-83.

Carlson RW, Sikic BI, 1983, Continuous infusion or bolus injection in cancer chemotherapy, Annals of Internal Medicine **99**, 828-33.

Cline M, Haskell C, 1980, Cancer Chemotherapy, WB Saunders Co., Philadelphia.

Collins JM, 1984, Pharmacologic rationale for regional drug delivery, Journal of Clinical Oncology **2**, 498-503.

Cox E, 1985, The Hickman catheter, Nursing Mirror **161**, 34-6.

Cunningham DC, et al, 1997, A randomised trial comparing ECF with FAMtx in advanced oesophago-gastric cancer, Journal of Clinical Oncology **15**(1), 261-7.

Davis MR, 1981, Guidelines for safe handling of cytotoxic drugs in pharmacy departments and hospital wards, Hospital Pharmacy **16**, 17-20.

Department of Health, 1988, Policy for Safe Handling of Cytotoxic Drugs, Health Management System and Personnel Division WHC(88)65, Her Majesty's Stationery Office, London.

Falck K, Grohn P, Sorsa M, 1979, Mutagenicity in the urine of nurses handling cytostatic drugs, Lancet i, 1250-51 (Letter to the editor).

Galassi A, Hubbard SM, Alexander A, et al, 1996, Chemotherapy administration: practical guidelines. In: Chabner BA, Longo DL (Editors), Cancer Chemotherapy and Biotherapy: Principles and Practice (Second edition), Lippincott-Raven, Philadelphia.

Garvey EC, Manganarro M, 1982, Nursing implications of hepatic artery infusion, Cancer Nursing **5**, 51-5.

Garvey EC, 1987, Current and future nursing issues in the home administration of chemotherapy, Seminars in Oncology Nursing **3**(2), 142-7.

Goodman M, 1991, Delivery of cancer chemotherapy. In: Baird SB, McCorkle R, Grant M (Editors), Cancer Nursing: A Comprehensive Textbook, WB Saunders Co., Philadelphia.

Graze P, 1980, Bone marrow failure: management of anaemia, infections and bleeding in the cancer patient. In: Haskell C (Editor), Cancer Treatment, WB Saunders Co., Philadelphia.

Harris CC, 1976, The carcinogenicity of anticancer drugs: a hazard in man, Cancer **37**, 1014-23.

Hirst M, Tse S, Mills D, et al, 1984, Occupational exposure to cyclophosphamide, Lancet i (8370), 156-88.

Hoffman DM, 1980, The handling of antineoplastic drugs in a major cancer center, Hospital Pharmacy **15**, 302-4.

Keizer JH, Pinedo HM, 1985, Cancer chemotherapy: alternative routes of administration - a review, Cancer Drug Delivery **2**, 147-69.

Knowles RS, Virden JE, 1981, Developing guidelines for working with anti-neoplastic agents, British Medical Journal **281**, 589-91.

Ladik CR, Stoehr GP, Maurer MA, 1980, Percutaneous measures in the preparation of antineoplastics, American Journal of Hospital Pharmacy **37**, 1185-8.

Lind J, Bush NJ, 1987, Nursing's role in chemotherapy administration, Seminars in Oncology Nursing **3**(2), 83-6.

Lokich J, Bothe A, Fine N, et al, 1982, The delivery of cancer chemotherapy by constant venous infusion, Cancer **50**, 2731-35.

Maki DG, Cobb L, Garman JK, et al, 1988, An attachable silver-impregnated cuff for prevention of infection with central venous catheters: a prospective randomised multicenter trial, American Journal of Nursing **85**, 307-14.

Markman M, Howell SB, Lucas WE, et al, 1984, Combination intra-peritoneal chemotherapy with cis-platin, cytarabine, and doxorubicin for refractory ovarian carcinoma and other malignancies principally confined to the peritoneal cavity, Journal of Clinical Oncology **2**, 1321-6.

Moores D, 1991, Malignant pleural effusions, Seminars in Oncology **18** (Suppl 2), 59-61

Nanninga AG, de Vries EGE, Willemse PHB, et al, 1991, Continuous infusion of chemotherapy on an outpatient basis via a totally implanted venous access port, European Journal of Cancer **27**(2), 147-9.

Neal AD, Wadden RA, Chiou WL, 1983, Exposure of hospital workers to airborne antineoplastic agents, American Journal of Hospital Pharmacy **40**, 597-601.

Nguyen T, Theiss J, Marney T, 1982, Exposure of hospital workers to mutagenic antineoplastic drugs, Cancer Research **42**, 4792-6..

Niewig R, Griedanus J, de Vries E, 1987, An outpatient education program for a continuous infusion regimen on an outpatient basis, Cancer Nursing **10**(4), 177-92.

Pritchard AP, David JA, 1988, The Royal Marsden Hospital Manual of Clinical Nursing Procedures (Second edition), Harper and Row Publishers, London

Rogers B, Emmett EA, 1987, Handling antineoplastic agents: urine mutagenicity in nurses, Image: Journal of Nursing Scholarship **19**, 108-13.

Schulmeister L, 1992, An overview of continuous infusion chemotherapy, Journal of Intravenous Nursing **15**(6), 315-21.

Scott PJ, 1989, Current practice in hospital waste disposal, Hospital Engineering **43**(2), 10-4.

Selevan SG, Lindbohm ML, Hornung RW, et al, 1985, A study of occupational exposure to antineoplastic drugs and fetal loss in nurses, New England Journal of Medicine **313**, 1173-8.

Smith IE, Walsh G, Jones P, et al, 1995, High complete remission rates with primary neoadjuvant infusional chemotherapy for large early breast cancer, Journal of Clinical Oncology **13**(2), 424-9.

Sotaniemi EA, Sutininen S, Arranto AJ, et al, 1983, Liver damage in nurses handling cytostatic agents, Acta Medica Scandinavica **214**, 181-9.

Staiano N, Gallelli JF, Adamson RH, et al, 1981, Lack of mutagenic activity in urine from hospital pharmacists admixing antitumour drugs, Lancet i (8220), 615-6.

Sticklin LA, Dubbelde K, Larson E, 1989, Nursing care of the patient receiving subcutaneous low-dose ARA-C therapy, Oncology Nursing Forum **16**, 365-69.

Swenson KK, Iricksson JH, 1986, Nursing management of intraperitoneal chemotherapy, Oncology Nursing Forum **13**(2) 33-7

Thompson AM, Kidd E, McKenzie M, et al, 1989, Long term central venous access: the patient's view, Intensive Therapy and Clinical Monitoring **17**, 14-7.

Tipton JM 1995, Principles of oncology nursing. In: Skeel RT, Lachant NA (Editors), Handbook of Cancer Chemotherapy (Fourth edition), Little, Brown and Co., Boston.

Waksvik H, Klepp O, Brogger A, 1981, Chromosome analyses of nurses handling cytostatic agents, Cancer Treatment Reports **65**, 607-10.

Williams WW, 1985, Infection control during parenteral nutrition therapy, Journal of Parenteral and Enteral Nutrition **9**, 735-46.

Winters V, Peters B, Coila S, et al, 1990, A trial with a new peripheral implanted vascular access device, Oncology Nursing Forum **17**, 891-6.

Woollons S, 1996, Infusion devices for ambulatory use, Professional Nurse **11**(10), 689-95.

Zimmerman PF, Larsen RK, Barkley EW, et al, 1981, Recommendations for the safe handling of injectable antineoplastic products, American Journal of Hospital Pharmacy **38**, 1693-5.

Zook-Enck D, 1990, Intraperitoneal therapy via the Tenckhoff catheter, Journal of Intravenous Nursing **13**, 375-82.

CHAPTER 7   GENERAL EFFECTS OF CANCER CHEMOTHERAPY

Although antineoplastic agents are undoubtedly useful in attempts to treat cancer their effects are not restricted only to malignant cells - normal cells may also be affected. It is the effects on normal cells that are described as the side-effects of chemotherapy and may determine whether or not treatment can be continued.

Since cellular damage is largely determined by the generation time (Tc) (Ch. 3), the degree of damage to normal tissues can be predicted by consideration of the Tc of the cells comprising that tissue. Thus, those cells that have a rapid mitotic rate [eg. bone marrow, hair follicles, GI epithelium, and reproductive cells (ovaries/testes)] are those which are most vulnerable to chemotherapy-induced damage. There are however, occasions when cell damage occurs irrespective of the cell cycle time. For example, although intracellular DNA may be damaged by cytotoxic therapy, normal cellular functions may continue until the time of replication when the DNA damage becomes manifest and the cell is unable to divide (mitotic death).

Cytotoxic drugs may, therefore, cause widespread cellular/tissue damage which results in site-specific side-effects. At the same time, generalised effects may occur including fatigue, lethargy, anorexia, taste changes, nausea and vomiting and pain. Indeed, one of the major effects separating antineoplastic agents from most other drugs is the frequency and severity of anticipated side-effects even when administered at usual therapeutic dosages (Skeel, 1995). Thus all those caring for patients receiving anticancer drugs must be familiar with both the expected and the unusual toxicities of the drugs their patients are receiving. Patients must be carefully monitored so that adverse reactions can be identified early and, where necessary, treatment modified before toxicity becomes life-threatening.

Thus, when chemotherapy is considered as a treatment for individual patients the benefits of that treatment must be established and it must be certain that such benefits outweigh the risk of potential acute/chronic toxicities. Acute toxicity may be more acceptable when the goal of treatment is cure or improved survival than it is when the goal is palliation; palliative therapy that results in serious or acute side-effects, causing further distress, is bad
110

palliative therapy (Ch. 15). However, when the potential for cure or prolonged survival exists the risk of chronic or delayed toxicity gains in importance, particularly when there is a choice between two equally effective drug regimes.

When drugs are to be given as an adjunct to other methods of treatment (eg. surgery, radiotherapy) the likelihood of enhanced side-effects must be considered. In such cases, although it is predicted that metastases are present, there may be no clinical evidence of disease; the patient may feel well and find it difficult to accept toxic side-effects. It is inevitable that some patients receiving adjunctive chemotherapy have, already, been cured by their previous therapy and so will be subjected only to its toxicities and not to its benefits.

The side-effects induced by chemotherapy may be discussed in three broad categories: acute, subacute and late or chronic.

Acute side-effects are those occurring during or shortly after administration (Table 7.1). Many of these are localised, affecting the site of venepuncture or the path of the vein selected for infusion; most are transient and respond well to symptomatic treatment. For example, a local allergic reaction can often be controlled by application of topical steroids. It is, however, important that patients are told about any expected reactions so that they can help to differentiate between a local allergic response and the pain associated with extravasation (Ch. 8).

Table 7.1   **Possible acute side effects of cancer chemotherapy**

Nausea and vomiting
Pain at insertion site or along vein selected for administration
Sensation of cold along path of vein
Flushing   -   along path of vein
                -    face
                -    body
Urticaria   -   along/adjacent to path of vein (localised)
                -    generalised
Abnormal taste/smell
Hypersensitivity reactions
Anaphylaxis
Extravasation

Acute systemic effects may also be seen. The most serious of these are hypersensitivity reactions which usually arise within 15 minutes of the start of therapy (p130-7). Other acute reactions (eg. hot flushes, dizziness and acute hypotension) may also occur; most can be easily overcome by ceasing administration and recommencing the infusion at a slower rate once the patient has recovered.

Subacute side-effects arise within 3-7 days of therapy (Table 7.2). Many of these (eg. anorexia, nausea and vomiting, stomatitis) can significantly affect the patient and are discussed in greater depth later in this book.

Other subacute effects (eg. malaise, lethargy, pain, urinary pigmentation) can cause marked distress if the patient is not aware that they may occur. For example, unexpected pigmentation of the urine (blue/green - mitoxantrone, red/orange - doxorubicin or epirubicin) can cause considerable concern; transient pain, affecting either the site of the tumour or the jaw, may follow vinca alkaloid therapy and can be controlled by analgesia. Steroid cover can often alleviate the flu-like symptoms that may follow bleomycin therapy.

Table 7.2.   **Possible short term side-effects of chemotherapy**

Bone marrow depression
Nausea and vomiting
Anorexia
Mucositis/stomatitis
Pain at site of tumour or in jaw
'Flu-like' syndrome
Malaise and lethargy
Diarrhoea or constipation

Long term side-effects are usually manifested at least 7 days after treatment (Table 7.3); many are cumulative and may lead to a necessary discontinuation or postponement of therapy or a change in the planned treatment regime. Many such toxicities may affect major body organs (eg. bone marrow, liver, kidneys) leading to life-threatening complications.

FACTORS WHICH ENHANCE OR PROLONG TOXICITY
Most toxicities are dependent on:
1. The drug(s) involved.
2. The dose.
3. The administration schedule.
4. The route of administration.
5. The individual concerned.

Table 7.3   **Possible long term side-effects of chemotherapy**

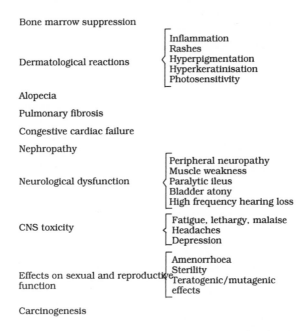

Bone marrow suppression

Dermatological reactions
- Inflammation
- Rashes
- Hyperpigmentation
- Hyperkeratinisation
- Photosensitivity

Alopecia

Pulmonary fibrosis

Congestive cardiac failure

Nephropathy

Neurological dysfunction
- Peripheral neuropathy
- Muscle weakness
- Paralytic ileus
- Bladder atony
- High frequency hearing loss

CNS toxicity
- Fatigue, lethargy, malaise
- Headaches
- Depression

Effects on sexual and reproductive function
- Amenorrhoea
- Sterility
- Teratogenic/mutagenic effects

Carcinogenesis

Similarly, both the duration and the severity of chemotherapy-induced toxicity can be exacerbated, or ameliorated, by many factors including interactions with other pharmacological agents, the patient's general condition and previous radiotherapy. Such factors must be considered when planning treatment for individual patients.

Pharmacological agents

As shown in Ch 3, interactions between cytotoxic drugs and other pharmacological agents can affect the efficacy or toxicity of chemotherapeutic regimes and so have significant effects on the success or failure or the patient's treatment. For example, patients suffering from chemotherapy-induced bone marrow depression, and, particularly, thrombocytopoenia, should not be given anticoagulant drugs (eg. heparin, salicylates) or non-steroidal anti-inflammatory drugs (eg. indomethacin, ibuprofen) which may exacerbate the risk of haemorrhage. Similarly, drugs, such as antihistamines and pheno-thiazines, must not be given in conjunction with procarbazine which inhibits monoamine oxidase; foods high in tyramine (eg. cheese, pickled herrings, alcohol and Chianti wine) should be also avoided.

Many other examples can be found. For instance, the toxicity of 6-mercaptopurine is greatly enhanced by allopurinol which inhibits its metabolism and the nephrotoxicity associated with methotrexate is exacerbated by both cisplatin and aminoglycoside antibiotics, such as gentamycin, kanamycin and neomycin. Such nephrotoxicity may be reduced by alkalinisation and hydration.

The patient's condition

A variety of physiological and nutritional deficits may increase the risks of chemotherapy. For example, hepatic abnormalities will enhance the toxicity of those drugs detoxified by the liver. Similarly, the likelihood of toxic effects is increased when renal dysfunction is present since, when excretion is impaired, the active drug, or its metabolites, may remain in the circulation for a prolonged period increasing the exposure of normal tissues to its cytotoxic effects.

Thus both hepatic and renal function may influence the choice and dose of the drugs employed and the treatment schedule; both must be assessed before chemotherapy is commenced. The patient's nutritional condition may also affect the efficacy of treatment enhancing the likelihood of toxic effects. At the same time, chemotherapy-related side-effects may contribute to a decline in the patient's nutritional condition (see Ch. 12).

MULTIMODAL THERAPY

The integration of more than one antineoplastic therapy into a treatment regime for individual patients is described as multimodal therapy (Scofield et al, 1991) and designed to improve the therapeutic outcome while reducing the associated toxicity. Such therapy may include adjuvant and neo-adjuvant therapy (Ch. 5), induction chemotherapy and bone marrow transplantation (Ch. 9) or treatment with biological response modifiers.

Although multimodal therapy is neither effective nor desirable for all kinds or stages of cancer it may provide the best opportunity to exploit the advantages of each treatment modality in treating individual patients (Dobelbower, 1995). Thus radiation may be used as an adjunct to chemotherapy or surgery; chemotherapy may be used as an adjuvant to surgery or radiotherapy or all three modalities may be combined in treating a single individual.

All methods of anticancer therapy have side-effects; when they are combined it must be remembered that the potential morbidity is also combined. The impact may, therefore, be significant, particularly when the effects are synergistic rather than additive (Dobelbower, 1995). Ideally, the toxicity of therapy should be no greater than the sum of the side-effects of each modality (Scofield et al, 1991).

Surgery plus irradiation
Even at relatively low doses, radiation will impair wound healing due to its effects on the proliferation of fibroblasts; wound breakdown is likely. Radiotherapy after lymph node dissection may increase the incidence of lymphoedema while previous abdominal surgery may enhance radiation injury to the intestine (Holmes, 1996).

Chemotherapy with radiotherapy
The effects of radiation may occur immediately or be delayed for months or even years after therapy has been completed (Holmes, 1996). Combining chemotherapy with radiotherapy may enhance both its immediate and delayed effects. For example, use of actino-mycin-D, doxorubicin, bleomycin, 5-fluorouracil or hydroxyurea can exacerbate cutaneous reactions while the threshold dose for radiation-induced pneumonitis is significantly reduced when radio-therapy is given in conjunction with doxorubicin, actinomycin-D, hydroxyurea, vincristine or procarbazine (Dobelbower, 1995).

COMMON TOXICITIES
Some toxic effects are relatively common amongst cancer chemotherapeutic agents. These include:
1. Bone marrow suppression.
2. Nausea and vomiting.
3. Disruption of the gastrointestinal epithelium.
4. Alopecia.

Other toxicities are less common. Examples include:
1. Neurotoxicity (eg. vincristine).
2. Haemorrhagic cystitis (cyclophosphamide).
3. Pulmonary fibrosis (bleomycin).
4. Anaphylaxis (eg. L-asparaginase).

Such specific effects will be discussed in the relevant chapters; only generalised effects will be covered here.

FATIGUE

Although many patients can continue to work and enjoy their usual activities throughout therapy others will experience varying degrees of fatigue and malaise. Affected patients will feel tired, lethargic and weak; this may interfere with the ability to participate in 'normal' events and may influence their perception of their condition and contribute to a decline in quality of life. Such patients may require considerable reassurance that this is a normal reaction to therapy and does not, of necessity, indicate a worsening of their condition. Thus it is important that patients are prepared for the possibility of its occurrence as this may influence their response to fatigue.

Fatigue arises for two main reasons. Firstly, energy demand is increased both by the processes involved in malignancy *per se* and by the need for increased anabolism necessary to repair damage to normal cells. This may be exacerbated by malnutrition and cancer cachexia (see Ch. 12). Secondly, chemotherapy results in cellular destruction which, in turn, is associated with the release of both cellular debris and waste products into the circulation.

Interventions suitable for the patient with fatigue

It must be recognised that many aspects of fatigue are subjective so that the extent of the distress experienced by individual patients must be assessed. Care is then directed towards helping the patient to maintain the optimum level of activity consistent with his disease status.

A combination of direct intervention and patient education will help to establish priorities and determine the most appropriate ways in which energy will be expended. Activities that will maintain or build on current levels of functioning should be encouraged (Morris, 1982). For example, eliminating some activities may help the patient to cope with his reduced energy reserves.

Before this can be achieved careful assessment is required to identify the factors contributing to fatigue and the resultant changes in lifestyle. It is, therefore, important to develop understanding of the meaning of this symptom to the patient as this may affect his willingness or ability to overcome its effects on particular aspects of his life. For example, an individual for whom work is an important source of satisfaction satisfaction but who places less emphasis on his social or recreational activities, may prefer to restrict participation in social events than take time away from work (Nail, 1992).

The patient should be taught to take measures designed to help him to conserve his energy so that he can continue with at least some of his normal work and/or social and recreational activities if this is what he wants to do. Wherever possible, he should be encouraged to maintain his usual activities but, at the same time, he should be advised to pace himself to take account of his need for additional rest. His family and friends should be encouraged to provide assistance in performing daily tasks such as house-work, meal preparation and grocery shopping. The patient should be encouraged to rest when tired, to take regular rest periods and to increase his sleeping pattern by, for example, going to bed early at night or, perhaps, staying in bed later in the morning. Maintenance of a normal food intake, and optimal nutritional status, will help to boost the energy supply and help to reduce fatigue.

ANOREXIA

A decreased appetite is common in cancer patients. Although its aetiology is not fully understood it is clearly a complex process involving many physiological and psychological factors which may be exacerbated by both the therapeutic and side-effects of chemotherapy (Table 7.4). Thus, many patients undergoing such therapy will develop anorexia that may, in turn, have a significant impact on both their physiological and psychological condition.

Table 7.4   **Factors contributing to anorexia in patients receiving cytotoxic therapy**

Fatigue, malaise, lethargy
'Flu-like' syndrome
Changes in taste sensation
Xerostomia
Mucositis/stomatitis
Pharyngitis/oesophagitis
Nausea and vomiting
Diarrhoea/constipation
Emotional/psychological responses to disease or treatment
? Toxic products released by the tumour
Metabolic disturbances

Anorexia also contributes to a marked decline in nutritional status (Ch. 12). Aggressive nutritional support may be required, particularly since it is known that patients who are well-nourished are better able

117

to tolerate their treatment; malnutrition significantly increases morbidity (Holmes and Dickerson, 1987). Thus every attempt must be made to persuade the patient to eat. It must be recognised, however, that the degree and extent of anorexia are subject to considerable individual variation and are, in addition, variable within the same individual at different times.

This means that interventions which work initially may not work for that patient when attempted for the second or third time (Schnipper, 1985). Both the patient and his family may need considerable reassurance and must be assured that the loss of appetite and early satiety (feelings of fullness), which may follow just a few mouthfuls, are largely outside the patient's control. This can be particularly important as the provision of food can be regarded as a means of demonstrating care and affection for loved ones; its rejection can be seen to be hurtful and taken to signify rejection of the person rather than just the food. This can cause feelings of guilt at not eating and lead to unnecessary pressure and tension between patient and family. Appropriate teaching, of both the patient and his family, combined with counselling and the setting of realistic goals, can help to overcome such effects. Suitable interventions include:

- Frequent small snacks (2-3hrly) may overcome early satiety.
- 'Make every mouthful count' by encouraging the use of high protein, high energy foods (ie. use nutrient-dense foods).
- Ensure that pain is well controlled. Anticipate the need for analgesia so that the patient is not distracted from eating by the presence of pain.
- When nausea is present ensure this is well-controlled by regular antiemetic therapy (Ch. 11).
- Reduce unpleasant environmental stimuli to a minimum (eg. bedpans or commodes and other unpleasant smells and sights. At home, reduce cooking smells).
- Use alcohol (eg. sherry, wine, etc.) to stimulate appetite.
- Take note of taste changes and overcome these where possible (see below).
- Be flexible and enable the patient to eat when he is hungry.

Although anorexia is a complex and disturbing symptom for both the nurse and the patient there is considerable potential for minimising its effects (Schnipper, 1985).

The nutritional care of the chemotherapy patient is discussed further in Chapter 12.

TASTE ABERRATION

Taste changes are common and may be exacerbated by a variety of chemotherapeutic agents. They are due primarily to damage to the taste buds together with salivary changes. There is no uniform pattern of change although alterations in sweet and bitter thresholds are reported as the most common (DeWys and Walters, 1975; Calman, 1982). This means, for example, a lowered urea (bitter) recognition threshold or an elevated sucrose (sweet) threshold. A lowered bitter threshold may be manifested by aversion to red meat or a sudden dislike of coffee, tea or chocolate and a decreased response to sweet tastes by the need for food/drinks to be sweeter before they are recognised as sweet.

However, as there is no standard pattern of taste change, each patient must be individually assessed; it is not possible to suggest any single way in which the problem can be overcome. Limited evidence suggests that improvement may follow an objective response to treatment (DeWys, 1978).

LEARNED FOOD AVERSION

Taste aberrations are important not only because they contribute to anorexia but also because they may lead to the development of food aversions which are not uncommon in cancer patients. Such aversions may also be due to a learned response to the association between symptoms and disease/treatment (Bernstein and Bernstein, 1981; Leathwood et al, 1986). This is regarded as a variant of classical conditioning when a conditioned stimulus (such as taste) becomes associated with an unconditioned response (eg. pain or discomfort) (Bolles, 1975). For example, animal studies have shown that just one pairing of a food with GI discomfort due to radiotherapy will cause continued avoidance of that food even after treatment has been completed. Such effects are likely to cause aversion to those novel food(s) consumed around the time discomfort is experienced. Similar effects have been noted during/after cancer chemotherapy and may cause aversion to even favourite foods. Indeed, studies (eg. Holmes, 1993) reveal that affected patients commonly avoid one or more foods after the start of therapy (Table 7.5). However, no relationships could be demonstrated between its incidence and either the type of disease or the drugs used in therapy. Thus the care of patients with food aversion can only be planned on an individual basis. Dietary modification, avoiding disliked food(s), usually overcomes the problem. However, when the diet is very restricted, advice may be required from a dietician or nurse-nutritionist.

Table 7.5   **Food/drink commonly avoided by cancer patients receiving chemotherapy** (Holmes, 1993)

Chocolate	Coffee
Citrus fruit	Tea
Red meat	Red wine
Cheese	

Care of the patient suffering taste aberration

Appropriate care is directed towards overcoming the effects of taste aberration so as to maintain an adequate food and fluid intake. Since some evidence suggests a relationship between trace mineral deficiencies, particularly zinc deficiency, and taste aberration (Hambidge et al, 1972) it is possible that zinc supplementation may help to overcome hypoguesia (diminished taste) and dysguesia (loss of taste) in some patients. This is not, however, likely to be beneficial when the changes are due to destruction of the taste buds.

As previously observed, taste changes are highly variable so that each patient must be individually assessed if those factors that may be contributory to taste change and that may, in turn, decrease food intake, are to be identified. Changes in the taste of 'normal' foods may significantly alter usual eating patterns causing distress to the patient who can no longer enjoy his favourite foods and stress for the carer who may find it difficult to persuade him to eat. It is, therefore, important that both the patient and his family understand that this is a consequence of the disease and/or its treatment. The patient must be persuaded to eat; this is best achieved by attempting to identify of a variety of acceptable foods and planning the diet with these in mind.

Clearly the presence and degree of taste alteration must be assessed. Common complaints include:

- A decreased recognition of sweet tastes so that additional sugar is necessary for this to be recognised. This can be beneficial in those patients requiring a high energy intake.
- Conversely, there may be an increased recognition of sweet tastes; care must be taken to ensure that the patient is not given foods/drinks which are too sweet as this may

discourage consumption.

- Changes in the recognition of bitter tastes. This poses particular problems with regard to protein-containing foods. Beef and pork are those most commonly rejected although any protein (eg. fish, eggs, poultry) may be affected. Other foods, such as those that are naturally sour or bitter (eg. tomatoes, lemons and other citrus fruit, coffee, tea and chocolate), may also be rejected (Holmes, 1993).

- At times, the patient may complain of a persistent metallic taste that is not related to any specific food. This is difficult to overcome. Clearly, canned products should be avoided; the use of plastic cutlery may be helpful. Chewing plain, soft mints during and after administration of chemotherapy has been found to be helpful (Pehanrich, 1983).

- Hypoguesia or dysguesia may lead to a condition described as 'mouth blindness' (McCarthy-Leventhal, 1959) when food is described as tasting like 'cotton wool', 'chalk' or 'charcoal'. Since these are all difficult to chew and swallow the inevitable difficulty in eating can have a major effect on the patient's food intake.

All these effects may have a significant impact on the patient's nutritional status; regular assessment is essential (Ch. 12).

Appropriate interventions

Once taste changes are recognised and affected foods identified an appropriate diet can be planned which excludes foods for which the patient has expressed a dislike or aversion. Alternatively, spices, herbs and other flavourings (eg. onions, garlic, fruit juices) can be added to foods in an attempt to mask taste changes. This can be difficult to achieve, particularly in hospitals, and considerable ingenuity may be needed before successful solutions are identified.

However difficult, it is important that patients are persuaded to eat as it is vital that nutritional status is maintained; this may have a significant impact on the quality of his life. Alternative approaches can be tried to tempt patients to consume an adequate diet.

- Serve foods hot or warm; this will help to intensify its taste.
- As odour and appearance are important in stimulating the appetite and tempting patients to eat, ensure that all food smells 'good' and looks attractive (ie. is well-presented).
- Ensure that foods are moist and easy to eat. Add sauces,

121

gravies and dressings or, alternatively, use 'artificial saliva' to increase the amount of moisture in the mouth - food must be in solution before it can be tasted. Do not encourage fluids to be taken with meals as this promotes satiety and may limit the amount consumed.

- Since small amounts of food may be better tolerated provide small, nutrient-dense meals or snacks at frequent intervals (eg. 6 times a day). Large amounts may be very off-putting to some patients.
- Ensure that any liquids taken are nutritious (eg. milk drinks, fruit juices).
- Teach the patient to recognise the importance of food which should be regarded as an important part of treatment and can, if necessary, be presented as a form of 'medicine' that must be taken regularly.

Taste alteration may be a permanent consequence of the disease or its treatment, and since cancer is rarely acutely fatal (Shils, 1977), this may become a chronic disability. It is, therefore, vital that patients are helped to come to terms with taste changes and taught how best to overcome their effects and maintain their food intake.

PAIN

Many patients receiving chemotherapy may be suffering from pain due to either their primary disease or to secondary deposits. Indeed, the pain associated with malignant disease is often chronic and disabling and may totally disrupt the life of many sufferers. The severity and extent of pain and discomfort are largely dependent on the location of the tumour(s) as well as the type of treatment received; individual perceptions of pain and behavioural responses may also influence its degree (Cleeland and Bruera, 1995). Tumours involving or causing pressure on bones, viscera or nerves may cause significant pain. Chemotherapy too may cause pain largely through its side-effects, such as stomatitis, hepatitis or diarrhoea. Alternatively, chemotherapy may be used in an attempt to achieve systemic pain relief through a reduction in tumour size.

Since, as can be seen, pain is not a simple phenomenon but a complex sensation having both physical and psychological components, caring for affected patients is a considerable challenge since each patient's experience of pain will be different. No two people, even those with the same medical diagnosis, will either feel or report the same level of pain. Thus, the expression of pain will vary considerably with the individual whether this be acute, chronic (benign) or chronic (malignant) (Sofaer, 1989) (Table 7.6).

Table 7.6   **Types of pain** (based on Sofaer, 1989)

Acute pain	Pain that is of sudden onset and which has a foreseeable end (eg. postoperative pain)
Chronic pain (benign)	Pain that lasts beyond the 'expected' time for healing; no apparent end in sight. May/may not be associated with ongoing pathology (eg. chronic back pain)
Chronic pain (malignant)	Pain associated with malignant disease that usually occurs towards the end of life.

Acute and chronic pain are different entities (Sofaer, 1989) and so require different treatment. Acute pain is often regarded as a 'warning' indicating tissue damage thus reducing activity and acting as protection against further damage; chronic pain, on the other hand, is usually persistent and may be destructive, particularly when it is associated with terminal illness.

Pain assessment

Effective assessment is central to effective management so that pain must be explicitly investigated during the initial consultation and at all follow-up visits or admissions. The history should elicit:

- Onset, course and location
- Severity
- Quality
- Exacerbating/relieving factors
- Effects on functional status and social interactions.

This information helps to develop understanding of the aetiology, characteristics, and pathophysiology of the individual's pain thus aiding its management.

Elucidating the pathophysiological basis of pain is important. For example, visceral pain results from activation of nociceptors present in the cardiovascular and respiratory systems and the GI and genito-urinary tracts. The term 'nociceptive pain' refers to the pain syndrome attributed to the activation of these receptors. Visceral pain is poorly localised and may be referred to a cutaneous site distant from the lesion; it may be associated with tenderness at this site (Coyle and Foley, 1991). Such pain, described as deep, aching or gnawing, usually responds well to opioid drugs.

Somatic pain is usually well-localised and often has an aching, throbbing or sharp quality and is usually constant. It results from activation of nociceptors in cutaneous and deep tissues and is often associated with, for example, tumour metastasis to the bone and musculoskeletal tissues. Such pain may be responsive to cortico-steroids and non-steroidal anti-inflammatory agents.

The term 'neuropathic pain' is applied to pain syndromes resulting from peripheral or central neural injury (Tasker et al, 1983) due to, for example, tumour invasion, surgery, radiotherapy or chemo-therapy. Neuropathic pain may be described as burning, tingling or 'electrical' pain and results in symptoms such as parasthesiae and peripheral neuropathy. Because it is sustained by processes within the nervous system itself, neuropathic pain may persist even after the underlying cause is eliminated (Popp and Portenoy, 1994).

Pain relief
Attempts at pain relief must be based not only on an assessment of the physical contributors to its causation but also on assessing the factors influencing the individual's perception of his pain and his responses to it. Such responses may be affected by a wide variety of factors including not only the type of pain but psychosocial factors such as age, sex and cultural background. Thus each patient must be assessed and treated on an individual basis. (For reviews of pain theories and factors influencing the perception of pain see Latham, 1987; McGuire and Yarbro, 1990; Portenoy, 1992).

Assessment is, however, complex since, unlike many other symptoms, pain is not always obvious unless it is made explicit through verbal or non-verbal communication. Similarly, the severity of pain cannot be directly measured. It is, therefore, important to remember that the management of cancer pain falls into two main categories: primary control through reversal of the specific patho-physiological factors causing the pain (eg. infection, inflammation, anxiety) and, secondly, control of symptoms by altering the perception of pain by the central nervous system.

The concept of the WHO three-step 'analgesic ladder' (World Health Organisation, 1986) is useful in managing cancer pain since the sequence in which drugs are given is adjusted to follow the course and intensity of the patient's pain (Figure 7.1).

Figure 7.1   **WHO three-step analgesic ladder** (WHO, 1986)

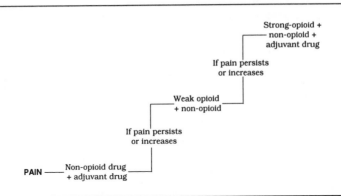

A non-opioid drug should be tried first (Table 7.7). If this is ineffective, when given at the recommended dose and frequency, a drug in the weak opiate group is added to the regime. When this combination fails to relieve pain a strong opioid is substituted (Step III). Initially this is given orally, in tablet or elixir form, moving to subcutaneous or intravenous administration as required. Adjuvant drugs (Table 7.8) are added at each step if required.

Table 7.7   **Drugs used in pain relief in cancer**

Category	Drug
Non-opioids	Aspirin
	Paracetamol
	Ibuprofen
	Fenoprofen
	Diflunisal
	Naproxen
	Pentazocine
Weak opioids	Codeine
	Dextropropoxyphene
Strong opioids	Morphine
	Meperidine
	Methadone
	Pethidine
	Buprenorphine
	Hydroxymorphone
	Levorphanol

Table 7.8 **Examples of adjuvant drugs used in pain control**

Anticonvulsants	Carbamazepine
	Phenytoin
Psychotropics	Prochlorperazine
	Chlorpromazine
	Haloperidol
	Diazepam
	Amitryptylline
Non-steroidal anti-inflammatory drugs	Diflunisal
	Flurbiprofen
	Ibuprofen
	Naproxen

The patient should be closely observed to ensure that the treatment continues to match his pain and minimise side-effects. Non-steroidal anti-inflammatory drugs (NSAID) may be added to the regime and phenothiazines, anticonvulsants and tranquillisers may be used as an adjunct to therapy both to control the nausea sometimes caused by narcotics and to decrease pain perception.

Recurring cancer pain must be treated with a continuous schedule of drug therapy whether or not pain is present at the time of administration. Anxiety due to anticipation of pain is known to increase the perception of that pain confirming the need for regular medication; 'prn' schedules are less effective. Carers should also be aware of alternative pain relief measures [eg. relaxation, distraction techniques and visualisation] which may help to control pain. Similarly, pain relief measures previously used by the patient can, where appropriate, be incorporated in the patient's care plan.

This approach takes account of the individual nature of pain and may enable the patient to play an active role in his care. The single most important intervention is a caring, sympathetic and supportive relationship with the patient which clearly indicates a recognition of his current difficulty and provides reassurance that every possible attempt is being made to alleviate his distress.

Comprehensive reviews of the management of cancer pain are given by Twycross and Lack (1983), World Health Organisation (1986) and McGuire and Yarbro (1990).

RECALL PHENOMENON

Administration of certain cytotoxic agents (eg. doxorubicin and actinomycin-D) can reactivate (recall) previous radiation-induced skin

126

reactions. Such patients should be carefully monitored for signs of a reactivated skin reaction (see p185-186).

DEVELOPMENT OF SECOND MALIGNANCIES

As many of the antineoplastic agents are themselves mutagenic and/or carcinogenic secondary neoplasms may be a complication of anticancer therapy. Examples include an increased incidence of bladder cancer in patients with ovarian carcinoma or myeloma treated with alkylating agents, most notably cyclophosphamide (Jones et al, 1983) (see p287-288).

While this risk, which arises some years after apparently successful therapy, is of little importance in palliative care it may be significant when treatment is directed towards cure or control of disease and prolongation of life. Careful follow-up care is required. Nonetheless, for most patients, the benefits of chemotherapy strongly outweigh the possible risks from this delayed complication.

REFERENCES

Bernstein IL, Bernstein ID, 1981, Learned food aversions and cancer anorexia, Cancer Treatment Reports **65** (Suppl), 43-7.

Bolles RC, 1975, Learning Theory, Rhinehart and Wilson, New York.

Calman KC, 1982, Cancer cachexia, British Journal of Hospital Medicine **27**, 28-34.

Cleeland CS, Bruera ED, 1995, Managing cancer pain. In: Skeel RT, Lachant NA (Editors), Handbook of Cancer Chemotherapy, Little, Brown and Co., Boston.

Coyle N, Foley KM, 1991, Alterations in comfort: pain. In: Baird SB, McCorkle R, Grant M (Editors), Cancer Nursing: A Comprehensive Textbook, WB Saunders Co., Philadelphia.

DeWys WD, Walters K, 1975, Abnormalities of taste sensation in cancer patients, Cancer **36**, 1888-96.

DeWys WD, 1978, Changes in taste sensation and feeding behaviour in cancer patients, Journal of Human Nutrition **32**, 447-53.

Dobelbower RR, 1995, Principles and practice of radiation therapy. In: Skeel RT, Lachant NA (Editors), Handbook of Cancer Chemotherapy, Little, Brown and Co., Boston.

Hambidge KM, Hambidge C, Jacobs M, et al, 1972, Low levels of zinc in hair, anorexia, poor growth and hypoguesia in children, Paediatric Research **6**, 868-76.

Holmes S, Dickerson JWT, 1987, Malignant disease: nutritional implications of disease and treatment, Cancer and Metastasis Reviews **6**, 357-81.

Holmes S, 1993, Food avoidance in patients undergoing cancer chemotherapy, Supportive Care in Cancer **1**, 326-30.

Holmes S, 1996, Radiotherapy: A Guide for Practice, Asset Books, Leatherhead.

Jones R, Frank R, Mass T, 1983, Safe handling of chemotherapeutic agents: a report from the Mt Sinai Medical Center, Ca: A Cancer Journal for Clinicians **33**(5), 258-63.

Latham J, 1987, Pain Control, Lisa Sainsbury Foundation Series, Austen Cornish Publishers Limited, London.

Leathwood PD, Ashley DV, Moennoz DV, 1986, Anorexia and cachexia in cancer, Nestlé Research News 1985/86, Nestec, Switzerland.

McCarthy-Levanthal EM, 1959, Post-radiation mouth blindness, Lancet ii, 1138-9.

McGuire DB, Yarbro CH (Editors), 1990, Cancer Pain Management, Grune and Stratton Inc., Orlando, Florida.

Morris ML, 1982, Tiredness and fatigue. In: Norris CM (Editor), Concept Clarification in Nursing, Aspen Systems Corporation, Rockville.

Nail LM, 1992, Fatigue. In: Groenwald SL, Frogge MH, Goodman M, Yarbro CH (Editors), Treatment modalities, Part III from Cancer Nursing: Principles and Practice (Second edition), Jones and Bartlett Publishers, Boston.

Pehanrich M, 1983, A tip for the taste buds ..., Oncology Nursing Forum **10**, 59.

Popp B, Portenoy RK, 1994, Pain. In: Macdonald JS, Haller DG, Mayer RJ (Editors), Manual of Oncologic Therapeutics (Third edition), JB Lippincott Co., Philadelphia.

Portenoy RK, 1992, Cancer pain: pathophysiology and syndromes, Lancet **339**, 1026-31.

Schnipper IM, 1985, Symptom management: Anorexia, Cancer Nursing **8** (Suppl), 33-5.

Scofield RP, Liebman MC, Popkin JD, 1991, Multimodal therapy. In: Baird SB, McCorkle R, Grant M (Editors), Cancer Nursing: A Comprehensive Textbook, WB Saunders Co., Philadelphia.

Shils ME, 1977, Nutritional problems induced by cancer, Medical Clinics of North America **63**, 1009-25.

Skeel RT, 1995, Antineoplastic drugs and biologic response modifiers: classification, use, and toxicity of clinically useful agents. In: Skeel RT, Lachant NA (Editors), Handbook of Cancer Chemotherapy, Little, Brown and Co., Boston.

Sofaer B, 1989, Care of the person in pain. In: Hinchcliff S, Norman SE, Schober JE (Editors), Nursing Practice and Health Care, Edward Arnold, London.

Tasker RR, Tsudn T, Hawrylshyn, P 1983, Clinical neurophysiological investigation of deafferentation pain. In: Bonica JJ, Lindblom U, Iggo A

(Editors), Advances in Pain Research and Therapy, Volume 5, Raven Press, New York.

Twycross RG, Lack SA, 1983, Symptom control in Far Advanced Cancer: Pain Relief, Pitman Medical Books, London.

World Health Organisation, 1986, Cancer Pain Relief, World Health Organisation, Geneva.

CHAPTER 8　　HYPERSENSITIVITY, ANAPHYLAXIS AND EXTRAVASATION

Hypersensitivity, anaphylaxis and infiltration (extravasation) are the most significant and most dangerous emergency situations likely to arise during chemotherapy administration. In view of the need for immediate treatment, either to save the patient's life or to minimise residual disability, these effects are discussed in some depth.

HYPERSENSITIVITY REACTIONS

Although hypersensitivity reactions (HSR) may occur with almost any antineoplastic agent both the degree of risk and the type of reaction are subject to considerable variation (Weiss, 1992). Thus, while some reactions may be serious, even life-threatening (eg. anaphylaxis) others may be less significant (eg. urticaria) (Table 8.1).

Table 8.1　　**Gell-Coombs classification of allergic response**
(Based on Gell et al, 1975)

Type I	Immediate reaction mediated by antibodies and resulting from passive sensitisation. May be either an antigen-antibody reaction (anaphylaxis) or a direct antigen (anaphylactoid) reaction. Effects can be seen locally, (eg. urticaria) or be more generalised, such as rashes and angioneurotic oedema. Reactions can be mild or extremely severe causing shock.
Type II	Antibodies react with the antigen on cell membranes causing cell damage or death. Effects depend on the nature of the affected cells.
Type III	Soluble antigen-antibody complexes become localised at a reaction site and initiate an inflammatory response.
Type IV	Delayed hypersensitivity reaction; long period of onset, often 24-48hrs after contact with the allergen. Mediated by sensitised lymphocytes and causes local tissue damage.

Most such reactions are mediated through immunological mechanisms due to interactions between antigens and antibodies. In some cases, however, the mechanism(s) through which hyper-sensitivity arises is unknown. For example, bleomycin may cause severe skin reactions and, in rare cases, a reaction characterised by high fever, hypotension and cardio-respiratory collapse (Brown, 1987). Although its aetiology is unknown this is believed to be a form

130

of anaphylaxis and may, in extreme cases, lead to death. It is clear, however, that it does not involve any immunological mechanism; it is thought that bleomycin, in some way, stimulates the release of pyrogenic substances from leucocytes.

Those administering antineoplastic drugs *must* be familiar with those drugs most likely to cause hypersensitivity (Table 8.2) so that, prior to administration, appropriate action can be taken to prevent or treat reactions that occur.

Table 8.2   Some drugs likely to cause hypersensitivity reactions

	Type of reaction
High risk	
Cisplatin	Type I and Type II
Etoposide	Type I
L-asparaginase	Type I
Mechlorethamine (topical)	Type IV
Melphalan (IV)	Type I
Teniposide	Type I and Type II (rare)
Paclitaxel	Type I
Moderate risk	
Bleomycin	Hyperpyrexia
Cyclophosphamide	Type I
Doxorubicin/daunorubicin	Type I
Methotrexate	Type I, Type III (?)
Procarbazine	Type I, Type III (?)
Low risk	
Busulphan	Type I, Type III (?)
Chlorambucil	Type I
Cytosine arabinoside	Type I
5-Fluorouracil	Type I
Hydroxyurea	Type III (?), hyperpyrexia
Mechlorethamine (IV)	Type I, Type II (?)
Mitomycin-C	Type I

An allergy history must be obtained from all patients although this may not predict a reaction to chemotherapy. However, when hyper-sensitivity can be anticipated, the patient must be warned, told what to expect and what action will be taken if an untoward reaction occurs. He should be advised of the signs and symptoms and told to report them immediately. Such patients may be extremely anxious and require considerable support and reassurance.

Anaphylaxis (Type I reaction)

Anaphylactic reactions are the most significant and most dangerous of the allergic responses. Injection of a specific allergen (antigen), in this case a drug, stimulates the production of immunoglobulin E (IgE) which becomes fixed to the mast cells in the tissues and to the membrane of basophils present in the circulation. On second, or subsequent, exposure to the antigen this binds with IgE on the surface of mast cells and basophils triggering immediate degranulation and a release of histamine, and other vasoactive amines (eg. serotonin), platelet activating factor, slow-reacting substance A and eosinophil chemotactic factor (Figure 8.1).

Figure 8.1   **Diagrammatic representation of a Type 1 reaction**
(Based on Taussig, 1979)

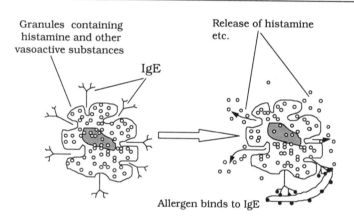

Mast cell or basophil with absorbed IgE   **Allergic response**

These factors exert pharmacological effects on smooth muscle (contraction) and blood vessels (increased permeability) as shown below:

Histamine:
1. Increases vascular capacity due to vasodilation.
2. Increases capillary permeability and causes marked loss of plasma from the circulation into the tissues.
3. Causes dilation of the arterioles and a decrease in arterial pressure.

These effects lead to a dramatic decrease in cardiac output and a fall in arterial pressure, due, in part, to hypovolaemia. This can lead to death within a few minutes unless treatment is immediate (ie. administration of adrenaline to oppose the effects of histamine).

Platelet activating factor (PAF) results in the release of serotonin (5-hydroxytryptamine) which augments the action of histamine further increasing capillary permeability.

Slow-reacting substance-A (SRS-A) induces a prolonged contraction of certain of the smooth muscles, particularly of the bronchioles. This may cause an asthma-like attack and, at times, death by suffocation.

Eosinophil chemotactic factor attracts eosinophils to the site of the reaction. Their role is to control the reaction by destroying the mediators released from the mast cells and/or basophils. They contain histaminase, an enzyme that inactivates histamine, together with other enzymes to destroy PAF and SRS-A.

Anaphylactic reactions (anaphylactic shock) are, fortunately, rare but may occur when an antigenic substance, such as some of the chemotherapeutic agents, enters the circulation.

Signs and symptoms of anaphylaxis
The patient may initially complain of agitation, dizziness, nausea or crampy abdominal pain all of which may be accompanied by an acute urge to urinate or defecate; generalised itching, tightness in the chest or inability to speak may also develop. Respiratory distress, hypotension and facial oedema may also occur (Garvey, 1987). Other signs and symptoms include those listed in Table 8.3. Anaphylaxis usually arises within the first 15 minutes of the start of therapy.

Table 8.3   Signs and symptoms of anaphylaxis

Mild reaction	Flushing, headache, itching of skin, nausea and/or vomiting, weakness and giddiness, dyspnoea, feeling generally unwell.
Moderate reaction	Wheezing, angioneurotic oedema (particularly of the face).
Severe reaction	Sudden hypotension, tachycardia, changes in level of consciousness.
	Hoarseness and breathing difficulties leading to bronchospasm due to oedema of the upper respiratory tract. May lead to respiratory arrest.
	Cardiac arrest due to severe shock.

Local or generalised urticaria (hives). Antigen entering specific skin areas leads to a localised anaphylactoid reaction. This, in turn, leads to local histamine release which causes vasodilation and an immediate 'red flare'; increased capillary permeability leads to localised erythema of the skin in the affected area.

Angioedema, localised oedema due to the increased capillary permeability, affects particularly the face, lips, eyelids, hands and feet.

Respiratory distress, stridor and cyanosis. Both histamine and SRS-A cause contraction of smooth muscle which may affect the bronchioles causing an acute, asthma-like attack thus inhibiting air intake and reducing both oxygen uptake and carbon dioxide elimination. This, with hypovolaemia, leads to cyanosis.

Hypotension is due to hypovolaemia combined with a reduction in both cardiac output and arterial pressure.

Cardiac arrest. The severe shock caused by anaphylaxis may result in cardiac arrest when immediate resuscitation procedures must be instigated (Table 8.4).

Table 8.4   Resuscitation procedure (anaphylaxis)

1. Lay patient flat.
2. Call for help. Do *not* leave patient alone.
3. Clear patient's airway.
4. Administer adrenaline as described in text.
5. Commence mouth-to-mouth resuscitation and/or cardiac massage as required.
6. Continue resuscitation procedures until help arrives or patient recovers.
7. Continue to monitor patient closely even following recovery.

Management of anaphylaxis

Since the immediate cause of anaphylaxis is iatrogenic it is the responsibility of all those administering chemotherapy to do all that is possible to prevent its occurrence. Thus, prior to administration, the patient must be carefully assessed to establish whether he has previously experienced an allergic response or has a history of drug reactions.

The patient should be asked if he has previously reacted unfavourably to any drug or to an insect bite or sting; if he has then he should be asked to describe the reaction experienced. Such information is important since repeated exposure to a known antigen

134

increases the likelihood of an allergic response. Similarly he should be asked whether or not he believes he is allergic to 'anything' and, if so what and how the allergy is manifested.

On occasions the patient may report the 'normal' side-effects of previous therapy in the mistaken belief that these indicate an allergic reaction. Since many patients do not have access to sufficient information they may be unable to distinguish between an allergic response and the expected side-effects.

The medical history should be explored to identify any respiratory problems, such as asthma or hay fever or the presence of eczema, which may suggest a history of allergy and indicate the need for caution when prescribing or administering drugs. Vital signs, temperature, pulse, blood pressure and respiratory rate, should be recorded to provide baseline data.

However, although anaphylaxis, and other allergic reactions, are more likely in those with a history of allergies, it must be recognised that a drug reaction can develop at any time in any individual. Similarly, although anaphylaxis is more likely after a number of exposures to a particular antigen, it can, on occasions, arise in the absence of any previous exposure (sensitisation).

Drugs associated with potential HSR must be delivered with caution and all those involved in drug administration should ensure that they are familiar with the signs of a hypersensitivity reaction and with the actions to be taken if this should occur.

Prior to administration, the availability of emergency equipment should be ascertained. This should include at least 3 ampoules of 1mg/ml adrenaline (1:1000 solution), 3 x 1ml syringes, 3 x 21G needles (Royal College of Nursing, 1988). Clear instructions for the management of anaphylaxis and of cardiac arrest should be attached; resuscitation equipment should be available. At the same time, the patient must be taught to recognise the symptoms of an allergic response and to recognise the need to report these immediately should they occur.

Treatment

Anaphylaxis is always an emergency situation requiring immediate treatment as listed below:

1. As soon as anaphylaxis is suspected stop infusion of the drug; leave the needle in place.
2. Symptoms, both subjective and objective, should be

evaluated as quickly as possible. Patients must be assessed rapidly to ensure that an open airway is present and maintained. Supplemental oxygen must be given when respiratory symptoms are present. Endotracheal intubation may be needed. When laryngeal oedema is present and causing respiratory distress, tracheostomy may be necessary.

3. Call for medical and emergency support; ensure that the attending physician is notified immediately.

4. Inform the patient that a drug reaction is suspected; provide reassurance that this can be treated.

5. The patient should lie flat, with his feet slightly raised.

6. Remember that the patient could collapse at any time. Do *not* leave him alone.

7. If anaphylactic shock is suspected, administer adrenaline into a limb other than that used for drug administration. This should be injected slowly taking about 1 minute for delivery of the total dose.

In an adult, the initial dose required is 0-3-0.5mg adrenaline (0.3-0.5ml of a 1:1000 solution) given intravenously (Quan and Skeel, 1995). This should reverse the patient's symptoms in the majority of cases but, if after 10 minutes, there is no response the dose may be repeated up to a total of three doses. For milder reactions, 0.2-0.3ml of 1:1000 adrenaline may be given subcutaneously and repeated twice at 15 minute intervals. In the rare event of life-threatening anaphylaxis, 0.5mg of adrenaline should be given intravenously; this dose may be repeated once after 10 minutes if this is needed. However, because of the cardiovascular stress caused by adrenaline its use should be avoided in relatively minor allergic reactions.

In a child, the required dose is calculated according to the following formula:

$$10\mu g \text{ adrenaline per kg body weight.}$$

This may be repeated up to a total dose of 500µg. (British Medical Journal, 1981).

The dose of adrenaline required in case of anaphylaxis should be calculated before drug administration is commenced.

Other forms of hypersensitivity reaction

Table 8.1 outlines the various forms of hypersensitivity reactions any of which may occur in response to administration of chemotherapy.

The principles of such reactions are outlined below.

Type II (antibody-cell surface) reactions involve direct damage to body cells due to the action of an antibody (usually IgM or IgG). The target of such damage is often the erythrocytes which, after reacting with the antibody, may be destroyed resulting in haemolytic anaemia. In drug-induced haemolytic anaemia the drug itself, or one of its reactive metabolites, becomes attached to the red cell membrane; antibodies against the drug or its derivatives, lead to destruction of the cell.

Type III reactions. Tissue damage is caused by antigen-antibody complexes that exert toxic effects. When this is localised in or around the walls of blood vessels an inflammatory response is initiated which can result in vasculitis in, for example, the joints, skin, kidney or heart.

Type IV (delayed hypersensitivity) reactions develop 24-48 hours after contact with the antigen, particularly in the skin. Such reactions typically begin after a few hours, although they may not be recognised as such, reaching a peak after 48 hours. They usually take the form of erythematous induration (red, hard swelling) which can, ultimately, result in contact dermatitis, granuloma formation or rejection of homografts.

When a patient has previously reacted adversely to a chemo-therapeutic agent preventive measures must be instigated prior to any subsequent treatment. If the drug is not an essential component of the treatment regime it should be discontinued or an analogue substituted. When this is not possible or advisable the patient should be prepared for treatment with a regime including, for example, prednisone, diphenhydramine and cimetidine. However, many units, and individual physicians, employ individual regimes for this purpose. Adrenaline, corticosteroids and diphenhydramine must be available when treatment is administered; emergency (resuscitation) equipment should also be nearby. In these circumstances it is usually recommended that the drugs are administered by a physician.

EXTRAVASATION

Extravasation is a rare but recognised complication of cancer chemotherapy. The term describes the infiltration of intravenous fluids or drugs into the perivascular or subcutaneous tissues surrounding the site of infusion. The incidence of extravasation is believed to be between 0.1% and 7% (Montrose, 1987; Boyle and Engelking, 1995).

If the infiltrated fluid has no vesicant properties, the effects, whilst uncomfortable, are usually temporary and include localised inflammation and swelling and, on occasions, pain. Infiltration of a vesicant agent (Table 8.5) may, however, have serious consequences. Although initial signs and symptoms may resolve without treatment, tissue damage may increase in severity over time and, in severe cases, can progress to ulceration and/or necrosis exposing under-lying tissues and blood vessels leading in turn to loss of mobility and, at times, secondary infection. The degree of tissue damage depends on the quantity and concentration of the drug that is infiltrated and the response to that tissue to the drug (Davis et al, 1995).

Table 8.5   Drugs with vesicant or irritant properties

Vesicant drugs: Capable of causing a blister and gradual tissue destruction and/or necrosis if infiltrated.

Amsacrine	Mechlorethamine
Carmustine*	Melphalan*
Dacarbazine*	Mitomycin-C
Actinomycin-D	Mithramycin
Daunorubicin	Rubidonmycin
Epirubicin	Streptozocin*
Estramustine phosphate	Vinblastine
Etoposide*	Vincristine
Idarubicin	Vindesine
Maytasine	Vinorelbine

* When given at standard doses

Irritant drugs: Capable of producing perivenous pain at injection site or along path of the vein either during the injection.

Carmustine*	Mithramycin
Dacarbazine*	Teniposide
Streptozocin*	

* When given at standard doses

The initial signs and symptoms reported or observed are variable but may include altered sensation (eg. pain, stinging or burning) at the injection site, erythema, swelling, induration or a change in the features of the infusion (eg. resistance or absence of blood return on aspiration) (Davis et al, 1995).

Extravasation can usually be avoided by means of a good injection (administration) technique but, even when the greatest care and skill are employed, accidents will occasionally occur. The severity of the reaction is dependent on the drug involved, the amount leaking into the tissues and the length of exposure (Brown and Hogan, 1992). Injuries resulting from extravasation include hyperpigmentation, burning, erythema, inflammation, ulceration, necrosis, pain, tissue loss or loss of mobility (Montrose, 1987).

Toxic local reactions, both vascular and extravascular, account for between 2-5% of all the adverse reactions associated with anti-neoplastic drugs. The time of onset may vary from minutes to hours or weeks and the extent from minor skin discoloration to severe local necrosis of the dermis and underlying structures. The extent of the damage is usually obvious within 7-10 days after most extra-vasations (Brown and Hogan, 1992).

Factors increasing the risk of extravasation

A variety of factors may increase the likelihood of localised reactions. These include:

- Anatomical and physiological factors related to individual patients
- The drug concerned
- Previous or concurrent radiotherapy
- Poor venepuncture techniques.

Anatomical and physiological factors. Local reactions are most likely in the elderly or debilitated and in those with generalised vascular disease. Thus Ignoffo and Friedman (1980) suggested that venous integrity, vessel diameter and local blood flow are implicated in their development. Similarly, patients with elevated venous pressure (eg. those with superior vena cava syndrome), or ineffective lymphatic drainage (eg. those with lymphoedema) are more sus-ceptible to localised reactions since decreased flow and/or increased venous pressure increases both the local drug concentration and the duration of exposure. Thus, when venous drainage is impaired, it is advisable to avoid injecting vesicant drugs into the affected extremity.

Such reactions also appear to be associated with the site of injection and may also be more severe when extravasation affects a previously irradiated site (Brown and Hogan, 1992). The optimal site for injection of vesicant drugs is the forearm which has superficial veins and sufficient soft tissue to prevent damage to the nerves and tendons. Extravasation in the wrist or hand may result in significant damage to both nerves and tendons causing permanent disability; extravasation in the antecubital fossa cannot be easily detected.

However, it is not only the site of injection that is important but also the technique of venepuncture employed. For example, a vein may be punctured several times before cannulation is achieved thus increasing the likelihood of leakage from the vein. Thus if multiple puncture sites are necessary, a different vein should be selected. When this is not possible, a point proximal to previous puncture points should be used to avoid leakage from distal sites. Most cases of extravasation are caused by inappropriate technique or by failure to take appropriate action as soon as extravasation is recognised.

Pharmacological factors. The extent of local tissue damage depends on both the amount of the drug extravasated and the duration of exposure. This means that vesicant drugs, appropriately diluted, must be given with extreme caution. Once the cannula has been inserted the following general principles should be applied:

1. Drugs should be diluted in the appropriate amount of fluid to avoid high drug concentrations. Refer to the manufacturer's specific instructions.
2. The guidelines for administration of intravenous drugs should be closely followed.
3. Infuse 5-10ml normal saline prior to the administration of chemotherapy both to ensure patency of the vein and to test its integrity. Observe closely for signs of extravasation. If infiltration is apparent select another site that, if using the same arm, should be proximal or lateral to the initial site; points distal to the puncture must be avoided.
4. If multiple drugs are prescribed vesicant agents must be given first; if more than one drug is a vesicant inject that with the least amount of diluent first; separate each drug by flushing the cannula/tubing with 3-5ml normal saline.
5. Drugs should usually be administered over a minimum of 3 minutes, or approximately 5ml per minute (see Table 8.6 with regard to specific agents). Flush the cannula with normal saline after administration of 2ml of vesicant drugs; assess for blood return to ensure correct placement of the needle. Follow administration with a least 5-10ml of normal saline to flush the needle and tubing and to ensure complete delivery of the drug.

Table 8.6   **Principles of administration of some vesicant agents**
(subject to local modification)

Drug	Administration
Actinomycin-D	Dilute in 10ml normal saline. Administer by slow injection (3-5 minutes) directly into the vein or through tubing of fast-running IV infusion.
Doxorubicin	Dilute in normal saline to provide 2mg/ml. Slow injection (5 minutes) into vein or through tubing of fast-running IV infusion.
Melphalan	Slow injection (3-5 minutes) directly into the vein or through the tubing of fast running IV infusion.
Mitomycin-C	Dilute in normal saline/sterile water to provide 0.5mg/ml; administer by slow direct injection or infuse in 500ml 5% glucose over 1 hour.
Mithramycin	Dilute in normal saline and administer slowly over 3-5 minutes or by slow infusion over 2-6 hours.
Mechlorethamine	Dilute in 10ml normal saline; administer by slow injection (2-3 minutes) or through tubing of fast-running IV infusion.
Daunomycin Rubidomycin	Infuse in 30-60ml over 5-10 minutes. Do *not* administer by direct bolus; allergic reactions possible.
Streptozocin	Infuse in 200ml fluid over 15-30 minutes or over 6 hours in a large volume of fluid. Do *not* inject directly into a vein.
Vinblastine Vincristine Vindesine	Dilute in normal saline and administer over 1-2 minutes or into tubing of fast-running IV infusion. Give only through a central line.

6. Observe for signs of extravasation.

7. Repeatedly ask the patient if he feels any pain, stinging or burning; discontinue administration immediately if extravasation is suspected.

8. The site of infusion must be closely observed both during and for several hours following administration so as to detect signs of infiltration, such as erythema, localised oedema, leakage of intravenous fluid or discomfort/pain.

9. Record details of administration carefully to provide a point of reference in the event of later problems.

The risk of extravasation highlights the need for those giving chemotherapy to be familiar with vesicant agents and to be able to distinguish these from irritant drugs. The latter may cause pain and inflammation at either the site of administration or along the path of the vein through which they are administered but, unlike, vesicants, cause no permanent damage. Similarly they must be familiar with the hospital policy with regard to the management and reporting of extravasation when this occurs. An 'extravasation kit' must be available whenever vesicant drugs are administered (Table 8.7).

Table 8.7   Contents of an extravasation kit

Assorted needles (19G, 21G, 25G, 27G)
Tape
Instant cold pack
Heat pack
Dexamethasone injection (8mg in 2 ml)
Hydrocortisone cream (1%)
Syringes (2ml, 5ml, 10ml, 20ml)
Alcohol swabs
Appropriate antidotes (eg. 10% sodium thiosulphate, hydrocortisone (100mg vial), etc.)
Latex gloves
Policy/procedure for management of extravasation
Documentation for recording the event

Radiotherapy. The risk of local reactions is enhanced in patients who have previously received radiotherapy to the infusion site. Similarly those receiving radio-potentiating antineoplastic drugs (eg. Doxorubicin, paclitaxel) may develop cutaneous reactions in previously irradiated areas even though these may be distant from the infusion site. Thus, wherever possible, infusions should not be given through areas that have previously been irradiated; areas previously subjected to radiotherapy should be carefully observed for any signs of a localised reaction.

Management of extravasation

All those administering chemotherapy must be familiar with local policy with regard to the management of extravasation of chemo-therapeutic agents. The required intervention varies with the drug involved (Table 8.8); the required antidote should be available when-ever a vesicant drug is to be administered. Despite variations in local policy and required antidotes certain general principles can be applied as outlined below.

Extravasation should be suspected if the patient complains of burning, stinging or any other change at the injection site. This should, however, be distinguished from the 'flare reaction' that may follow administration of, for example, doxorubicin and daunorubicin and is manifested by a localised redness or blistering (the nettle rash effect) (Goodman, 1986; Pritchard and David, 1988). Induration, swelling or leakage may be observed. If resistance is felt on the plunger of a syringe, or there is an absence of free flow in an infusion, infiltration should be suspected.

Table 8.7   Examples of drugs and antidotes used in the management of extravasation

Drug	Antidote	Dose
Actinomycin-D	Sodium thiosulphate 10% or ascorbic acid	Dilute 4 ml of antidote in 6ml sterile water; give 4ml. 1ml of 50mg/ml solution.
Carmustine	Sodium bicarbonate 8.4%	5ml.
Doxorubicin Daunorubicin	Hydrocortisone or dimethyl sulphoxide (50-100% solution) or sodium bicarbonate 8.4% + dexamethasone (4mg/ml)	5mg. Apply topically. 5ml. 1ml.
Mechlorethamine	Sodium thiosulphate 10%	Dilute 4 ml of antidote in 6ml sterile water; give 4ml.
Mithramycin	Sodium EDTA 150mg/ml	1ml.
Mitomycin-C	Dimethyl sulphoxide (50-100% solution) or Sodium thiosulphate 10%	Apply topically. Dilute 4 ml of antidote in 6ml sterile water; give 4ml.
Vinblastine Vincristine	Hyaluronidase (150U/ml)	1-3ml.

Once extravasation has occurred the physician should be informed and treatment should be initiated immediately:

1. Chemotherapy should be discontinued.
2. Any residual medication, and 3-5ml of blood, should be withdrawn so as to remove some of the drug from the area.
3. If an intravenous antidote is required this should be

instilled prior to removal of the needle.

4. Remove the needle or cannula.

5. If recommended use a 25-27G needle to aspirate the subcutaneous 'bleb' to remove as much of the drug from the tissues as possible.

6. If a subcutaneous antidote is required administer this into the area of infiltration using a 25-27G needle; use a new needle for each injection.

7. Apply a topical steroid cream or ointment if required and cover with a sterile occlusive dressing. Avoid applying pressure to an area where infiltration is suspected. Continue this for as long as erythema persists.

8. Apply heat or cold to the area according to local policy. This is a controversial area since there is a dichotomy of views. Those advocating the immediate application of heat suggest that this is required to increase vasodilation, facilitate fluid absorption and decrease local drug concentration. Those recommending the use of cold compresses suggest that, since cold causes vasoconstriction, this will decrease absorption of the chemotherapeutic agent into the tissues thus localising the extent of tissue damage. It has also been suggested that a reduction in temperature will decrease the ability of the drug to disrupt cellular metabolism and reduce the destructive effects of enzymes released during the inflammatory response.

9. Elevate the affected limb and/or encourage movement and maintain this for 48 hours.

10. Clearly document the incident in the patient's records detailing the actions taken.

The rationale underlying this approach is based on the need to minimise cellular damage by:

a. Altering the local pH to enhance inactivation of the drug.

b. Reducing the ability of the drug to bind to DNA.

c. Removing as much of the drug as possible, diluting that which remains and neutralising its effects.

d. Reducing inflammation   (Ignoffo and Friedman, 1980)

If, after 48 hours, the reaction has settled the patient may begin to use his arm normally although he should be advised to keep it elevated as much as possible. However, since ulceration usually occurs 3-4 weeks after the extravasation close observation will be necessary (Larson, 1985). Where tissue breakdown occurs, sterile dressings will be required. It is, however, worth noting that the majority of extravasations do not progress beyond a mild reaction even in the absence of pharmacological intervention (Birdsall and Naleboff, 1988). However, if there is immediate evidence of ulceration, or if pain, blistering or ulceration persist surgical treatment may be required to prevent chronic ulceration. Where tissue breakdown occurs sterile dressings will be necessary.

REFERENCES

Birdsall C, Naleboff AF, 1988, How do you manage chemotherapy extravasation? American Journal of Nursing **88**, 228-30.

Boyle D, Engelking C, 1995, Vesicant extravasation: myths and realities, Oncology Nursing Forum **22**, 57-67.

British Medical Journal, 1981, Treatment of anaphylactic shock, British Medical Journal **282**, 1011-12.

Brown J, 1987, Chemotherapy. In: Groenwald SL, Frogge MH, Goodman M, Yarbro CH (Editors), Cancer Nursing: Principals and Practice, Jones and Bartlett Publishers, Boston.

Brown JK, Hogan CM, 1992, Chemotherapy. In: Groenwald SL, Frogge MH, Goodman M, Yarbro CH (Editors), Cancer Nursing: Principles and Practice (Second edition), Jones and Bartlett Publishers, Boston.

Davis ME, DeSantis D, Klemm K, 1995, A flow sheet for follow up after chemotherapy extravasation, Oncology Nursing Forum **22**(6), 979-81.

Garvey EC, 1987, Current and future nursing issue in the home administration of chemotherapy, Seminars in Oncology Nursing **3**(2), 142-7.

Gell PGH, Coombs RRA, Lachmann PJ, 1975, Clinical Aspects of Immunology (Third edition), JB Lippincott Co., Philadelphia.

Goodman MS, 1986, Cancer: Chemotherapy and Care, Bristol Laboratories, Gransville.

Goodman M, 1991, Delivery of cancer chemotherapy. In: Baird SB, McCorkle R, Grant M (Editors), Cancer Nursing: A Comprehensive Textbook, WB Saunders Co., Philadelphia.

Ignoffo RJ, Friedman MA, 1980, Therapy of local toxicities caused by extravasation of cancer chemotherapeutic drugs, Cancer Treatment Reviews **7**, 17-27.

Larson DL, 1985, What is appropriate management of tissue extravasation by agents? Plastic and Reconstructive Surgery **75**, 397-402.

Anaphylaxis, hypersensitivity and extravasation

Montrose PA, 1987, Extravasation management, Seminars in Oncology Nursing **3**(2), 128-32.

Pritchard AP, David JA, 1988, The Royal Marsden Hospital Manual of Clinical Nursing Procedures (Second edition), Harper and Row, Publishers, London.

Quan WD, Skeel RT, 1995, Critical care issues in oncology and bone metastasis. In: Skeel RT, Lachant NA (Editors), Handbook of Cancer Chemotherapy (Fourth edition), Little, Brown and Company, Boston.

Royal College of Nursing (Community Nursing Association), 1988, Anaphylaxis Guidelines for all Nurses and Health Visitors Working in the Community Settings, Royal College of Nursing, London.

Taussig MJ, 1979, Processes in Pathology, Blackwell Scientific Publications, Oxford.

Weiss RB, 1992, Hypersensitivity reactions, Seminars in Oncology **19**(5), 458-77.

CHAPTER 9　　BONE MARROW SUPPRESSION

The function of normal bone marrow is essential to life. Since the cells it produces (leucocytes, platelets and erythrocytes) are responsible for the transport of oxygen and carbon dioxide, for the maintenance of immune status and for haemostasis, its destruction may have far-reaching effects. Cancer chemotherapeutic agents are, by design, intended to interfere with cell replication either by killing tumour cells (cytotoxicity) or by causing cessation of growth (cytostasis). However, since such therapy cannot yet be targeted only against malignant cells, damage to normal but rapidly dividing cells, such as the bone marrow, is likely. Myelosuppression, therefore, frequently accompanies cancer therapy and is the most likely dose-limiting toxicity.

Bone marrow suppression may be rapid in onset and recover quickly or be cumulative and delayed and, at times, cause severe and prolonged pancytopoenia. Reduced bone marrow reserves, due to prior or concurrent radiation of significant amounts of the bone marrow, can increase myelotoxicity (Table 9.1).

Table 9.1　　**Percentage bone marrow affected by normal radio-therapeutic techniques** (Based on Dritschilo and Sherman, 1981)

Area of Irradiation	Estimated Percentage of Bone Marrow Affected
Chest wall/lymphatics	15 - 20
Pelvic	15 - 25
Abdominal	20 - 25
Pulmonary/mediastinal	20 - 25
Mantle	20 - 50
Cranial	25 - 45
Total nodal	60 - 70
Craniospinal	60 - 75
Total body	100

DEVELOPMENT OF BLOOD CELLS

To understand the potential damage that chemotherapy may cause to the bone marrow it is helpful to review the normal development of blood cells. All cells are believed to develop from a pluripotent stem cell which differentiates and matures into different blood cells.

Leucocytes

The white blood cells (WBC) comprise five different types of cell (McConnell, 1986) which can be separated into two groups: granulocytes which have granules in their cytoplasm and the lymphocytes and monocytes that contain no granules.

The granulocytes (also known as polymorphonuclear cells) include the neutrophils, eosinophils and basophils. The most important are the neutrophils that comprise the majority of the WBC and provide the 'first line of defence' against infection. When infection is present there is an increased percentage of neutrophils in the circulation and, usually, an overall increase in the number of WBC (leucocytosis). The eosinophils are active against parasites and allergens while basophils play a role in the production of histamine (Ch. 8) and in fibrinolysis. The lymphocytes both provide cell-mediated immunity (T-cells) and produce antibodies (B-cells) which represent the second 'line of defence' against infection acting to destroy remaining micro-organisms and removing debris. Monocytes act as phagocytes engulfing mycobacteria and fungi.

Platelets

Platelets are formed from the megakaryocytes released from the bone marrow which, on release, break into tiny fragments known as platelets. They play a key role in haemostasis and are central to coagulation. Platelets are important in maintenance of capillary integrity; they adhere to sites of injury in the blood vessel wall creating a 'plug' thus reducing or stopping blood loss. They also release Factor III, central to the initiation of clot formation, and also participate in the retraction of clots as healing takes place.

Erythrocytes

Red blood cells are essential for the transport of oxygen and carbon dioxide in the circulation; they also play a central role in acid-base balance in acting as a buffer in the bloodstream. A decline in the number of circulating red blood cells results in reduced oxygen transport resulting in development of the signs and symptoms of anaemia and impaired tissue oxygenation (p156-158).

Implications for treatment

As not all bone marrow cells are actively dividing at the same time 15-50% stem cells are in the resting (G_0) phase of the cell cycle and so are not damaged by cell cycle phase specific agents. Phase specific agents (such as the antimetabolites) tend to cause a rapid decline (nadir) (7-30 days) associated with a rapid recovery while cell cycle phase non-specific agents (eg. daunorubicin) cause nadirs occurring within 10-14 days of administration with recovery in 21-24 days. Lastly, the cell cycle non-specific agents (eg. the nitrosoureas) produce delayed and prolonged bone marrow suppression in which the lowest point is reached 26-63 days after treatment and recovers in 35-89 days.

Such factors are considered in the planning of treatment regimes. For example, drugs causing an early nadir combined with rapid recovery (21-28 days) can be given every 3-4 weeks while those causing delayed bone marrow suppression can be administered only at 6-8 week intervals. Some drugs (eg. nitrosoureas) may have a cumulative effect causing severe and less easily reversed bone marrow suppression, decreasing the bone marrow reserve and resulting in prolonged leucopoenia and thrombocytopoenia.

Colony stimulating factors

In view of the significant problems associated with bone marrow suppression there have been many attempts to overcome the myelo-suppressive effects of anticancer drugs. Many of these focus on the use of haemopoietic growth factors that, under normal circumstances, act to regulate the proliferation, maturation, regulation and activation of blood cells (Clark and Kamen, 1987).

These factors, known as colony stimulating factors (CSFs), hold great promise for the treatment and management of myelo-suppression and have, in general, been named after the major target cell on which they exert their effects. Thus, for example, granulocyte-macrophage CSF (GM-CSF) targets both granulocytes and macro-phages while G-CSF targets the granulocytes with particular affinity for the neutrophils (Parkinson, 1995). GM-CSF not only exhibits its predominant effects on granulocytes and macrophages but also potentiates the functions of neutrophils (Parkinson, 1995).

The therapeutic applications of CSFs are under active investigation in both disease-related and treatment-induced myelosuppression. Studies have shown that GM-CSF and G-CSF can significantly reduce or prevent the myelosuppression caused by chemotherapy (eg. Thompson et al, 1989; Crawford et al, 1991; Trillet-Lenoir et al, 1993). These initial trials are encouraging and lead to the hope that CSFs will have a significant impact on cancer treatment enabling higher doses of chemotherapy to be used while minimising its effects on the bone marrow.

COMPLICATIONS OF BONE MARROW SUPPRESSION

Chemotherapy does not affect mature blood cells (which are no longer actively dividing) rather it damages the stem cells thus decreasing the ability of the bone marrow to replace depleted blood cells. As all blood cells have a fixed life span (Table 9.2) the effect of chemotherapy can largely be predicted. The lowest point reached in the peripheral blood is called the nadir (Table 9.3)

Table 9.2 **Life-span of individual blood cells**

Type of cell	Life-span
White blood cells	6 hours
Platelets	8-10 days
Erythrocytes	120 days

As neither the platelets nor the white blood cells are stored in any significant quantity, the effects of bone marrow suppression are first seen on these cells. The first to be affected are the neutrophils followed by a decrease in circulating platelets; erythrocytes will be affected some weeks later. Bone marrow toxicity is generally temporary recovering once treatment ceases. However, if the haemopoietic system is affected by primary or secondary malignant deposits, resumption of normal activity is less predictable.

Assessment of bone marrow function is essential before chemotherapy commences and before periodic or cyclical treatment is given, particularly when myelosuppressive drugs are employed. Additional blood counts should be carried out at the time of the predicted nadir or when symptoms of bone marrow toxicity are displayed (eg. bleeding or pyrexia).

Table 9.3   Examples of drugs causing bone marrow suppression

Drug	Expected nadir (days)	Recovery (days)
Mechlorethamine	7-15	28
Melphalan	10-12	42-50
Busulfan	11-30	24-54
Chlorambucil	14-28	28-42
Cyclophosphamide	8-14	18-25
Cisplatin	14	21
Cytosine arabinoside	12-14	22-24
5-fluorouracil	22-24	16-24
Methotrexate	7-14	14-21
Daunorubicin	10-14	21
Vindesine	5-10	10
Etoposide	9-14	20-22
Actinomycin-D	14-21	22-25
Mitomycin-C	28-42	42-56
Procarbazine	25-36	36-50
Mitoxantrone	8-10	>2 weeks

The care of vulnerable patients is directed towards the prevention or alleviation of symptoms resulting from the impact of chemotherapy. The care required by patients suffering from bone marrow suppression is directly related to its consequences that are major causes of both morbidity and mortality.

Leucopoenia

Leucopoenia is the most serious form of myelosuppression. As leucocytes play a major role in the resistance to infection, leucopoenia (a deficiency of white blood cells (WBC) below the normal limit of 5×10^9/litre) significantly increases the risk of infection. The decrease in lymphocytes and granulocytes also suppresses cellular and humoral immunity and studies have shown that it is the patients' natural flora that causes approximately 85% of infections in those who are neutropoenic. This is exacerbated by malnutrition, the effects of age, recent surgery and drugs (eg. corticosteroids) (Sarna, 1980). Prevention of infection is, therefore, an important goal of care. Medical management may include prophylactic antibiotics and/or antiviral agents.

Care of the patient with leucopoenia

Since the integrity of the skin and mucous membranes provides an important barrier to infection, invasive procedures should be kept to a minimum. However, when they are unavoidable, meticulous aseptic

151

care and observation are essential, particularly when the patient is also thrombocytopoenic. The bedridden patient is particularly vulnerable, due to the risk of pressure sores and hypostatic pneumonia; regular turning and pressure area care are essential.

When leucopoenia is marked, the patient may be cared for in protective isolation (reverse barrier care) which will, ideally, be carried out in a single room with filtered air to reduce the risk of air-borne infection. Sterile equipment and linen must be used and staff caring for the patient should be screened for possible infection. A clean gown and mask are worn at the bedside and hands must be washed thoroughly under running water before attending to the patient. Only immediate family are allowed to visit and they, too, must wear a gown and mask and should avoid physical contact with the patient. This may be difficult for the patient to cope with since isolation can result in significant sensory deprivation. Staff must, therefore, be aware of the emotional/psychological effects of isolation and provide comprehensive supportive care.

However, opinions vary as to the degree of protective isolation that is required (Pritchard and David, 1988) and not all units will subscribe to this approach. In general, however, the greater the level of protection the lower the risk of infection.

Teaching patients and their family about the risk of infection and its prevention, as well as ways of minimising the risk, are important interventions (Brandt, 1984; Henschel, 1985). However, those who are neutropoenic often fail to manifest the usual signs of infection (ie. inflammation or pain). Pyrexia, usually the first sign of infection, may arise only slowly and a temperature of 38.3°C in a neutropoenic patient can result in death within 48hrs if untreated because sepsis develops so rapidly (Carlson, 1985). Infection is, therefore, a medical emergency in those with neutropoenia.

Oral hygiene is particularly important in the care of these patients. The mouth should be rinsed with normal saline or a mild antiseptic mouthwash (such as glycothymoline) every 2 hours. When the patient is unable to maintain his own oral hygiene this task must be performed for him. A copious fluid intake (2-3 litres/day) will be beneficial. Immune status can be enhanced, to some extent, by means of a high protein, high energy diet. Supplementation with vitamin C may also be beneficial.

Routine samples, including specimens of urine, stools and sputum and swabs from the skin, nose and throat, should be taken for

152

bacterial culture. Swabs are also taken from any suspicious sites, such as an intravenous cannula or urinary catheter.

Thrombocytopoenia

Since platelets have a rapid turnover (life-span 8-10 days) they are particularly sensitive to chemotherapy and, as previously observed, damage to the stem cells prevents their replacement. The onset of thrombocytopoenia is more gradual than that of leucopoenia and the nadir often occurs later than that of the white blood cells. Similarly, recovery from leucopoenia usually precedes that of the platelets.

Thrombocytopoenia, characterised by bleeding in any site, may be the first sign of bone marrow suppression. Petechiae and purpuric areas may appear in the skin or mucous membranes and bleeding may occur from the nose, gums, GI or genitourinary tract.

The risk of serious bleeding increases as the platelet count decreases; the likelihood of spontaneous bleeding is significant once the platelet count falls to $<20 \times 10^9$/litre (normal range 200-300 x 10^9/litre). Minor bleeding, such as occult blood in the stools, may occur when the platelet count reaches 50×10^9/litre although this does not, of necessity, signal the onset of an acute haemorrhage. The platelet count is not, however, an absolute indicator of the likelihood of bleeding as this may be affected by many factors including the rate of decline in the platelet count or the concurrent presence of infection.

Care of the patient with thrombocytopoenia

The specific care required by thrombocytopoenic patients varies with the individual, the associated symptomatology and the severity of his condition. There are, however, several common problems and general considerations that are applicable to all affected patients.

Close observation must be maintained on all patients suffering from thrombocytopoenia so that any signs of bleeding are rapidly detected (Table 9.4). Thus the urine and stools should be routinely tested for the presence of blood and any vomit should also be closely observed.

Bleeding may affect the gums or nasal mucosa and epistaxis is common. If menstruation has not been suppressed by treatment, prolonged and heavy vaginal bleeding may occur; vaginal bleeding may also occur in post-menopausal women. There is also the possibility of internal bleeding signs and symptoms of which include

153

Bone marrow suppression

pallor, weakness, rapid deep respirations (air hunger), a rapid weak pulse and hypotension. Mental and neurological status should also be closely monitored due to the risk of cerebral dysfunction resulting from intracranial haemorrhage.

Table 9.4   **Assessment of the thrombocytopoenic patient**

GI tract	Observe vomit for signs of bleeding (haematemesis); monitor stools for the presence of occult blood or frank malaena.
Cutaneous signs	Inspect skin and mucous membranes for presence of petechiae and/or purpuric rashes. Monitor for the presence of ecchymoses or bleeding from gums or nose or prolonged oozing from venepuncture sites.
Genitourinary tract	Monitor urine for the presence of blood; assess for abnormal menstruation (pre-menopausal women) or unexpected vaginal bleeding (post-menopausal women).
Respiratory tract	Assess secretions/sputum for the presence of blood.
Central nervous system	Monitor for any change in neurological function (eg. blurred vision, disorientation, headaches, altered level of consciousness or mental state, changes in pupil size or reactivity to light).

Measures to prevent bleeding

Since haemorrhage is a life-threatening complication of thrombo-cytopoenia every attempt must be made to prevent its occurrence. Measures can be taken to reduce the risk of bleeding. For example, drugs that inhibit prostaglandin synthesis, or that interfere with platelet production or function, will increase the risk of bleeding (Barton-Burke et al, 1991); such medications must, therefore, be avoided and include all aspirin-containing drugs and non-steroidal anti-inflammatory agents. Such drugs may also irritate the gastric mucosa.

Other factors that will increase the risk of bleeding include infiltration of the bone marrow by tumour cells (eg. leukaemia) or radiation-induced bone marrow suppression (Table 9.1). The frequency of invasive procedures should be reduced to a minimum. When subcutaneous or intramuscular injections are essential, a small gauge needle must be used and gentle pressure applied to the site after administration until it is clear that any bleeding has stopped (usually about 15 minutes).

154

Trauma to the body tissues must be avoided so that the patient must be handled gently and, if he is confined to bed, he should be turned every 1-2 hours to reduce pressure to the tissues; pressure-relieving devices should be employed. He should be instructed about the importance of avoiding bumps, scratches, and cuts; severe injury can result should he fall. An electric razor should be used to help to maintain the integrity of the skin and, to avoid damage to the gums and mucous membranes, a very soft toothbrush should be used for cleaning the teeth. Regular mouthwashes and irrigation can help maintain oral hygiene; the use of toothpicks and dental floss should be avoided. Constipation should be prevented; aperients and/or stool softeners may be given to maintain bowel function (Table 9.5).

Table 9.5   Commonly used laxatives

Bulk-forming agents eg. bran, ispaghula husk, methylcellulose, psyllium preparations	Absorb water and swell thus increasing stool bulk; stimulate rectal reflexes and promote defaecation.	May cause intestinal obstruction in those with intestinal diseases. Can cause flatulence.
Faecal softeners and lubricants eg. arachis oil, dioctyl sodium sulphosuccinate and glycerol	Used primarily as enemas or suppositories. Valuable when rapid purgative effect is needed.	Used when bulk laxatives would be useful but are contraindicated due to intestinal pathology.
Gastrointestinal stimulants eg. senna, danthron, bisacodyl	Act on bowel stimulating peristalsis and reducing reabsorption of water and electrolytes.	Abuse may lead to fluid or electrolyte imbalance and colonic atony.
Osmotic laxatives eg. lactulose, magnesium sulphate	Decrease water re-sorption causing retention of large amounts in both small and large intestine thus causing increased peristalsis.	May cause abdominal discomfort and flatulence.

Care during a bleeding episode

The patient must remain in bed during a bleeding episode although, since he may not be experiencing any discomfort, he may find it difficult to remain inactive. He may also be apprehensive and fearful so that his feelings must be acknowledged and reassurance given. Thus emotional/psychological support is essential particularly when bleeding is acute as this can be very frightening. Rapid intervention, such as the application of an ice pack or direct pressure, may be required. The patient must not be left alone since the nurses' presence can provide comfort and reassurance. Staff should listen to the patient and answer any questions he may have.

Platelet transfusions (p158) may be given when the platelet count falls below 10×10^9/litre or during episodes of active bleeding although it must be recognised that this is only a palliative measure; the risk of bleeding continues until the bone marrow has recovered.

Anaemia

Anaemia is rare following bone marrow suppression related to chemotherapy although it may arise due to the cumulative effects of some anticancer drugs (eg. cisplatin). Like thrombocytopoenia, the likelihood of anaemia is enhanced by the presence of tumour infiltration of the bone marrow or by radiation-induced damage to the marrow; it is also potentiated by bleeding/haemorrhage, such as that resulting from thrombocytopoenia. Chemotherapy-induced anaemia may exacerbate that caused by the disease itself or the anaemia that may accompany chronic disease.

As the life span of red blood cells is considerably longer than that of leucocytes or platelets ($\approx$120 days) treatment-induced anaemia may not develop for some time after treatment and can usually be treated with transfusion of either packed red cells or whole blood. It is often due to a chemotherapy-induced decrease in erythrocyte production although acute anaemia may also result from bleeding episodes due to thrombocytopoenia.

The patient must be observed for signs and symptoms of anaemia (Table 9.6) so that care can be directed towards its treatment. Regardless of its cause the patient will manifest signs and symptoms that are attributable to tissue and organ hypoxia since anaemia decreases the capacity of the blood to transport oxygen. The severity of the symptoms depends on the degree of anaemia present.

Initially, the patient will experience general fatigue, lassitude, shortness of breath on exertion and anorexia. These are non-specific symptoms which can be difficult to differentiate from the general effects of disease and treatment. Complaints of headache, dizziness and 'tingling' of the extremities are common; diarrhoea or constipation may be present. The mucous membranes and skin become pale and the nail-beds pallid and, as hypoxia leads to a fall in the basal metabolic rate, the patient may feel cold.

156

Table 9.6   **Signs and symptoms of anaemia**

Dyspnoea on exertion
Palpitations
Tiredness/weakness
Anorexia
Dysphagia
Glossitis
Parasthesiae
Intermittent claudication
Angina pectoris
Oedema of ankles
Pallor, particularly affecting the mucous membranes

In severe cases
Faintness/giddiness
Tinnitus
Headache
Spots before the eyes

---

becomes pale and the nail-beds pallid and, as hypoxia leads to a fall in the basal metabolic rate, the patient may feel cold.

Palpitations may also be present as the heart rate increases in an attempt to reverse the oxygen deficiency. If the condition is severe circulatory and renal dysfunction may develop causing oedema and, on occasions, angina pectoris due to myocardial hypoxia.

Care of the patient with anaemia

The care required depends on the severity of the anaemia and is directed towards alleviating the patient's discomfort and preventing any complications. Since the anaemic patient will tire easily he should be encouraged to rest at intervals throughout the day. When the anaemia is severe bedrest may be required until his haemoglobin level approaches normality (8.1-9.9mmol/l); this necessitates attention to pressure area care and prevention of hypostatic pneumonia and deep vein thrombosis.

A light, varied and easily digestible diet should be given which is high in energy and protein and which will provide the nutrients necessary for erythropoeisis. This may be difficult to achieve in the anorexic patient (see Ch. 7) so that frequent small meals/snacks and nutrient-dense liquids may prove more acceptable.

Since severe anaemia may cause marked dyspnoea, the patient may be more comfortable if he is nursed with the head of the bed elevated or in the sitting position well supported with pillows.

Dyspnoea, in addition to anaemia *per se*, may result in a sore and painful mouth so that thorough oral hygiene becomes essential.

Blood transfusion may be given to correct anaemia. This may involve administration of either whole blood or packed red blood cells that provide the same oxygen carrying capacity as whole blood but in a reduced volume of fluid thus reducing the risk of circulatory overload.

A patient who is fatigued and lethargic due to anaemia may have difficulty in believing that his symptoms are not due to a progression of his disease, particularly if this is accompanied by a range of chemotherapy-induced side-effects. He may, therefore, require considerable support and reassurance. His concerns should be identified and factual information provided in an attempt to convince him that his condition will improve once his anaemia has been corrected.

BLOOD COMPONENT THERAPY

Bleeding, and other haematological complications, are often due not to direct effects of the disease but rather, as has been observed, to indirect effects of either the tumour itself or of its treatment. Thus transfusion therapy is often required. Since whole blood can exacerbate the risk of haemorrhage, through dilution of clotting factors and platelets (Smith, 1987), it is common to administer only the specific blood component needed by the patient.

Blood components can be obtained from three sources: the general 'pool' of blood donors (homologous), the patient's own blood (autologous) or from designated donors when a particular person is recruited specifically for the purpose.

Platelet transfusion

Platelets are transfused both in cases of bleeding and/or as a prophylactic measure. As previously described, platelet transfusion may be given when the platelet count falls below 10×10^9/litre, when the patient is clinically symptomatic or during episodes of bleeding; prophylactic transfusion may be considered when the count falls to 20×10^9/litre.

When surgery is contemplated in the thrombocytopoenic patient the platelet count must be raised, through transfusion, to at least 60 $\times 10^9$/litre; if intracranial surgery is to be undertaken the platelet count must reach 100×10^9/litre. In all such cases, the bleeding time must be checked prior to surgery and should be within two minutes of the upper limit of normal (3-8 minutes). Prior to intra-cranial surgery the bleeding time must be normal.

Since some patients undergoing chemotherapy may require frequent platelet transfusion they should be typed for HLA (histo-compatibility locus) antigens as there is an increasing risk of alloimmunisation and the development of antiplatelet antibodies after multiple transfusions. As transfused platelets usually survive for only two days, transfusion is regarded only as a palliative measure and the risk of haemorrhage persists until the bone marrow has recovered. In the absence of normal platelet production, it is easy to see why multiple transfusions may be required. Alloimmunisation may limit the effectiveness of such transfusion. However, by restricting exposure to individual platelet donors (eg. histocompatible family members) reactions may be decreased (Smith, 1987).

Available types of platelets for transfusion are those obtained from random donors, a single donor or those which have been HLA-matched to individual patients. Platelets obtained from random donors are those most commonly used; single donor and HLA-matched platelets are generally reserved for those who fail to respond to randomly obtained cells, those who may be candidates for bone marrow transplantation or those expected to need multiple trans-fusions (Smith, 1987). On occasions, the patient's platelets may be collected and returned to the blood stream after marrow toxic therapy has been given. When platelets are to be given to severely immuno-suppressed patients (eg. following BMT) they, like all other blood components, should be irradiated to prevent graft-versus-host disease (Graze, 1980) (see p164 and p168-172).

Management of a patient receiving platelet transfusion
The patient's previous transfusion history, as well as his experiences during transfusion, should be evaluated as should his understanding of the purpose and rationale underlying his treatment. His level of anxiety and concern should be established and reassurance provided. Unless the patient has previously displayed a reaction to platelet infusion, platelets are usually administered rapidly bearing in mind the volume of fluid to be given and the patient's physiological condition; action may be required to facilitate the flow of the transfusion.

Vital signs (temperature, pulse, respiration and blood pressure) must be assessed prior to transfusion to provide a baseline against which future changes can be judged; monitoring should continue throughout the transfusion and for an hour or two after its completion. The platelet count is monitored prior to, and 1 hour after, transfusion (Daly et al, 1980). Premedication may be given prior to transfusion so as to reduce the chills and fever that often accompany transfusion of 'foreign' platelets; both pyrexia and chills may lead to early destruction of transfused platelets.

One of the most common causes of an inadequate increase in platelets following transfusion is immune platelet destruction. Transfused platelets are destroyed rapidly by recipient antibodies directed at antigens on the surface of the platelets, primarily HLA-A and B antigens (Lee and Schiffer, 1995). Multiple transfusion of red blood cells or platelets may expose the patient to numerous foreign HLA antigens leading, in some cases, to the development of allo-antibodies (antibodies to other human antigens) (Gmur et al, 1983); these antibodies may cause the immune destruction of platelets.

The patient should be closely monitored for signs of an allergic reaction (Ch. 8) and the physician notified should this occur. Platelet transfusions are not, however, routinely discontinued if an allergic reaction occurs although the patient may require rapid treatment, and considerable support and reassurance may be necessary.

Granulocyte transfusion

Granulocytes are important in determining the host's response to, and defence against, infection; their production is stimulated in the presence of inflammation and infection. However, when bone marrow function has been reduced by chemotherapy, the response to infection is suboptimal so that, in the presence of infection, some oncologists will provide exogenous granulocytes to support the patient until his bone marrow recovers and is able to produce an adequate number of white blood cells.

Granulocyte transfusion may be used to reduce the risk of infection in the granulocytopoenic patient or to assist in the treatment of infection in the compromised patient. Its use is, however, controversial (Dutcher, 1986) and used only rarely because of limited effect and multiple side-effects (Deisseroth and Wallerstein, 1989). As a result, the following criteria are used in making the decision to transfuse granulocytes:

1.　Granulocyte count <5 cells x 10^9/litre.

2. Pyrexia in excess of 38°C which has failed to respond to antimicrobial therapy.
3. Documentary evidence of gram-negative sepsis.
4. Reduced bone marrow function which is not expected to recover for 5-10 days.
5. A diagnosis in which induced remission is likely or with a prognosis which warrants aggressive supportive therapy.
6. The availability of donors.

(DeVita et al, 1982; Abrams and Deisseroth, 1985)

Granulocytes are collected, by means of a variety of cell separators, from ABO and HLA-compatible matched donors, often family members. Although such therapy is known to be effective, the ratio of cost to benefit is high (Wright, 1984). Since the half-life of white blood cells is only about 6 hours, transfusion must commence immediately after collection. For this reason also it is usual for transfusions to be continued for at least 4 consecutive days. Alternatively, they may be continued until the infection subsides or signs of bone marrow recovery are seen.

Patients are usually premedicated with both corticosteroids and analgesic or antipyrexial agents prior to receiving granulocyte transfusion. This is designed to reduce the pyrexia and chills which accompany a transfusion reaction. HLA and blood group (ABO) compatibility will help to prevent a transfusion reaction and will also enhance the survival time of transfused granulocytes although HLA-compatible granulocytes are not usually administered to patients who are expected to undergo subsequent bone marrow transplantation.

Management of a patient receiving granulocyte transfusion

The infusion is given through a standard blood administration set, with a Y-connector, through which isotonic saline solution is given concurrently, into a large bore central vein or through a large bore cannula so as to prevent damage to, or destruction of, the granulocytes. The transfusion should be slow infusing 200-300ml over 2-3 hours although, over the first hour, only 50-75ml should be given and the patient must be closely observed for signs of a transfusion reaction. This is necessary since it is likely that some of the donor's erythrocytes are mixed with the granulocytes. Once transfusion is completed the infusion bag should be rinsed, using 30-40ml isotonic saline, to remove any granulocytes adhering to its surface. This 'rinsing fluid' is then infused into the patient.

161

Since complications are likely, the patient should be closely observed and vital signs monitored both prior to the infusion and throughout its course. Thus temperature, pulse, blood pressure and respiration should be measured every 15 minutes for the first half an hour after which half hourly recordings are required until the transfusion is completed. Four hourly recordings should continue for at least 24 hours.

If the patient becomes pyrexial the infusion is continued, but at a reduced rate. However, if hypotension develops it may be necessary to discontinue the transfusion, particularly if the decrease in blood pressure exceeds 10mmHg. Similarly, the development of an allergic reaction (Ch. 8) necessitates immediate discontinuation of the infusion, at least until the attending physician has been notified. The transfusion may be continued after administration of corticosteroids and/or antihistamines. Anaphylactic reactions may occasionally arise (p132-136), characterised by extreme dyspnoea and hypotension. The transfusion is stopped immediately; adrenaline, antihistamines and steroids are given to treat this potentially lethal complication.

Some patients may also develop the pulmonary symptoms of fluid overload or of white cell sequestration in the lungs. The latter is not uncommon, particularly in the presence of pulmonary infection when granulocytes migrate to the site of the infection. These symptoms, particularly dyspnoea and cyanosis, are most likely when the transfusion is administered too rapidly (Graze, 1980).

Red blood cell transfusion

Whole blood is not usually required to treat the anaemia associated with cancer or its treatment unless there has been acute blood loss. Packed red blood cells provide the same oxygen-carrying capacity as whole blood but in a reduced volume (ie. without plasma). They are usually administered when haemoglobin falls below 8g/dl or when the haematocrit falls below 25 per cent (Lichtiger and Huh, 1985).

As in all cases in which blood transfusion is required, the compatibility of the transfusion with the patient's red blood cells (ABO and rhesus compatibility) must be assured to reduce the risk of haemolytic reactions. However, when long-term transfusions are needed, patients may become sensitised to the platelets and granulocytes present in packed red cells thus increasing the risk of transfusion reactions. For this reason, leucocyte poor (buffy coat poor)

162

packed red blood cells, which are comparatively free of both white blood cells and platelets, are often preferred since they provide red cells while reducing the risk of sensitisation to the other blood components (Pisciotto, 1989). Nonetheless the patient should be closely observed for signs of a non-haemolytic reaction (pyrexia, chills, headache, nausea and vomiting) which may occur immediately or within 24 hours of the transfusion.

Care of the patient undergoing red blood cell transfusion
In general, the care of the cancer patient receiving blood transfusion does not differ from that required by other patients although some aspects may require additional thought. For example, due to the need for repeated venepuncture, a reduced number of suitable veins may be available for transfusion. Secondly, due to the demands of chemotherapy, and other intravenous drugs (eg. antibiotics), it may be necessary to deliver the units of blood individually between the administration of other medications. Alternatively, a second cannula, or a double/triple lumen central line may be inserted to enable blood or blood products to be given in conjunction with other therapy.

Plasma products
Plasma products, such as fresh frozen plasma (FFP) and cryoprecipitate may be used to treat coagulopathies due to secondary disease states (eg. disseminated intravascular coagulation - p305). FFP is used to replace coagulation factors, particularly in the presence of multiple clotting deficiencies (Pisciotto, 1989) when 2-4 units are transfused every 6hrs. thus replacing 20-30% of the normal level of each of the clotting factors. Cryoprecipitate, prepared from FFP, performs a similar function.

Complications of blood component therapy
Complications of transfusion are common (Lee and Schiffer, 1995) and are characterised by the timing of their occurrence: acute or delayed. They may also involve immunological or non-immunological mechanisms (Berkman, 1984; Walker, 1987). Many can be ameliorated or prevented.

The term 'transfusion reaction' generally refers to the immediate immune reactions that can occur from blood component therapy. Signs and symptoms vary from urticaria and pruritis to pyrexia with rigor and, rarely, respiratory decompensation and hypotension;

anaphylaxis is rare but may arise (Ch. 8).

Acute haemolytic reactions may occur, usually as a result of red blood cell ABO incompatibility (Greenwalt, 1981). Such reactions are, fortunately, rare but may lead to shock, disseminated intravascular coagulation (p302-306) and/or acute renal failure any of which may be fatal. The severity of the reaction is entirely dependent on the amount of incompatible blood transfused and the time taken before appropriate interventions are instigated.

A delayed haemolytic reaction may occur gradually or lead to sudden and dramatic fall in haemoglobin. This too represents an immunological reaction occurring slowly over a period of time after the transfusion due to a recall memory immune (anamnestic) response. Affected patients develop sudden pyrexia accompanied by jaundice and a marked fall in haemoglobin.

Febrile reactions (non-haemolytic) are the most common reaction to any transfusion; they are usually mediated by the immune system. They are caused by an antibody-antigen response in which host antibodies are directed against antigens present on lymphocytes, granulocytes or platelets in transfused blood components. Pyrexia may arise early in the course of the transfusion or some hours after the transfusion has ceased.

Transfusion-associated graft-versus-host disease (TGVHD) is a rare complication of transfusion therapy occurring most commonly in severely immunocompromised patients (Leitman, 1985). TGVHD results from the infusion of immunocompetent T-lymphocytes present not only in whole blood but also in granulocyte, platelet and red blood cell fractionated components (Lee and Schiffer, 1995).

The true incidence of GVHD is unknown but is reported to be increasing, particularly in those with Hodgkin's and non-Hodgkin's lymphoma and those who have undergone allogeneic bone marrow transplantation (Lee and Schiffer, 1995). The use of irradiated blood components has been recommended to prevent GVHD in severely immunocompromised patients (Weiden, 1984).

WITHHOLDING OF CHEMOTHERAPY

When bone marrow suppression is severe it may be necessary to adjust the dose of chemotherapy required or to withhold therapy until there are signs of bone marrow recovery. The need to delay therapy is dependent on a variety of factors including the patient's baseline haematological profile, the chemotherapeutic regime to be followed and the availability of blood component support (Cline and Haskell, 1980). Guidelines for the withholding of treatment include a leucocyte count <4 x 10^9/litre and/or platelets below 100 x 10^9/litre. Drugs may be withheld for varying periods, usually a minimum of one week, to allow bone marrow recovery.

Most patients regard any interruption to their treatment as a significant disappointment and anxiously await the results of their blood count. Health care practitioners must recognise the significance of the 'waiting period' until results are available and provide appropriate support and reassurance. Similarly, they must help the patient to cope during temporary withholding of therapy.

BONE MARROW TRANSPLANTATION (BMT)

BMT is increasingly used to treat leukaemia, lymphoma and other malignancies (McConn, 1987). It has also been used to treat patients with aplastic anaemia and severe immunodeficiency diseases [such as acquired immunodeficiency syndrome (AIDS)] (Saikh, 1987) (Table 9.7). In such cases allogeneic transplantation is employed to reduce the risk of graft-versus-host disease (GVHD).

Table 9.7 Examples of diseases treated with bone marrow transplantation

Malignant disease	Haematological malignancies (eg. acute and chronic leukaemias, myelosclerosis and pre-leukaemias)
	Non-haematological disease such as lymphoma, multiple myeloma, neuroblastoma and some solid tumours.
Non-malignant disease	Severe aplastic anaemia, thalassaemia major, cyclic neutropoenia.
Immunological deficiencies	Acquired immunodeficiency disorder, combined immunodeficiency disorders, Wiskott-Aldrich syndrome.
Inborn errors of metabolism	Chronic granulomatous disease, Batten's disease, mucopolyscharidosis and lipidosis.

Two types of matching tests are used to minimise this risk. The first, HLA-matching, relies on the use of antibodies to identify the antigens. The second depends on a mixture of donor and recipient cultured lymphocytes [mixed lymphocyte cultures (MLC)] which are

165

tested for the ability of either the donor or recipient to react, by blastogenesis, to the antigens of the other (recipient or donor). However, it is not always possible to match bone marrow cells between donor and recipient except, perhaps, between identical twins; GVHD may develop in any patient undergoing allogeneic transplantation. The surviving immunologically-competent cells of the host are reacting against foreign components present in the transplanted bone marrow in an attempt to destroy it as the body would destroy any foreign antigen. However, if the transplant is successful, the donated stem cells will mature in the recipient's bone marrow taking over the functions of the diseased/absent stem cells.

Autologous bone marrow transplantation (Table 9.8) provides a means of overcoming bone marrow suppression; healthy marrow is 'harvested' from the patient before myelosuppressive therapy is given. Alternatively, marrow may be reinfused during relapse following high-dose conditioning in an attempt to destroy all malignant cells (eg. Yeager et al, 1986). The marrow is preserved and returned to the patient, by infusion, after treatment but before the expected nadir of myelosuppression occurs. Since this approach relies on re-infusion of the host's bone marrow there is no likelihood of GVHD.

Table 9.8   Types of bone marrow transplant

Autologous	Involves the patient's own marrow which is collected and preserved and later reinfused.
Syngeneic	Relies on marrow donated by an identical twin; ensures compatibility with the recipient.
Allogeneic	Use of an HLA-matched donor, usually a family member although unrelated donors have been used successfully in those in whom no related donor is available.

Bone marrow transplantation

Conditioning therapy is used to prepare the patient for BMT. This consists of high-dose chemotherapy and/or total body irradiation or both, the intention being to totally eradicate the patient's marrow and any residual tumour cells as well as to help to prevent graft rejection by the immune system (Thomas, 1983). The most common chemotherapeutic agent employed in conditioning regimes is cyclophosphamide; other drugs (eg. busulfan, etoposide, daunomycin, cytosine arabinoside, 6-thioguanine) may also be used. Total body irradiation

(TBI) offers optimal cell kill by penetrating all those areas that are most resistant to anticancer drugs [eg. CNS, skin and testes) (Thomas and Fefer, 1985; Holmes, 1996).

Patients undergoing such treatment are often severely debilitated, and may be seriously ill, due to both the side-effects of disease and to the prior conditioning regime. However, the hope of a cure is often a strong motivating factor so that, although they may be unrealistically optimistic, they may also be anxious and fearful about their forth-coming treatment and the probable need for subsequent isolation.

It is important to recognise that the conditioning regime itself would be fatal if the patient were not 'rescued' by BMT, a relatively simple and straightforward procedure bearing similarity to a blood transfusion; the marrow is transfused through a central line over the course of several hours. Complications may include volume overload and, occasionally, pyrexia, chills or a rash; these can be treated with antipyretics, antihistamines and/or decreasing the rate of the infusion. Rarely, pulmonary abnormalities may arise as a result of fat emboli; these are treated as they would be if they resulted from any other cause.

Complications of BMT are common and result from:

1. The conditioning regime.
2. Graft-versus-host disease.
3. Problems associated with the primary disease.

(Sullivan and Storb, 1984; Buchsel and Parchem, 1988)

Immunosuppressive drugs are given to prevent rejection. Bone marrow aspiration is performed weekly; if the graft is successful, blood cells (erythrocytes, leucocytes and platelets) will begin to develop in the 'new' bone marrow. However, until the graft has taken, the patient is particularly vulnerable to infection, bleeding and the side-effects of both radiotherapy and chemotherapy; opportunistic infections are common as commensal organisms, which are part of the body's normal flora, become pathogenic. Examples include those affecting the mouth, throat and oesophagus (eg. *candida albicans* and *herpes simplex*) which may exacerbate pre-existing mucositis.

Acute complications (Table 9.9) arise several days after BMT and can affect multiple organ systems; the majority are the result of the conditioning regime (Bearman et al, 1988) combined with the lack of functioning bone marrow and iatrogenic factors resulting from the treatments employed to treat other complications. It is important to recognise that the complications are closely interrelated; one

167

complication can lead to another and the treatment of one can exacerbate another (Storb and Thomas, 1985). It is also important to note that the clinical onset of many complications may be subtle and the clinical manifestations of a variety of complications can be the same (Ford and Ballard, 1988). Thus patients who have undergone BMT require close observation and careful assessment.

Table 9.9 **Potential acute complications of bone marrow transplantation**

Gastrointestinal	Mucositis affecting the oral cavity, oesophagus, gastric or intestinal mucosa.
	Lower bowel toxicity leading to nausea and vomiting and/or diarrhoea.
Acute graft-versus-host disease	Maculopapular rashes; generalised erythro-oedema.
	Hepatic disorders leading to elevation of liver enzymes, right upper quadrant pain, hepatomegaly and jaundice.
	Green, watery diarrhoea, abdominal pain and cramping, anorexia, nausea and vomiting.
Renal insufficiency	Decreased urine output, proteinuria, hypertension, renal failure, thrombocytopoenic purpura, thirst, dizziness. Distension of neck veins, peripheral oedema. Elevation of serum creatinine.
Veno-occlusive disease	Weight gain, ascites, elevation of serum bilirubin. Encephalopathy, upper right quadrant pain associated with hepatomegaly.
Infection	Bacterial, viral or fungal infections.
Alopecia	Loss of body hair.

Haemorrhage may occur at any time after transplantation; it is, however, most likely in the first month after BMT when the patient is unable to produce megakaryocytes and, therefore, platelets. Epistaxis is the most commonly seen form of bleeding (Ford and Ballard, 1988); it may also occur from the mouth and GI tract (Spencer et al, 1986) or the genitourinary tract (Brugieres et al, 1989). Cranial bleeding is not unlikely and the patient must be closely observed for signs of raised intracranial pressure. Availability of blood products is, therefore, an essential part of the transplant procedure.

Despite prophylaxis, relying on immunosuppressive therapy, the patient is also at risk of graft-versus-host disease (GVHD) which occurs when the transplanted marrow tissue rejects that of the host (Thomas et al, 1975) since the immunologically competent cells (specifically the T-lymphocytes) of the graft recognise the patient as 'foreign' and its cells, therefore, react against the host. GVHD developing within 3 months of the transplant is referred to as acute graft-versus-host disease; that arising more than 3 months after transplantation is known as chronic graft-versus-host disease (Graze and Gale, 1979). GVHD primarily affects three body systems: the skin, the liver and the GI tract (Table 9.10).

Table 9.10   Acute graft-versus-host disease

Stage	Skin	GI tract	Liver
Mild	Maculopapular rash covering <25% of body surface.	Green and watery diarrhoea (500ml-1 litre per day).	Elevated bilirubin (2-3mg/dl).
Moderate	Maculopapular rash covering 25-50% of body surface.	Green and watery diarrhoea in excess of 1 litre/day but less than 1500ml.	Elevated serum hepatic enzymes and bilirubin (3-6mg/dl).
Severe	Generalised erythro-oedema.	Green and watery diarrhoea >1500ml/day.	Elevated serum hepatic enzymes, bilirubin (6-15mg/dl).
Life-threatening	Severe desquamation and formation of bullae.	Pain, paralytic ileus.	Elevated serum hepatic enzymes, bilirubin >15mg/dl.

The onset of GVHD coincides with engraftment. GVHD-related complications are responsible for approximately 10% of deaths after BMT (Meyers, 1986). Acute GVHD typically begins with a punctate maculopapular rash affecting particularly the palms of the hands and soles of the feet; if untreated, this progresses to severe erythema, wet desquamation and blistering, similar to second degree burns, and carries the risk of secondary infection (Ford and Ballard, 1988). Pain may be present in the right upper quadrant of the abdomen and hepatomegaly may be found on palpation. Circulating levels of the hepatic enzymes and bilirubin may be elevated; the development of jaundice indicates progressive liver involvement (Sullivan and Parkman, 1983). GI involvement is primarily manifested by nausea, vomiting, anorexia, abdominal pain and cramping; profuse green watery diarrhoea is a typical early symptom (Sullivan and Parkman,

1983; Ford and Ballard, 1988).

The chronic condition can present in a similar fashion but more often presents as a multi-system disease very similar to the collagen-vascular diseases; it is most commonly seen in those who had acute GVHD (Appelbaum, 1995). Both forms of GVHD can lead to areas of hypo- or hyperpigmentation, loss of elasticity, contractures and ulceration.

Care after bone marrow transplantation

One of the most important aspects in management of patients after BMT is the prevention of GVHD. This is achieved by a combination of preventive isolation and immunosuppressive medication. Isolation may delay the onset of GVHD and to decrease its incidence; it may also increase survival (Meyers, 1986). The aim of immunosuppressive medication is to remove or inactivate T-lymphocytes thus preventing 'attack' on body organs (Storb and Thomas, 1985).

Cyclosporine is an immunosuppressive agent acting specifically against T-lymphocytes thus permitting the growth of other bone marrow cells (Press et al, 1986). Methotrexate, in low doses, will slow growth of the bone marrow thus reducing T-cell production. Studies have shown that these two drugs, used in combination, are more effective than either agent used alone (Sullivan and Parkman, 1983; Storb et al, 1986). Other approaches to prevention include mono-clonal antibodies designed to achieve T-cell depletion, lectin agglutinin and T-cell immunotoxins (Freeman, 1988).

Should GVHD occur despite prophylactic therapy, treatment includes increasing the dose of cyclosporine and administration of monoclonal antibodies against T-cells, horse antithymocyte globulin and corticosteroids (Appelbaum, 1995). Single-agent prednisone is the standard treatment for chronic GVHD and is effective in between 50% and 75% of cases; cyclosporine, azathioprine and thalidomide may also be useful. Because affected patients are also susceptible to bacterial infection, prophylactic antibiotics (eg. trimethoprin, sulpha-methoxazole and/or penicillin) are also employed.

Intensive nursing care is required during the immediate post-transplant period which is stressful and traumatic for both the patient and his family due to the range of side-effects he may be experiencing, the uncertainties involved in bone marrow trans-plantation and the need for prolonged isolation and hospitalisation. This places a considerable strain on the health care team as they must not only care for the patient but must also support his family, particularly when one of the family has been the bone marrow donor.

Appropriate interventions include all those applicable to those patients suffering bone marrow suppression; other factors must also be taken into account. These include:

- Reverse barrier care is used to 'protect' the patient
- Monitoring of the patient's temperature every 4 hours is essential to enable rapid treatment to be initiated when infection is present
- Prophylactic mouthwashes (eg. normal saline or hydrogen peroxide) must be given to prevent mucositis and stomatitis and reduce the risk of secondary infection
- The patient's personal hygiene must be maintained at an optimal level. Daily baths, using an antiseptic, are recommended
- The perianal area is especially vulnerable to infection, particularly when diarrhoea is present. Meticulous perianal care is essential
- When an intravenous infusion is in progress the insertion site should be closely observed for signs of infection. A bacteriostatic ointment may be prescribed
- If intestinal mucositis and diarrhoea are severe total parenteral nutrition is essential to offset post-treatment malnutrition (Ch. 12).

The success or failure of a bone marrow transplant can usually be determined within 10-20 days when, if it is successful, the blood cells will begin to develop within the bone marrow. If remission has been achieved, fewer than 5% of the cells present in the marrow will be blast cells. The granulocytes will increase more rapidly than platelets although both will gradually develop and reach normal levels. Since red cells develop more slowly it may be several weeks before the haematocrit rises.

Skilful assessment and careful management are essential for the patient with GVHD, since both the condition itself, and the therapy employed in its prevention/treatment, may have adverse effects (Ford and Ballard, 1983). Care includes management of the burn-like wounds, profuse diarrhoea and abdominal pain and/or cramping (Parker and Cohen, 1983). Fluid and electrolyte balance must be monitored carefully; fluid replacement, total parenteral nutrition and infusion of blood components may be required.

Bone marrow suppression

Continuing support and observation is required throughout the recovery period and following discharge. Bone marrow aspiration and haematological studies are carried out regularly both to ensure progress is maintained and to permit early detection of any relapse.

Patients should be advised to avoid crowds and to stay away from any individual (even a family member) suffering from any form of infectious disease for 3-6 months after discharge from hospital since their immune function will be compromised for some time following even a successful bone marrow transplant.

Although bone marrow transplantation is now curing patients who were otherwise incurable, provided that the bone marrow is replaced with marrow from a healthy donor, it remains a procedure not without risk. The care of such patients poses a considerable challenge. Health care professionals play a vital role not only in preparing the patient for treatment but also in paying close attention to his physical needs, the educational needs of both the patient and his family and in providing emotional/psychological support and reassurance. Although it is a traumatic experience, bone marrow transplantation gives the patient a better chance to live a normal life.

REFERENCES

Abrams RA, Deisseroth A, 1985, Use of blood and blood products. In: DeVita VT, Hellman S, Rosenberg SA (Editors), Cancer: Principles and Practice of Oncology (Third edition), JB Lippincott Co., Philadelphia.

Appelbaum FR, 1995, Allogeneic bone marrow transplantation for treatment of malignancy. In: MacDonald JS, Haller DG, Mayer RJ (Editors), Manual of Oncologic Therapeutics (Third edition), JB Lippincott Co., Philadelphia.

Barton-Burke M, Wilkes GM, Berg D, et al, 1991, Cancer Chemotherapy: A Nursing Process Approach, Jones and Bartlett Publishers, Boston.

Bearman SI, Appelbaum FR, Buckner CD, et al, 1988, Regimen-related toxicity in patients undergoing bone marrow transplant, Journal of Clinical Oncology **6**, 1562-8.

Berkman PT, 1984, The spectrum of transfusion reactions, Hospital Practice **19**, 205-19.

Brandt B, 1984, A nursing protocol for the client with neutropenia, Oncology Nursing Forum **11**, 24-8.

Brugieres L, Hartmann O, Travagli JP, et al, 1989, Haemorrhagic cystitis following high-dose chemotherapy and bone marrow transplantation in children with malignancies. Incidence, clinical course and outcome, Journal of

172

Clinical Oncology **7**, 194-9.

Buchsel PC, Parchem C, 1988, Ambulatory care of the bone marrow transplant patient, Seminars in Oncology Nursing **4**, 41-6.

Carlson AC, 1985, Infection prophylaxis in the patient with cancer, Oncology Nursing Forum **11**(2), 24-8.

Clark SC, Kamen R, 1987, The human hematopoietic colony stimulating factors, Science **246**, 1229-37.

Cline M, Haskell C, 1980, Cancer chemotherapy, WB Saunders Co., Philadelphia.

Crawford J, Ozer H, Stoller R, et al, 1991, Reduction by granulocyte colony-stimulating factor of fever and neutropenia induced by chemotherapy in patients with small cell cancer, New England Journal of Medicine **325**, 164-7.

Daly PA, Schiffer CA, Aisner J, et al, 1980, Platelet transfusion therapy. One hour posttransfusion increments are valuable in predicting the need for HLA-matched preparations, Journal of the American Medical Association **243**, 435-8.

Deisseroth A, Wallerstein R, 1989, Use of blood and blood products. In: DeVita VT, Hellman S, Rosenberg SA (Editors), Cancer: Principles and Practice of Oncology (Third edition), JB Lippincott Co., Philadelphia.

DeVita VT, Hellman S, Rosenberg SA, 1982, Cancer: Principles and Practice of Oncology, JB Lippincott Co., Philadelphia.

Dritschilo A, Sherman D, 1981, Radiation and chemical injury in bone marrow, Environmental Health Perspectives, June, 62-5.

Dutcher JP, 1986, Platelet and granulocyte transfusions in cancer patients, Advances in Immunology and Cancer Therapy **2**, 211-49.

Ford RC, Ballard B, 1988, Acute complications after bone marrow transplantation, Neurology Clinics **6**, 377-87.

Freeman SE, 1988, An overview of bone marrow transplantation, Seminars in Oncology Nursing **4**, 9-14.

Gmur J, von Felton A, Osterwalder B, et al, 1983, Delayed alloimmunisation using random single donor platelet transfusions: a prospective study in thrombocytopoenic patients with acute leukaemia, Blood **62**, 473-9.

Graze P, 1980, Bone marrow failure: management of anemia, infections and bleeding in the cancer patient. In: Haskell C (Editor), Cancer Treatment, WB Saunders and Co., Philadelphia.

Graze PR, Gale RP, 1979, Chronic graft versus host disease: a syndrome of disordered immunity, American Journal of Medicine **60**, 611-20.

Greenwalt TJ, 1981, Pathogenesis and management of haemolytic transfusion reactions, Seminars in Hematology **18**, 84-94.

Henschel L, 1985, Fever patterns in the neutropenic patient, Cancer Nursing **8**, 301-5.

Bone marrow suppression

Holmes S, 1996, Radiotherapy: A Guide for Practice, Asset Books, Leatherhead.

Lee EJ, Schiffer CA, 1995, Haematologic effects. In: MacDonald JS, Haller DG, Mayer RJ (Editors), Manual of Oncologic Therapeutics (Third edition), JB Lippincott, Co., Philadelphia.

Leitman SF, 1985, Post transfusion graft-versus-host disease. In Smith DM, Silvergleid AJ (Editors), Special Considerations in Transfusing the Immunocompromised Patient, American Association of Blood Banks, Arlington.

Lichtiger B, Huh YO, 1985, Transfusion therapy for patients with cancer, Ca: A Cancer Journal for Clinicians **35**, 311-6.

McConn R, 1987, Skin changes following bone marrow transplantation, Cancer Nursing **10**, 82-4.

McConnell EA, 1986, Leukocyte studies: what the counts tell you, Nursing **86**, 42-3.

Meyers JD, 1986, Infection in bone marrow recipients, American Journal of Medicine **81** (Suppl 1A), 27-38.

Parker N, Cohen T, 1983, Acute graft-versus-host disease: a nursing perspective, Nursing Clinics of North America **18**, 569-77

Parkinson DR, 1995, Principles of therapy. In: Skeel RT, Lachant NA (Editors), Handbook of Cancer Chemotherapy (Fourth edition), Little, Brown and Co., Boston.

Pisciotto PT (Editor), 1989, Blood Transfusion Therapy - A Physician's Handbook (Third edition), American Association of Blood Banks, Arlington.

Press OW, Schaller RT, Thomas ED, 1986, Bone marrow transplant complications. In: Toledo-Pereyra LH (Editor), Complications of Organ Transplantation, Marcel Dekker Inc., New York.

Pritchard AP, David JA, 1988, The Royal Marsden Hospital Manual of Clinical Nursing Procedures (Second edition), Harper and Row Publishers, London.

Saikh BS, 1987, Acquired immunodeficiency syndrome and related malignancies. In: Skeel RT (Editor), Handbook of Cancer Chemotherapy, Little Brown and Co., Boston.

Sarna G, 1980, Oncologic emergencies. In: Sarna G (Editor), Practical Oncology, Houghton Mifflin, Boston.

Smith MR, 1987, Infections and bleeding. In: Skeel RT (Editor), Handbook of Cancer Chemotherapy, Little, Brown and Co., Boston.

Spencer GB, Hackman RC, McDonald GB, et al, 1986, A prospective study of unexplained nausea and vomiting after marrow transplantation, Transplantation **42**, 602-7.

Storb R, Thomas ED, 1985, Graft-versus-host disease in dog and man. The Seattle experience. In: Moller G (Editor), Immunological Reviews No. 88, Munksgaard, Copenhagen.

174

Storb R, Deeg HJ, Whitehead J, et al, 1986, Methotrexate and cyclosporine compared with cyclosporine alone for prophylaxis of acute graft-versus-host disease after bone marrow transplantation for anaemia, New England Journal of Medicine **314**, 729-35,

Sullivan KM, Parkman R, 1983, The pathophysiology and treatment of graft-versus-host disease, Clinical Haematology **123**, 774-89.

Sullivan KM, Storb R, 1984, Allogeneic bone marrow transplantation, Cancer Investigation **2**, 27-38.

Thomas ED, Storb R, Clift RA, et al, 1975, Bone-marrow transplantation, New England Journal of Medicine **292**, 832-43 and 895-902.

Thomas ED, 1983, Bone marrow transplantation: a life-saving applied art, Journal of the American Medical Association **249**, 2528-36.

Thomas ED, Fefer A, 1985, Bone marrow transplantation. In: DeVita VT, Hellman S, Rosenberg SA (Editors), Cancer: Principles and Practice of Oncology (Third edition), JB Lippincott, Philadelphia.

Thompson JA, Lee DJ, Kidd P, et al, 1989, Subcutaneous granulocyte-macrophage colony-stimulating factor in patients with myelodysplastic syndrome: toxicity, pharmacokinetics and haematologic effects, Clinical Oncology **7**, 151-5.

Trillet-Lenoir V, Green J, Manegold C, et al, 1993, Recombinant granulocyte colony-stimulating factor reduces the infectious complications of cytotoxic chemotherapy, European Journal of Cancer **29A**, 319-24.

Walker RH, 1987, Special report: transfusion risks, American Journal of Clinical Pathology **88**, 951-61.

Weiden P, 1984, Graft-versus-host disease following blood transfusions, Archives of Internal Medicine **144**, 374-8.

Wright D, 1984, Leukocyte transfusions: thinking twice, American Journal of Medicine **76**, 637-44.

Yeager AM, Kaizer H, Santos GW, et al, 1986, Autologous bone marrow transplantation in patients with acute nonlymphocytic leukaemia, using ex vivo marrow treatment with 4-hydroperoxycyclophosphamide, New England Journal of Medicine **315**, 141-8.

CHAPTER 10   CUTANEOUS SIDE-EFFECTS

Although they may cause significant distress for affected patients mucocutaneous side-effects, with the exception of stomatitis, are not usually considered to be amongst the important toxicities of chemo-therapeutic agents. Nonetheless, it is important that their occurrence is recognised and treatment instigated where appropriate. When changes can be anticipated the patient should be informed of the likelihood of their development so that they are prepared for any alterations in function or appearance that may occur.

ALOPECIA

Alopecia is often identified as the single most distressing side-effect of chemotherapy (Coates et al, 1983; Baxley et al, 1984) and, indeed, presents such a devastating prospect that it may lead to a patient's refusal to accept the prescribed therapy (Cline, 1984; Klopovich and Clancy, 1985).

Since hair follicles undergo rapid cell division they are vulnerable to the toxic effects of cytotoxic drugs due to their high level of metabolic activity. This is due to two different mechanisms (Crounse and VanScott, 1960). Firstly, if damage is severe, the stem cells of the hair follicle are damaged leading to atrophy; the hair then falls out spontaneously (Chernecky and Yasko, 1986). Alternatively, lesser damage leads to the production of thinner and weaker hair that may break off at the scalp (Dunagin, 1984). At any given time, 85-90% of scalp hair follicles are in active division; body hair follicles divide less frequently (Crounse and VanScott, 1960).

Hair loss is most common when higher doses of chemotherapy are employed; drugs of lower intensity, or at lower doses, reduce the mitotic rate causing partial atrophy of the follicle. The extent of alopecia is influenced by a variety of drug- and patient-related factors and, contrary to patient belief, most anticancer drugs do not cause hair loss.

The degree and duration depend on the drug, or combination of drugs, and the dose of drug employed; its pharmacokinetics and route of administration are also important. For example, cyclo-phosphamide in excess of 500mg/m^2 will produce alopecia after two cycles have been administered; low doses of doxorubicin (>50mg/m^2)

will have similar effects (Siepp, 1989). Other agents known to cause alopecia are shown in Table 10.1. Thus alopecia is a side-effect of some but not all antineoplastic drugs; the reasons for this variation are not entirely clear (Welch and Lewis, 1980).

Table 10.1   Examples of chemotherapeutic agents which may cause alopecia

Actinomycin-D	Ifosfamide
Bleomycin	Mechlorethamine
Busulphan	Methotrexate (without folinic acid rescue)
Cyclophosphamide	Mitomycin-C
Cytosine arabinoside	Mitoxantrone
Daunorubicin	Paclitaxel
Doxorubcin	Teniposide
Etoposide	Vincristine
5-Fluorouracil	Vinblastine
Hydroxyurea	Vindesine

Hair loss is not, however, specific to cancer chemotherapy and may be a reaction, albeit uncommon, to a variety of drugs (Levantine and Almeyda, 1973) (Table 10.2).

Table 10.2   Other drugs which may cause alopecia

Antibiotics	**Hormones**
Gentamycin	Testosterone
Streptomycin	Oestrogens
Tetracycline	
Anticoagulants	**Miscellaneous**
Warfarin	Levodopa
Heparin	Lithium carbonate
Anticonvulsants	Methysergide
Phenobarbitone	Propanolol
Phenytoin	Radiation

Alopecia occurs approximately two weeks after treatment begins and, unlike that associated with radiotherapy, may be widespread affecting not only the hair on the scalp but also that on the face and body. There is, however, considerable individual variation in the pattern of hair loss so that some patients may experience total alopecia while others may lose only patches of hair. The loss may be gradual lasting for several days during which hair may litter the patient's bed each morning causing marked distress (Clement-Jones, 1985); wearing a hair-net in bed can help to reduce the debris. Some patients, particularly those with long hair, may prefer to have their hair cut to reduce the stress and anxiety associated with watching their hair fall out slowly. The patient should be reassured that the hair loss associated with chemotherapy is generally temporary and that regrowth usually begins after the cessation of treatment; regrowth is usually clinically evident within 4-6 weeks (Chernecky and Yasko, 1986). He should, however, be warned that, at times, the regrowth may be of a different colour and/or texture.

Patient-related factors that may contribute to the occurrence of alopecia include the rate of scalp hair growth, which is subject to considerable individual variation, as well as the general condition of the hair; damaged hair is more susceptible to chemotherapy-induced damage. The general medical condition is also important and factors, such as chronic stress and/or malnutrition may potentiate hair loss (Table 10.3).

Table 10.3   Medical conditions that may cause alopecia

Hormonal dysfunction:	Hypo/hyperthyroidism
	Hypoparathyroidism
Addison's disease	
Prolonged pyrexia	
Herpes zoster (shingles)	
Pernicious anaemia	
Protein-energy malnutrition	

Attempts to reduce the incidence of alopecia due to cancer chemotherapy are controversial and a variety of techniques have been employed. These include the use of a scalp tourniquet (peripheral constriction) and methods of scalp cooling (hypothermia) the aim being to reduce blood flow to the scalp and minimise the contact between anticancer drugs and the dividing stem cells of the hair follicles (Figure 10.1). Peripheral constriction will cause obstruction of the blood flow through the superficial capillaries. Hypothermia will result in constriction of those capillaries; it will also decrease metabolic activity in the hair follicles and may restrict the uptake of temperature-dependent drugs (eg. doxorubicin) (Keller and Blausey, 1988). In either case, therefore, the procedure will temporarily reduce the blood flow thus decreasing the amount of drug able to reach the hair follicle and

178

disrupt hair production (Cline, 1984).

However, because both approaches reduce drug concentrations in the scalp this may provide a sanctuary for metastases. Thus, neither technique should be used in patients with leukaemia, lymphoma or other tumours which have the potential for scalp metastases.

Figure 10.1   The skin and a hair follicle

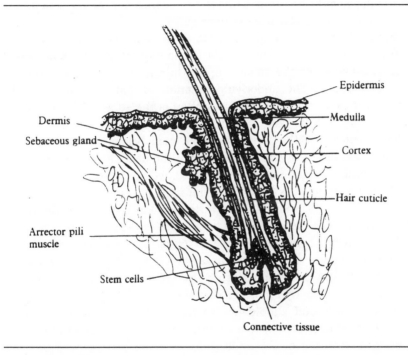

There is confusion in the literature with regard to the efficacy of these techniques both with regard to their role in preventing hair loss and with regard to the risk of scalp metastases. Clearly, if the latter were proven this would cast doubt on the advisability of using such procedures (Tierney, 1987). However, the results of studies to date are equivocal and some workers (eg. Middleton et al, 1981; Siepp, 1985) suggest that scalp cooling should not be used in patients with advanced metastatic disease that may spread to the skin or soft tissues while others suggest that the risk of scalp metastases is minimal (eg. Dean et al, 1983). It seems appropriate, therefore, that patients be advised of the remote risk of scalp metastases when

179

cooling is offered. Similarly, they should be informed that these techniques do not guarantee that alopecia will be prevented. Such methods have been found to be most useful when doxorubicin is used due largely to its short half life (30 minutes) which normally results in total hair loss in 90% of cases.

Many patients, however, receive a combination of drugs when the effectiveness of scalp constriction/hypothermia is reduced. Neither technique should be used without the permission of the consulting physician or in the absence of informed consent from the patient.

Scalp tourniquet. The first reports of the successful use of a scalp tourniquet occurred in the 1960's (Hennessy, 1966; Simister, 1966) when occlusion of the blood supply to the scalp was reported to prevent alopecia. The underlying rationale is that pressure from the tourniquet causes temporary constriction of the superficial veins of the scalp (Cline, 1984). This is achieved using either a pneumatic or a tube tourniquet. Either is applied one inch below the hair line and continued behind the ears to the nape of the neck; the lower margin of a pneumatic tourniquet should be just above the eyebrows.

A tube tourniquet is knotted at the nape of the neck ensuring that the tubing is tight enough to begin to 'wrinkle' the skin at the top of the forehead. The patient should be advised not to move his head or to talk since moving the facial muscles tends to loosen the tubing. This technique has one major disadvantage as it is not possible to control the pressure on the scalp tissue; this lack of control may lead to damage of the underlying nerves due to compression.

A pneumatic cuff should be inflated gradually to 50mmHg above the patient's systolic blood pressure. This enables distribution of a uniform pressure over the underlying tissue so that there is less risk of nerve compression and it has been suggested (Lovejoy, 1979) that it is physiologically safe to inflate the cuff to as much as 170mmHg for periods of up to one hour. Peripheral constriction should not, however, be used when the patient is hypotensive or when his platelet count is <50 x 10^9/litre. A cuff is usually applied 5 minutes before intravenous chemotherapy is given and kept in place for 10-15 minutes after administration is completed.

Both these procedures are extremely uncomfortable and may cause headache or feeling of pressure that can be controlled by mild analgesia given half an hour prior to application of the tourniquet. Since verbal communication is discouraged the patient should be provided with pencil and paper to enable him to communicate with

180

staff when required. It should be noted, however, that the value and effectiveness of this technique are questionable and, although some have reported good results (eg. Hennessy, 1966) others have found it ineffective (eg. Lovejoy, 1979).

Scalp cooling is most commonly achieved using an 'ice cap' although a thermocirculator, relying on the circulation of cold air, may be employed. A commercially available ice cap may be used. Alternatively, a 'home made' cap can be manufactured from hot/cold packs containing a gel that crystallises at between -15°C and -18°C. These should be held together, using waterproof tape, and moulded into shape using a wig stand. The cap is then bandaged into position on the stand and placed in a deep freeze for at least 24 hours.

Whichever technique is employed the procedure must be carefully explained to the patient who must be assured that it can be discontinued at any time without detrimental effects on his chemo-therapy. Before the ice cap is applied the patient's hair must be thoroughly wetted and a crepe bandage, previously soaked in cold water, is wrapped tightly around his head. This should be evenly applied forming a thin layer over the scalp. These procedures will compress the hair preventing air from becoming trapped between the scalp and the cap which, in turn, will improve conduction of the cold to the scalp. The cap is then placed on the patient's head ensuring that it fits closely covering the entire head and hairline; additional ice packs can be added if required. The whole is then bandaged in place to ensure that contact is maintained between the scalp and the pack.

The pack is applied 15 minutes before chemotherapy is given and kept in place for at least 30 minutes after completion of therapy (Dean et al, 1979; Hunt et al, 1982) so that cooling is maintained until plasma levels of the drug have dropped.

As this is an uncomfortable procedure, and the cap itself is extremely heavy, the head and neck should be well supported with pillows. A towel should be placed around the shoulders to catch drips as the ice melts. Warm blankets should be provided to keep the patient as comfortable as possible.

Once treatment is completed the bandages and ice cap should be removed carefully so as to prevent damage to the hair and scalp. The patient should be encouraged to rest since removal of the weight may result in dizziness. The hair should be towelled dry, using a soft towel and the patient encouraged to restyle it gently.

The focus of most research in this area has been therapy with doxorubicin (eg. Maxwell, 1980) or cyclophosphamide (eg. Parker, 1987) showing that hair loss can be reduced and sometimes prevented. An additional approach to prevention includes the use of high doses of vitamin E (tocopherol) which, in high doses (1600iu/day), may prevent alopecia (Wood, 1985). Replication studies replicate have, however, been unsuccessful (Perez et al, 1986).

Care of the patient with alopecia

Alopecia may have profound psychological effects on affected patients so that the stress associated with both the anticipation and the experience of hair loss must not be overlooked. The possibility must be discussed with the patient before treatment commences so that appropriate measures can be planned to minimise changes in appearance. Whether it involves head or body hair the effect on the individual can be devastating, significantly altering their appearance and body image, so that considerable psychological support may be required. Understanding and support from both the caring team and the patient's family and friends are essential.

Appropriate interventions include not only forewarning the patient but discussing with him the alternative courses of action and appropriate care. When the treatment plan suggests that hair loss is likely it is advisable for a wig to be selected before the loss occurs since it is easier to select a wig of an appropriate colour and style when hair loss is not apparent. Alternatively, a photograph can be used to help in selection. It is often beneficial if the wig is worn before hair is lost as this may help adjustment. However, some wigs cause scalp irritation so that some patients may prefer to wear a scarf, turban or hat to conceal hair loss. When facial hair is lost an eyebrow pencil and false eyelashes may help to restore body image.

Hair should be washed gently every 4-7 days using a mild shampoo. It should be left to dry naturally since hair dryers and other heated appliances should not be used; similarly, hair sprays, dyes and permanent waving solutions should not be applied as these may increase the fragility of the hair. Excessive brushing/combing should be avoided.

These measures will not, however, prevent hair loss and it is essential that those caring for affected patients recognise the difficulties the patient is facing. Genuine concern must be shown for affected patients and suggestions made as to how some of the changes in appearance can be overcome. Allowing the patient to voice his concern, anger or resentment is also valuable. Ongoing support is often needed to allow the patient to work through, or grieve over, his loss. Reassurance that hair will grow back is also helpful.

DERMATOLOGICAL REACTIONS

The skin provides a protective and flexible covering for the body. It is also the largest body organ receiving approximately a third of the oxygenated blood supply. It comprises three layers: the epidermis (outer layer), the dermis and subcutaneous tissue (Figure 10.1). The epidermis is subject to continued renewal through active cell division in the basal layers which undergo keratinisation to produce 'scales' that are shed from the surface.

The skin provides protection against the environment. It is the 'first line of defence' against bacteria and other foreign substances and physical trauma. Damage to the skin thus breaches this barrier increasing the permeability to bacteria, etc.. Additional functions include a role in the regulation of body temperature, sensory perception and the production of vitamin D. Lastly, because the skin is a highly visible part of the body, it plays a significant role in the communication of feelings and the maintenance of body image.

Certain chemotherapeutic agents can cause skin reactions including urticaria, erythema and pruritis. Other unusual reactions include hyperpigmentation, vasculitis, flushing and changes in the nails including, rarely, nail loss (Nixon, 1976); photosensitivity may also occur. However, with the exception of local necrosis due to extravasation (p138-46), skin reactions are rarely dangerous. They may, nonetheless, cause the patient significant distress.

Urticaria. Transient erythema or urticaria usually occurs within a few hours of chemotherapy administration then gradually disappears. It may be generalised or localised at the site of administration. It must, however, be differentiated from other disorders, such as *herpes zoster*, or an allergic reaction although, as shown in Ch. 8, an allergic response may initially be manifested by urticaria so that this can be difficult. Such reactions occur infrequently but have been reported following treatment with L-asparaginase and cisplatin. Other drugs that may cause such effects include chlorambucil, melphalan, methotrexate and thiotepa.

Hyperpigmentation, like urticaria, may be either localised or generalised. It may, for example, affect the nail beds or the oral mucosa or may affect the skin surfaces along the veins used for drug administration. Changes are usually seen within 2-3 weeks of chemo-therapy administration and last for 2-3 months after treatment is completed. Drugs which may cause hyperpigmentation include busulfan, adriamycin, bleomycin, thiotepa and 5-fluorouracil (5-FU). When the reaction can be predicted the patient should be warned that it is likely and that it will gradually disappear when treatment ceases. It may, nonetheless, be distressing for the individual particularly when the face is affected as it may be, for example, by actinomycin-D.

Pruritis is a mainifestation of many medical conditions both benign and malignant. It may, occasionally, arise as a consequence of treatment with anticancer drugs when it is primarily due to either a hypersensitivity reaction or to dry skin and scaling caused by chemotherapy-induced damage to sebaceous or sweat glands (Lokich and Moore, 1984).

Photosensitivity reactions can occur following administration of a variety of antineoplastic agents including actinomycin-D, bleomycin, dacarbazine, 5-FU, methotrexate and vinblastine; they may also be due to a variety of other drugs (eg. analgesics, antidepressants, anti-microbial agents or non-steroidal anti-inflammatory agents) (Hawk, 1986). Since patients with cancer are often taking a variety of both prescription and non-prescription drugs such reactions are not unlikely and can occur during treatment or reactivate a previous skin reaction due to sunburn when drugs are given soon after exposure to the sun.

When such reactions develop the patient must be advised to avoid exposure to the sun. Loose cotton clothing will be the most comfortable. However, when exposure cannot be avoided, an effective sun screening product (high sun protection factor) should be applied.

Hyperkeratinisation, resulting in swelling and thickening of the skin, most commonly affecting the hands but also the feet, elbows and gluteal areas, may accompany administration of bleomycin, 5-FU, doxorubicin and high dose cytosine arabinoside (Lokich and Moore, 1984). This condition, known as hand-foot syndrome, is characterised by painful and intense erythema of the palms and soles and may affect the function of the hand and be associated with sensory impairment or parasthesiae of the fingers (Halnan et al, 1972). It may, albeit rarely, progress to cause ulceration or gangrene. Although, with the exception of gangrene, these changes are largely reversible once treatment is discontinued, they may indicate the development of pulmonary fibrosis. Therapy is often withheld until the symptoms subside and resumed at a lower dose. However, the symptoms often reappear necessitating the cessation of therapy.

An *acne-like reaction* may develop and is manifested initially by erythema, particularly on the face. This rapidly progresses to the papules and pustules characteristic of acne. Such a reaction often accompanies administration of actinomycin-D and will gradually disappear once treatment is discontinued.

Changes in the finger or toe nails are often seen during chemotherapy, particularly that involving cyclophosphamide or doxorubicin; it has also been reported in therapy with melphalan, 5-FU, daunomycin and bleomycin. This most often leads to pigmentation which results in the deposition of pigment at the base of the nail causing transverse dark bands that correlate with the times at which drugs were administered. At times, a partial separation of the nail plate may be observed.

RECALL PHENOMENA
Since both radiotherapy and chemotherapy cause damage to or destruction of stem cell populations their combined use may lead to exaggerated effects on the skin and mucous membranes, even when administration is separated by time (p127). Administration of certain cytotoxic agents can reactivate skin reactions in patients who have previously developed radiation-induced desquamation (dry or wet). It has been suggested, however, that such reactions result not from reactivation (or recall) of previous damage but rather the addition of chemotherapy-induced damage to that previously caused by radiation (Phillips, 1980).

Some areas of the skin are particularly vulnerable to damage, such as those where two skin surfaces are in contact (eg. face or perineum) or when skin integrity has been disrupted (eg. surgical wounds). When such areas have previously been exposed to radiation they should be closely observed for signs of a recall reaction.

Skin reactions are usually progressive increasing in intensity throughout the course of treatment. Initially, a sensation of warmth may be felt in the affected area. The first real indication of a reaction is erythema which is similar to that seen following exposure to sunlight. The colour may vary from a mild reddening to marked inflammation due to capillary dilation; slight oedema may be present.

This initial reaction may be followed by dry desquamation when

185

Cutaneous effects

the skin becomes very dry, due to damage to the sebaceous and sweat glands, and the patient may complain of itching, flaking and cracking of the skin. This may then proceed to further inflammation, oedema and moist desquamation characterised by the formation of blisters, exudative ulceration and/or loss of the epithelial layers of the skin. This is can be extremely painful so that therapy may be discontinued to allow time for the skin to recover.

Care of patients experiencing skin reactions

Successful care depends on assessment and continued evaluation of the prescribed therapy. Anticipation of the potential for reactions enables effective patient education to be planned and directed towards early recognition of the signs and symptoms and appropriate interventions. This allows the patient to maintain an element of control and may be important since his actions and behaviours may be critical in preventing complications.

When skin reactions can be anticipated the patient should be taught the fundamentals of skin care that are designed to prevent irritation or stress to the skin surface and to maintain its integrity. The area should be kept clean and dry. It may be washed gently using tepid water, a mild soap and a soft cloth; a gentle, patting motion is advised. The area should be thoroughly but gently dried, again using a patting motion, and a soft towel. A baby dusting powder may be applied as this is soothing to irritated skin.

Wherever possible, the affected area should be exposed to the air although exposure to sunlight should be discouraged. Extremes of temperature should be avoided (eg. hot water bottles, electric blankets or ice packs) even though they may appear to be soothing. Clothing should be loose and non-constricting and harsh fabrics should be avoided; 100% cotton is ideal. Dryness and itching may occur due to impaired function of the sebaceous and sweat glands. The patient should be advised not to rub or scratch the skin; cosmetics and lotions should not be applied although a steroid cream (eg. hydrocortisone 1%) may be prescribed to control irritation; this should, however, be avoided where possible so as to avoid thinning of the epidermis. Pure lanolin may be soothing and prevent skin breakdown.

The risk of infection is great when moist desquamation is present which is characterised by intense erythema, blistering and ulceration. It may be intensely painful due to damage to the nerve endings; it is likely to produce a serous exudate. The area must be kept clean and

186

dry but may be cleansed with half-strength hydrogen peroxide and normal saline applied with an irrigating syringe to prevent friction. Although exposure to the air will be beneficial the affected area may be covered with a non-constrictive, non-adhesive or hydrogel dressing. If a dressing is required this must be changed as soon as it becomes damp. Swabs should be sent for bacteriological examination if infection is suspected; systemic or topical antibiotics will be prescribed if, and when, they are necessary.

Moist desquamation may be persistent, particularly in folds of skin; dry, non-adherent or hydrogel dressings may be required for some time after treatment. Alternatively, desquamation may leave a scab that will adhere to the affected surface and, if removed, will simply be renewed thus prolonging the time required for healing. Erythema may also persist taking some weeks to subside; the affected area may remain irritating and susceptible to damage so that the patient should be advised to continue to wear loose clothing so that friction is minimised.

REFERENCES

Baxley KO, Erdman LK, Henry EB, et al, 1984, Alopecia: effect on cancer patient's body image, British Medical Journal **291**, 423-4.

Chernecky CC, Yasko JM, 1986, In: Yasko JM (Editor), Nursing Management of Symptoms associated with Chemotherapy, Adria Laboratories, Columbus, Ohio.

Clement-Jones V, 1985, Cancer and beyond: the formation of BACUP, British Medical Journal **291**, 1021-3.

Cline BW, 1984, Prevention of chemotherapy-induced alopecia: a review of the literature, Cancer Nursing **7**, 22-8.

Cline M, Haskell C, 1980, Cancer chemotherapy, WB Saunders and Co., Philadelphia.

Coates A, Abraham S, Kaye SB, et al, 1983, On the receiving end - patient perception of the side effects of cancer chemotherapy, European Journal of Clinical Oncology **19**, 203-8.

Crounse RG, VanScott EJ, 1960, Changes in scalp hair roots as a measure of toxicity from cancer chemotherapeutic drugs, Journal of Investigational Dermatology **35**, 83-90.

Dean JC, Salmon SE, Griffith KS, 1979, Prevention of doxorubicin-induced hair loss with scalp hypothermia, New England Journal of Medicine **301**, 1427-9.

Dean JC, Griffith KS, Cetas TC, et al, 1983, Scalp hypothermia: a comparison of ice packs and the KoldKap in the prevention of doxorubicin-induced alopecia, Journal of Clinical Oncology **1**, 33-7.

Dunagin WG, 1984, Dermatologic toxicity. In: Perry MC, Yarbro JW (Editors), Toxicity of Chemox, Greene and Stratton, Orlando, Florida.

Halnan KE, Bleehan NM, Brewin TB, et al, 1972, Early clinical experience with bleomycin in the UK in a series of 108 patients, British Medical Journal **4**, 635-8.

Hawk J, 1986, Sunlight and the skin, Occupational Health **38**, 60-2.

Hennessy JD, 1966, Alopecia and cytotoxic drugs (Letter to the Editor) British Medical Journal **2**, 1138.

Hunt J, Anderson J, Smith I, 1982, Scalp hypothermia to prevent adriamycin-induced hair loss, Cancer Nursing **5**, 25-32.

Keller JF, Blausey LA, 1988, Nursing issues and management of chemotherapy-induced alopecia, Oncology Nursing Forum **15**(5), 603-7.

Klopovich PM, Clancy BJ, 1985, Sexuality and the adolescent with cancer, Seminars in Oncology **1**, 42-8.

Levantine AV, Almeyda J, 1973, Drug reactions 23: drug-induced alopecia, British Journal of Dermatology **89**, 549-3.

Lokich JJ, Moore C, 1984, Chemotherapy-associated palmar-plantar erythrodysthesia syndrome, Annals of Internal Medicine **101**, 798-800.

Lovejoy NC, 1979, Preventing hair loss during adriamycin therapy, Cancer Nursing **2**, 117-21.

Maxwell M, 1980, Scalp tourniquets for chemotherapy-induced alopecia. American Journal of Nursing **80**, 900-3.

Middleton J, Franks D, Buchanan RB, et al, 1981, Failure of scalp hypothermia to prevent hair loss when cyclophosphamide is added to doxorubicin and vincristine, Cancer Treatment Reports **69**, 373-5.

Nixon DW, 1976, Alteration in nail pigment with cancer chemotherapy, Archives of Internal Medicine **136**, 1117-21.

Parker R, 1987, Preventing hair loss during adriamycin therapy, Cancer Nursing **2**, 117-21.

Perez JE, Macchiavelli M, Leone BA, et al, 1986, High-dose alpha-tocopherol as a preventive of doxorubcin-induced alopecia, Cancer Treatment Reports **70**, 1213-4.

Phillips TL, 1980, Tissue toxicity of radiation-drug interactions. In: Sokol GH, Maickel RP (Editors), Radiation Drug Interactions in the Treatment of Cancer, John Wiley and Sons, Chichester.

Seipp CA, 1989, Adverse effects of treatment: hair loss. In: DeVita VT, Hellman S, Rosenberg SA (Editors), Cancer Principles and Practice of Oncology, JB Lippincott Co., Philadelphia.

Siepp CA, 1985, Scalp hypothermia: indications for precaution, Oncology Nursing Forum **10**, 12-5.

Simister JM, 1966, Alopecia and cytotoxic drugs (Letter to the Editor), British Medical Journal **2**, 1138.

Tierney AJ, 1987, Preventing chemotherapy-induced alopecia in cancer patients: is scalp cooling worthwhile? Journal of Advanced Nursing **12**, 303-10.

Welch D, Lewis K, 1980, Alopecia and chemotherapy, American Journal of Nursing **80**, 903-5.

Wood LA, 1985, Possible prevention of adriamycin-induced alopecia by tocopherol (Letter to the Editor), New England Journal of Medicine **312**, 1060.

CHAPTER 11   GASTROINTESTINAL SIDE-EFFECTS

The effects of chemotherapy on the gastrointestinal (GI) tract are often dramatic and result in a variety of uncomfortable and distressing side-effects including damage to the oral cavity, pharynx, and oesophagus, mild to severe nausea and/or vomiting, diarrhoea or constipation. Such effects can be devastating, particularly for the patient who has previously suffered only minor discomfort as a result of his disease when treatment-induced side-effects can be seen to confirm the serious nature of their disease. Since many of these effects can be predicted appropriate therapy can be planned even before treatment commences. Appropriate care and intervention may significantly affect the patient's ability to cope with GI side-effects.

EFFECTS ON THE ORAL CAVITY

The oral cavity is lined by a layer of rapidly dividing mucosal cells which are extremely vulnerable to the effects of antineoplastic therapy. As such cells are also exposed to repeated physical, chemical, thermal and microbial insults the mouth can become a focal point for a variety of complications of chemotherapy (Table 11.1). Indeed, studies show that 40% of adults (Sonis et al, 1978) and 90% of children (Sonis and Sonis, 1979) treated with antineoplastic drugs develop some form of oral complication. Younger patients (ie. those under 20yrs) are those who most commonly develop oral mucositis (Raybould and Ferretti, 1990). Similarly, patients with impaired renal and/or hepatic function are at an increased risk of oral complications due to the reduced metabolism and/or excretion of antineoplastic drugs; persistent blood or tissue levels of cytotoxic agents will delay re-epithelialisation (Raybould and Ferretti, 1990). Furthermore, since the oral cavity has a diffuse bacterial flora and an almost ubiquitous presence of chronic, often asymptomatic, infection (Sonis, 1983) it is an important site of entry for pathogenic organisms, particularly in the immunocompromised patient. Thus, unless oral effects are recognised and treated early, they may become so severe that they prevent completion of an adequate course of chemotherapy and systemic infection, originating in the mouth, may be life-threatening (McElroy, 1984).

Table 11.1   Effects of chemotherapy on the oral cavity

Generalised effects
        Xerostomia
        Altered taste perception
Inflammatory changes
        Mucositis
        Ulceration
Infectious complications
        Periodontal infection/disease
        Dental caries
        Gingivitis
        Viral infections (eg. *herpes simplex*)
        Fungal infections (eg. *candida albicans*)
Indirect effects secondary to myelosuppression
        Gingival bleeding
        Atrophy of tongue and buccal mucosa

Although various oral problems may arise they are, fundamentally, due to either the direct effects of chemotherapy or to the indirect effects of myelosuppression or immunosuppression when leucopoenia renders the patient vulnerable to infection. Any drug causing myelosuppression may, therefore, indirectly cause stomatitis. Thus, although virtually all anticancer drugs can cause oral damage the extent to which this occurs is variable. For example, although mucosal ulceration may follow treatment with cyclophosphamide or phenylalanine mustard, this is rarely seen after treatment with other alkylating agents. Stomatitis has been reported to affect 48% to 75% of all patients receiving 5-FU (Greenwald, 1973) and may be dose-limiting. Dose-limiting oral toxicities may also follow administration of actinomycin-D and methotrexate (Raybould and Ferretti, 1990).

Direct effects usually arise within 4-7 days of therapy resolving once treatment is completed; indirect effects occur within 12-16 days usually coinciding with the nadir of the white blood cell count when patients are profoundly neutropoenic (Lockhart and Sonis, 1979); healing occurs as the neutrophil count returns to normal.

Stomatitis/mucositis

Stomatitis results from damage to the mucous membranes of the mouth and is largely unpreventable. Since these membranes are continually subjected to considerable trauma the cells are highly proliferative so as to replace those which are lost or damaged. Thus chemotherapy, through inhibition of cellular replication, means that production of new cells is insufficient to maintain mucosal integrity; the mucosa thins and the signs and symptoms of mucositis appear. Eliminating pre-existing dental disease - as a source of mucosal ulceration and trauma - prior to therapy can reduce the frequency and/or severity of oral complications.

Mucosal reactions usually occur in two stages. First, the mucosa thins and becomes erythematous; ulceration may occur. A reduced food and fluid intake, due to other side-effects of therapy (eg. nausea and vomiting), together with some degree of xerostomia, compounds the problem allowing plaque and debris to accumulate on the teeth and mucosal surfaces. This renders the mucosa an ineffective barrier to secondary, opportunistic infection.

In the early stages mild erythema and, possibly, some loss of taste develop. The patient may complain of tenderness and, perhaps, increased salivation that will decrease as the reaction proceeds. The mucosa is increasingly inflamed and dry and xerostomia becomes apparent. If the condition remains untreated the tongue becomes swollen and the papilli inflamed; the surface becomes coated, small blisters may develop and a line of demarcation appears separating the damaged and healthy tissue. The inflammatory response continues to intensify; if untreated, the blisters turn into ulcerated lesions. Even minor trauma may cause painful erosions and ulceration predisposing to secondary infection.

However, despite its severity, mucositis is self-limiting and usually resolves 2-4 weeks after chemotherapy is completed. Cyclical regimes may, however, subject the mucosa to repeated chemical insults thus inhibiting resolution and increasing the severity of the response. Secondary infection must be treated since local infection can rapidly become systemic and life-threatening, particularly in those who are immunocompromised (McElroy, 1984).

The indirect effects of chemotherapy initially affect the gingiva where pre-existing infection may predispose to further destruction and infection. Once gingival breakdown has become established, ulcerative lesions and surface necrosis may spread to any area of the mucosa (Sonis, 1983). Secondary infection and haemorrhage are common but, due to myelosuppression, the cardinal signs of inflammation may be absent. However, the greater the degree and duration of neutropoenia the greater is the risk of infection.

Opportunistic infections are usually of bacterial or fungal origin; viral infections are comparatively rare and usually involve *herpes simplex*. Both fungal and bacterial infections are usually precipitated by commensal organisms present in the oral cavity although they may also be due to infections introduced into the mouth from the environment (eg. in food and drink).

The commonest infections are candidiasis (thrush), herpetic lesions of the lips/mucosa and staphylococcal infections (Campbell, 1987). Thrush is manifested by soft white plaques on the mucosa and tongue; angular cheilitis is likely. In the absence of treatment the plaque will gradually erode the tissue causing haemorrhage and severe pain and providing entry sites for further infection (Eilers et al, 1988). Oral Nystatin may be prescribed to treat mild cases; amphotericin-B or ketoconazole may be needed to prevent systemic dissemination. Chlorhexidine rinses have shown some effect in modifying candidiasis (Weisdorf et al, 1989).

Herpes simplex is the most common viral pathogen associated with myelosuppressive chemotherapy. Lesions most commonly originate on the lips but may rapidly spread to form a generalised stomatitis with irregular ulcers and painful, bleeding gums. Such infections may progress to affect the pharynx and oesophagus. Unless secondarily infected, they usually regress within 7-10 days. The most important systemic effect of herpetic infection is the break-down of local barriers that may facilitate the entry of commensal microorganisms into the circulation leading to systemic infection (Raybould and Ferretti, 1990). *Herpes simplex* infection itself may also spread to other organs resulting in, for example, oesophagitis, pneumonitis or widely-disseminated disease.

Mucositis is exacerbated when nutritional status is poor, particularly when there are deficiencies of the B complex vitamins (especially folic acid, riboflavin (B_2) and cyanocobalamin (vitamin B_{12}), vitamin C and zinc). Other factors causing dryness and/or trauma to the mucous membranes, such as oxygen therapy, mouth breathing, dehydration and poor oral hygiene, may all contribute to an exacerbation so that care must be taken to minimise their effects.

Care of the patient with stomatitis

Stomatitis causes significant distress for affected patients posing difficulties related to pain control and inhibition of food and fluid intake; it increases the risk of systemic infection. Thus, when stomatitis can be anticipated, the oral cavity should be regularly assessed, starting before treatment, noting areas of dryness, inflammation, ulceration or other breaks in mucosal integrity and the presence of infection, so that appropriate care can be instigated. Such assessment is the first step in planning successful care. Body temperature should be monitored and swabs taken for bacterial culture from any lesion or when infection is suspected. Successful care is often dependent on teaching the patient to identify and manage oral hygiene so as to prevent oral complications and promote oral comfort.

Although a number of measures can be used to treat stomatitis, it is important to enlist the patient's help in achieving this. Regular care is essential to promote and maintain a satisfactory state of health in the tissues and secretions of the oral cavity and may be achieved by either reinforcing an existing oral care regime, teaching the patient the techniques required or by performing care for the dependent or disabled patient. Thus the purposes of oral care are:

- Prevention of infection, periodontal disease and gingival bleeding
- Prevention of further damage to oral structure so as to allow completion of treatment
- Improvement of general well-being.

The teeth must be gently brushed after every meal and at bedtime, using a soft tooth-brush. The Bass technique of is believed to be *'the best at meeting the requirement of proper oral hygiene and is relatively simple for the patient to learn'* (Trowbridge and Carl, 1975). This involves using a small soft tooth-brush placed at a 45° angle between the gums and teeth and moved in short, horizontal strokes. The lingual surfaces of both the upper and lower anterior teeth are cleaned using the tip or heel of the tooth-brush (Dudjak, 1987).

The mouth should be regularly rinsed using warm saline solutions or non-alcohol containing mouthwashes, such as 0.5% chlorhexidine (1ml chlorhexidine in 200ml water); alcohol will enhance dryness and cause desiccation of the membranes. The commonly used glycerine and lemon swabs should also be avoided. In fact, as long ago as 1969, Wiley suggested that glycerol or lemon were neither acceptable cleansers nor effective oral care agents. Commercial mouthwashes containing detergents should also be avoided as detergent removes mucins from the tissues. It is generally believed that it is the frequency and regularity of oral care that maintains the oral condition rather than the specific agent involved (Dudjak, 1987).

As the basic value of any mouthwash depends primarily on its mechanical actions in washing away loose debris, as well as its physical action of moistening the mouth and softening the oral mucosa, normal saline, glycothymoline and even water will be effective mouthwashes and leave subjective feelings of freshness; they will also provide temporary relief of xerostomia (Daeffler, 1980).

The efficacy of preventative oral care in reducing the morbidity associated with the oral complications of cytotoxic therapy has been clearly demonstrated (eg. Beck, 1979; Overholser et al, 1982). Thus oral care should be undertaken in all 'at risk' patients including those who are dependent and those who are immunosuppressed. However, when reactions are severe using toothbrush, or even a foam stick, may be unbearable; gentle oral syringing may be required. This is soothing and will help to decrease the risk of infection.

The mouth should be cleaned every 2 hours using hydrogen peroxide, normal saline or other mild mouthwash; the lips can be kept moist using petroleum jelly, pure lanolin or other lip salve. When mucous and serous secretions are reduced, artificial saliva can be used to maintain comfort. Several products are available and should be used as often as needed to ensure patient comfort. However, the volume used must be the minimum necessary to maintain internal lubrication since excessive quantities of artificial saliva simply serve to enhance discomfort (Navazesh and Ship, 1983). 1-2ml will often maintain lubrication for as long as 12 hours.

Trauma to the mucous membranes must be avoided. Loose dentures, for example, may cause friction to the gums and provide a food trap so that, unless they can be adapted or relined, dentures are best worn only when necessary (eg. when eating). All irritant substances should be avoided as they may aggravate mucositis. These include alcohol, tobacco and hot spicy foods although, when the patient is psychologically dependent on alcohol or tobacco, which are often used as supports to alleviate stress and anxiety, considerable empathy and understanding will be needed.

Regular analgesia may be needed both to promote comfort and to ensure an adequate food intake. Topical anaesthetics prior to meals may also enhance the ability to eat although some patients find their analgesic properties unpleasant, particularly on the tongue. They may also affect taste sensation further inhibiting food intake. Adequate nutrition is essential if cellular repair and regeneration is to occur. Dietary manipulation including nutritious but soft and bland foods is essential (see Ch. 12).

Xerostomia

Some chemotherapeutic drugs (eg. procarbazine) may adversely affect salivary flow. Initially salivation may be stimulated causing drooling and hypersalivation; subsequent changes may lead to inhibition of the acinar cells causing xerostomia and reducing the lubricating qualities of saliva so that it adheres to the mucosa and teeth making eating, swallowing and chewing difficult. Xerostomia may also interfere with chemical digestion and taste perception.

Xerostomia is also associated with other complications including increased dental caries and periodontal disease, mucositis, disturbed oral sensations and changes in taste sensation (eg. Holmes, 1991). As dryness of the mouth is distressing and uncomfortable, and can also limit the ability to communicate, its effects cannot be over-emphasised. Appropriate care is, therefore, vital to patient comfort and quality of life as well as in preventing additional complications.

Care of the patient with xerostomia

The patient should be taught to avoid trauma to the mucous membranes and to adopt measures which will maintain the moisture of the membranes and maintain or enhance protective mechanisms. An increased fluid intake, sipped frequently throughout the day, highly flavoured lozenges and sugar-free chewing gum will help to keep the membranes moist. Affected patients should be advised to avoid sugar, and sugar-containing products, since the combination of xerostomia and sucrose enhances the development of dental caries.

The role of normal saliva is important in controlling the balance of the oral flora; its absence significantly increases the risk of infection by permitting both the development of microbial plaque and the emergence of a highly cariogenic microflora. This explains the increased incidence of *candida albicans*, and other infections, seen in xerostomic patients and stresses the need for a regular and effective mouth care regime as previously described.

PHARYNGITIS

Mucositis may, at times, extend to include the pharynx and oesophagus causing extreme discomfort; on occasions it may be so severe as to necessitate discontinuation of the treatment to allow healing to take place. Pharyngitis is manifested by a sore throat, an irritant, hacking cough and varying degrees of dysphagia all of which may significantly affect food and fluid intake and influence the patient's willingness or ability to talk due to the discomfort this causes.

Treatment includes rest, a liquid or soft diet, aspirin or other analgesic agents and warm saline gargles. Alternatively throat irrigation may be more effective since gargling will not reach all parts of the pharynx and, by stretching the inflamed tissue, may increase discomfort by increasing tension and pain. Irrigation is achieved by attaching a rubber tube, to which an irrigating tip is attached, to an irrigation can filled with the desired solution heated to the appropriate temperature. This is then hung above the patient's head while the patient leans over a collecting basin so that fluid runs back out of the mouth. The nozzle is inserted into the mouth, without touching the base of the tongue or uvula (which will cause gagging), and, while holding the breath to prevent aspiration, the patient directs the solution so as to ensure that all parts of the throat are irrigated. The tubing must be clamped at intervals to enable the patient to breathe and rest since 1-2 litres of fluid are used. The irrigating solution may be normal saline, sodium bicarbonate or a mild antiseptic; sodium bicarbonate is particularly effective when secretions are tenacious. Solutions are used as hot as the patient can tolerate although they should never be hotter than 120°F (48.8°C).

Gargling and throat irrigations are soothing and will both aid comfort and help to loosen and remove secretions. They also increase the surface blood supply by causing local vasodilation. Local anaesthetics and antiseptics may also be applied using a throat spray.

Oral care is important in patient care and, as it is refreshing, will help to both to maintain comfort and to prevent drying and cracking of the lips and reduce the risk of secondary oral infection. Antitussive agents may be prescribed for the relief of the patient's cough.

OESOPHAGITIS

Oesophagitis should be considered if the patient complains of difficult or painful swallowing. It results from the effects of treatment on the rapidly dividing cells of the oesophageal mucosa causing inflammation (mucositis) and, in severe cases, ulceration that may be so severe as to necessitate the discontinuation of treatment until healing has taken place. It may also result from candidal infection. Even when the condition is not severe, it may be extremely uncomfortable and can significantly limit food and fluid intake.

Oesophagitis is manifested by:
- Sore throat

- Sensation of a 'lump' in the throat
- Difficulty in swallowing, particularly of solid foods (dysphagia)
- Pain on swallowing (odynophagia).

It may be accompanied by a severe and constant substernal pain that closely resembles that associated with myocardial infarction; this must be excluded before the diagnosis is confirmed. Once oesophagitis is confirmed the goals of care become:

1. Alleviation/minimisation of pain and discomfort.
2. Provision of optimal nutritional and fluid replacement.

Care of the patient with oesophagitis

Care is designed to prevent further irritation of the oesophageal mucosa so that, in the acute phase, a liquid diet is advised as this is less abrasive to the inflamed area. When solids can be tolerated, foods given should be bland and soothing; frequent small meals will help to prevent gastric distension and reduce gastric acid secretion.

Gastric reflux must be prevented and the irritating ability of the gastric juices decreased. Antacids will help to reduce gastric acidity and Gaviscon™, a mixture of alginic acid and aluminium hydroxide, is useful as it floats on the surface of the gastric acid pool reducing the movement of acid into the oesophagus. Although milk and milk products can be soothing high protein foods should usually be avoided during the acute phase as protein stimulates the production of gastrin thus increasing pressure on the cardiac sphincter and, in turn, increasing the risk of gastric reflux.

Foods that are soft and smooth will be easier to swallow; adding gravy or sauces can be helpful. Hot or spicy foods are best avoided; cold foods or those served at room temperature are recommended. Alcoholic or carbonated drinks may be irritant and acidic foods, such as citrus fruit or fruit juices, uncomfortable. Dry or hard foods (eg. biscuits, raw fruit and vegetables) may be difficult to swallow. However, as each patient is an individual he will identify those foods that are most acceptable.

Food brought in from home may be more appealing than mass-produced, hospital food and, as affected patients are at considerable nutritional risk, this should be encouraged where possible. A liquid nutritional supplement may be an appropriate adjunct to treatment, particularly when food intake is severely restricted; alternatively enteral or total parenteral nutrition may be needed (Ch. 12). Affected patients may require nutritional counselling from a dietician or nutrition nurse specialist.

Systemic analgesics, prior to meals, may provide general relief from oesophageal pain whilst liquid preparations, such as Mucaine™ or liquid aspirin solutions, may provide local relief.

Because the gag reflex may be decreased or absent a nurse or family member should always be present when the patient is eating so that swift action can be initiated should complications result. Certain general measures will, however, be valuable when caring for the dysphagic patient. These include:

1. Elevation of the head of the bed to reduce the risk of regurgitation and inhalation of the gastric content.
2. To reduce the risk of regurgitation still further, no food should be taken within 2-3 hours of going to bed.
3. Provision of a high energy, moderate protein, pureed or liquid diet which provides for all nutrient requirements including the trace nutrients (minerals and vitamins).
4. Where necessary, stagnating oesophageal content should be removed by careful lavage using a wide-bore tube. This is necessary to prevent inhalation during sleep, to reduce mucosal inflammation and to improve swallowing. Great care is required during this procedure to avoid further damage to the oesophageal mucosa.

Once the acute phase has subsided a high energy, high protein diet is essential to promote recovery and cellular regeneration. The importance of maintaining hydration and providing an adequate diet cannot be stressed highly enough

INDIGESTION, NAUSEA AND VOMITING

These unpleasant symptoms are commonly experienced by cancer patients; they may be extremely distressing and cause considerable discomfort. Although different, the similarities between them mean that it is convenient for these symptoms to be considered together.

Indigestion is the term used to describe a feeling of discomfort in the epigastric region or the back of the throat; it may be accompanied by heartburn, regurgitation of the acidic gastric contents, belching, distension and/or nausea. Nausea describes a feeling of discomfort, again in the back of the throat and the epigastric region, which frequently occurs in a wave-like fashion. It is often associated with the need to vomit and so often precedes vomiting. Nausea may be accompanied by pallor, cold clammy skin, hypersalivation, faintness, tachycardia and, occasionally, diarrhoea. It may also be associated with a decrease in gastric activity.

Vomiting is an involuntary reflex. It is a somatic response that involves forceful ejection of the contents of the stomach and, at times, those of the duodenum and jejunum, through the oral cavity. It is immediately preceded by a widespread autonomic reaction that results in rapid breathing, hypersalivation, dilation of the pupils, diaphoresis (sweating), pallor, and tachycardia; bradycardia is common during the process of vomiting (Nord and Sodeman, 1985).

It is not entirely clear why these symptoms arise during chemotherapy although, as is well-recognised, their occurrence is dependent on drug dosage, duration of therapy and individual response. Thus, when associated with chemotherapy, the degree and extent of vomiting are variable; they are also dependent on the emetogenic potential of the drugs administered (Table 11.2).

Table 11.2   Emetogenic potential of some chemotherapeutic agents

Mild	Moderate	Severe
Bleomycin	Anthracyclines	Actinomycin-D
Chlorambucil	Cytosine arabinoside	Carmustine
5-fluorouracil	Carboplatin	Cisplatin
L-asparaginase	Etoposide	Dacarbazine
Hydroxyurea	Hexamethylamine	Lomustine
Melphalan	Ifosfamide	High dose methotrexate
Methotrexate	Mitoxantrone	Mechlorethamine
Mitomycin-C	Nitrosoureas	High dose cyclophosphamide
6-mercaptopurine	Procarbazine	
Vinca alkaloids	Streptozocin	

Pathophysiological mechanisms

Nausea and vomiting follow stimulation of the vomiting reflex coordinated by the emetic centre located in the medullary lateral reticular formation of the brain (Figure 11.1). This receives afferent stimuli from four main sources: the chemoreceptor trigger zone (CTZ), the vestibular area, the cerebral cortex and limbic system and peripheral stimuli arising from the GI tract through the vagus nerve; stimuli transmitted by the vagus reach the brain through the nucleus of the solitary tract (NTS).

Figure 11.1   Schematic representation of the vomiting reflex

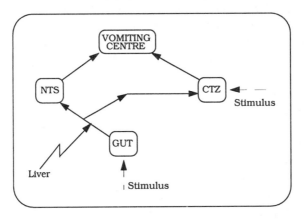

Physiological stimulation of both the emetic centre and the CTZ is thought to be mediated by a variety of neurotransmitters including acetylcholine, dopamine, histamine, serotonin and noradrenaline. Awareness of such factors forms the basis of many of the antiemetic therapies which are often designed to block neurotransmitter receptors thus inhibiting the mechanisms responsible for the initiation of at least some nausea and vomiting.

The CTZ, located in the area postrema of the IVth ventricle, is stimulated by specific drugs and chemicals and by cellular by-products present in the blood stream. It is believed that cells destroyed by anticancer drugs release toxic waste products that stimulate both the CTZ and the vomiting centre.

The vomiting centre thus receives stimuli from both the CTZ and the NTS; it may also be stimulated by afferent impulses arising in the vestibular area which transmits impulses to both the cerebellum and the emetic centre. This latter mechanism is primarily associated with motion sickness and is, therefore, believed to play little role in the nausea and vomiting induced by cancer chemotherapy.

Vagal stimuli may be initiated in the presence of GI pathology, such as inflammation, oedema or irritation of the GI tract. Thus nausea and vomiting may, in some cases, arise as secondary responses to other side-effects, such as mucositis.

The cerebral cortex and limbic system are stimulated by the senses, anxiety and pain as well as by increases in intracranial pressure (Yasko, 1985); they are also influenced by prior experiences. This mechanism is believed to be responsible for anticipatory and

201

conditioned psychological stimuli and is, therefore, the mechanism that causes the patient to become nauseated at the sights, sounds and smells associated with the hospital *per se* or other factors associated with drug administration. Such effects are particularly likely if the patient has previously associated chemotherapy with these symptoms. Indeed, a number of studies have suggested a psychological component of chemotherapy-induced nausea and vomiting (eg. Morrow, 1984; Rhodes et al, 1986), particularly with anticipatory symptoms; this suggests a conditioned response.

Anticipatory nausea and vomiting are usually experienced on the day preceding drug administration although they may start on entering the hospital. Morrow and Rosenthal, (1996) reported that 25% of patients will experience anticipatory nausea and vomiting by their fourth cycle of treatment. Such symptoms have been associated with a variety of factors such as susceptibility to motion sickness, age (50yrs or less) and post-treatment responses to prior chemotherapy (eg. Rhodes et al, 1986; Coons et al, 1987; Headly, 1987).

Types of emesis
Acute chemotherapy-induced emesis
For most previously untreated patients nausea and vomiting typically arise between 90 minutes and 3 hours after chemotherapy has been administered and persist for 2-6 hours (Gralla and Axelrod, 1990). Such effects are, undoubtedly, dose-related. Important exceptions to this are intravenous carboplatin or cyclophosphamide following which vomiting occurs 9-18hrs after the start of therapy.
Delayed chemotherapy-induced emesis
Delayed emesis is most commonly associated with highly emetogenic drugs (Table 11.2), especially high-dose cisplatin (at doses greater than 100mg/m^2) (Gralla and Axelrod, 1990). Although nausea and vomiting may be well-controlled during the immediate post-therapy period, they may arise 1-4 days later. Delayed emesis is usually less severe than that arising acutely but it may, nonetheless, result in considerable discomfort and interfere with appropriate nutrition.
Anticipatory emesis
Anticipatory symptoms (see above) are often the result of poorly-controlled emesis during prior therapy and are most commonly associated with highly emetogenic chemotherapy (Table 11.2). They are learned (conditioned) responses to something that is associated with the true stimulant. Learned stimuli thus include the thoughts,

202

sights, tastes and odours associated with therapy. Because such symptoms are learned responses they occur after the first dose of chemotherapy has been given, especially when vomiting has not been controlled effectively; they may increase with successive cycles. This highlights the need for effective emetic control during the early stages of therapy.

Non-chemotherapy-induced emesis

Although nausea and vomiting can often be attributed to therapy such symptoms may arise independently of treatment. Associated causes may include fluid and electrolyte imbalances, cerebral or hepatic metastases, uraemia, intestinal obstruction, infection or septicaemia. Other medications (eg. opiates, antibiotics, bronchodilators) and other conditions, such as gastritis, may also be contributory factors (Gralla and Axelrod, 1990) (Table 11.3). Such causes may require a different approach to management so that the cause must be clearly established before treatment is instigated.

Table 11.3   Causes of vomiting in the cancer patient

Fluid and electrolyte abnormalities
    eg. hypercalcaemia
       hypovolaemia
       water intoxication
       adrenocortical insufficiency
Bowel obstruction
Peritonitis
Metastasis involving the central nervous system
    eg. brain
       meninges
Hepatic metastases
Renal dysfunction
Uraemia
Local infections/septicaemia
Iatrogenic factors
    eg. chemotherapy
       narcotics
       exposure to radiation
Psychogenic factors
    eg. fear and anxiety
       emotional responses to disease or treatment

Care of the patient suffering nausea and vomiting

Although there have been marked improvements in the management of chemotherapy-induced nausea and vomiting these symptoms continue to cause considerable distress for significant numbers of patients and may necessitate marked changes in the normal patterns of activity (Craig and Powell, 1987). Their frequency, duration and severity are subject to considerable individual variation. The severity and likelihood can be exacerbated by various factors including the nature of drugs(s) prescribed, the treatment schedule and a poor nutritional status.

Nausea and vomiting will interfere with normal nutrition and, if prolonged, compromise nutritional status causing weight loss and malnutrition. They may lead to dehydration through fluid loss or a failure to maintain fluid intake and, together with a loss of gastric secretions, cause fluid and electrolyte imbalance. Control of nausea and vomiting is, therefore, essential to enhance both physiological and psychological comfort, prevent malnutrition and dehydration, maintain mobility and eliminate fatigue; appropriate care may enable therapy to be continued.

The care required includes both medication to alleviate the symptoms and supportive measures; nutritional status must be carefully monitored (p229-238). Close observation and assessment are valuable in preventing both indigestion and nausea, particularly when they are, for example, associated with ingestion of certain foods or drugs that may be withheld. Specific factors aggravating nausea and vomiting include:

1. Food and drink.
2. Movement or position change.
3. The mention or sight of chemotherapeutic drugs.
4. Equipment (eg. syringes).
5. Specific odours (eg. antiseptics).

Measures appropriate in the management of indigestion and nausea vary depending upon the individual concerned. Certain general principles can, however, be applied.

1. Ensure that patients are aware that such symptoms may arise as a result of treatment and do not, of necessity, indicate further spread of the disease. Stress that they are not inevitable and their occurrence is subject to considerable individual variation; not all patients are affected.
2. Record the onset, duration and intensity of symptoms. Identify any aggravating factors.
3. Explore remedies that have previously been found helpful

in relieving of indigestion and/or nausea. Are they appropriate for use in the current situation?

4. Encourage the regular use of prescribed antiemetics. Such drugs appear to be more effective when taken regularly to maintain optimal blood levels; a prophylactic approach to such therapy is recommended. Antiemetics, given 30-60 minutes before therapy and every 4hrs for at least 24hrs thereafter, may help to minimise nausea and vomiting. The response to any interventions employed must be carefully evaluated.

5. Encourage affected patients to rest in a comfortable position, where possible in a quiet and peaceful environment. Ensure that the environment is clean, comfortable and odour-free; nausea can be triggered by unpleasant sights and smells.

6. Have a vomit bowl nearby but out of sight of the patient It must, however, be recognised that some patients may prefer this to be visible and readily available.

7. Provide fresh air by enabling the patient to rest near an open window or even, weather permitting, out of doors.

8. Encourage the patient to experiment with different foods served at different temperatures until acceptable foods are identified.

9. Use distraction techniques to reduce feelings of nausea. Listening to music, a favourite television programme or talking to members of the health care team, relatives or friends can all provide distraction.

Behavioural techniques (eg. hypnosis, progressive muscle relaxation and guided imagery (visualisation)) have all been used in attempts to reduce nausea and control vomiting, particularly that associated with cancer chemotherapy (Redd and Hendler, 1983). However, their use is controversial and so is often discouraged, perhaps because they are not really understood. When used by a properly trained and prepared member of the health care team they are not harmful and may provide the patient with a sense of control over his symptoms. Such techniques are, however, time-intensive and require a one-to-one approach; this may explain why they are only rarely used within the National Health Service care provision. They are, however, widely used by many of the so-called 'alternative' practitioners.

Gastrointestinal side-effects

When vomiting is the prevalent symptom additional interventions and observations may be required:

1. The frequency of vomiting, as well as the amount and type of vomit, must be carefully monitored.
2. An accurate fluid balance chart must be maintained and the patient carefully observed for signs of dehydration and electrolyte imbalance (Table 11.4).
3. The patient should be encouraged to refrain from eating whilst vomiting persists. Advise the patient to drink as much as possible sipping liquids slowly.
4. Frequent mouth care and mouthwashes must be offered to maintain comfort, particularly after vomiting.
5. Stay with the patient during episodes of vomiting thus providing both physical and psychological support.

When the condition is severe intravenous fluids may be necessary to replace electrolytes or to prevent or correct dehydration; total parenteral nutrition may be required (p244-246).

Table 11.4   Signs of dehydration (fluid deficit)

Thirst
Poor skin turgor
Dryness of skin and mucous membranes
Decreased salivation - oral discomfort (may interfere with speech)
Tongue dry and furrowed
Dysphagia - particularly of solid foods
Concentrated urine of a high specific gravity (>1030)
Constipation - production of hard, dry stools; faecal impaction
Eyes appear sunken
Elevated body temperature
Blood pressure and pulse volume normal in early stages
Apprehension, restlessness
Apathy, weakness, disorientation

LATE STAGES

Oliguria - may lead to acidosis
Eyes severely sunken
Blood pressure and pulse rate and volume fall
Coma

LABORATORY FINDINGS

Elevated haemoglobin
Elevated serum sodium (hypernatraemia)
Decreased serum potassium (hypokalaemia)

206

ANTIEMETIC THERAPY

Nausea and vomiting were once the most feared side-effect related to chemotherapy; for many years such symptoms were considered to be unavoidable and only partially alleviated by means of antiemetics. However, even today, despite significant improvements in antiemetic management, there is still considerable individual variation in both the incidence and severity of chemotherapy-induced nausea and vomiting; psychological effects may augment such effects. It may, therefore, take several attempts before a suitable and effective drug is identified for individual patients. At times, a combination of drugs, or an antiemetic with steroids, antihistamines or sedatives, is needed.

Many of the available antiemetics are dopamine-receptor antagonists (eg. substituted benzamides, butyrophenones and phenothiazines). Indeed, recognition of the major role of the dopamine receptor represented a major development in the management of chemotherapy-induced emesis and now enables highly emetogenic agents, such as cisplatin, to be given safely and humanely (Grunberg, 1997). Combined with steroids (eg. dexamethasone) and neuroleptics (eg. lorazepam) it enables antiemetic protection to be provided for 60-70% of those treated with cisplatin-based regimes (Kris et al, 1985).

Metoclopramide is a procainamide derivative that has both central and peripheral antiemetic actions. It is a dopamine blocker which acts on both the CTZ and the GI tract (Harrington et al, 1983) and increases gastric emptying and GI motility; it is also mildly antagonistic to serotonin and exhibits anticholinergic activity.

Side-effects include sedation, diarrhoea and extrapyramidal effects such as muscle twitching, ataxia and restless, together with agitation and anxiety (Table 11. 5). Such effects may be controlled, in part at least, by diphenhydramine (Tsavaris et al, 1991).

Table 11.5   Side-effects of dopamine antagonists

Hypotension	
Sedation	
Agitation	
Diarrhoea	
Extrapyrimidal effects such as:	Restlessness
	Akasthisia
	Oculogyric crises
	Torticollis

Gastrointestinal side-effects

Phenothiazines (eg. prochlorperazine, promethazine), once the most commonly used antiemetics, are also potent blockers of the dopamine receptors and selectively inhibit the CTZ; they also directly inhibit both the vomiting centre and autonomic effects from the vagus nerve. Some drugs [eg. chlorpromazine] may also have a tranquillising effect.

Phenothiazines are primarily administered orally but may also be given rectally (as suppositories) although the efficacy of this route has not been established. However, when oral preparations cannot be given (eg. when the patient is vomiting) and parenteral administration is inappropriate (eg. in outpatients), the rectal route may provide a suitable alternative. Side-effects are minimal but may include sedation, orthostatic hypotension and occasional extrapyrimidal effects; hypersensitivity may occur (Ch. 8).

Butyrophenones. Drugs from this group (eg. haloperidol) are potent inhibitors of the CTZ; they also block dopamine-mediated stimuli, decrease vestibular stimuli and exert anxiolytic activity. Since they are not associated with hypertension or cardio-respiratory effects such drugs are useful in elderly or debilitated patients. They may, however, cause insomnia and tolerance may develop after repeated doses (Grant, 1987).

Cannabinoids (delta-9-tetrahydrocannabinol), derived from marijuana, possess significant antiemetic properties, particularly against the nausea and vomiting associated with cancer chemotherapy (Sallan et al, 1980). They also produce an elevation of mood, sedation and a reduced recognition of pain together with an improvement in appetite all of which may be desirable in the cancer patient. However, cannabinoids are also associated with a variety of toxic effects including hallucinations, dysphoria and syncope and, on occasions, frank psychosis (Grant, 1987); depression of the immune system may also occur. These drugs must be used with extreme caution particularly in the elderly or debilitated patient. Their use is controversial and health care professionals must remember that the use of cannabis (marijuana) *per se* is currently illegal in the UK.

Antihistamines [eg. cyclizine] are effective in decreasing vestibular stimuli and may help both to increase the effectiveness of antiemetics and decrease the incidence of toxic effects. Their action as histamine blockers may also decrease GI-vagal stimuli. Their effects are, however, generally inferior to those of the phenothiazines in controlling chemotherapy-induced vomiting (Frytak and Moertel, 1981).

5-HT$_3$ antagonists. Antiemetic therapy has improved significantly in recent years due largely to the introduction of 5-hydroxy-tryptamine receptor antagonists, particularly when they are used in conjunction with corticosteroids (Latreille et al, 1995). Serotonin (5-hydroxytryptamine (5-HT)) is an important neurotransmitter, the highest concentration of which is found in the enterochromaffin cells of the intestinal tract.

Several of these drugs (eg. ondansetron, granisetron, tropisetron) have been shown to possess antiemetic effects that are superior to or at least equivalent to high dose metoclopramide with only few, insignificant side-effects (Marty et al, 1990) and, when combined with dexamethasone, are particularly effective in treating acute emesis (Bleiberg, 1996). They are less effective in controlling delayed emesis occurring 24hrs or more after the administration of chemotherapy (Bleiberg, 1996; Grunberg, 1997).

5-HT$_3$ antagonists have been shown to be effective in controlling the vomiting associated with a wide-range of anticancer drugs (eg. Green et al, 1988; Marschner et al, 1988). They may be given orally or intravenously as either a single dose or a continuous infusion. Studies have shown that oral administration of bioequivalent doses is generally as effective as intravenous preparations (eg. Fraschini et al, 1991). This has significant advantages.

Although the use of such drugs involves considerable cost, oral administration may reduce the need for hospitalisation or the use of hospital supplies. They may, therefore, be of particular value in the outpatient setting and for those cared for at home (Grunberg, 1997); they may also help to reduce the occurrence of anticipatory nausea and vomiting in subsequent cycles of chemotherapy.

The prevention of delayed-onset emesis also requires some consideration. It is suggested that this is best achieved using dexa-methasone routinely over the first 3-5 days, particularly with high-dose chemotherapy regimes (Warr, 1997). Evidence suggests that a dopamine-receptor antagonist (eg. metoclopramide) may improve the efficacy of dexamethasone in controlling this distressing symptom.

Steroids. Although the mechanism of action is unknown, cortico-steroids may be used as antiemetic agents. Long-term use, however, is undesirable due to their adverse effects on the immune system and the risk of Cushing-like symptoms.

The most effective glucocorticoid used as an antiemetic is dexa-methasone which can control chemotherapy-induced emesis in the majority of patients; methylprednisolone is also used although it is only moderately effective.

Interventions related to food and drink

Some patients experience symptoms that may, temporarily at least, be refractive to pharmacological intervention. When this occurs food and drink should not be given enterally. Intravenous hydration should be commenced or increased to compensate for GI losses. Serum electrolytes should be carefully monitored; deficits must be corrected; parenteral nutrition may be necessary (p244-246). Undernoursihed patients - and children whose growth and development depend on an adequate nutrient intake - are of particular concern in this regard.

For those patients whose symptoms are less extreme, a number of measures can be attempted. However, acceptable foods and drinks will vary from patient to patient so that an individual approach to care is essential. Several general principles may, however, be useful:

1. Encourage the patient to experiment with eating patterns or types of foods in an attempt to reduce nausea and vomiting, For example he may find it helpful to avoid eating or drinking for 1-2 hours prior to chemotherapy and for up to 2 hours after administration. Alternatively, restricting the intake to clear fluids only both before and after chemotherapy may be helpful.
2. Ensure that antiemetic drugs are taken as prescribed.
3. Avoid fatty, spicy, highly salted or sweet foods as well as those with strong odours. Bland foods (eg. cottage cheese, mashed potatoes, eggs) may be better tolerated.
4. Ensure that food smells do not linger; the odour of hot food may aggravate nausea. Common examples of foods that may create such problems include: cooked cruciferous vegetables (eg. cabbage, cauliflower, broccoli), fish, strong cheeses and fried foods.
5. Foods which are cold, or are served at room temperature, are generally tolerated better than hot foods.
6. Eating solid foods alone may be better tolerated than when solids and liquids are combined.
7. Encourage the patient to eat and drink slowly taking small mouthfuls and ensuring that these are well chewed before they are swallowed.

8. A clear liquid diet may help to minimise nausea although this should not be adhered to for longer than 2-3 days. Fruit juices, clear soups and carbonated drinks may prove acceptable. Some patients find soda water, or a mixture of soda water and milk, has a settling effect.

9. Stressful stimuli may be reduced by manipulating the external environment to remove the sights, smells and sounds which may contribute to the condition.

It should again be emphasised that responses to treatment-induced nausea and vomiting are highly individual. Some patients are resilient and able to tolerate food shortly after the acute emetic period has passed; others experience considerable difficulty. The effects may be compounded by both physical and psychological factors.

EFFECTS ON THE SMALL INTESTINE
Diarrhoea
The intestinal epithelium is subject to continuous trauma during the normal processes of digestion and absorption. As a result, the cells of the intestinal mucosa are highly proliferative to replace cells lost from normal 'wear and tear'. These cells have a short life-span; the renewal rate is shortest in the small intestine (2 days) and longest in the distal part of the large intestine (2-6 days). Chemotherapy, by inhibiting normal cell replication, may disrupt cell replacement so that epithelial integrity is disturbed, the mucosa becomes inflamed and oedematous and the absorptive surface area is decreased. Such damage leads to mucosal irritability and, in turn, a rapid transit time potentiating nausea and vomiting, diarrhoea, abdominal distension, cramping, and flatulence.

Diarrhoea and cramping most often accompany therapy involving antimetabolites (such as cytosine arabinoside, 5-FU and methotrexate) as well as actinomycin-D, doxorubicin and hydroxyurea (Mitchell and Schein, 1982). The degree and duration of such symptoms depend on the drug, the dose schedule and duration of therapy. The most severe cases have been observed following sequential administration of high dose 5-FU and cytosine arabinoside; GI toxicity constitutes a major dose-limiting factor of these agents. In the absence of secondary infection, mucosal regeneration takes place about 2 weeks after therapy is completed or discontinued (McDonald and Tirumali, 1984).

However, not all the diarrhoea occurring in cancer patients is due to chemotherapy. Other causes include prior radiation to the abdo-pelvic region, concurrent antibiotic therapy, GI tumours, anxiety and stress, faecal impaction or intestinal infection; an inappropriate diet may also be a contributory factor. Malabsorption is also common due not only to diarrhoea but also to direct effects on the absorptive surface of the intestine the structure of which is designed to enhance absorption through its large surface area (Figure 11.2).

Figure 11.2   Diagrammatic representation of the intestinal villi

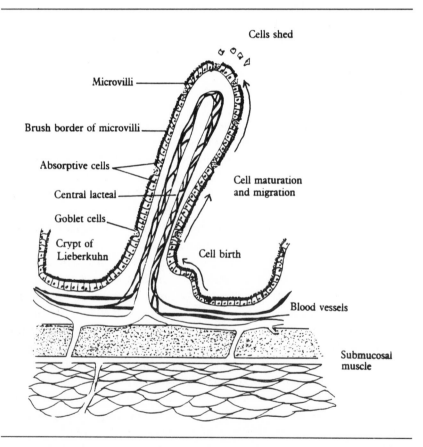

The villi and microvilli are responsible for both digestion and absorption since the microvilli produce many of the enzymes needed for digestion before nutrients can be absorbed by the villi. The epithelial cells of the villi divide rapidly and so are particularly vulnerable to the effects of chemotherapy becoming flattened and atrophic; the mucosa becomes ulcerated and the absorptive surface reduced. The composition and concentration of the intestinal enzymes are reduced so that neither food nor water can be adequately digested or absorbed exacerbating diarrhoea and compromising nutritional status. Recognition of the risk of malnutrition, effective monitoring and the instigation of appropriate preventive measures and/or nutritional support are, therefore, essential (Ch. 12).

Care of the patient with diarrhoea

Since diarrhoea is a symptom that can often be anticipated, particularly in those receiving antimetabolites, nitrosoureas and hydroxyurea, the patient must be informed of the likelihood of its occurrence so that it is not perceived as an exacerbation of his disease. Diarrhoea is a debilitating and distressing side-effect that may significantly alter his pattern of activity; comprehensive supportive care may be needed.

As in all areas of care, a thorough assessment is needed before treatment to provide a baseline against which to judge the extent and severity of diarrhoea. This should be designed to establish the usual pattern of elimination, the current nutritional status and the patient's usual coping strategies so that he can be helped to come to terms with his symptoms.

The patient should be instructed to keep a record of the frequency and characteristics (colour, odour, consistency, quantity) of any diarrhoea and to report its occurrence to a member of the caring team. Stools should be observed for the presence of blood; description of any associated pain should be obtained. Such factors can help in determining the cause of diarrhoea. Once the aetiology is known, it is possible to develop appropriate plans for management. Appropriate antidiarrhoeal medication can help to reduce the symptoms and relieve abdominal cramping. Various drugs may be given to reduce inflammation. Drug effectiveness must be monitored; adjustments are made to the therapeutic regime as required.

When diarrhoea is severe or intractable care should be directed towards reducing bowel activity. Bedrest is often required although this can be difficult to achieve in the presence of diarrhoea; hospitalisation may be needed. Bedrest, particularly in the debilitated patient, carries the risk of pressure sores so that pressure area care is essential, particularly with regard to the anal area which may be inflamed, sore and excoriated from diarrhoea and accidental leakage. Loss of bowel control can be very embarrassing and stressful for the patient who may, for example, need a bedpan at meal times when others are eating when he may be concerned about his 'antisocial behaviour'. Distress is increased if a bedpan is not available and soiling of the bed results. This may be interpreted as a return to childhood leading to a loss of self-esteem; considerable emotional support and reassurance may be required; sensitive care can help to reduce these concerns.

The nurse's attitude is particularly important as the patient may be sensitive and require reassurance that giving and clearing bedpans and changing beds are something which nurses expect to do rather than an unpleasant chore. A clean, covered bedpan or commode can be left at the bedside to reassure the patient. An air freshener should be available.

Losses of large amounts of fluid may result in dehydration and electrolyte imbalance (Table 11.4); accurate records of fluid balance must be maintained and the patient closely observed for signs of toxicity. He should be encouraged to drink at least 3 litres/day and should be advised not to restrict this to water but to consume other liquids (eg. fruit juices, clear soups) to increase his potassium and sodium intake. Carbonated drinks, unless allowed to 'go flat', should not be encouraged, as they may exacerbate diarrhoea. As extremes of temperature may aggravate diarrhoea, fluids should be served at room temperature.

Electrolyte balance must be closely monitored and losses, especially of potassium and sodium, replaced early. This can, initially, be achieved by including foods/drinks high in potassium in the diet (eg. baked potatoes, bananas, orange juice) or by potassium supplements. Intravenous replacement are given when necessary, using saline solutions with added potassium. If intravenous feeding must be continued for longer than 72 hours, 3% amino acid solutions should be given to prevent protein catabolism particularly when food intake is restricted. On occasions, complete bowel rest may be required; total parenteral nutrition (TPN) may be needed (p244-246). For others, a liquid diet can be helpful; low osmolality, low residue nutritional formulae may help maintain the nutrient intake but, again, TPN may be required when malabsorption is present and

214

weight loss continues.

When an oral diet can be tolerated this should be high in both protein and carbohydrate and should leave very little residue in the intestinal tract. Foods that are either irritant or stimulating to the GI tract should be avoided and soft, bland, easily digestible foods selected. The diet suggested in Table 11.5 is appropriate.

Table 11.5   Diet suitable for the patient with severe diarrhoea

	Permitted	Not allowed
Meat, fish, eggs, poultry, meat substitutes	Any meat, poultry or fish, eggs, cottage cheese, hard cheese.	Fried meats or sausages. Dried peas, beans and legumes. Nuts and seeds.
Dairy products: milk, cheese, yoghurt	Milk, cottage cheese, hard, cheese, yoghurt - without fruit.	Yoghurt with fruit.
Breads and cereals	White bread or rolls, cream crackers, water biscuits, rusks, plain biscuits, rice, pasta, corn, well-cooked oatmeal.	Wholegrain cereals and bread, wholemeal pasta, cereals with dried fruit and/or nuts.
Vegetables	Potatoes without skin, asparagus, green beans, squash or marrow, carrots.	Other vegetables, dried beans, peas, nuts, seeds, peanut butter (crunchy).
Fruit	Bananas, apples (in any form, cooked or raw), grape juice and other fruit juice (strained). Avocados.	All other fruit.
Desserts	Any desserts without fruit, seeds or nuts (eg. milk puddings, egg custards, ice creams, sponge puddings).	Fruit, nuts and seeds other than those identified.
Soups	Creamed or clear soups not based on vegetables.	Vegetable soups except those made with permitted vegetables.
Snacks	Plain biscuits, potato crisps, pretzels and rice snacks.	Nuts and seeds. Popcorn.
Drinks	Any drinks other than those listed in the next column.	Coffee, hot chocolate, beer, liquor, carbonated drinks.

For some patients, however, milk/milk products should be avoided as they may exacerbate diarrhoea. This is due to the effects on the GI mucosa which may affect the concentration of the digestive enzymes inducing an absence of lactase, the enzyme necessary for digestion of milk, causing lactose intolerance (Hyams et al, 1982). Undigested lactose ferments in the intestine causing distension, flatulence and severe cramping. Affected patients may, however, be able to tolerate yoghurt and other fermented milk products since lactose may be destroyed by the action of lactobacilli, the microorganism used to promote fermentation. Milk substitutes and non-dairy creamers can be used to make food and drinks more palatable. When required, low osmolality, lactose-free nutritional supplements can be given.

Mucosal irritation must be carefully assessed and perianal care meticulous to prevent the occurrence of secondary, opportunistic infection and to aid patient comfort and help to prevent the development of pressure sores. Anal irritation can be reduced by use of a topical anaesthetic but, when this is ineffective, a low dose steroid may be prescribed. Since diarrhoea, and the concurrent debilitation, are exhausting frequent rest periods must be planned.

Constipation

Constipation describes the slow movement of faeces through the intestine which is associated with hard, dry stools that tend to accumulate in the descending colon where fluid absorption continues dehydrating the stools still further (Holmes, 1987). The frequency of defaecation is decreased and associated with undue straining and may leave the patient with a sensation of incomplete evacuation (Johnson and Gross, 1985). Constipation can cause considerable discomfort, abdominal pain and distension and a feeling of fullness. Headache, associated with anorexia, nausea and vomiting, is common. Such symptoms may, in turn, create nutritional problems, especially if abdominal pain and distension preclude oral intake.

Chemotherapy can cause constipation directly or indirectly. For example, adynamic ileus, constipation, colicky abdominal pain and distension are frequent complications of vinca alkaloid therapy and indicate drug-associated neurotoxicity. Symptoms may develop within 3 days of drug administration and may not resolve for 2-3 weeks. Older patients, and those receiving high-dose therapy, are most susceptible to such toxicities. Other chemotherapy-associated causes include diminished oral intake, use of opioid analgesia and anticholinergic medications prescribed as treatment for diarrhoea or emesis (McDonald and Tirumali, 1984). Similarly, environmental factors, such as a change in normal routines due to hospitalisation or attempts to use a bedpan, may also alter normal patterns of defaecation causing constipation.

Previous disorders, such as haemorrhoids, diverticular disease anal fissures, or perianal abscesses, can cause pain or difficulty with defaecation; affected individuals may ignore the need to defaecate. Still other conditions, such as neurological dysfunction, cerebral or spinal tumours or pelvic disease, may disrupt intestinal innervation thus giving rise to severe constipation.

Finally, constipation may be iatrogenic when it may be associated with both medical and surgical treatment or with hospitalisation *per se*. Other drugs that may be involved include antacids containing calcium and aluminium and many of the antidepressant, anaesthetic and anticonvulsant agents which act on the central nervous system or alter the transmission of nerve impulses. Constipation carries particular dangers for those patients who are either thrombocytopoenic or leucopoenic when straining at stool may, for example, increase intracranial pressure causing cerebral haemorrhage; areas of mucosa, torn on contact with hard dry faeces, may become infected resulting in the development of perianal or perirectal abscesses.

Constipation is an uncomfortable and distressing symptom so that, when it can be anticipated, every attempt should be made to prevent its occurrence by prophylactic means rather than employing methods of treatment once the condition has developed.

Care of the patient with constipation

A wide range of preparations are available, as both over-the-counter purchases and prescribable products, to treat constipation. These include bulk producers, stool softeners and lubricants, osmotic laxatives and chemical stimulants (Table 9.5). A range of suppositories and enemas may also be used to stimulate defaecation. Their use is not, however, generally recommended in cancer, particularly in those who are myelosuppressed.

The emphasis should be on prevention rather than treatment of constipation. This should include:

1. Slow introduction of a high fibre diet. Provide, for example, wholegrain breads and cereals, fruit and vegetables, nuts and legumes.
2. Ensuring an adequate fluid intake (at least 3 litres/day).
3. Ensuring adequate physical activity, within the limits of the

general medical condition.

4. Where possible, encouraging the use of the toilet or a bedside commode; avoid the use of bedpans. Ensure privacy.
5. Attempting to 'retrain' defaecation by encouraging defaecation at the same time each day.
6. Providing a hot drink approximately half an hour before 'planned' defaecation to stimulate the gastrocolic reflex.

Care should be taken in applying these principles to those with GI disease or intestinal obstruction. Patients should be closely monitored to ensure the success of the regime. Clearly, this regime involves the patient in his care and so can be used whether the patient be in hospital or at home. Its success is dependent on careful and thorough patient education.

REFERENCES

Bateman DN, Darling WM, Boys R, et al, 1989, Extrapyramidal reactions to metoclopramide and prochlorperazine, Quarterly Journal of Medicine **264**, 307-11.

Beck S, 1979, Impact of a systematic oral care protocol in stomatitis after chemotherapy, Cancer Nursing **2**, 185-9.

Bleiberg H, 1996, Antiemetic treatment: what have we achieved? Topics in Supportive Care in Oncology No. 20, pp9-10.

Campbell S, 1987, Mouth care in cancer patients, Nursing Times **83**, 59-60.

Coons H, Levanthal H, Nerenz D, et al, 1987, Anticipatory nausea and emotional distress in patients receiving cis-platin-based chemotherapy, Oncology Nursing Forum **14**, 31-8.

Cotanch P, Strum S, 1987, Progressive muscle relaxation as antiemetic therapy for cancer patients, Oncology Nursing Forum **14**(1), 33-7.

Craig JB, Powell BL, 1987, Review: the management of nausea and vomiting in clinical oncology, American Journal of Medical Science **293**, 34-44.

Daeffler R, 1980, Oral hygiene measures for patients with cancer, Cancer Nursing **3**, 347-56.

Dudjak LA, 1987, Mouth care for mucositis due to radiation therapy, Cancer Nursing **10**, 131-40.

Eilers J, Berger AM, Peterson MC, 1988, Development, testing and application of the oral assessment guide, Oncology Nursing Forum **15**, 325-30.

Fraschini G, Ciociola A, Esparza L, et al, 1991, Evaluation of three oral doses of ondansetron in the prevention of nausea and emesis associated with cyclophosphamide-doxorubicin chemotherapy, Journal of Clinical Oncology **9**, 1268-74.

Frytak S, Moertel CG, 1981, Management of nausea and vomiting in the cancer patient, Journal of the American Medical Association **245**, 393-6.

Gralla RT, Axelrod R, 1990, Treatment of emesis. In: MacDonald JS, Haller DG, Mayer RJ (Editors), Manual of Oncologic Therapeutics (Third edition), JB Lippincott Co., Philadelphia.

Green JA, Watkin SW, Hammond P, et al, 1988, The efficacy and safety of GR38032F in the prophylaxis of ifosfamide-induced nausea and vomiting, Abstracts of papers presented at the 13th Congress of the European Conference for Medical Oncology, Lugano, Switzerland. Produced by Glaxo.

Greenwald ES, 1973, Cancer chemotherapy (2nd Edition), Medical Examination Publishing Co., New York.

Grunberg SM, 1997, Innovative approaches in the treatment of emesis, Supportive Care in Cancer **5**, 9-11.

Harrington RA, Hamilton CW, Brogden RN, et al, 1983, Metoclopramide: an updated review of its pharmacological properties and clinical use, Drugs **25**, 451-94.

Headly J, 1987, The influence of treatment time on chemotherapy-induced nausea and vomiting, Oncology Nursing Forum **14**, 43-7.

Holmes S, 1987, Disturbances of the nutrient supply. In: Boore JRP, Champion R, Ferguson MC (Editors), Nursing the Physically Ill Adult, Churchill Livingstone, Edinburgh.

Holmes S, 1991, Oral complications of specific anticancer therapy, International Journal of Nursing Studies **28**, 343-60.

Holmes S, 1996, Radiotherapy: A Guide for Practice, Asset Books, Leatherhead.

Hyams JS, Batrus CL, Grand RJ, et al, 1982, Cancer chemotherapy-induced lactose malabsorption in children, Cancer **49**, 646-50.

Johnson BL, Gross J, 1985, Handbook of Oncology Nursing, John Wiley and Sons, New York.

Kris MJ, Gralla RJ, Clark RA, et al, 1985, Consecutive dose-finding trials adding lorazepam to the combination of metoclopramide plus dexamethasone: improved subjective effectiveness over the combination of diphenhydramine plus metoclopramide plus dexamethasone, Cancer Treatment Reports **69**, 1257-62.

Latreille J, Stewart D, Laberge F, et al, 1995, Dexamethasone improves the efficacy of granisetron in the first 24h following high dose cisplatin chemotherapy, Supportive Care in Cancer **3**, 307-13.

Lockhart PB, Sonis ST, 1979, Relationship of oral complications to peripheral blood leukocyte and platelet counts in patients receiving cancer chemotherapy, Oral Surgery **48**, 21-8.

Marschner N, Nagel G, Bruntsch U, et al, 1988, Oral GR38032F as anti-emetic

219

prophylaxis in patients receiving cyclophosphamide-containing chemotherapy regimens, Abstracts of papers presented at the 13th Congress of the European Conference for Medical Oncology, Lugano, Switzerland. Produced by Glaxo.

Marty M, Pouillart P, Scholl S, et al, 1990, Comparison of the 5-hydroxy-tryptamine 3 (serotonin) antagonist ondansetron (GR38032F) with high dose metoclopramide in the control of cisplatin-induced emesis, New England Journal of Medicine **322**, 816-21.

McDonald GB, Tirumali N 1984, Intestinal and liver toxicity of antineoplastic drugs, Western Journal of Medicine **140**, 250-9.

McElroy TH. 1984, Infection of the patient receiving chemotherapy for cancer: oral considerations, Journal of the American Dental Association **109**, 454-6.

Mitchell EF, Schein PS, 1982, Gastrointestinal toxicity of chemotherapeutic agents, Seminars in Oncology **9**, 52-7.

Morrow GR, Rosenthal SN, 1996, Models, mechanisms and management of anticipatory nausea and emesis, Oncology **53**(Suppl 1), 4-7.

Morrow GR. 1984, Clinical characteristics associated with the development of anticipatory nausea and vomiting in cancer patients undergoing chemotherapy treatment, Journal of Clinical Oncology **2**, 1170-9.

Navazesh M, Ship II, 1983, Xerostomia: diagnosis and treatment, American Journal of Otolaryngology **4**, 283-92.

Nord NJ, Sodeman WA, 1985, The stomach. In: Sodeman WA, Sodeman TM (Editors), Sodeman's Pathologic Physiology: Mechanisms of Disease, WB Saunders Co., Philadelphia.

Overholser D, Peterson D, Williams L, et al, 1982, Periodontal infection in patients with acute nonlymphocytic leukaemia: prevalence of acute exacerbation, Archives of Internal Medicine **142**, 551-4.

Raybould TP, Ferretti GA, 1990, Oral care of the cancer patient. In: MacDonald JS, Haller DG, Mayer RJ (Editors), Manual of Oncologic Therapeutics (Third edition), JB Lippincott Co., Philadelphia.

Redd W, Anderson G, Minagawa R, 1982, Hypnotic control of anticipatory emesis in patients receiving chemotherapy, Journal of Counselling and Clinical Psychology **50**(3), 14-9.

Redd WH, Hendler CS, 1983, Behavioural medicine in comprehensive cancer treatment, Journal of Psychosocial Oncology **1**, 3-17.

Rhodes V, Watson P, Johnson M, 1986, Association of chemotherapy-related nausea and vomiting with pre-treatment and post-treatment anxiety, Oncology Nursing Forum **13**, 41-7.

Rhodes VA, Watson PM, Johnson MH, 1985, Patterns of nausea and vomiting in chemotherapy patients: preliminary study, Oncology Nursing Forum **12**, 42-8.

Sallan SE, Cronin C, Zelen M, Zinberg NE, 1980, Antiemetics in patients receiving chemotherapy for cancer, New England Journal of Medicine **302**, 135-8.

Sallan SE, Cronin CM, 1985, Nausea and vomiting. In: DeVita VT, Hellman S, Rosenberg SA (Editors), Cancer: Principles and Practice of Oncology, JB Lippincott Co., Philadelphia.

Shafer WG, Hine MK, Levy BM, 1974, A Textbook of Oral Pathology (Third edition), WB Saunders Co., Philadelphia.

Sonis AL, Sonis ST, 1979, Oral complications of cancer chemotherapy in pediatric patients, Journal of Pedodontics **3**, 122-8.

Sonis ST, Sonis AL, Lieberman A, 1978, Oral complications in patients receiving treatment for malignancies other than of the head and neck, Journal of the American Dental Association **97**, 468-72.

Sonis ST, 1983 Epidemiology, frequency and distribution, mechanisms and histopathology. In: Peterson DE, Sonis ST (Editors), Oral Complications of Cancer Chemotherapy, Martinuus Nihjoff, The Hague.

Trowbridge J, Carl W, 1975, Oral care of the patient having head and neck irradiation, American Journal of Nursing **75**, 2146-9.

Tsavaris N, Zamanis N, Zinelis A, et al, 1991, Diphenhydramine for nausea and vomiting related to cancer chemotherapy with cisplatin, Journal of Pain and Symptom Management **6**(8), 461-5.

Warr D, 1997, Standard treatment of chemotherapy-induced emesis, Supportive Care in Cancer **5**(1), 12-6.

Weisdorf DJ, Bostrum B, Raether D, et al, 1989, Oropharyngeal mucositis complicating bone marrow transplantation: prognostic factors and the effect of chlorhexidine mouth rinses, Bone Marrow Transplantation **4**, 89-95.

Wiley S, 1969, Why glycerol and lemon juice? American Journal of Nursing **69**, 343-4.

Yasko JM, 1985, Holistic management of nausea and vomiting caused by chemotherapy, Topics in Clinical Nursing **7**, 26-38.

CHAPTER 12   NUTRITIONAL CARE OF THE CHEMOTHERAPY PATIENT

The nutritional condition of a cancer patient undergoing chemotherapy is affected by both the disease and its treatment. Thus nutritional care cannot be discussed without first considering the nutritional effects of cancer itself (see Holmes and Dickerson, 1988). The effects of chemotherapy may exacerbate nutritional decline.

NUTRITIONAL EFFECTS OF MALIGNANCY

Malnutrition affects 40% of those hospitalised for cancer treatment (Landel et al, 1985); it is associated with varying degrees of weight loss, a poor prognosis, a reduced response to therapy, prolonged or enhanced morbidity of therapeutic side-effects and reduced quality of life. Weight loss may arise even before the diagnosis is confirmed and is often one of the most disabling aspects of cancer leading to distressing and potentially life-threatening symptoms (eg. secondary infection). It occurs at different stages in the disease and does not directly correlate with the histological type or site of the tumour, the extent of metastasis, duration of disease or food intake. Weight loss leads to marked decline in muscle mass and body fat leading to wasting and physical weakness and provoking anxiety for patients and carers. This condition is known as cancer cachexia, the term 'cachexia' being derived from the Greek 'kaxos' and 'hexis' (poor condition). It appears to result from two opposing effects: the host's attempt to isolate and 'starve' the tumour and an attempt by the tumour to alter host metabolism so as to satisfy its needs (Laviano et al, 1996).

A number of symptoms characterise cachexia including anorexia, early satiety, marked weight loss, muscle weakness, anaemia and oedema (Langstein and Norton, 1991) which result from the cumulative effects of various factors including alterations in the energy demand and disturbances of carbohydrate, protein and fat metabolism. Combined with the primary symptoms, these exacerbate nutritional decline. For example, malabsorption may potentiate nutrient deficiency while pain, depression, fatigue and other symptoms, may potentiate anorexia; treatment-induced effects may exacerbate this still further. Thus the onset of cachexia may

222

negatively affect both the quality and the length of life. It also accounts for more than 20% of all cancer deaths which are directly attributable to malnutrition and tissue wasting (Daly et al, 1992).

In view of the significant morbidity and mortality associated with cachexia considerable research has been devoted to attempts to identify ways of overcoming it . Better understanding and reversal of its deleterious effects would not only improve well-being but also life expectancy in many patients (Gelin and Lundholm, 1992). Yet malnutrition can often be avoided (Shils, 1977) and, as cancer is often a chronic disease, emphasises the need for nutritional support to be initiated early in the disease process; it is easier to prevent malnutrition than to rehabilitate the already malnourished. The short-term benefits of nutritional care may markedly improve the quality of life (Torosian et al, 1983; Holmes and Dickerson, 1991).

PATHOPHYSIOLOGY OF MALNUTRITION

The development of malnutrition is complex (Table 12.1) and both cancer itself and its treatment may be contributory factors. Its extent is also influenced by the location of the tumour; malnutrition is more common with tumours at specific sites (eg. head and neck, GI tract, central nervous system and lung (Ollenschlager et al, 1988)). The incidence varies from approximately 9% in breast cancer to 80% in oesophageal tumours (Larrea et al, 1992). However, no patient and no tumour are excluded.

Table 12.1   Factors contributing to malnutrition in cancer patients

Metabolic disorders - altered metabolism of fat, protein, carbohydrate, vitamins, minerals and electrolytes
Anorexia
Taste aberrations
Dysphagia
Malabsorption
Food aversion
Early satiety
Emotional/psychological consequences of disease and treatment
Treatment-induced side-effects

Protein-energy malnutrition (PEM) is the most common form of malnutrition arising when dietary protein and energy intake are insufficient to meet individual needs. An inadequate intake leads to depletion of body stores to meet the nutrient demand; fat and protein are catabolised to provide energy leading to a loss of both subcutaneous fat and muscle mass. Visceral proteins (eg. serum albumin) are also depleted. However, in cancer, PEM reflects not only reduced consumption but also an increased demand for nutrients. Tumours may act as 'parasites' drawing nutrients from the host. When dietary intake fails to meet the nutrient demands of both host and tumour, body stores are catabolised and weight falls. Yet Morrison (1976), argued that 'normal' individuals increase their intake when energy requirements are increased. Clearly, this does not occur in cancer and food intake does not keep pace with nutrient needs. Indeed, some patients fail even to maintain their current weight, despite intakes of 3-4000kcal/day (Heber et al, 1985).

Thus, in the absence of obvious causative factors, such as co-existent endocrine disorders or sepsis, it seems that malignancy *per se* induces profound nutritional abnormalities. These are manifested by significant metabolic changes (Table 12.2) resulting in an increased demand for energy and leading to depletion of body protein (from muscle) and fat (from subcutaneous tissue). Although anorexia may contribute to body tissue depletion it is quite clear that inadequate food consumption alone cannot account for these effects; other factors must also contribute to their development.

Table 12.2   Examples of the metabolic changes which may be associated with cancer

Metabolic change	Effect	Manifestations
↑ energy expenditure	↑ energy demand ↑ basal metabolic rate ↑ protein catabolism	Weight loss Loss of subcutaneous fat Loss of body protein Muscle weakness
Alterations in glucose metabolism	Impaired glucose tolerance ↑ anaerobic glycolysis ↑ gluconeogenesis ↓ sensitivity to insulin ↓ energy production	Hyperglycaemia Protein depletion → muscle weakness
↓ protein synthesis		Protein depletion → muscle weakness Immunodepression
↑ fat catabolism		Loss of subcutaneous fat Decrease in total body fat Weight loss

Possible mechanisms of metabolic change

Even when adequate nutrients are supplied, nutritional support often fails to replenish body stores (Espat et al, 1995). Research indicates that some tumours produce substances that induce metabolic derangements. Beutler and Cerami (1986) were among the first to suggest that the immune system may be significant in mediating such effects. Later evidence (Moldawer et al, 1992) suggests that abnormalities are primarily due to host-derived cytokines, such as tumour necrosis factor (TNF), interleukin-1 (IL-1), interleukin-6 (IL-6) and interferon-γ (IFNγ). These cytokines, produced by the immune system, act at multiple target sites (eg. bone marrow, adipocytes, hepatocytes and neurones) to produce complex biological responses that may ultimately lead to the development of cachexia.

Progressive malignancy is also known to be accompanied by an acute phase response (Cooper and Stone, 1979) similar to that evoked by other tissue injuries (eg. inflammation or sepsis) which can cause cachexia if prolonged and untreated (Gelin and Lundholm, 1992). The similarity in physiological responses suggests involvement of common mediator(s) such as the cytokines (eg. TNF). Although the effects of cytokines are primarily protective they may also exert adverse effects through both autocrine and paracrine actions (Figure 12.1). For example, IL-1 'activates' the immune system in response to exogenous stimuli but, when produced by tumour-infiltrating macrophages, stimulates the release of colony-stimulating factor-1 (CSF-1) from tumour cells (Evans et al, 1989).

Figure 12.1   The action of cytokines

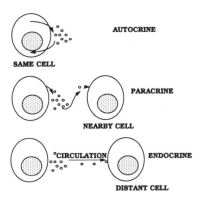

225

TNF induces anorexia and weight loss in animals (eg. Langstein and Norton, 1991) appearing to account for at least some of the wasting accompanying malignancy (Torti et al, 1985). TNF and IL-1 may, together, maintain tumour growth by stimulating neo-angiogenesis within cancer-bearing tissues (Moldawer et al, 1992); IL-6 potentiates anorexia (Busbridge et al, 1989). However, although IL-1 is known to contribute to the development of cachexia in some patients, it is unlikely to be the major cause (Fearon, 1992).

Fluid and electrolyte disturbances

Fluid and electrolyte disturbances are common; in advanced cancer, both intra- and extracellular water are increased thus masking body tissue loss. The value of body weight as an indicator of nutritional depletion therefore declines as the disease progresses. Hypo-natraemia and hypercalcaemia are the most common electrolyte disturbances. Indeed malignancy is the most common cause of hypercalcaemia in hospital patients. Complications of both the disease and its treatment may cause other electrolyte abnormalities and acid-base imbalance. Weight loss and hypercatabolism can stimulate sodium and potassium loss although serum levels remain in the normal range. Hypocalcaemia may arise in the presence of hypoalbuminaemia. Monitoring serum electrolytes is essential.

Impaired food intake

Food intake may be impaired by many factors (Table 12.1). The location of a tumour may affect ingestion, digestion or absorption and malignancy anywhere in the body may cause malabsorption through secondary intestinal changes (Wangel and Deller, 1966). Specific nutritional problems related to chemotherapy include nausea and vomiting (Ch. 11), anorexia, taste aberrations, stomatitis, pharyngitis (Ch. 7) and diarrhoea (Ch. 11).

Anorexia (Ch. 7) commonly compounds cancer-associated weight loss; various factors contribute to its development. For example, metabolic effects may generate spurious signals that are interpreted centrally as indicators of satiety (Mattes et al, 1987) so that the patient feels full whether or not he has eaten adequate amounts. Serotonin, and other neurotransmitters, have been the focus of most research in this area. For example, Krause et al (1979a; 1979b) have shown that cerebral serotonin levels correlate closely with the onset of anorexia. This, together with evidence that serotonin plays a role in generating satiety (eg. Lehr and Goldman, 1973; Kruk, 1976), suggests that it may be linked to the development of anorexia; others, however (eg. von Meyendfeldt et al, 1980), have shown that inhibiting serotonin synthesis does not eliminate anorexia; other mechanisms must also be involved. Although such work offers the possibility of clinical intervention to control anorexia, further work is required.

Behavioural and symptomatic factors: Although metabolic changes are clearly important contributors to malnutrition, the contribution of behavioural and symptomatic factors cannot be overlooked. For example, emotional responses may adversely affect appetite and there are times in the disease trajectory when patients are particularly vulnerable to emotional distress. Considerable stress is experienced before the diagnosis is confirmed. Confirmation may promote further emotional trauma; a weight loss of 5-10lbs is not unusual during this period, primarily due to psychological or emotional factors rather than to the disease itself (Holland et al, 1977).

Previous attitudes and beliefs about cancer and its treatment may combine with continued fear of recurrence, appearance of new symptoms (whether or not they are disease-related) and anxiety related to cancer treatments, contributing to the causation of anorexia (Schmale, 1979). Thus anorexia may be experienced as an emotional response throughout the course of the disease.

Similarly, depression may accompany continued progression of the disease and may provide a psychological basis for anorexia and would, therefore, be expected to improve with antidepressive therapy. However, anorexia is generally unresponsive to tricyclic drug therapy (Wesdorp et al, 1983) and, since Plumb et al (1976) showed that, although physical symptoms are common, non-physical signs of depression (eg. feelings of worthlessness, guilt, suicidal tendencies) are not significant, it is suggested that depression does not contribute significantly to its aetiology. In any case, Holland et al (1977) claim that symptoms suggestive of depression reflect the physical rather than the psychological condition.

Physical discomfort: Any type of physical discomfort may depress food intake; control of distressing symptoms is essential. Such discomfort may include the stomatitis, xerostomia, pain, nausea and vomiting or diarrhoea caused by chemotherapy.

Taste changes: Alterations in appetite and anorexia may both be attributable to taste change that, together with an altered sense of smell (anosmia), may lead to disinterest in food. Positive taste

227

experiences are important in triggering the physiological responses central to food ingestion and digestion. For example, the volume of salivary and gastric secretions depends, in part, on individual taste experiences. Thus, in the presence of taste changes, the taste stimulus may be inadequate to stimulate an appropriate physiological response thus contributing to malnutrition and weight loss (Ch. 7).

Learned Food Aversion (Ch. 7) is not uncommon and may play a major role in decreasing food consumption (eg. Bernstein and Bernstein, 1981; Leathwood et al, 1986).

Psychosocial factors influencing nutritional status

A number of psychosocial factors may be associated with nutritional depletion in cancer. For example, as has been shown, both emotional and behavioural factors may contribute to a reduced food intake. Similarly, depression may be accompanied by a marked decline in food consumption (Schmale, 1979). Social factors may also contribute to nutritional depletion (see below).

Hospital-related factors

Hospitalisation may, itself, adversely affect eating patterns due to the timing of meals and/or the types of food available as this may disrupt the patient's normal routine; cultural factors may influence the type(s) of food that patients are able/willing to eat. For example, if a patient's usual diet includes spicy or highly seasoned foods - and he is undergoing treatment that causes oral inflammation and pain - this may no longer be tolerated.

Eating behaviour is influenced by a wide variety of social, cultural, psychological and physiological factors (Novin and van der Weele, 1977) all of which may be disrupted by cancer or its treatment, compounding the nutritional problems to which affected patients are exposed. Eating is normally a social event but, in hospitals, there are rarely common eating places and patients may be left to eat in isolation, in bed or at the bedside, reducing social interaction. Food is often served in large, impersonal portions that seem to take no note of individual needs or requests. It is difficult to allow for individual likes and dislikes but, in cancer, a flexible and individual approach is essential if food intake and, therefore, nutritional status is to be maintained.

Some procedures can potentiate nutritional decline. For example, although investigations are essential in hospital care they may be associated with unnecessarily prolonged starvation; this may be extended by pre- and postoperative fasting. Missing meals is sometimes unavoidable but alternative provision must be made to ensure that food intake is maintained. However, administrative changes have made this more difficult (Garrow, 1994). Catering services may be provided on tightly controlled contracts; additional meals, or snacks, often require dietetic referral and hygiene regulations prohibit preparation or storage of food in ward kitchens. Thus those patients fasted overnight for diagnostic tests, and absent from the ward at lunch, may wait as long as 24hrs between meals. It is little wonder that patients often lose more weight in hospital (Garrow, 1994). This may be exacerbated when necessary assistance or feeding aids are not available to patients in need. The importance of attempting to overcome such difficulties cannot be overemphasised.

NUTRITIONAL MANAGEMENT OF THE CHEMOTHERAPY PATIENT

The preceding discussion shows that patients undergoing chemotherapy may have a compromised nutritional status before treatment begins and, as has been shown, many of its side-effects may have nutritional consequences and exacerbate malnutrition. In addition, many may have received prior therapy that may have long-lasting nutritional consequences (Table 12.3). Thus nutritional care is an essential part of the care of the patient undergoing active therapy to help them to cope and to enhance both the therapeutic response and the quality of life. It is clear that appetite and the ability to eat are important factors in determining the quality of life (Padilla, 1986).

Nutritional assessment

Although prevention of malnutrition must be the primary aim, nutritional care is often considered only after severe depletion is present. The initial care plan for all chemotherapy patients must include nutritional assessment both to determine the risk of nutritional depletion and to provide background data against which the severity of future changes can be assessed. Regular follow-up assessment should be carried out at least once a month even after nutritional support has been instigated. This enables care to be dynamic and responsive to the patient's changing needs.

The overall goals of such care are:
1. To prevent or correct nutritional deficiencies.
2. To prevent or minimise weight loss.

Table 12.3 Some treatment-induced nutritional effects

Surgery	Oropharyngeal	Chewing/swallowing difficulties. Dependence on enteral (tube) feeding.
	Oesophagectomy	Gastric stasis. Hypochorhydria. Diarrhoea/steatorrhoea.
	Gastrectomy	Achlorhydria and lack of intrinsic factor → vitamin B_{12} malabsorption. Hypoglycaemia. Dumping syndrome. General malabsorption.
	Intestinal: jejunal	Malabsorption.
	ileum	Vitamin B_{12} deficiency, bile salt deficiency; diarrhoea. Severe malabsorption.
	massive	Acidosis.
	Ileostomy/colostomy	Fluid/electrolyte imbalance.
Radiotherapy	General	Radiation syndrome. Anorexia.
	Head and neck	Altered taste sensation, xerostomia, damage to, or loss of, teeth; mucositis.
	Lower neck or mediastinum	Oeophagitis, pharyngitis, dysphagia; fibrosis, oesophageal stenosis or stricture.
	Abdomen/pelvis	Acute/chronic bowel damage, diarrhoea, malabsorption; intestinal fistulae, fibrosis or stenosis.
Chemotherapy		Anorexia, nausea and vomiting, diarrhoea or constipation; stomatitis or mucositis. Intestinal ulceration, malabsorption; fluid and electrolyte imbalance Nitrogen and calcium losses
	Corticosteroids	Hyperglycaemia

Nutritional assessment is the essential first step in care provision and is important for all patients whether in hospital or at home. This is the process through which the nutritional condition is established and represents the degree to which individual needs for nutrients are met by the nutrient consumption. If carried out effectively nutritional assessment helps to:

- Identify existing/potential problems
- Identify the cause of current problems
- Provide baseline data for subsequent assessment
- Determine the response to nutritional intervention.

Clinical observation, anthropometry, biochemical analyses and dietary evaluation are the general methods of assessment; this should also include socioeconomic and pyschosocial factors. Much of this information should be provided through a thorough medical and nursing assessment. Discussion with family and friends may provide valuable additional information. Current drug therapy should also be identified, including not only cytotoxic therapy but also vitamins and other 'over-the-counter' medicines and 'recreational' drugs (Holmes, 1986). Additional health problems (ie. diabetes mellitus or renal disease) must be recognised as these may also affect nutrition.

Clinical examination includes observation of the general condition and, with a complete physical examination, reflects overall nutritional status. Although the physical signs and symptoms of malnutrition may not be evident until the condition is advanced, weight loss, for example, may be visible to the naked eye. Particular attention should be paid to the skin, hair, mouth, teeth and general skin and muscle tone since they may provide evidence of nutritional deficiency. Common signs indicating malnutrition include: dry, flaky skin, dull or sunken eyes, oral lesions, muscle wasting or oedema; sparse or thin hair may also be evident. Psychosocial factors requiring consideration include levels of anxiety, fear or depression all of which may potentiate anorexia.

Anthropometric data, physical measurements reflecting nutritional status, are central to a physical examination (Table 12.4). Some, such as height, indicate past or chronic nutritional status while others (eg. triceps skinfold thickness (TSF), midarm circumference (MAC) reflect the current nutritional condition and are used to assess skeletal energy reserves. Such data is most useful when obtained over a period of time; the initial data provides an important baseline for subsequent assessment.

The degree of energy depletion is determined by the height:weight ratio, TSF and MAC. Weight and height are the most common measures of nutritional status but, because their importance is not recognised, they are often measured sloppily and inconsistently. Since weight loss is associated with increased morbidity and mortality in cancer the importance of accurate measurement cannot be overemphasised.

If weight is to be measured accurately patients should be weighed before breakfast and with an empty bladder. The same scales should be used, and the same clothes worn, each time a patient is weighed.

Table 12.4   Anthropometric measurements in nutritional assessment

	Purpose	Technique
Body weight	Provides basis for other anthropometric measures. Sum of all body constituents - repeated measures will indicate changes.	Use same scale, clothing and time of day. Empty bladder and bowel before weighing.
Height	Represents past (chronic) nutritional status. Used with weight to calculate ideal body weight.	See text.
Ideal body weight (IBW)	Once calculated provides an indication of nutritional status. A current weight 70-80% IBW indicates moderate malnutrition; <70% IBW = severe malnutrition.	Calculated from height and weight using standard tables.
Usual body weight (UBW)	Once usual body weight has been established it becomes possible to calculate the percentage weight change. Useful indicator of nutritional change.	$\% \text{ UBW} = \dfrac{\text{Current weight (kg)}}{\text{UBW (kg)}} \times 100$ $\% \text{ weight change} = \dfrac{\text{UBW (kg) - current weight (kg)}}{\text{UBW (kg)}} \times 100$
Midarm circumference (MAC)	Reflects body protein and fat content.	Measure circumference of upper arm at mid-point between acromial process of scapula and olecranon process of ulna using a non-stretch tape measure.
Triceps skinfold thickness (TSF)	Estimates subcutaneous fat and energy reserves.	Measure at same point as MAC using callipers. Take average of 3 readings. Ensure skin and fat lifted clear of underlying tissue prior to measurement.
Midarm muscle circumference (MAMC)	Provides further evidence with regard to body energy and protein reserves.	Estimated indirectly from MAC and TSF. MAMC = MAC (cm) - (3.142 x TSF (cm))
Arm muscle area (AMA)	Provides further evidence with regard to body energy and protein reserves.	$\text{AMA (cm}^2) = \dfrac{(\text{MAMC} - 3.142 \times \text{TSF})^2}{4 \times 3.142} - 6.25 \text{ (Females)}$ $\text{AMA (cm}^2) = \dfrac{(\text{MAMC} - 3.142 \times \text{TSF})^2}{4 \times 3.142} - 10.0 \text{ (Males)}$

[Note: These measurements provide only an approximate guide to changes in energy reserves. They are of most value when used to monitor patients over a period of time].

Height should be measured as described:
1. The patient should be barefoot or wearing only socks or stockings.
2. His feet should be together with heels against the wall or measuring board.

3. He should be standing erect, not slumped or stretching, and looking straight ahead.
4. A horizontal bar is then lowered to rest flat against the top of the head.
5. Height is read to the nearest 0.5cm.

To determine whether weight is appropriate for height this is compared with standard tables. However, such figures can be misleading if they are used to determine whether an individual is at some 'desirable' weight (Durnin and Fidanza, 1985) as the concept of 'ideal body weight' is derived from life assurance tables. Tables relating weight/height to mortality have limitations since the information is derived from a restricted, and possibly unrepresentative, sample of applicants for life assurance. It is also important to realise that, in cancer, the recorded body weight may be distorted by the presence of oedema, ascites or tumour mass. Nonetheless, when current weight is compared with the usual body weight (prior to diagnosis), this provides a guide to the degree of weight change; weight loss is *always* significant. It is also important to remember that, although the current weight may be appropriate for height, this may still be significantly below the usual weight. Estimation of percentage weight change is therefore a more sensitive indicator of tissue gain or loss.

Triceps skinfold thickness (TSF) provides a measurement of subcutaneous fat and, once measured, is compared with reference standard tables (see Goodinson, 1987a) (Figure 12.2). Because the amount of fat located in the subcutaneous tissues varies with age and sex it is important that tables used to evaluate skinfold measurements are age and sex specific. Midarm circumference (MAC) provides a sensitive indicator of lean body mass and, therefore, of skeletal protein reserves (Figure 12.3). When MAC and TSF are combined it is possible to obtain an even better assessment of energy and protein nutriture, through indirect determination of arm muscle and fat area.

The arm muscle area provides a good indication of the lean body mass and, therefore, skeletal protein reserves. This is particularly valuable in assessing patients who are likely to be protein-energy malnourished (such as cancer patients) (see Wright and Heymsfield, 1979; Gibson, 1990). Since changes in both fat and protein mass provide good indicators of nutritional change they should be studied at the initial assessment and serially to evaluate the nutritional changes resulting from cancer and its treatment.

233

Figure 12.2   **Measurement of triceps skinfold thickness**

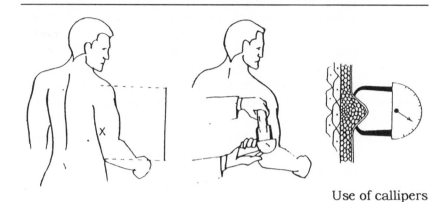

Use of callipers

Measured at a point over the triceps muscle midway between the acromium and olecranon process of the posterior aspect of the arm

Figure 12.3   **Measurement of midarm muscle circumference**

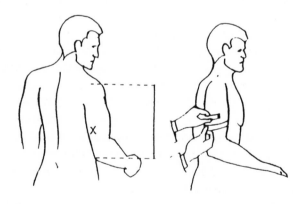

Identifying the mid-point   Measuring the circumference at the mid-point of the arm

Biochemical analyses provide important information and, as the most specific of all assessment techniques, can detect covert nutritional deficiencies. For example, serum albumin and transferrin are indicative of visceral protein levels; serum transferrin also reflects body protein synthesis. As hypoalbuminaemia is associated with an increased incidence of complications after cancer therapy, serum albumin can be used to identify vulnerable patients (eg. Kokal, 1985).

Immunocompetence is also significantly reduced by malnutrition. Cell-mediated immunity is particularly vulnerable. The total lymphocyte count reflects immunocompetence as well as visceral protein stores and is decreased in PEM. Skin sensitivity tests to recall antigens can be used to reflect T-cell-mediated immunity. When cell-mediated immunity is impaired, the response to antigens to which individuals have previously been exposed is diminished; there may be a complete lack of response (anergy). Daly et al (1979) have shown that those who are anergic have, on average, lost 20kg more than those individuals with a functioning immune system.

However, as concurrent disease and/or chemotherapy may also cause immunosuppression the value of these techniques in affected patients may be limited. Indeed, since metabolic changes are common, altered biochemistry may reflect the presence of malignancy itself rather than nutritional abnormalities. Nonetheless, when taken in conjunction with other measures of nutritional status, biochemical tests may be useful (see Goodinson (1987b).

Dietary evaluation may include both assessment of actual food and drink consumption and a history of prior intake and usual dietary habits. However, obtaining a dietary history is a difficult and often frustrating aspect of nutritional assessment as it is difficult to record food intake without influencing eating patterns although the extent of change depends on the understanding of the need for measurement and to what degree individuals are influenced by what they think staff want to know. An awareness of this risk is essential in assessing the data obtained. The most common methods of assessing food consumption are shown in Table 12.5.

Standard food tables can be used to establish actual nutrient consumption. Alternatively, the food group method (Table 12.6) can provide a crude measure of nutrient consumption; this will enable detection of gross deficiencies of protein, iron, calcium and some vitamins although this can be more difficult when the diet comprises many mixed or unusual foods that cannot be easily classified. It must, however, be recognised that the simple act of measuring food intake may markedly affect the amount and type of food consumed and the nutrient composition may be altered by the method of preparation and storage after cooking.

Table 12.5   Recording of dietary intake

	Method	Comment
24 hour recall	Interview/questionnaire designed to establish everything eaten in previous 24hrs and to obtain an estimate of the quantity.	Contains inherent sources of error due to difficulty of recalling everything that has been eaten; previous day's intake may not be typical; patient may not be telling the truth.
Food frequency questionnaire	Provides information on the frequency of consumption of individual foods (eg. how often they are eaten per day, week or month).	Can validate 24hr recall and clarify food consumption. May be selective looking at only areas believed to be deficient or global attempting to gain an overall impression of the diet.
Food diary	Patient records everything he eats/drinks over a defined period, usually 3-4 days. Often includes both week days and weekends.	Requires more time, understanding and motivation from the patient but, if recorded immediately after eating, provides accurate data. Problems include non-compliance, inaccuracy in recording or atypical intake on recording days.
Direct observation	Enables precise recording of food presented/consumed especially if food and waste are weighed. Should be as unobtrusive as possible; most easily achieved when meals provided for the patient.	The most time-consuming, expensive and difficult method of obtaining dietary data. When weighed intakes are required can lead to problems with patient compliance.

As a result, an accurate assessment of nutritional status relies on a combination of the methods described as it is neither possible nor accurate to judge the adequacy of the diet by looking at the intake alone. Serum and tissue levels of nutrients must also be evaluated and a thorough physical examination undertaken to assess the clinical evidence of a deficiency state.

A *dietary history* allows information regarding usual dietary habits to be obtained and should be a standard part of the assessment of every cancer patient. This can help to:

- Establish whether the diet is sufficient

Table 12.6   The basic food groups

	Number of servings per day	What is a serving?
Meat group	2 or more	2-3oz lean, cooked meat, poultry or fish 1 egg 4oz cooked, dried beans, peas or legumes 4 tbspns peanut butter
Milk group (adults)	2 or more	8oz milk - whole, skimmed, buttermilk or evaporated milk 1.5 oz Cheddar-type cheese 8 oz cottage cheese 6 oz yoghurt 6oz ice cream
Vegetable and fruit group	4 or more	6oz vegetable 1 apple, banana, potato ½ medium grapefruit or melon
	plus 1 or 2 (vitamin C)	Grapefruit, orange, orange juice Brussels sprouts Green peppers Melon/lemon Cabbage, cress, spinach, cauliflower Potatoes, sweet potatoes, yams Tomatoes
	1 at least every other day (vitamin A)	Dark green, yellow or orange vegetables and fruit (eg. carrots, pumpkin, spinach, sweet potatoes, squash or apricots)
Bread and cereal group	4 or more	1 slice of bread 1 oz cereal 4-6oz cooked cereal, pasta, or rice

- Determine food likes, dislikes and preferences
- Evaluate current and previous eating patterns
- Provide information about social and environmental factors influencing the ability to purchase, obtain or prepare food
- Allow factors inhibiting food consumption (eg. chewing, swallowing difficulties, anorexia, nausea, and vomiting, taste changes, oral discomfort) to be identified
- Identify concurrent illness (eg. diabetes or renal disease)
- Identify any dietary changes due to disease or treatment.

In obtaining such a history, discussion with family and friends may provide further useful information. A dietary history thus helps both to identify areas of difficulty for specific patients and to enable a nutritional care plan based on individual likes and dislikes, preferences and habits to be developed thus helping to increase the likelihood of compliance with any dietary regime. An alternative, and time-saving regime, is to give the patient a questionnaire to complete supplementing this with information derived from family and friends.

NUTRITIONAL SUPPORT

All patients should be encouraged to eat a varied and well-balanced diet that includes foods from all the food groups (Table 12.6) in amounts sufficient to maintain, or increase, body weight. To minimise weight loss, and facilitate repair and regeneration of damaged tissues, a high energy, high protein diet is recommended. Items consumed should be selected from as wide a variety of foods as possible as this will help to ensure that vitamin and mineral requirements are met; supplements may be required. Methods of increasing the energy and protein content of the diet are shown in Table 12.7.

Table 12.7   Some ways of increasing the energy and protein content of the diet

Energy
Use single or double cream instead of milk
Butter toast when it is hot and will absorb greater amounts of butter
Add cream, evaporated milk or ice cream to milky drinks and deserts
Eat cream soups rather than clear soups
Add mayonnaise, salad dressings, gravies and sauces to meals and sandwiches
Eat potatoes, pasta, rice or bread at least twice a day
Have honey, jam, jelly or syrup with bread or toast and add to milk puddings
Add fruit or full-fat yoghurt to breakfast cereals
Eat between-meal snacks, such as nuts, crisps, sweets, chocolate or dried fruits
Add sugar to deserts and beverages
Fry foods rather than grilling them, eat baked potatoes with butter and/or cheese or sour cream

Protein
Fortify whole milk with skimmed milk powder, egg or ice cream
Add yoghurt to the daily diet
Eat additional eggs, milk, fish, poultry or eggs
Add eggs and/or cheese to salads, casseroles and sauces
Add ice cream, skimmed milk powder or eggs to desserts

Modification of the nutrient intake

Many patients cannot meet their nutritional needs through oral intake alone and additional support is needed. A voluntary food intake falling below 80% of the required amounts of energy and protein (Table 12.8) indicates the need for support.

Table 12.8   Energy and protein needs of patients undergoing chemotherapy

Energy
Females

At ideal body weight (IBW)	=	IBW x 39.4kcal/kg per day
With weight loss	=	IBW x 44.4kcal/kg per day

Males

At ideal body weight (IBW)	=	IBW x 44.4kcal/kg per day
With weight loss	=	IBW x 48.4kcal/kg per day

When weight loss exceeds 1kg/week an additional 4.4kcal/kg is added to the daily intake until ideal body weight is reached.

Protein

IBW x 2g protein/kg/day

The strategy selected for modifying the food intake to ensure an adequate supply of nutrients will depend on the specific feeding problem and the degree of nutritional depletion. The oral route is the preferred method of feeding although this may be difficult when the patient is suffering from anorexia, nausea, dysphagia or taste aberration Nonetheless, eating must be encouraged by modifying both the food and its presentation; suitable approaches have been discussed in the relevant chapters.

However, individual patients may require particular dietary changes that can pose difficulties in the hospital environment since the attitude to patient feeding is often surprisingly inflexible and many patients find hospital food unfamiliar and unacceptable. It may be valuable to enlist the help of relatives and/or friends to provide foods which the patient 'fancies' and will enjoy.

There is little doubt that control of those symptoms limiting food intake can help considerably so that regular administration of anti-emetics, analgesics or antidiarrhoeal medications are simple measures that can be extremely effective. However, food intake can also be limited by early satiety when the patient feels hungry at the start of a meal but finds he is unable to eat more than a few mouthfuls. In this case, as when caring for those with anorexia, frequent small meals may be more acceptable and nutritional supplements may help to ensure an adequate nutrient intake.

The timing of meals deserves some consideration. Many patients complain of a decreased ability to eat as the day progresses, the morning being the best time for eating. The reasons for this are not entirely clear but it may result from a sluggish digestion and reduced rate of gastric emptying due to a reduction in the secretion of gastric enzymes combined with atrophy of both the GI mucosa and the gastric muscle itself (DeWys, 1979). Thus affected patients should be encouraged to eat their largest meal early in the day and to consume frequent, small but nutrient-dense snacks or drinks thereafter.

Enteral feeding and nutritional supplements

When patients are unable to eat sufficient food to meet their nutritional needs additional support is essential. This can be achieved in several ways. For example, additional milky drinks, such as milk shakes, can be given to boost the nutrient intake; whole milk provides 160kcal and 8g protein per 200ml. However, despite its value as a nutritional supplement, milk cannot be given to those patients with intestinal damage who are also lactose intolerant or to those who cannot tolerate, digest or absorb a normal diet. In some such cases, a liquid nutrition formula can be used to overcome some of these difficulties and provide either total or supplemental support.

Individual food consumption must be monitored and the caring team must then decide when alternative methods of feeding are needed. Such modifications may necessitate a simple change in the texture of foods (eg. a soft or pureed diet) or the need for specialist nutritional approaches.

Liquid diets may be derived from normal foods (homogenised) or commercially-prepared. Although the latter are more convenient, microbiologically safer and of consistent nutrient composition, those based on normal foods may be more psychologically acceptable to both patient and carer. Liquid formulas may be used as tube feeds, 'sip' feeds or between-meal supplements; they may also be incorporated into 'normal' foods to increase their nutrient density.

The many formulae available mean that it is possible to consider individual needs when selecting feeds. For example, if fat digestion is impaired, a feed containing readily-absorbed fats (medium chain triglycerides) may be given while, for the lactose intolerant, lactose-

240

free formulae can be selected. Complete formulae provide all the essential nutrients while modular products provide sources of either protein or carbohydrate and can be used to increase the intake of specific nutrients by increasing the nutrient density of a normal diet. These include products such as Maxipro™ and Maxijul™ (Scientific Hospital Supplies); a variety is now available.

Liquid formulae may be based on either whole protein or protein isolates. Whole protein feeds are derived from eggs, milk or meat and are relatively palatable, less expensive and lower in osmolarity than those based on protein isolates. Since they contain intact and complex nutrients they require normal digestion and absorption so that their use is limited to those patients with normal GI function. Hydrolysed formulae contain 'pre-digested' protein, together with simple carbohydrates and fat, and require little digestion and absorption. Their protein is derived from soya beans, milk or eggs. Both types of supplement are available in lactose-free formulations and so can be used for the lactose intolerant patient and are useful adjuncts to the care of the cancer patient.

One problem that may be encountered is that most, but not all, supplements currently available are sweet and so may be rejected by many patients, particularly those suffering from taste aberration. Taste fatigue is common; liquid diets rapidly become monotonous and are associated with the lack of satisfaction derived from chewing. As wide a variety as possible should be offered, including some savoury flavours, if necessary adjusting this to suit the patient.

When supplements are used as the sole source of nutrition the major complications are diarrhoea and crampy abdominal pain secondary to the high osmotic load. When the caloric density exceeds 1.5kcal/ml the high solute load can cause dehydration and azotaemia. Both these effects can be overcome by decreasing the tonicity of the feed by adding water and, unless fluid restriction is required, the fluid intake should approximate 1ml/kcal/day.

Feeds containing dietary fibre may be useful and help to maintain GI function; they may also help to promote feelings of satiety thus overcoming the feelings of hunger often associated with liquid diets.

When precisely defined quantities of nutrients are required defined formula and elemental diets can be used both of which will meet the basal requirement for both macro- and micronutrients. Defined formula diets may be based on either hydrolysed protein or free amino acids, simple sugars and very little fat; they are somewhat unpalatable and various flavouring agents are needed to disguise their organic (bitter) flavour. They cannot, therefore, be used when there is a sensitivity to bitter tastes; in fact, they are rarely given by the oral route.

Elemental diets, based on free amino acids, simple sugars and a minimal amount of fat, have some advantages over other liquid diets as they are totally bulk-free; many are almost fat free. Minimal digestion is needed before such nutrients can be absorbed so that most pancreatic, biliary and small intestinal secretions are not necessary for absorption; furthermore, absorption can occur even when the absorptive surface area is markedly reduced or when the small intestinal mucosa has been disrupted by either radiotherapy or chemotherapy.

Tube feeding

When oral nutrient intake is inadequate but GI function is normal, tube feeding is the method of choice for providing nutritional support. Compared with parenteral feeding this is more effective in preserving intestinal function and promoting efficient nutrient use (Goodwin and Wilmore, 1988); it is also less expensive and less likely to cause complications.

Tube feeding may be used to supply nutrients to patients who have a functional GI tract but who are unable, or unwilling, to take adequate food orally. Feeds may be administered through various routes (Table 12.9).

A nasoenteric tube is preferred when there is no obstruction between the nasopharynx and stomach/duodenum. The tube selected should be the smallest possible that will permit the passage of the selected feeding formula. They are usually made of silicon-rubber or polyurethane and do not stiffen or crack even after prolonged use. Most are weighted with either tungsten or mercury which eases its passage into the stomach, jejunum or duodenum. Permanent feeding access is indicated for long-term feeding; this is usually achieved through an enterostomy, most commonly a gastrostomy. Percutaneous gastrostomy under endoscopic control (PEG) is increasingly popular as a means of tube placement for patients who require nutritional support but are poor surgical risks (Payne-James and Silk 1988). When compared with other forms of gastrostomy PEG is less costly, the complication rate is low and insertion is relatively straightforward (Taylor and Goodinson-MacLaren, 1992).

Table 12.9   Placement of feeding tubes (from Holmes, 1987)

	Advantages	Disadvantages
Nasogastric	Usually well-tolerated as stomach acts as 'reservoir' holding and releasing feeds at a controlled rate and enhancing absorption thus avoiding dumping syndrome.	The risk of aspiration is high. Contraindicated when patient is vomiting, has GI bleeding or total intestinal obstruction
Nasoduodenal	Risk of aspiration reduced as both lower oesophageal and pyloric sphincters inhibit gastric reflux. Feeds can be both digested and absorbed provided correct formula is given.	Dumping syndrome is likely since the stomach is bypassed.
Nasojejunal	Aspiration is extremely unlikely (as above).	Dumping syndrome is common, particularly when hypertonic feeds are given or feeds are administered too quickly.
Oesophagostomy	Usually well tolerated. Stomach used as a 'reservoir'; controlled release of food prevents dumping syndrome.	Risk of aspiration is high. Thoracic duct injury may occur.

The most common placement methods are the 'pull-through' (Gauderer-Ponsky) and 'push-through' (Sachs-Vine) techniques. The first requires introduction of a guidewire through the abdominal wall. This is pulled out through the mouth by an endoscope, attached to the PEG and used to pull it into place in the abdominal wall. The latter involves threading the PEG over the guidewire, pushing this through the abdominal wall from inside. In either case, the tube is secured to the external abdominal wall; the tip is positioned in the gastric antrum. Longer tubes may be positioned in the duodenum or jejunum. Once the PEG is well-established, a gastrostomy button may be inserted into the tract formed by the gastrostomy. Unlike the gastrostomy tube, which protrudes and may snag in clothes or interfere with sexual activity, this lies almost flush with the skin.

Administration of feeds
Selection of feeding solutions depends on the mode of administration as well as the patient's nutritional condition. Many of the liquid supplements can be given as tube feeds and will meet the basal requirement for all nutrients.

Regardless of the route through which feeds are to be given, they may be administered continuously or by intermittent bolus and either pump-controlled or controlled by gravity. Although continuous feeding is preferred, as it decreases the risk of diarrhoea, bolus feeding is often used, and is certainly more convenient when the patient is treated at home provided that feeds are tolerated and cause no unpleasant symptoms. Bolus feeds have several advantages, such as increased patient mobility and ease of maintenance, and also similarity with the physiological aspects of 'normal' eating. However, uncontrolled bolus feeding may cause nausea, diarrhoea, abdominal cramps and vomiting and, therefore, an increased risk of aspiration. Slow, gravity drip feeds, or those delivered by pump over a 30-40 minute period, are generally better tolerated.

Continuous feeding is usually carried out over 16-20 hours to maximise tolerance and increase absorption. It may be carried out overnight. Volumetric pumps provide the safest and most accurate method of continuous infusion and ensure the passage of viscous solutions through a fine bore tube. A pump should always be used when feeding through a duodenostomy or jejunostomy to prevent dumping syndrome. The maximum flow rate should be about 125ml/hr; the rate of administration and the concentration of the solution should be increased gradually over several days to decrease side-effects. Most commercial feeds provide 1-2kcal/ml. However, when caloric density exceeds 1.5kcal/ml, the high osmolarity may cause dehydration and azotaemia. This can be overcome by adding water to dilute the feed; unless fluid restriction is necessary, intake should approximate 1ml/kcal/day.

The major complications of tube feeding are diarrhoea and crampy abdominal pain secondary to the high osmotic load. However, whenever enteral feeding is employed, there is a potential risk of aspiration of vomit. This can be prevented by elevating the head of the bed, avoiding night feeds, placing the distal end of the tube beyond the pylorus (although this may increase the risk of dumping syndrome) and carefully evaluating gastric retention. When the residual volume exceeds 75-100ml, feeds should be withheld.

Parenteral feeding

Although parenteral feeding is the least preferred method of nutritional support it must be considered whenever the GI tract is non-functional. When this method of feeding is the only source of nutrients it is referred to as total parenteral nutrition (TPN). It may also be given to support an inadequate oral intake (supplemental parenteral nutrition).

Supplemental nutrition is often given by infusing fluids into a peripheral vein. Such fluids must be isotonic/hypotonic so as to prevent phlebitis and irritation of the vein, and consist of solutions of dextrose, amino acids or lipid emulsion together with vitamins, trace elements and electrolytes. The same nutrients are supplied by TPN but at higher concentrations which are hyperosmolar. Peripheral venous nutrition is usually used on a short term basis (5-7 days) and is useful only for repletion of mild to moderate depletion when nutrient needs, although greater than normal, are not excessive.

TPN depends on placement of a long-term feeding access device into a large diameter vein, usually the subclavian vein, where the rapid and copious blood flow quickly dilutes the concentrated and hypertonic solutions required to satisfy the patient's nutritional needs without exceeding his daily fluid tolerance. This necessitates placement of a central line (see p94).

Energy (calories) is usually provided by a carbohydrate such as glucose (dextrose) or fat (lipid) which is a concentrated source of energy providing 9kcal/g compared with the 4kcal/g provided by carbohydrate. Fats are infused in 10% or 20% solution to ensure adequate provision of essential fatty acids thus preventing deficiency. Adequate calories must be given to ensure that administered protein (as amino acids) can be used to synthesise body tissues rather than to supply energy. Minerals, trace elements, vitamins and electrolytes are added to the parenteral solution at the time of preparation. Insulin may also be added since endogenous insulin secretion may be inadequate when hypertonic glucose is administered.

TPN is, however, an expensive procedure requiring continuous monitoring. It carries the risk of serious complications that can be categorised as mechanical, metabolic and infective (Table 12.10). However, Mullen (1981) reviewed the incidence and severity of complications in cancer patients as compared with non-cancer patients concluding that there was no difference between the two groups so that there are no additional hazards in this group of patients. Thus, TPN is often used to maintain nutritional status in those patients who have lost GI function but who are free of disease as well as in the severely malnourished individual for whom active treatment is contemplated. When used in appropriate patients, there

doubt that TPN improves the response to anticancer therapies
o improves the quality of life (Torosian et al, 1983).
can also be used at home provided that the patient, and/or
relatives, have been trained to cope. There must also be
supportive and regular follow-up. Home TPN can permit a return to a
normal life and work thus significantly improving the quality of life.

Table 12.10   Potential complications of total parenteral nutrition

Mechanical	Pneumothorax	Injury to brachial plexus
	Haemothorax	Injury to subclavian artery
	Hydrothrorax	Central vein thrombophlebitis
	Thoracic duct injury	Arteriovenous fistula
	Cardiac perforation	Air or catheter embolism
	Catheter misplacement	Endocarditis
	Subclavian haematoma	
Metabolic	Dehydration and electrolyte imbalance	Hyperchloraemic acidosis
	Hyperosmolar hyperglycaemia (non-ketotic)	Hyperammonaemia
		Azotaemia
	Hyper/hypophosphataemia	Trace element deficiency
	Hypocalcaemia	Rebound hypoglycaemia on cessation of treatment
	Hypomagnesaemia	
Infective	Entry site - contamination during insertion	
	Catheter 'seeding' from blood-borne or other (distant) infection	
	Contamination of feeding solution	

Psychological aspects of nutritional support

Nutritional support may have a number of psychological and social
consequences the occurrence of which increases with the length of
the period of support (Gulledge, 1987): patients may require
considerable support and encouragement. Artificial feeding may
cause feelings of frustration, loss of control and independence and,
for some, suggests a return to childhood; the presence of a feeding
tube may cause disgust, anger and concern or anxiety at alterations
in body image This may necessitate significant changes in lifestyle
markedly altering family and social activities many of which focus
around food and drink (Gulledge, 1987). A loss of libido is common.

PATIENT COMPLIANCE

Regardless of which method of feeding is used patient compliance
and co-operation are essential if nutritional care and support is to be

successful. Thus the patient must understand the reasons for such care. It is also essential that both the patient and his family are aware of the problems that may arise and their possible solutions. Teaching should take place at an early stage and should continue alongside periodic nutritional assessment. Specific goals should be established and directed towards a tangible means of feedback, such as body weight or improvement in general well-being.

THE TERMINAL PATIENT

Clearly the patient with cancer, who is also receiving chemotherapy, is at considerable nutritional risk; problems may persist long after therapy has been completed. An awareness of these effects, together with an understanding of their cause, will help the caring team to plan appropriate preventive measures. However, although an important part of the total care of all patients, it must be recognised that nutritional support will not cure cancer although it can improve the patient's response to treatment as well as his quality of life. It can be very disturbing for the patient and his family to observe the continuing muscle wasting and physical weakness that accompany starvation so that nutritional support can play an important supportive role. However, it is of questionable benefit for the patient in whom antineoplastic therapy has failed and who has no realistic expectations of a positive outcome. Thus there comes a time when unwanted nutritional support should not be continued since an extension of life may prolong suffering. It may be more appropriate to suggest that the patient should eat what, if any, food is wanted and that he is given emotional and psychological support and comfort. Nutrition no longer matters; the pleasurable aspects of food and eating should be emphasised with little concern about its quantity or its nutrient content.

REFERENCES

Bernstein IL, Bernstein ID, 1981, Learned food aversions and cancer anorexia, Cancer Treatment Reports **65** (Suppl), 43-4.

Beutler B, Cerami A, 1986, Cachectin and tumour necrosis factor as two sides of the same biological coin, Nature **110**, 584-8.

Busbridge J, Dascombe MJ, Hoopkins S, et al, 1989, Acute central effects of interleukin-6 on body temperature, thermogenesis and food intake in the rat, Proceedings of the Nutrition Society, **38**, 48A.

Nutritional care of the chemotherapy patient

Cooper EH, Stone J, 1979, Acute phase reactant proteins in cancer. In: Klein G, Weinhouse S (Editors), Advances in Cancer Research, Academic Press, New York.

Daly JM, Dudrick SJ, Copeland EM, 1979, Evaluation of nutritional indices as prognostic indicators in the cancer patient, Cancer **43**, 925-31.

Daly JM, Redmond HP, Gallagher H, 1992, Perioperative nutrition in cancer patients, Journal of Parenteral and Enteral Nutrition **16** (Suppl 6), 100S-109S.

DeWys WD, 1979, Anorexia as a general effect of cancer, Cancer **43**, 2013-4.

Durnin JVGA, Fidanza F, 1985, Evaluation of nutritional status, Bibliotheca Nutrition et Dietetics **35**, 20-30.

Espat NJ, Moldawer LL, Copeland EM, 1995, Cytokine-mediated alterations in host metabolism prevent nutritional repletion in cachectic cancer patients, Journal of Surgical Oncology **58**, 77-81.

Evans R, Duffy TM, Blake SS, et al, 1989, Regulation of systemic macrophage IL-1 gene transcription: the involvement of tumour-derived macrophage growth factor CSF-1, Journal of Leukocyte Biology **46**, 428-32.

Fearon KCH, 1992, The mechanisms and treatment of weight loss in cancer, Proceedings of the Nutrition Society **51**, 251-65.

Garrow J, 1994, Starvation in Hospital (Letter to the Editor), British Medical Journal **306**, 934.

Gelin J, Lundholm K, 1992, The metabolic response to cancer, Proceedings of the Nutrition Society **51**, 279-84.

Gibson RS, 1990, Principles of Nutritional Assessment, Oxford University Press, Oxford.

Goodinson SM, 1987a, Anthropometric assessment of nutritional status, Professional Nurse **2**, 388-93.

Goodinson SM, 1987b, Biochemical assessment of nutritional status, Professional Nurse **2**, 8-12.

Goodwin CW, and Wilmore DW, 1988. Enteral and parenteral nutrition. In: Paige, DM, Jacobson HN, Owen GM, Sherwin R, Solomons N, Young VR (Editors) Clinical Nutrition second edition, St Louis: C.V. Mosby Co., pp476-503.

Gulledge AD, 1987, Psychosocial issues of home parenteral and enteral nutrition, Nutrition in Clinical Practice **2**, 183-94.

Heber D, Byerly CO, Cheblowski RT, 1985, Metabolic abnormalities in the cancer patient, Cancer **55** (Suppl), 225-9.

Holland, JCB, Rowland J, Plumb M, 1977, Psychological aspects of anorexia in cancer patients, Cancer Research **37**, 3425-8.

Holmes S, 1986, Nutritional needs of medical patients, Nursing Times **82**(17), 34-6.

Holmes S, 1987, Artificial feeding, Nursing Times **83**, 49-58.

248

Holmes S, Dickerson JWT, 1988, Malignant disease: nutritional implications of disease and treatment, Cancer and Metastasis Reviews **6**, 357-81.

Holmes S, Dickerson JWT, 1991, Food intake and quality of life in cancer patients, Journal of Nutritional Medicine **2**, 359-368.

Kokal WA, 1985, The impact of antitumour therapy on nutrition, Cancer **55**, 273-8.

Krause R, James JH, Ziparo V, et al, 1979a, Brain tryptophan and the neoplastic anorexia-cachexia syndrome, Cancer **44**, 1003-8.

Krause R, James JH, Humphrey C, et al, 1979b, Plasma and brain amino acids in Walker-256 carcino-sarcoma bearing rats, Cancer Research **39**, 3065-9.

Kruk ZL, 1976, Dopamine and 5-hydroxytryptamine inhibit feeding in rats, Nature, New Biology **246**, 52-7.

Landel AM, Hammond, WG, Meguid MM, 1985, Aspects of amino acid and protein metabolism in cancer bearing states, Cancer **55** (Suppl), 230-7.

Langstein HN, Norton JA, 1991, Mechanisms of cancer cachexia, Hematology and Oncology Clinics of North America, **5**, 103-6

Larrea J, Vega S, Martinez T, et al, 1992, The nutritional status and immunological situation of cancer patients, Nutricion Hopitalaria **7**, 178-82.

Laviano A, Renvyle T, Yang Z-J, 1996, From laboratory to bedside: new strategies in the treatment of malnutrition in cancer patients, Nutrition **12**(2), 112-22.

Leathwood PD, Ashley DV, Moennoz DV, 1986, Anorexia and cachexia in cancer, Nestlé Research News 1985/86, Néstec Ltd., Switzerland.

Lehr D, Goldman W, 1973, Continued pharmacologic analysis of consummatory behaviour in the albino rat, European Journal of Pharmacology **23**, 197-200.

Matte's RD, Arnold C, Boraas M, 1987, Management of learned food aversion in cancer patients receiving cancer chemotherapy, Cancer Treatment Reports **71**, 1071-8.

Moldawer LL, Rogy MA, Lowry SF, 1992, The role of cytokines in cancer cachexia, Journal of Parenteral and Enteral Nutrition **15** (Suppl 6), 43S-49S.

Morrison SD, 1976, Control of food intake in cancer cachexia: a challenge and a tool, Physiology and Behaviour **17**, 705-9.

Mullen JL, 1981, Complications of total parenteral nutrition in the cancer patient, Cancer Treatment Reports **65**, (Supplement 5), 107-15.

Novin D, van der Weele DA, 1977, Visceral involvement in feeding, Progress in Physiology and Psychology **7**, 193-241.

Ollenschlager G, Konkol K, Modder B, 1988, Indicators for and results of nutritional therapy in cancer patients, Recent Results in Cancer Research **108**, 172-84.

Padilla G, 1986, Psychological aspects of nutrition and cancer, Surgical Clinics of North America **66**, 1121-34.

Payne-James JJ, Silk DBA, 1988, Enteral nutrition: background indications and management, Clinical Gastroenterology **2**, 815-47.

Plumb M, Holland J, Park S, et al, 1976, Depression of symptoms in patients with advanced cancer: a controlled assessment Psychosomatic Medicine **36** (Abstr), 459.

Schmale AH, 1979, Psychological aspects of anorexia: areas for study, Cancer **43**, 2087-92.

Selby P, Hobbs S, Viner C, et al, 1987, Tumour necrosis factor in man: clinical and biological observations, British Journal of Cancer **56**, 803-78.

Shils ME, 1977, Nutritional problems induced by cancer, Medical Clinics of North America **63**, 1009-25.

Taylor S, Goodinson-MacLaren S, 1992, Nutritional Support: A Team Approach, Wolfe Publishing Ltd., London.

Torosian MH, Mullen JL, Miller EE, 1983, Enhanced tumour response to cycle specific chemotherapy by parenteral amino acid administration, Journal of Parenteral and Enteral Nutrition **7**, 337-45.

Torti FM, Dieckmann B, Beutler B, et al, 1985, A macrophage factor inhibits adipocyte gene expression: an in vitro model of cachexia, Science **229**, 867-9.

von Meyendfeldt MF, Chance WT, Fischer JE, 1980, Investigation of serotonergic influence on cancer-induced anorexia, Neuroscience Abstracts **6**, 525-6.

Wangel AG, Deller DJ, 1966, Malabsorption syndrome associated with carcinoma of the bronchus, Gut **6**, 73-6.

Wesdorp RIC, Krause R, von Meyendfeldt MF, 1983, Cancer cachexia and its nutritional implications, British Journal of Surgery **70**, 352-5.

Wright RA, Heymsfield S, 1979, Nutritional Assessment, Blackwell Scientific Publications, Oxford.

CHAPTER 13   EFFECTS ON SEXUAL FUNCTION

Cancer affects all aspects of life and most of those diagnosed with the disease will have concerns about its possible sexual effects as well as those of its treatment (Glasgow et al, 1987; Smith 1989). This is particularly important when it is recognised that cancer is often a chronic disease. The quality of life of sufferers is of paramount importance thus sexual function, as an important component of the quality of life, takes on increasing relevance. This is true whether or not the individual is undergoing chemotherapy. Yet health care providers often overlook this aspect of care. This may arise for a number of reasons including lack of knowledge or awareness of the impact of the disease and its treatment on sexual function and a general discomfort about discussing such issues with patients.

Clearly the significance of sexual issues varies considerably so that each patient *must* be treated as an individual with his own unique set of fears, worries and needs. Each must be individually assessed and care prescribed on an individual basis.

SEXUAL FUNCTION

The World Health Organisation (1975) describes sexual health as *'the integration of somatic, emotional, intellectual and social aspects of sexual being in ways that are positively enriching and that enhance personality, communication and love'* thus demonstrating that it incorporates not only the sexual act but also the ability to maintain interpersonal relationships and communicate in a meaningful fashion with significant others.

Psychosocial factors

Optimal sexual function is also dependent on a variety of psycho-social factors (Table 13.1). For example, an adolescent may face a variety of issues in this area including learning to give or receive love, developing relationships with the opposite sex and choosing marital or sexual partner(s) (Woods, 1990). Most adults will focus on sexual activity and gratification within a stable relationship. Sexual activity and interest persist into later life and older adults are no less vulnerable to changes in their sexual functioning (Woods, 1990).

Table 13.1   Psychosocial factors which may affect sexual function

Age
Alteration in body image
Reduced self-esteem
Attitudes, beliefs and misconceptions
Anxiety and depression
Role changes
Emotional separation
Physical separation
Availability of a partner
Hospitalisation

Body image and self-esteem are important contributors to the way individuals perceive their sexuality. Developing cancer may cause significant changes in self-esteem, some of which are transient and others permanent. There is little doubt that cancer can exert negative effects on self-esteem whether or not changes in body image are apparent (Folz, 1987). If the patient must also adjust to changes in his physical appearance, his sexual function may be further compromised; this may exacerbate pre-existing anxiety and depression.

Anxiety and depression are commonly observed in cancer patients (eg. Andersen, 1985). Indeed clinical depression may be found in between 17 and 25% of all patients hospitalised for the treatment of cancer (Petty and Noyes, 1981). Both anxiety and depression may have significant effects on sexual function.

Similarly, the changing roles within the family may threaten an individual's self-esteem (Johnson, 1986) and, in turn, lead to sexual dysfunction. This should be considered when planning care for affected patients. Thus it is not surprising that many patients feel that they have lost control of their lives. It is not surprising if these effects monopolise the patient's thinking and obliterate his/her desire for a sexual relationship.

The direct effects of cancer on sexual function are dependent on the nature of the disease and the area of the body involved. For example, disease invading the vulva, vagina, cervix, or breast may affect a woman's sexual function and involvement of the testes, urinary tract or penis that of the male. Tactile responsiveness may be affected by neurological involvement and vascular changes may cause physiological dysfunction. Hormonal effects may disturb sexual function through hormonal imbalance.

The clinical manifestations of the disease, such as malaise, fatigue, and physical weakness, may cause a gradual reduction in libido and treatment of the disease may necessitate hospitalisation and physical separation of the patient and his or her partner. Emotional separation can also result from the difficulties associated with both accepting and living with the diagnosis. These effects may combine to make it difficult to establish or maintain an intimate relationship and the stress engendered may cause a fragile relationship to deteriorate.

The partner is also vulnerable to psychological effects that may impact on normal sexual expression. The patient's family have to adjust to many changes and depression and anticipatory grieving lead to an almost constant emotional stress. Anxiety and depression may affect their sexual function and interest.

In addition, the physical condition of the patient may cause fears that he is too sick for sexual activity or that he will, in some way, be hurt should sexual activity be attempted. The partner may feel guilty about making sexual overtures to someone who is experiencing the trauma of cancer or its treatment or be concerned that they may 'catch' the disease. Furthermore, a partner may find it difficult to 'switch' roles between that of care-giver and that of sexual partner (Lamb, 1991).

For all these reasons, sexual expression may decrease and may reinforce the patient's belief that he is 'dirty' or 'unclean'. The side-effects of chemotherapy may further decrease the patient's self-esteem through alterations in his body image thus exacerbating sexual difficulties. Fatigue, weakness, nausea and vomiting may also make sexual relationships difficult.

SEXUAL DYSFUNCTION

The sexual response in both males and females is initiated by a combination of tactile, visual and psychological factors (Table 13.2). Psychologically this compromises two main changes - an increase in venous blood flow (vasocongestion) and an increased muscle tension (myotonia) (Woods, 1990) which are dependent on intact neurological function and an appropriate hormonal environment. According to Woods (1990), sexual dysfunction may affect the areas of excitement (desire or interest), arousal (readiness) and orgasm (release) and may arise, as has been shown, from a variety of external or internal factors.

Table 13.2   Cycle of sexual response

Phase	Female	Male
Excitement (desire or interest) (parasympathetic response)	Lubrication of vagina. Size of clitoris and labia minora increased. Increased sensation felt in clitoris and labia minora. Neuro-muscular tension, breasts enlarge, erection of nipples. Upward movement of uterus.	Erection of penis; testicles drawn up towards body. Erection of nipples. Increase in cardiac and respiratory rate.
Plateau (readiness) (parasympathetic response)	Vagina expands and contractions begin. Clitoris retracts. Uterus draws up further.	Circumference of penis increases. Testes enlarge; lubricating fluid released from Cowper's gland.
Orgasm (sympathetic response)	Uterus contracts, deeper portion of vagina becomes distended. Pelvic thrusts with associated general muscular contractions.	Ejaculation; pelvic thrusts associated with generalised muscular contraction.
Resolution (satisfaction) (parasympathetic response)	Congestion of organs subsides. Uterus and vagina gradually return to pre-excitement state. General release of tension.	Congestion of organs subsides. Loss of erection and return to pre-excitement state. General release of tension.

Note: All of these reactions depend on libido. Progression between stages may be disrupted by fear, anxiety, anger and lack of privacy. To progress between stages hope, safety, contentment and privacy are necessary.

EFFECTS OF CHEMOTHERAPY

Even when the disease itself has caused no anatomical alterations, disturbances to body image may arise as a result of side-effects of its treatment. Such effects may also cause unpleasant or distressing symptoms that may also disrupt the patient's perceptions of his body image with the effect that patients may withdraw from any social interactions.

For some patients, self-esteem is dependent on their physical abilities and productivity. Changes in such abilities due, for example, to fatigue and/or muscle wasting, may, therefore, have a profound impact on affected individuals. Because productivity is so important to them they may attempt to meet their goals thus increasing their fatigue, perhaps to the point of exhaustion. Thus chemotherapy itself may affect the patient's sexuality either directly or indirectly affecting not only sexual function but also reproductive ability and foetal development.

The degree of dysfunction is related not only to the age and general condition of the patient but also to the drugs employed and the dose and duration of the chemotherapy regime. Indeed, many of the drugs used in cancer treatment may have profound and often lasting effects on the ovaries and testes altering both germ cell production and endocrine function (McInnes and Schilsky, 1996) (Table 13.3).

Table 13.3   Examples of drugs causing infertility
(Based on McInnes and Schilsky, 1996)

CERTAIN	HIGHLY LIKELY
Chlorambucil	Adriamycin
Cyclophosphamide	Vinblastine
Phenylalanine mustard	Cytosine arabinoside
Mechlorethamine	Cisplatin
Busulfan	Nitrosoureas
Procarbazine	Etoposide
	Amsacrine

UNLIKELY
Methotrexate
5-fluorouracil
6-mercaptopurine
Vincristine
Interferon

Effects on the female

The mature ovary plays a dual role: the production of hormones (oestrogen and progesterone) and the release of ova. Cytotoxic therapy may cause fibrosis resulting in amenorrhoea; vaginal epithelial atrophy and endometrial hypoplasia occur and patients may experience menopausal symptoms (eg. hot flushes or symptoms of oestrogen deficiency, such as vaginal dryness and dyspareunia). The primary cause of these effects is ovarian failure and follicle destruction (eg. Montz et al, 1991).

The onset and duration of amenorrhoea appear to be related to both the dose of drug delivered and the age of the patient. Younger patients (<40yrs) generally seem better able to tolerate larger cumulative doses before amenorrhoea develops and also have a greater likelihood of resumption of menses once treatment is complete (Priestman, 1989; McInnes and Schilsky, 1996) although this may not occur for 6-12 months.

If subsequent pregnancy is desired it should be remembered that all the ova present in the ovaries were exposed to the effects of chemotherapy so that genetic effects may affect the unborn child (see p262); genetic counselling is essential for such patients and their partners. However, it must also be recognised that many women who have undergone such treatment have successfully given birth to normal infants.

Until comparatively recently, no techniques existed to enable affected women to maintain their fertility following chemotherapy that ablates ovarian function. Although oocyte freezing and storage have been partially effective, the most consistent results have been achieved when embryos have been preserved (through cryo-preservation (freezing)) for later intrafallopian or intrauterine transfer (Abdalla et al, 1989). Oocytes are harvested before therapy and fertilised *in vitro* by husband or donor sperm prior to storage in liquid nitrogen. Once chemotherapy is complete, the endometrium is prepared appropriately using hormonal therapy and the embryo is transplanted.

Permanent sterility may result in acute manifestations of the menopause so that the patient may need considerable psychological support and reassurance that sterility affects neither femininity nor sexual drive/desire. Where hormonal replacement therapy is not contraindicated this can be a useful adjunct to treatment. Additional advantages include prevention of post-menopausal osteoporosis and a diminished risk of premature atherosclerosis (Quantock and Beynon, 1995).

Attempts to protect the ovaries from chemotherapy-induced damage have focused on the use of oral contraceptives to promote ovarian suppression (eg. Chapman and Sutcliffe, 1981) although, to date, results have been disappointing (Falkson and Falkson, 1989; Whitehead et al, 1993).

As has been observed, a loss of libido, a decrease in vaginal muscle tone and dyspareunia are also common which, when combined with a loss of body hair and the diagnosis of cancer *per se*, may significantly affect the patient's self-image and self-esteem resulting in feelings of unattractiveness and undesirability. Such problems are likely to persist unless action is taken to prevent or minimise their impact. However, most women experiencing such difficulties are able to overcome them with the use of a vaginal hormone cream (unless this is contraindicated), vaginal dilation and pelvic floor exercises (Schrover et al, 1984a; 1984b; 1986).

Encouraging open discussion of the patient's feelings and anxieties is important. Open communication with her partner is also essential if the patient is to be helped to come to terms with these effects. This is a sensitive area and one in which health care professionals, particularly nurses, have been shown to be reluctant to initiate discussion (Faulkner and Maguire, 1984). Since this is an area where patients are also loathe to ask questions the opportunity for discussion must be presented; it is then up to the patient if she wishes to take up this opportunity.

Some units prefer to advise that intercourse be avoided during treatment although, provided that an effective method of birth control is employed, and provided the vagina is not affected by mucositis or ulceration, sexual intercourse can usually be continued during therapy. This can significantly improve the patient's quality of life and greatly improve her general well-being. When the vagina is dry, a water-based lubricant, such as K-Y Jelly™, will improve lubrication and prevent discomfort/pain. However, a decrease in libido is to be expected during treatment.

Birth control, usually reliant on barrier methods of contraception, must be continued for at least 2 years after treatment to enable hormone levels, particularly oestrogen, to return to normal and to prevent stillbirth or chromosomal damage (Table 13.4). Oral contraceptives may be used but should be avoided by those with hormone-dependent tumours.

When menstruation has not been suppressed by treatment the patient should be asked to inform a member of the caring team when menses is expected, particularly when chemotherapy-induced bone marrow suppression is present, as thrombocytopoenia may result in unusually heavy blood loss. On occasions, continuous administration of oral contraceptives may be prescribed to suppress menstrual bleeding.

When menstruation occurs, the degree of blood loss should be closely monitored, by a daily pad/tampon count, and the duration of flow noted. If this is significant blood replacement therapy may be necessary.

Table 13.4   Barrier methods of contraception

Condom	Sheath of latex rubber or PVDC designed to cover the erect penis and contain the semen that is ejaculated. It is advisable to use condoms in conjunction with a spermicide (jelly, foam or cream). A female equivalent is available; this slots into the vagina and functions in a similar fashion.	If the patient is female, it may be helpful if a water-based lubricant (such as K-Y jelly™) is used to prevent trauma to the vaginal mucosa. A small number of people are allergic to either the rubber, the lubricant or the spermicide. In this case, a hypoallergenic brand should be used (eg. Durex Allergy™ (London Rubber Company)).
Diaphragm	Shallow dome of rubber or plastic with a metal rim also encased in rubber. The rim may be a flat compressible band (flat spring) or a wire-spiral, also covered in rubber (coil spring). This fits over the cervix acting as a barrier to prevent sperm reaching the uterus. A spermicide (jelly, foam or cream) should also be used.	A very few women may be unable to use a diaphragm (the vagina may be too long or the cervix too short). A few may be allergic to the rubber or the spermicide although this is less of a problem than it is with condoms.
Cervical cap	Made of rubber/plastic and designed to fit snugly over the cervix to prevent sperm entering the cervical canal. Should be used with a spermicide (jelly, foam or cream).	These devices cannot be used by all women. May be worn continuously, except during menstruation; some suggest that, like the diaphragm, the cap be removed about 6 hours after intercourse.
Vault cap	Dome made of rubber or plastic that fits across the top end of the vagina covering the cervix. Held in place by suction, air being expelled when the cap is pushed into place.	Not as easy to use as the diaphragm but may be useful for those women in whom the vaginal muscles are weak or when the cervix is split, torn or very short.

Effects on the male

The adult testis functions as both an endocrine and an exocrine gland in producing spermatozoa and testosterone (McInnes and Schilsky, 1996). Chemotherapy may, through its effects on rapidly dividing cells, result in aplasia of the germinal epithelium reducing spermatogenesis, often leading to a total absence of sperm (azoospermia); such sperm as are produced may display altered morphology, motility and/or chromosomal abnormalities (Martin, 1993). In general, cytotoxic therapy has little effect on Leydig cells so that testosterone secretion continues and there are few changes in secondary sexual characteristics. However, although uncommon, Leydig cell dysfunction may occur and is detected by an increase in serum luteinising hormone and, if uncompensated, a fall in testosterone secretion. This may result in testicular atrophy.

The recovery of spermatogenesis is unpredictable (Priestman, 1989) so that sterility may be permanent or temporary. This is probably related to the age of the patient and the total dose of chemotherapy received (McInnes and Schilsky, 1996). In addition, a man undergoing chemotherapy may be advised to ensure that he does not father a child for at least 2 years after the completion of therapy. Effective methods of birth control are, therefore, essential (Table 13.4). When sterility is a matter of particular concern the possibility of 'sperm banking' should be discussed with the patient. This involves the cryopreservation of semen, and its subsequent use for artificial insemination. This can help to overcome this problem for some patients. It must, however, be recognised that this approach is only of value if the semen is of good quality since freezing, in itself, may decrease sperm motility. Thus, although sperm banking can be useful, it does not guarantee success. If it is unsuccessful artificial insemination by donor (AID) may be considered.

Impotence and gynaecomastia may also arise and can have significant effects on both body image and self-esteem. Impotence may begin 2-3 weeks after treatment commences and persist for some weeks after its cessation; on occasions recovery is incomplete. It arises for several reasons including the anxiety, worry, concern and depression that may follow the diagnosis of cancer, the fatigue, lethargy and weakness often associated with chemotherapy and the side-effects of therapy, such as diarrhoea, nausea and vomiting.

Impotence can have a dramatic effect of affected patients who may require considerable support. When this is a matter of concern to the patient considerable reassurance is often needed. When impotence is expected to be permanent, testosterone implants may be beneficial and the patient should be referred to the appropriate specialist for care and treatment of his condition.

A loss of the ability to engage in sexual intercourse need not, however, prevent the patient from participating in other ways of satisfying

259

his sexual needs; sexual counselling may be beneficial and help the patient, and his partner, to identify alternative behaviours. For example, hugging and kissing can demonstrate continuing affection.

Both partners should be included in counselling to encourage communication of their fears, needs and anxieties. Again the patient may be embarrassed or reluctant to discuss his problems so that carers must make it clear that they understand and give the patient the opportunity to talk if this is what he wishes to do.

General care of the patient suffering from sexual dysfunction

If health care workers are to help the patient to deal with sexual problems they must first be comfortable with their own sexuality and attitudes as well as their counselling skills (Webb, 1987). Contact with the self as a sexual being will be evident to others and will convey comfort to them (Fetter, 1987). If this is not the case help should be sought from a trained counsellor.

Staff must be aware of the sexual implications of the treatment the patient is receiving if appropriate supportive care is to be given. Careful assessment of the patient is required. The literature contains many references to the issue of sexual assessment (eg. Chapman and Sughrue, 1987); many of these are specific to cancer patients. The following data will provide information on which to base such care:

1. The usual pattern of sexual activity and the changes enforced by both the disease and the treatment.
2. The desire and opportunity for sexual activity.
3. The partner's desire and patterns of coping with sexual deprivation.

Such an assessment must be carried out in privacy ensuring that adequate time is available for the patient to express their concerns and anxieties and for discussion to take place. Patients are often glad to be given the opportunity to discuss their sexual concerns and to know that help is available. It is important that the counsellor is non-judgmental and he/she must accept and support the patient's feelings and beliefs about his sexual behaviour. Since nurses have the most enduring relationship with the patient, the task of identifying such problems often falls to this professional group although specialist advice should be available when this is required.

It is difficult to identify any way in which the physiological and psychological effects of malignant disease and its treatment can be avoided so that the predominant role of the health care professional is in helping the patient to come to terms with them and to develop appropriate coping mechanisms.

Appropriate assessment, when combined with the carer's knowledge of both the patient and the sexual effects of the particular tumour and its treatment, will help them to predict potential problems and direct her counselling appropriately. Since many of the side-effects of the disease, as well as chemotherapy itself, may also affect sexuality, through their effects on body image and self-esteem (eg. alopecia, oral mucositis, diarrhoea, nausea and vomiting), this must also be considered when offering advice for the management of such effects. For example, an awareness of the presence of dypsnoea could lead a carer to ask whether this interferes with the patient's sexual activity. This demonstrates both awareness and understanding and legitimises sexuality as an appropriate area for discussion helping both the patient and his/her partner to cope more effectively with the problems they may face. As the patient's partner knows and understands the patient he or she should always be involved in discussion with both members of the caring team and the patient. This may facilitate development of a supportive and caring relationship. Most patients will adjust to these effects although the time required for such adjustment is highly variable.

In general, health care professionals need not worry about discussing sexual problems with their patients since many are relieved that their anxiety is recognised. A patient will, in any case, indicate quite clearly whether or not they wish to pursue the discussion and patients generally recognise carers as professionals and quickly become quite comfortable in discussing such matters. The older patient may, however, find such open communication more difficult. Caring and sensitive care can, eventually, overcome such difficulties.

Temporary sexual difficulties are often self-limiting resolving once the patient has had time to adapt to the presence of the disease and its treatment or to the loss of a body part (eg. breast or testicle) or a change in their usual appearance. Engendering a positive and hopeful outlook is a clear role for health care workers who can also emphasise many of the positive aspects of sexuality by complementing the patient on her beautiful hair or encouraging the use of make up or everyday clothes. These actions may also help to enhance self-perception of body image and encourage the patient to regain their self-esteem. The partner can play a positive reinforcing role although, it must be recognised, they too may have problems in coping with the changes in their loved one.

For those who are able to maintain sexual activity, effective birth control is essential so that contraceptive advice may be required. For others, however, even the physical expression of simple affection may be impaired by, for example, the precautions required to prevent infection (eg. protective isolation); kissing may be impossible when stomatitis is present. Such patients should be encouraged to express their feelings openly and honestly and to communicate these to their partners. This can have marked effects on the relationship when the realisation that both partners are experiencing difficulties and frustrations can help to engender feelings of closeness. Both partners must be aware that alterations in the normal sexual pattern creates difficulties for them both and that resolution may require time, patience and understanding.

If pregnancy should occur during treatment a termination may be advised due to the risk of teratogenic effects leading to congenital malformations (see below). These are particularly likely if metho-trexate or alkylating agents are given during pregnancy (Cline and Haskell, 1980).

GENETIC (TERATOGENIC) EFFECTS

Teratogenic effects refer to the ability of toxic compounds, such as cancer chemotherapeutic agents, to produce alterations in a foetus following exposure. Thus, chemotherapy, particularly during the first trimester, has been related to congenital abnormalities. The alkylating agents and antimetabolites are those anticancer drugs most commonly associated with foetal malformations. Treatment during the second or third trimester does not generally increase the incidence of congenital abnormalities (Kaempfer, 1988) although it may cause premature birth or infants of low birth weight.

Clearly, an undesired pregnancy carrying the risk of genetic abnormality is an added stress for the patient undergoing treatment for cancer and, it is often difficult to predict when a patient (male or female) receiving chemotherapy is infertile and sterility may only be temporary, the need for effective birth control cannot be stressed highly enough. It has been suggested that this should continue for at least two years after therapy so as to prevent conception. This will allow time for the recovery of spermatogenesis or ovarian function following therapy (Kaempfer, 1988; Lowitz, 1988).

REFERENCES

Abdalla HI, Babee RJ, Kirklan A, et al, 1989, Pregnancy in women with premature ovarian failure using tubal and intrauterine transfer of cryopreserved zygotes, British Journal of Gynaecology **96**, 1071-5.

Andersen BL, 1985, Sexual functioning morbidity among cancer survivors, Cancer **55**, 1835-42.

Chapman J, Sughrue J, 1987, A model for sexual assessment and intervention, Health Care for Women International **8**, 87-99.

Chapman RM, Sutcliffe SB, 1981, Protection of ovarian failure by oral contraceptives in women receiving chemotherapy for Hodgkin's disease, Blood **58**, 849-51.

Cline MJ, Haskell CH, 1980, Cancer Chemotherapy, WB Saunders and Co., Philadelphia.

Falkson G, Falkson HC, 1989, CAF and nasal buserelin in the treatment of premenopausal women with metastatic breast cancer, European Journal of Clinical Oncology **25**, 737-40.

Faulkner A, Maguire P, 1984, Teaching ward nurses to monitor mastectomy patients, Clinical Oncology **10**, 383-9.

Fetter MP, 1987, Reaching a level of sexual comfort, Health Education **18**, 6-8.

Folz AT, 1987, The influence of cancer on the self concept and quality of life, Seminars in Oncology Nursing **3**, 303-12.

Glasgow M, Halfin V, Althausen AF, 1987, Sexual response and cancer, Ca: A Cancer Journal for Clinicians **37**, 322-32.

Johnson J, 1986, Sexual concerns of the cancer patient, Nursing Republic of South Africa Verpleging **1**(10), 24-5.

Kaempfer SH, 1988, Reproductive planning. In: Baird SB (Editor), Decision Making in Oncology Nursing, BC Becker, Toronto.

Lamb MA, 1991, Alterations in sexuality and sexual functioning. In: Baird SB, McCorkle R, Grant M (Editors), Cancer Nursing: A Comprehensive Textbook, WB Saunders Co., London.

Lowitz BB, 1988, Pregnancy and sexual function. In: Casciato DA, Lowitz BB (Editors), Manual of Clinical Oncology (Second edition), Little, Brown and Co., Boston.

Martin RH, 1993, Detection of genetic damage in human sperm, Reproductive Toxicology **7**, 47-51.

McInnes S, Schilsky RL, 1996, Infertility following cancer chemotherapy. In: Chabner BA, Longo DL (Editors), Cancer Chemotherapy and Biotherapy: Principles and Practice (Second edition), Lippincott-Raven, Philadelphia.

Montz DL, Wolff AJ, Gambone JC, et al, 1991, Gonadal protection and fecundity in cyclophosphamide-treated rats, Cancer Research **51**, 2124-6.

Effects on sexual function

Petty F, Noyes R, 1981, Depression secondary to cancer, Biologic Psychiatry **16**, 1203-20.

Priestman TJ, 1989, Cancer Chemotherapy: An Introduction (Third edition), Springer-Verlag, London.

Quantock C, Beynon J, 1995, HRT and the nurse, Nursing Standard **9**(40), 20-1.

Schrover LR, von Eschenbach AC, 1984a, Sexual and marital counselling with men treated for testicular cancer, Journal of Sexual and Marital Therapy **10**, 29-40.

Schrover LR, von Eschenbach AC, Smith DB, Gonzales J, 1984b, Sexual rehabilitation of urological cancer patients: a practical approach, Ca: A Cancer Journal for Clinicians **34**, 66-73.

Schrover LR, Gonzales J, von Eschenbach AC, 1986, Sexual and marital relationships after chemotherapy for seminoma, Urology **27**, 117-23.

Smith DB, 1989, Sexual rehabilitation of the cancer patient, Cancer Nursing **12**, 10-15.

Webb C, 1987, Sexual healing, Nursing Times **83**, 28-30.

Whitehead E, Shalet SM, Blackledge G, et al, 1993, The effect of combination chemotherapy on ovarian function in women treated for Hodgkin's disease, Cancer **52**, 265-9.

Woods NF, 1990, Human Sexuality in Health and Illness, (Third edition), CV Mosby, St Louis.

World Health Organisation, 1975, Education and Treatment in Human Sexuality. The Training of Health Professionals. Report of a WHO meeting, Technical Report Series No: 572, WHO, Geneva.

CHAPTER 14   LESS COMMON TOXIC EFFECTS

Almost any tissue or organ can be affected by chemotherapy. Although most toxicities affect rapidly proliferating tissues cellular damage can, at times, occur irrespective of the generation time. For example, although DNA may be damaged, normal function may continue until mitosis when DNA damage becomes manifest and the cell is unable to divide (mitotic death). Similarly, unique toxicities may occur only in response to specific chemotherapeutic agents.

GENITOURINARY AND RENAL TOXICITY

Haemorrhagic cystitis may affect patients treated with either cyclophosphamide or ifosfamide. This unique side-effect affects about 10% of all those treated with cyclophosphamide due to the irritant effects of its metabolites on the mucosal lining of the bladder, particularly acrolein and 4-hydroxycyclophosphamide (Figure 14.1). The risk is increased in those who have received prior pelvic radiation or by inadequate hydration before, during and after treatment. The severity may vary from mild cystitis to severe bladder damage with massive haemorrhage (Priestman, 1989) and may lead to significant scarring and, possibly, an increased risk of bladder carcinoma.

Figure 14.1   **Summary of the metabolism of cyclophosphamide**
(Based on Priestman, 1989)

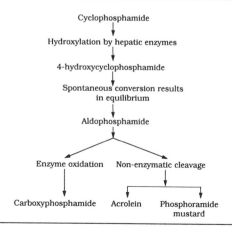

Care must be taken to prevent these serious complications by maintaining adequate hydration and encouraging regular and frequent urination. The dose of the drug concerned is another factor to be considered; when this exceeds $1g/m^2$ MESNA (sodium-2-mercapto-ethane-sulphonate) must be given simultaneously (Priestman, 1989). Indeed, MESNA, is the most effective agent for preventing cystitis and should be routinely administered to all those receiving high-dose cyclophosphamide as well as those with a history of drug-induced cystitis (Andriole et al, 1987). MESNA has no effect on the therapeutic activity of cyclophosphamide but reacts with acrolein and its 4-hydroxy metabolites converting them to harmless substances that will not damage the bladder mucosa. It is given in divided doses every 4hrs in doses equal to those of cyclophosphamide or ifosfamide (Andriole et al, 1987). Since MESNA has a relatively short half-life, administration must be continued for a period long enough to ensure complete deactivation of the toxic metabolites. This is particularly important in patients with impaired renal or hepatic function when drug metabolism or excretion may be inhibited.

Renal toxicity

As many cytotoxic drugs, or their metabolites, are excreted by the kidneys, renal function must be carefully evaluated before chemotherapy is given. Adequate renal function is also essential to ensure that the breakdown products, resulting from the destruction of both malignant and normal cells, are excreted. Renal insufficiency may necessitate adjustments or alterations to the planned therapy. The patient's hydration status is, therefore, important and fluid balance must be closely monitored, particularly when renal toxicity is likely. Administration of adequate fluids is, therefore, essential.

Some drugs (Table 14.1) may exert direct toxic effects on renal tissues; forced diuresis can help to prevent or minimise their impact. Clearly renal function must be closely monitored throughout treatment, and periodically after its completion.

When there are signs of renal toxicity, or the patient has pre-existing renal disease, the drug dosage must be reduced; alternatively urotoxic drugs may be withdrawn from the treatment plan. Thus some patients require intravenous hydration prior to chemotherapy to ensure an adequate urine output. Hyperuricaemia and uric acid nephropathy may be a problem for some patients leading to renal failure.

Table 14.1   **Drugs that may cause urotoxicity**

Drug	Some signs and symptoms	Effects on the kidney
Cisplatin	Decreased creatinine clearance leading to increased serum creatinine Hyperuricaemia Hypomagnesaemia Hypocalcaemia	Necrosis of proximal and distal tubules Disruption of resorptive mechanisms
Cyclophosphamide	Haemorrhagic cystitis Decreased urine output Hyponatraemia Increased urine osmolarity	Effects on bladder mucosa Direct effects on renal tubules
Methotrexate	Increased serum urea and creatinine concentrations	Precipitation in renal tubules
Nitrosoureas (effects often delayed until the completion of treatment)	Azotaemia Proteinuria Decreased creatinine clearance Progressive renal failure	Chronic nephritis, decrease in kidney size, glomerular sclerosis Atrophy of renal tubules
Streptozocin	Transient proteinuria Decreased creatinine excretion Hypokalaemia Glycosuria Phosphaturia Aminoaciduria	Tubular atrophy Diffuse nephritis
Vincristine	Hyponatraemia Syndrome of inappropriate secretion of antidiuretic hormone (SIADH)	Increased secretion of ADH

Acute uric acid nephropathy usually arises in those with large, rapidly growing tumours which are very responsive to chemotherapy. It results from massive tumour cell lysis, the release of intracellular mucoproteins and a subsequent production of uric acid (Portlock and Goffinet, 1986). It is most common in newly treated patients with leukaemia or lymphoma and can, generally, be prevented by administration of allopurinol, given prophylactically at least 12 hours before chemotherapy, combined with hydration. Allopurinol reduces the endogenous production of uric acid. The tumour lysis syndrome may also lead to other metabolic abnormalities including hypokalaemia, hyperphosphataemia and hypercalcaemia.

Less common toxic effects

Care of the patient receiving urotoxic drugs

Drug-induced cystitis may be due to a variety of pathological changes in the bladder wall including mucosal oedema and ulceration, sub-endothelial telangiectasis and haemorrhage and, at times, fibrosis of the detrusor muscles (Javadapour, 1982). Although secondary infection must be excluded, such cystitis is usually sterile. It is distressing and can be life-threatening when haemorrhage is severe (Kyle, 1982). Long-term effects may result leading to permanent contraction of the bladder and persistent urinary difficulties.

However, although rare, some patients show no evidence of bladder damage during therapy but develop bladder haemorrhage several months later on receiving a subsequent course of cytotoxic therapy (eg. cytosine arabinoside, methotrexate) (Tew et al, 1996). It is assumed that mucosal damage is incurred during the first course of therapy and that haemorrhage is precipitated by the irritation caused by the second drug. The patient should be warned of this possibility since it is frightening and may be mistaken for disease progression. He must be advised to increase and maintain his fluid intake (2-3 litres/day) to ensure rapid excretion of urotoxic meta-bolites and reduce their contact time with the bladder mucosa. However, when high-dose therapy is employed, a high fluid intake may be contraindicated due to the risk of inappropriate fluid retention. This is occasionally seen in those receiving doses of cyclo-phosphamide in excess of 50mg/kg and characterised by a marked fall in urine output 6-8hrs after administration that coincides with the peak excretion of alkylating metabolites in the urine. This is, however, self-limiting and is usually reversed within 12-16hrs (Tew et al, 1996).

Urinary retention can also be avoided by encouraging urination at least every two hours and ensuring that the bladder is emptied as soon as the urge to urinate is felt. It is particularly important that the bladder is emptied at night to avoid prolonged exposure of the mucosa to drug metabolites. The patient should be instructed to report all signs and symptoms indicative of cystitis so that a urine culture may be carried out to rule out the possibility of infection.

Cystitis

Cystitis is characterised by urinary frequency, and an urgency to void which may, at times, be almost continuous; pus, bacteria and mucus may be found in the urine, particularly when infection is

268

present. Micturition may cause burning, acute discomfort and pain (dysuria); low back pain and haematuria may occur. The cystitis accompanying administration of ifosfamide or cyclophosphamide may cause haematuria which, when severe, constitutes an emergency for which prompt treatment is required (see above).

Changes in urinary function may lead to feelings of shame, particularly if the symptoms result in incontinence; embarrassment is common and the symptoms themselves can lead to marked changes in normal patterns of activity. Affected patients may need a significant degree of emotional support. Such symptoms are very disturbing and distressing and must be recognised as such.

Care of the patient with cystitis

When urinary dysfunction is present a careful assessment is indicated to enable development of an appropriate care plan designed to minimise discomfort, promote continence and aid both psychological and physical comfort. The patient must be assured that this does not necessarily indicate disease progression. Thus, patients should be warned when cystitis is likely and be taught appropriate self-care measures to help to reduce its impact. To rule out infection, a sample of urine should be obtained for culture; where necessary, antibiotic therapy is given. Treatment is largely symptomatic.

The patient should be encouraged to maintain his fluid intake; an intake of 1 litre every eight hours will help to keep the urine osmolarity low, facilitate urination and reduce the risk of infection. The patient may also find it helpful to avoid substances that irritate the bladder mucosa (eg. tea, coffee, alcohol, tobacco and spicy foods). The risk of infection can also be reduced by teaching the patient measures designed to maintain an acidic urine (pH<7) which will inhibit bacterial replication in the bladder. Some workers suggest this is best achieved by giving daily doses of ascorbic acid (vitamin C) although the evidence regarding its efficacy is somewhat equivocal.

Dietary measures may help to acidify the urine so that the patient can be helped to select an appropriate diet. Daily measurement of the urinary pH will indicate whether or not these measures are effective.

Acid-base balance in foods. The potential acidity or alkalinity of a food refers to the end-products of its metabolism after digestion, absorption and utilisation. Most fruits and vegetables are rich in potassium, calcium and magnesium and so produce acids that can be used by the body (eg. carbonic acid). The end-products requiring excretion are, therefore, alkaline and will decrease the urinary acidity. Thus, when an acid urine is desired, the intake of most fruits and vegetables should be restricted. The exceptions are corn, plums, prunes and cranberries (see below).

A diet providing large quantities of protein will yield acidic waste products due to their high phosphorus, sulphur and iron content. Appropriate foods include eggs, meat, fish, poultry, milk or milk products, cereals/cereal products and bread. Neutral foods (ie. those producing neither excess alkaline nor acid residue) include sugar, tapioca, tea, coffee, butter, cooking oils, lard, cornflour and boiled sweets. Thus the required high energy, high protein diet, required for cellular repair and regeneration, can easily be achieved despite the need for some dietary changes to alleviate the symptoms of cystitis. However, to maintain an optimal nutritional status, vitamin and mineral supplementation may be required.

Many texts refer to the value of cranberry juice as a urinary acidulant as it contains quinic acid, which is metabolised to form hippuric acid and excreted in the urine. However, Sobota (1984) has indicated that it has only a small effect on urinary pH. It is clear, however, that cranberry juice does, indeed, inhibit bacterial growth and adherence to the bladder mucosa (Zafriri, 1989; Nazarko, 1995) and so may be useful in treating cystitis due to bacterial agents.

Pain may be significant; analgesics may be required. Relief may also be achieved by sitting in a warm bath. Good personal hygiene and efficient cleansing of the perineum, especially after defaecation, are extremely important in preventing ascending infection. Such cleansing is often difficult for the sick, the weak or the handicapped so that the carer must ensure that the patient is thoroughly cleansed.

Urgent treatment is needed when haemorrhagic cystitis is present; cytotoxic therapy must be discontinued immediately. Fluids, blood products and antispasmodics are needed; prophylactic antibiotics may also be given. An affected patient may be extremely anxious and fearful requiring a great deal of support and reassurance.

Various techniques have been attempted to achieve cauterisation of the bladder. However, continuous bladder irrigation, to prevent intravesicular clots, combined with transfusion to replace blood loss is usually effective (Tew et al, 1996). When bleeding is intractable, instillation of a 1% alum solution or dilute formaldehyde may reduce haemorrhage but may cause fibrosis and/or destruction of the bladder epithelium (Godec and Gleich, 1983; Goel et al, 1985). In extreme cases, when all local measures fail, cystectomy may be necessary (Tew et al, 1996).

Unless required for the purpose of bladder irrigation the use of in-dwelling catheters should be avoided as they are associated with bacteriuria, febrile urinary tract infection and sepsis. For the male, condom catheter drainage may be effective and, in females, appropriate padding and incontinence devices may prove acceptable alternatives. There will, however, be times when catheterisation is essential and when specific care will be required. Great care should be taken to prevent trauma during catheter placement and through-out the time during which the catheter remains in place (Table 14.2).

Table 14.2   Care of the patient with an indwelling catheter

During placement	Use strict asepsis Use generous amounts of sterile lubricant Use the smallest possible catheter Do not force the catheter
Subsequent care	**Males:** Secure catheter to abdomen to prevent rubbing of the penis at the scrotal junction **Females:** Secure catheter to thigh to prevent pulling
Prevention of infection	Keep drainage system closed at all times Obtain specimens through the needle aspiration port Ensure drainage bag is kept below level of the bladder Maintain accurate records of fluid intake and output and ensure an adequate fluid intake Ensure both the catheter and meatus are kept clean Ensure urine is kept acid Remove catheter as soon as possible

PULMONARY TOXICITY

Although unusual, pulmonary disturbances may be caused by a number of drugs (Table 14.3) and are generally manifested as pulmonary fibrosis; since lung damage is usually irreversible, such effects are potentially fatal. Most well-known of the drugs causing such toxicity are bleomycin, carmustine and busulfan (Weis and Trush, 1982). Patients must be closely monitored so that the causative agent(s) can be discontinued. However, early detection is difficult as the onset is often insidious and there is no test predictive of its occurrence nor is there an effective treatment (Cline and Haskell, 1980). Early changes are rarely evident on x-ray; damage that is visible on x-ray is already irreversible.

Table 14.3   Chemotherapeutic drugs causing pulmonary toxicity

Alkylating agents	Busulphan
	Cyclophosphamide
	Chlorambucil
	Melphalan
Nitrosoureas	Carmustine
Antitumour antibiotics	Bleomycin
	Mitomycin
Antimetabolites	Methotrexate
	Cytosine arabinoside
	6-mercaptopurine
Plant products	Etoposide
	Teniposide
Miscellaneous	L-asparaginase
	Procarbazine

The mechanism(s) through which pulmonary damage arises are not clearly understood. Two major mechanisms have been suggested. First, in some cases, the initial injury appears to occur in the endo-thelial cells which, in turn, initiates an inflammatory response in the cells lining the alveoli. The alveolar sacs become filled with exudate and diffusion of oxygen and carbon dioxide is inhibited. During the intermediate phase, fibroblasts infiltrate the alveolar walls and hyperplasia occurs. If this continues fibrotic changes will reduce pulmonary capacity. Secondly, it may be that immunological mechanisms are responsible for at least some cases of pulmonary toxicity when damage results from either an allergic reaction or from the deposition of antigen-antibody complexes in pulmonary tissues.

Bleomycin, for example, is preferentially distributed to the skin and lungs; both areas may show early signs of toxicity. Within the lungs there is a decrease in Type I pneumocytes and a redistribution of Type II pneumocytes into the alveolar spaces. At this stage, there may be symptoms of pneumonitis. The alveolar walls become thickened; collagen secretion is increased resulting in generalised interstitial fibrosis (Ginsburg and Comis, 1984). If damage continues, end-stage interstitial fibrosis leads to alveolar obliteration and dilation of the airspaces; pulmonary dysfunction is restrictive with functionally decreased lung volume, increased work of breathing and impaired gaseous exchange (Wickham, 1986).

Thus pulmonary toxicity results in impaired respiratory function which, over time, may progress to cause respiratory failure. The severity of pulmonary dysfunction may be exacerbated in the presence of chronic respiratory disease or infection of the respiratory tract. Radiotherapy, administered before or after chemotherapy, particularly that involving bleomycin, carmustine or busulfan, can increase the risk of pulmonary toxicity.

Effective care of patients with respiratory problems depends on an understanding of the underlying processes as well as of the complications that may arise as a result of the disease and its treatment. Care focuses on the relief of distressing symptoms and on prevention of common respiratory difficulties.

Each patient must be carefully assessed before appropriate care can be planned. Early physical findings include a dry hacking cough, fine râles with dyspnoea on exertion and a reduced diffusing capacity; little change is seen on chest x-ray. Later signs include dyspnoea at rest, tachypnoea and coarse râles accompanied by hypoxia due to the marked decrease in diffusion; x-ray will reveal signs of consolidation.

Evaluation of respiratory function depends on a combination of the medical history, physical examination, laboratory data and close observation. Four common problem areas can be identified: airway obstruction, hypoventilation and hypoxia, inadequate clearance of secretions and respiratory failure (Table 14.4).

Table 14.4   Examples of airway obstruction

Site of obstruction	Possible causes
Intraluminal	Secretions (mucus plugs)
	Neoplasm
	Foreign bodies
	Pneumonia
Wall of airway	Tumours
	Diffuse disease (eg. fibrosis, asthma, chronic obstructive airways disease)
Outside tracheobronchial tree	Tumours (eg. head, neck, thorax, abdomen)

Although the severity of the dysfunction determines the supportive measures required and the degree of assistance needed to maintain normal daily activity, certain general principles can be applied to the care of affected patients.

Common respiratory symptoms

Airway obstruction is characterised by both its position along the tracheobronchial tree and by whether it is an acute or chronic condition. It may arise in the lumen or the wall of the airway itself or outside the tracheobronchial tree. In general, the more central the obstruction the greater the disturbance to air flow. Management will differ depending on whether the condition is acute or chronic.

In acute obstruction, care is directed towards removing the obstruction (eg. tumour removal by surgery, chemotherapy or radiotherapy) or by providing an artificial airway (eg. tracheostomy). Chronic obstruction is managed by teaching the patient to identify those factors impairing his ventilatory function and to manage them using measures designed to increase expiratory flow and achieve optimal independence in the normal activities of living. Bronchospasm may be treated using drug therapy to promote relaxation of the bronchial muscles and increase vital capacity. Together with breathing exercises and relaxation techniques this will help to decrease anxiety and increase respiratory flow.

Airway obstruction may lead to both hypoventilation and hypoxia as gaseous exchange is inhibited when air movement is decreased. Hypoventilation arises when pulmonary function is reduced and is unable to maintain alveolar ventilation at a level appropriate to meet the metabolic demand; this may be of structural or functional origin. Functional causes include malnutrition and fatigue. Structural causes include tumours that obstruct the airway and treatment-induced effects, such as pneumonitis and pulmonary fibrosis which restrict lung expansion and ventilation; pneumonia, when exudate accumulates in the alveoli, has similar effects. Hypoventilation may, in turn, lead to hypoxia, hypercapnia and pneumonia.

Hypoxia (a decrease in oxygen tension) can, however, occur even in the absence of hypoventilation due to changes in the cardio-vascular-respiratory-haemopoietic system essential to satisfactory tissue oxygenation and to appropriate gaseous exchange. Hypoxia may, therefore, be due to a variety of causes including:

- Disturbances of the alveolar-capillary membrane, (eg. pulmonary fibrosis, emphysema) when fibrotic changes or oedema of the alveolar walls result in a decrease in the amount of oxygen diffusing into the bloodstream
- A reduced cardiac output
- Alterations in blood composition (eg. anaemia and a sub-

sequent decrease in haemoglobin). A reduced number of erythrocytes, or a less than normal complement of haemoglobin, reduces the amount of oxygen that can be taken up by the blood.

Hypoventilation may also lead to hypercapnia, the retention of carbon dioxide (CO_2) in excess of the normal range. Hypercapnia will develop more slowly than hypoxia because CO_2 is more soluble than oxygen and also diffuses more readily. Prevention of these conditions is essential. Symptomatic treatment includes drainage of pleural effusions, which inhibit thoracic expansion, use of bronchodilators, such as salbutamol, or drugs, such as digoxin, to improve cardiac output; blood transfusion may be used to correct anaemia.

Both airway obstruction and hypoventilation will inhibit the clearance of secretions from the respiratory tract. Unless preventive measures are taken, secretions will accumulate predisposing pneumonia; when this is combined with immunosuppression the risk is further increased. Care is, therefore, directed towards preventing infection and may include prophylactic antibiotics, treatment of the airway obstruction, endotracheal intubation, insertion of a tracheostomy to aid the removal of secretions or bronchoscopy designed to remove mucus plugs.

Respiratory failure

Respiratory failure results when the respiratory system cannot maintain adequate oxygenation and elimination of CO_2. The already compromised patient is at particular risk of respiratory suppression when certain drugs (eg. narcotics and some tranquillisers) are given; these should be used with caution in affected patients. Other causes include sepsis within the respiratory tract and interstitial fibrosis, both of which restrict lung expansion and obstruct of the major airways. Clearly diagnosis and treatment are essential to care of affected patients.

Care of the patient with a respiratory disturbance (Table 14.5)

Improving the quality of life is a major aim of care since respiratory disturbances may make 'normal' living impossible. The goals of care are, therefore, directed towards this aim and include:

- Promotion of optimal ventilation and oxygenation
- A decrease in the 'work' involved in respiration
- Prevention of infection.

Table 14.5   **Care of the patient with respiratory failure**

Prevention of infection	Prevent pneumonia as described. Ensure secretions removed by means of physiotherapy and postural drainage. Use aseptic techniques when suctioning is required.
Positioning Acute (short-term)	Turn head laterally with neck extended; inspect mouth for cause of obstruction. Insert artificial airway to relieve obstruction and maintain airway.
Chronic (long-term)	Get patient out of bed to maximise thoracic expansion, improve oxygenation and facilitate removal of secretions. Educate patient and family about management and appropriate care.
Oxygenation and mechanical ventilation	Maintain patency of airway; humidify inhaled air. When mechanical ventilation is employed, ensure endotracheal or tracheostomy tube well secured. Change ventilator tubing every 24hrs. Improve oxygen-carrying capacity by maintaining haemoglobin within normal limits, improving cardiac output and decreasing the work of breathing.
Prevention of the complications of mechanical ventilation	Maintain patency of airway; humidify inhaled air. Remove accumulated secretions. Prevent laryngeal or tracheal complications by securing the endotracheal tube, using low pressure cuffs or using minimal pressure occluding volume in the inflating cuff. Prevent barotrauma by minimising peak airway pressure, use of intermittent ventilation, prolonged expiratory time or decreased respiratory rate. Provide for mechanical emergencies - have Ambubag and mask at bedside.
Fluid balance	Ensure adequate hydration but restrict fluids if water retention is present. Administer diuretics when prescribed. Minimise the effects of positive pressure breathing; use intermittent mechanical ventilation. Minimise peak airway pressure.
General care	Control pain and stress. Sedate the patient when necessary. Maintain oral hygiene and pressure area care. Provide comfort and reassurance.

General principles can be applied as well as specific measures designed to overcome particular problems. Individual assessment of respiratory function is essential.

Table 14.6 provides an outline of the clinical findings associated with each of the respiratory problems discussed; these will provide a baseline against which to judge future changes. Continued regular assessment is essential to identify changes and, where appropriate, provide treatment at an early stage.

Table 14.6   Assessment of pulmonary function: clinical signs

	Medical history	Physical examination	Arterial blood gases	Chest X-ray	Pulmonary function tests
Airway obstruction	Dyspnoea and/or shortness of breath, cough haemoptysis, and recurrent upper respiratory tract infections	Cyanosis, increased rate of respiration, prolonged expiration. Use of accessory muscles of respiration. Stridor, tracheal shift. Flat or hyperresonant percussion; rhonci, râles and wheezing. Signs of consolidation, marked respiratory effort without air movement.	Po_2 - decreased Pco_2 - may be increased or decreased.	May show tumour, pneumonia or chronic obstructive airways disease.	Indicative of an obstructive defect.
Hypoxia and hypo-ventilation	Dyspnoea, tachypnoea, headache, lethargy, fatigue and restlessness, irritability and confusion.	Coma, cyanosis, tachycardia. Hypertension followed by hypo-tension. Decreased respiratory expansion, decreased breath sounds. Reduced diaphragmatic movement. Rhonci, râles, wheezing and signs of consolidation	Po_2 - decreased Pco_2 - may be increased	May show pulmonary oedema or fibrosis, tumour or pneumonia.	Indicative of an obstructive or restrictive defect.
Inadequate clearance of secretions	Cough with or without sputum. Change in colour, odour or consistency of sputum. Pyrexia. History of smoking and/or chronic obstructive airways disease.	Cyanosis. Increased work of breathing and increased respiratory rate. Use of accessory muscles of respiration Rhonci, râles, wheezing and signs of consolidation; systemic signs of dehydration.			
Respiratory failure	Rapid and progressive air hunger. Restlessness and confusion. Profuse sweating, headache. May also have a history of any of the symptoms listed above.	Tachycardia, hypo-tension, cyanosis Confusion, tremors. Decreased respiratory effort and respiratory rate. Papilloedema.	Po_2 - decreased Pco_2 - may be increased or decreased.	May show tumour, fibrosis, pneumonia or oedema.	Indicative of an obstructive or restrictive defect.

Table 14.7   Normal levels of blood gases

Arterial Po_2	80-104mmHg
Arterial Pco_2	36-42mmHg
Venous Po_2	45-46mmHg
Venous Pco_2	40-41mmHg
pH	7.35-7.45

The following parameters can aid detection of respiratory changes:

- Percussion - to identify areas of dullness
- Ascultation - to identify the presence of rhonci and râles
- Observation - to identify changes in the type, frequency and severity of coughing
- X-ray - to identify the presence and/or extent of pneumonitis, fibrosis, infection or obstruction
- Monitoring of blood gases and pH (Tables 14.7 and 14.8).

Respiratory difficulties (eg. pneumonitis) may be accompanied by a dry, persistent cough, dyspnoea on exertion, weakness and fatigue and, on occasions, pyrexia. Care is directed towards relief of symptoms as well as an improvement in pulmonary ventilation.

Table 14.8   The interrelationships between Po_2, Pco_2, pH and respiration

	Effects of decrease	Effect of increase
Po_2	Stimulates respiration; CO_2 'blown off'.	Increase has little effect on respiration.
Pco_2	Inhibition of respiration. When Pco_2 = 30mmHg or less ventilation decreases to 25% of normal.	Stimulates respiration. When Pco_2 reaches 50mmHg, ventilatory rate will triple.
pH	Respiration stimulated when pH is below 7.41; if pH <7.20 pulmonary ventilation quadruples.	When pH >7.41 respiration is inhibited. If pH >7.50 pulmonary ventilation decreased by 50%.

A persistent cough is debilitating and disabling and may, itself, cause profound fatigue and exhaustion; relief is, therefore, a major aim. Humidifying the air can significantly decrease the frequency of coughing. Inspired air is normally moistened within the respiratory tract by the moisture evaporated from the mucosal surfaces. Inflammation results in water depletion so that the mucus becomes viscous and impairs ciliary activity. Retention of this tenacious mucus increases airway resistance and promotes infection. Humidification is, therefore, important and can be achieved in a variety of ways. The choice depends mainly on:

- Whether or not the upper airway is bypassed
- The degree of mucosal dehydration
- The equipment available.

A steam kettle, vaporiser or room humidifier are the simplest methods available. In the home, a humidifier attached to the central heating system or a bowl of water close to a radiator may be adequate for this purpose. When oxygen therapy is required, bubbling the oxygen through water will increase its moisture content; the amount of water absorbed can be increased by using heated water. A more efficient method is delivery of water in an aerosol or nebulised form when the nebuliser produces a coarse spray of fluid which is directed into a stream of rapidly moving gas that is, subsequently, directed on to the walls of the container to reduce the size of the water particles. The usual diluent is sterile water although normal saline may be used. Hypertonic saline will promote liquefaction and elimination of accumulated secretions although this should not used unless prescribed by a physician. Medications, such as broncho-dilators [eg. salbutamol) may also be given in nebulised form thus avoiding systemic administration and the associated side-effects.

A high fluid intake (3 litres/day), when combined with high humidity, will help to liquefy secretions; unless such a fluid intake is contraindicated, at least 1 litre should be taken every eight hours. Warm fluids will be soothing when the cough is persistent. If the cough is inhibiting normal rest and sleep, a cough suppressant (eg. codeine linctus) may be given; cough lozenges or boiled sweets may also be helpful. Wherever possible, affected patients should be protected from irritant substances (eg. cigarette smoke, strong perfume) in the environment.

The patient should be encouraged to adopt a position that promotes optimal thoracic expansion and, therefore, improves both oxygenation and removal of any accumulated secretions. Ideally he will sit out of bed with his head and back bent slightly forward, his arms relaxed and supported (eg. leaning on forearm or elbow) and his feet flat on a firm surface. A similar posture can be adopted in bed

(Figures 14.2 and 14.3). The patient is generally the best guide as to the most comfortable possible; this is likely to be that providing the best alveolar ventilation.

Figure 14.2   **Positioning for optimal ventilation when sitting in a chair**

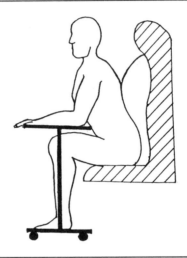

Prevention of infection

All the respiratory problems discussed are associated with a significant risk of pneumonia; prevention of infection is, therefore, essential. Strict asepsis must be maintained when caring for patients with respiratory disturbances both to decrease exposure to potentially infective organisms and to prevent cross-infection. This is particularly important when the patient has a temporary or permanent tracheostomy, is suffering from bone marrow depression or is otherwise immunosuppressed. On occasions, protective isolation (reverse barrier care) is required. Where possible, however, the length of the hospital stay should be reduced.

Optimal nutritional status must be maintained to enhance immunocompetence (Ch. 12). Care must be taken to ensure that the patient has adequate rest and sleep. The individual must be advised to avoid contact with any person (hospital staff, relatives, friends) thought to be suffering a respiratory tract infection, influenza or a cold.

Figure 14.3   Positioning for optimal ventilation when in bed

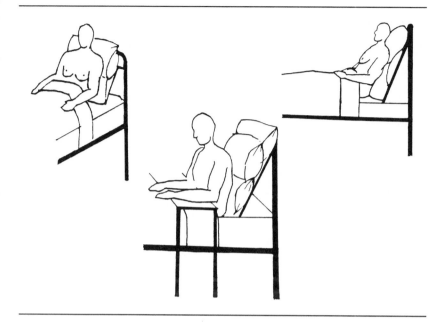

When necessary, coughing can be stimulated by irritating the pharynx using, for example, the tip of a suction catheter or application of digital pressure over the trachea just above the medial clavicular prominence. Prolonged exhalation may also stimulate coughing when the increased flow of air irritates the mucosa. When such measures are unsuccessful deep suctioning is required. Alternatively, when efficient access to the retained pulmonary secretions is essential to prevent the development of more serious respiratory problems (eg. pneumonia), a tracheostomy may be performed; this may also be needed when the upper airway is obstructed by tumour or laryngeal oedema, at least until treatment has effectively eliminated or reduced the obstruction.

Since the patient's respiration is often shallow, due to weakness and pain, alveolar ventilation is decreased. Deep breathing and coughing should be encouraged to prevent accumulation of secretions.

The patient should be encouraged to take regular deep breaths, inhaling deeply and relaxing the abdominal muscles. He should then lean forward and exhale as much as possible through pursed lips.

281

Less common toxic effects

Exhalation is most effective when the abdominal muscles are contracted so that pressure exerted on the lower abdomen may promote compression and aid in the elevation of the diaphragm during exhalation.

Breathing exercises should be carried out 2 or 3 times daily; their effectiveness may be increased if they are preceded by administration of a prescribed bronchodilator (eg. salbutamol) via a nebuliser.

Coughing is essential for removal of secretions from the respiratory tract and should not be suppressed unless it is non-productive or excessive and exhausting. The patient must be taught to cough effectively. Where possible, he should be in the sitting position; deep inspiration should be followed by a series of small, short coughs (short coughs require less energy and are less likely to cause airway collapse than a single, large and forceful exhalation).

Coughing can be assisted manually in those with weak abdominal muscles as previously described. The patient must be closely observed for signs of fatigue and allowed to rest when necessary; pain or unusual fatigue when coughing must be reported to the physician. The physiotherapist will advise when specific care and/or postural drainage is required.

NEUROTOXICITY

Reversible or irreversible neurotoxicity may occur with various anti-cancer drugs and may affect the central nervous system (CNS), the peripheral nervous system or the cranial nerves; on occasions all these systems may be affected (Table 14.9).

Neurotoxicity is usually temporary, resolving once treatment is completed although, at times, permanent neurological deficits may result (Cline and Haskell, 1980). Their occurrence, and severity, can be affected by the route of administration. For example, drugs given intrathecally may exhibit profound neurological effects that are not manifested when they are administered intravenously. One such drug is methotrexate which, given intravenously, exerts minimal neurotoxicity; although it is widely distributed in body water, it does not penetrate the nervous system. Severe neurotoxicity often accompanies high dose vincristine or cytosine arabinoside (Herzig et al, 1985). Neurotoxic effects are exacerbated by concurrent radiotherapy to the CNS.

Symptoms of toxicity may include cerebellar effects (eg. tremor, loss of balance and fine motor movements), severe peripheral neuro-

282

pathy, confusion and somnolence. Peripheral neuropathy may be manifested by a sensory loss in the extremities and auditory or visual impairment (Holden and Felde, 1987). By interfering with motor function, such symptoms may significantly affect normal life.

Table 14.9   Some commonly observed neurotoxicities

Drug	Route of administration	Neurotoxic effect	Signs and symptoms
Cisplatin	IV	Ototoxicity	Tinnitus/hearing loss.
Cytosine Arabinoside	Intrathecal	Acute arachnoiditis Meningeal irritation Necrotising leuko-encephalopathy	Nausea, vomiting, headache, stiff neck, lethargy, pyrexia. Hyperkinesis, ataxia, seizures, decreased motor skills.
5-fluorouracil	IV	Acute cerebellar syndrome	Ataxia, dizziness, slurred speech.
Methotrexate	IV (at high doses)	Transient CVA	Similar to cerebrovascular accident.
	Intrathecal	Meningeal irritation Acute arachnoiditis Paraplegic syndrome Encephalopathy Necrotising leuko-encephalopathy	Nausea, vomiting, stiff neck, headache, pyrexia, lethargy. Neurogenic bladder, leg pain, paraplegia (can be permanent). Confusion, dementia, seizures, spasticity, slurred speech, visual disturbances, quadraplegia. Hyperkinesis, seizures, ataxia, decreased motor skills.
Vincristine	IV	Peripheral neuropathy Neuropathy - cranial nerve - autonomic Encephalopathy	Loss of deep tendon reflexes, parasthesiae of extremities, muscle pain, and weakness. Vocal cord paresis, jaw pain, ptosis, diplopia. Constipation. Mental changes, confusion, coma.

Abnormalities in neurological function may, of course, be related to factors other than chemotherapy. For example, the primary tumour, or secondary deposits, may involve the nervous system; metabolic or electrolyte imbalances may cause neurological disturbance. Similarly, concurrent medical disease may be manifested through neurological defects. These may be difficult to differentiate from chemotherapy-induced neurotoxicity. Careful assessment is, therefore, required.

However, since the clinical manifestations of drug-induced toxicity are highly variable, it can be difficult to confirm the diagnosis. Similarly, the time of onset of neurotoxic effects varies; they can occur acutely within 2-3 hours of administration or be delayed for weeks, months or even years after treatment.

CARDIOTOXICITY

Both acute and chronic cardiotoxicity may directly result from chemotherapy (von Hoff et al, 1982) (Table 14.10). This is clearly a dose-limiting toxicity and is particularly associated with the anthracycline antibiotics, doxorubicin and daunomycin. This is of particular significance as many cancer patients are older adults and so may have pre-existing cardiac disease; a thorough cardiac assessment must be carried out prior to therapy. An electrocardiogram (ECG) should be performed before treatment and repeated regularly.

Table 14.10   Some examples of cardiotoxic drugs and their effects

Drug	Incidence	Toxicity
Amsacrine	5%	Ventricular fibrillation, cardiomyopathy
Cyclophosphamide	Rare	Haemorrhagic myocardial necrosis
Cisplatin	Not known	Cardiac ischaemia
Cisplatin-based combination therapy	Not known	Arterial occlusion, myocardial infarction, cerebrovascular accident
Actinomycin-D	Rare	Cardiomyopathy
Daunorubicin	0-41%	Transient ECG changes, cardiomyopathy
Doxorubicin	2.2%	Transient ECG changes, cardiomyopathy
5-fluorouracil	Rare	Angina 3-18hrs after drug administered

Acute cardiotoxicity occurs soon after administration of therapy and is manifested by ECG abnormalities (Tokaz and von Hoff, 1984). These are evidenced by sinus tachycardias, ST and T-wave changes and premature beats. Such changes are usually benign and reversible and do not necessitate alterations to treatment.

Rarely, a decrease in QRS voltage may occur; this is often irreversible and may be associated with the total dose received (Cortes et al, 1975). There have also been reports of life-threatening arrythmias and/or sudden death arising during or immediately after drug administration (Tokaz and von Hoff, 1984) although this is rare.

Subacute changes may cause fibrinous pericarditis associated

284

with myocardial dysfunction during the first 4-5 weeks of therapy (Kaszyk, 1986); again these are usually transient and reversible.

The most serious and dose-limiting cardiotoxicity is that causing *cardiomyopathy*. Damage to the myofibrils and subsequent degeneration are gradual; the maximum damage may not be seen for weeks or months after its completion (Kaszyk, 1986). It is more common for symptoms to arise soon after completion of treatment (Saltiel and McGuire, 1983). As myofibrillar damage increases, the heart is required to contract harder so as to compensate for the loss of pumping ability; hypertrophy occurs and the heart enlarges.

The signs and symptoms of cardiomyopathy are typical of those associated with congestive cardiac failure. These include a non-specific dry cough or tachycardia (Kaszyk, 1986). Dyspnoea and a non-productive cough are common and accompanied by ankle oedema and distension of the veins of the neck. Tachycardia, cardiomegaly and hepatomegaly may also be present. Once these signs and symptoms are present the patient has already developed irreversible damage for which, at present, there is no treatment. Clearly, cardiotoxic drugs must be discontinued as soon as cardiac damage is suspected. Supportive medical and nursing care must be provided for those who develop congestive cardiac failure.

HEPATIC TOXICITY

Hepatotoxicity is an uncommon but potentially serious problem in cancer therapy. Since both the hepatic artery and portal vein 'transport' cytotoxic agents to the liver from the bloodstream and the GI tract respectively, the liver is clearly vulnerable to toxic damage. It also plays a central role in drug metabolism so that it is, perhaps, surprising that hepatic damage is not more common. This can be explained, at least in part, by the fact that hepatocytes reproduce only slowly and, as a result, are less susceptible than those cells that are rapidly dividing (Perry, 1984).

Although most cytotoxic drugs are metabolised by the liver certain of them are particularly associated with hepatotoxicity (Table 14.11). It must, however, be remembered that any drug may have a hepatotoxic effect and others may produce idiosyncratic responses. As a number of disease or treatment-related factors may affect the liver it can be difficult to differentiate between these and chemotherapy-induced toxic effects (Table 14.12); a liver biopsy may be required.

Table 14.11   Examples of hepatoxic drugs

Agent	Effects produced
Amsacrine	Mild increase in serum bilirubin; rare hepatic failure. Elevated hepatic enzymes
Adriamycin	Elevated hepatic enzymes
Carmustine	Elevated hepatic enzymes; hepatitis
Chlorambucil	Elevated hepatic enzymes
Dacarbazine	Elevated hepatic enzymes
Daunomycin	Elevated hepatic enzymes
Methotrexate	Elevated hepatic enzymes; fibrosis, cirrhosis
Mithramycin	Acute necrosis; altered hepatic enzymes and clotting factors
L-asparaginase	Fatty changes; decreased serum proteins, impaired synthesis of clotting factors

The range of toxicity can include, for example, a transient elevation of hepatic enzymes (transaminases) arising from administration of cytosine arabinoside, cirrhotic changes due to methotrexate and liver necrosis with 6-mercaptopurine (Sallan et al, 1975).

Table 14.12   Factors contributing to hepatotoxicity in cancer

Malignant invasion	Immunosuppression
Primary hepatic tumour	Hepatic infection
Secondary deposits	Viral hepatitis

Concurrent administration of hepatotoxic agents (eg. anaesthetic agents, phenothiazines, oral contraceptives)

Previous/concurrent radiotherapy involving the liver

Transfusion of blood products

Graft-versus-host disease

Liver function should always be evaluated before chemotherapy is given and, when liver function is abnormal, drugs known to be hepatotoxic should be avoided. It must be remembered that abnormal liver function can also increase the toxicity of any drug (Cline and Haskell, 1980); affected patients must be closely monitored throughout the course of drug therapy, whether or not this is antineoplastic in nature.

Hepatic damage is first manifested by biochemical abnormalities; injury to the hepatocytes is demonstrated by elevation of the hepatic enzymes. Jaundice, ascites and hepatomegaly may also be present or may develop as the condition progresses.

The management of hepatic toxicity varies with the agent concerned. However, when other possible causes of damage have been eliminated, the suspected drug(s) may be discontinued. On occasions, a simple modification of the treatment regime and a reduction in the dose of the toxic agent will be sufficient to reverse hepatic damage enabling the planned treatment to be continued.

OCULAR TOXICITY
Toxicity to the eye is rare and it is not always possible to distinguish between this and pre-existing damage or malignant involvement. Such effects may include the formation of cataracts (busulphan), papilloedema (eg. procarbazine, cisplatin, chlorambucil), diplopia (eg. vincristine, vinblastine, procarbazine, chlorambucil), photophobia (eg. procarbazine, vincristine, vinblastine and 5-FU) and conjunctivitis (doxorubicin).

Neurotoxicity, affecting the CNS, may lead to secondary involvement causing blurred vision and impaired colour vision (Wilding, 1985). Such effects can be distressing (Holden and Felde, 1987). Problems encountered include mistaken colours, potential for injury and decreased appreciation of food and the environment in general. Bone marrow suppression may cause haemorrhage of the conjunctiva/retina secondary to thrombocytopoenia or anaemia.

LONG-TERM EFFECTS OF CHEMOTHERAPY
Individuals receiving chemotherapy are vulnerable not only to short-term side-effects but also to long-term effects that may arise some years later. These include, second malignant diseases, sterility or impaired gonadal function and teratogenic effects (Ch. 13).

Development of second malignancies
Since many antineoplastic drugs interact with DNA many are mutagenic and/or teratogenic. Some (eg. antitumour antibiotics, alkylating agents, epipodophyllotoxins and procarbazine) are known to be carcinogenic (Erlichman and Moore, 1996; King, 1996). Thus, for some patients, development of a second malignancy may be a long-term complication of chemotherapy. The pathology/histology of such a tumour will differ from that of the original tumour whereas, in metastatic disease, although the tumour may be in a variety of sites, this is of the same type as the original cancer.

Second malignancies may also develop as a result of the prolonged immunosuppression, often resulting from antineoplastic therapy; newly developed malignant cells may be able to develop and grow in an immunocompromised individual. The combined use of radiotherapy and chemotherapy may also contribute to their development since both of these interact with DNA and result in faulty transcription of genetic information (Kyle, 1982).

The risk of second malignancies is most common in those with Hodgkin's disease, multiple myeloma and acute leukaemia. It is, however, clear that, although the risk is real, and is often delayed for many years after apparently successful treatment, the number of patients affected is extremely small. At present the benefits of chemotherapy strongly outweigh the potential risks for the majority of patients. It is clear, however, that careful surveillance is necessary during the long-term follow-up of these patients.

REFERENCES

Andriole GL, Sandlund JT, Miser JS, 1987, The efficacy of Mesna (2-mercaptoethane sodium sulfonate) as a urinary protectant in patients with haemorrhagic cystitis receiving further oxazophosphorine chemotherapy, Journal of Clinical Oncology **5**, 799-803.

Cline MJ, Haskell CM, 1980, Cancer Chemotherapy, WB Saunders Co., Philadelphia.

Cortes EP, Lutman G, Wanka G, et al, 1975, Adriamycin cardiotoxicity: a clinico-pathologic correlation, Cancer Chemotherapy Reports **6**(2), 215-25.

Erlichman C, Moore M, 1996, Carcinogenesis: a late complication of cancer chemotherapy. In: Chabner BA, Longo DL, 1996, Cancer Chemotherapy and Biotherapy: Principles and Practice (Second Edition), Lippincott-Raven, Philadelphia

Ginsburg SJ, Comis RL, 1984, The pulmonary toxicity of antineoplastic agents. In: Perry MC, Yarbro JC (Editors), Toxicity of Chemotherapy, Grune and Stratton, Orlando, Florida.

Godec CJ, Gleich P, 1983, Intractable hematuria and formalin, Journal of Urology **130**, 688-91.

Goel AK, Rao MS, Bhagwat S, et al, 1985, Intravesical irrigation with alum for the control of massive bladder haemorrhage, Journal of Urology **133**, 956-7.

Herzig R, Hines J, Herzig G, et al, 1985, Cerebellar toxicity with high dose cytosine arabinoside, Journal of Clinical Oncology **5**, 927-32.

Holden S, Felde G, 1987, Nursing care of patients experiencing cisplatin-related peripheral neuropathy, Oncology Nursing Forum **14**, 13-7.

Javadapour N, 1982, Urologic emergencies. In: DeVita V, Hellman S, Rosenberg S, Cancer - Principles and Practice of Oncology. JB Lippincott Co., Philadelphia.

Kaszyk LK, 1986, Cardiac toxicity associated with cancer therapy, Oncology Nursing Forum **13**(4), 81-8.

King RJB, 1996, Cancer Biology, Addison-Wesley Longman Ltd., Edinburgh.

Kyle RA, 1982, Second malignancies associated with chemotherapeutic agents, Seminars in Oncology **9**, 131-42.

Nazarko L, 1995, The therapeutic uses of cranberry juice, Nursing Standard **9**(34), 33-5.

Perry MC, 1984, Hepatotoxicity. In: Perry MC, Yarbro JC (Editors), Toxicity of Chemotherapy, Grune and Stratton, Orlando, Florida.

Portlock CS, Goffinet DR, 1986, Manual of Clinical Problems in Oncology, Little, Brown and Company, Boston.

Priestman TJ, 1989, Cancer Chemotherapy: an Introduction (3rd edition), Springer Verlag, London.

Sallan SE, Zinberg AE, Frei F, 1975, Antiemetic effect of delta-9-tetra-hydrocannabinol in patients receiving cancer chemotherapy, New England Journal of Medicine **293**, 795-7.

Saltiel E, McGuire W, 1983, Doxorubicn cardiomyopathy, Western Journal of Medicine **139**(3), 332-41.

Sobota AE, 1984, Inhibition of bacterial adherence by cranberry juice: potential use for the treatment of urinary tract infections, Journal of Urology **131**, 1013-6.

Tew KD, Colvin M, Chabner BA, 1996, Alkylating agents. In: Chabner BA, Longo DL, 1996, Cancer Chemotherapy and Biotherapy: Principles and Practice (Second edition), Lippincott-Raven, Philadelphia.

Tokaz LK, von Hoff DD, 1984, The toxicity of anticancer agents. In: Perry MC, Yarbro JC (Editors), Toxicity of Chemotherapy, Grune and Stratton, Orlando, Florida.

van Hoff D, Rozencweig H, Piccart M, 1982, The cardiotoxicity of anticancer agents, Seminars in Oncology **9**(1), 23-33.

Weis RB, Trush DM, 1982, A review of the pulmonary toxicity of cancer chemotherapeutic agents, Oncology Nursing Forum **9**(1), 16-21.

Wickham R, 1986, Pulmonary toxicity secondary to cancer treatment, Oncology Nursing Forum **13**(5), 69-76.

Wilding G, Caruso R, Lawrence T, et al, 1985, Retinal toxicity after high-dose cisplatin-related peripheral neuropathies, Oncology Nursing Forum **14**, 13-9.

Zafriri D, 1989, Inhibitory activity of cranberry juice on adherence type 1 and type P fimbriated *Escheria coli* to eucaryotic cells, Antimicrobial Agents and Chemotherapy **33**(1), 92-8.

CHAPTER 15   EMERGENCY AND PALLIATIVE USES OF CHEMOTHERAPY

Patients with cancer may experience medical emergencies as a result of either the disease itself or its treatment. Ironically it is the success of anticancer treatment that has led to an increased likelihood of such complications as patients live longer and are subjected to increasingly aggressive therapies.

Chemotherapy can be used, with varying degrees of success, as an emergency or palliative treatment and can significantly improve the quality of life even when cure is unlikely. When cure is not possible the therapeutic goal becomes that of palliation which can be defined as prolongation of survival, relief of distressing symptoms and the maintenance of as near normal function as possible (Carter et al, 1987). The emphasis on improving distressing symptoms, rather than aiming for cure, means that therapy may be modified since the goals of palliation are such that acute side-effects are not tolerated; the risk of long-term effects is not, however, a major concern. The criteria for palliative care can be summarised as follows:

1.   The symptom must be sufficiently distressing and persistent to justify an effort to relieve it.

2.   The treatment required should be of short duration and make no additional demands on the patient.

3.   The treatment used must be adequate to meet the desired objective(s) without creating unnecessary side-effects.

Clearly treatment that adds to the patient's distress does not meet its objectives and is, therefore, regarded as bad palliative care.

PAIN RELIEF

The pain arising from malignant disease is often chronic and disabling and can totally disrupt the patients' life (p122-126). Treatment directed towards its relief is, therefore, essential. This cannot be achieved without accurate assessment. When it comes to assessing pain, the patient is the expert; each patient is unique with his personal perceptions of, and reactions to, his pain.

Relief of pain can be achieved in a variety of ways including:

1.   Appropriate explanation, which indicates understanding and concern, may help to reduce anxiety and raise morale.

290

2. Modification of the disease process using appropriate therapy.
3. Administration of analgesics and adjuvant drugs to elevate pain thresholds and alter pain perception.
4. Interruption of pain pathways (eg. using nerve blocks or neurosurgical techniques).
5. Immobilisation may help to reduce or alleviate pain (eg. internal fixation of a pathological fracture).
6. Diversion or distraction therapy may occupy the patient's attention thus helping to reduce his perception of pain.

(Based on Twycross and Lack, 1986).

Systemic chemotherapy may be used in combination with localised radiotherapy when lesions are extensive.

INCREASED INTRACRANIAL PRESSURE

An increase in intracranial pressure affects many cancer patients either due to their disease or its treatment (p201). This condition is manifested by periodic frontal or biooccipital headaches, projectile vomiting and mental torpor accompanied by papilloedema. The patient may develop personality changes, is often unsteady and may be incontinent of urine and/or faeces. Such effects require immediate treatment if coma and/or death are to be avoided (Adams and Victor, 1985; Salcman and Kaplan, 1986). Other, more specific, symptoms may occur depending on the site of the lesion.

Factors contributing to increased intracranial pressure include primary cerebral tumours, metastatic deposits in the brain/skull, metabolic encephalopathies, vascular disorders, infection and treatment related side-effects. Any increase in brain mass, due, for example, to tumour growth, haemorrhage or infection with exudate, increases pressure in the skull; as fluid accumulates, cerebral oedema develops affecting either the intracellular or extracellular spaces.

Primary brain tumours are most common in those over 50 years of age when they comprise 5% of all neoplasms. In adults, most brain tumours are gliomas or glioblastomas; pineal tumours (13% of all brain tumours); pituitary adenomas (10-15%), acoustic neuromas (5%), and miscellaneous neoplasms make up the remainder (Portlock and Goffinet, 1986).

Localised, extracellular (vasogenic) oedema is characterised by changes in the blood-brain barrier which result in an increase in its permeability allowing plasma proteins to 'leak' through vessel walls drawing fluid from the capillaries into the surrounding tissue. This causes compression of the surrounding vessels obstructing blood flow and increasing localised swelling and can be precipitated by primary and metastatic tumours, haemorrhage, necrosis, irritation or infection of cerebral tissues.

Infection of the central nervous system (CNS) is not common in cancer. The incidence is greatest in those with tumours affecting the CNS or in lymphoma or leukaemia. Insertion of an Ommaya or Rickam reservoir (Ch. 6) also creates a potential source of infection. An inflammatory response to infection will cause exudation thus increasing intracranial pressure. Cerebral irritation may result, for example, from the direct effects of radiotherapy or the indirect effects of tumour cell breakdown. Although those who have received whole brain irradiation, involving at least 60Gy, may develop cerebral necrosis this is more common when irradiation to the CNS has been combined with intrathecal treatment with methotrexate. Such effects are commonly delayed for some years after therapy and may be related to radiation-induced damage to the blood-brain barrier which increases the toxic effects of methotrexate. Alterations to the blood-brain barrier may enable other chemotherapeutic agents to enter the CNS and cause unexpected neurotoxicity.

The early signs and symptoms of increased intracranial pressure (Table 15.1) indicate the need for careful assessment, particularly in those patients identified to be at risk. Frequent objective evaluation is required (Table 15.2); serial observations are valuable for comparison when new signs and symptoms develop.

Table 15.1   Signs and symptoms indicating raised intracranial pressure

Alterations in mental status - restlessness, irritability, confusion
Altered level of consciousness
Elevated blood pressure
Gradual decrease in pulse and respiratory rate
Motor and sensory changes
Headache
Nausea - with/without projectile vomiting

NB. Diagnosis is clinically difficult until overt signs and symptoms are present.

Table 15.2   **Assessment of neurological function**

Level of consciousness	Alert, lethargic, obtunded, stuporous, coma?
Mental status	eg. Disorientation, disordered behaviour.
Respiratory pattern	Rate and depth of respiration, pattern changes, periods of apnoea, Cheyne-Stokes respiration, hyperventilation.
Pupil reactions	i) Responsiveness. ii) Placement of eyes a. at rest. b. on stimulation.
Eye movements	Conjugate (move together) or dysconjugate (deviation of one eye)?
Motor responses	Paresis or paralysis? Posture, reflexes.
Vital signs	Temperature, pulse, blood pressure.

Management

Until comparatively recently the only way in which increased intra-cranial pressure could be treated was by means of surgical intervention. Now, although some patients still require surgical treatment, a variety of medical measures can preclude the need for surgery. The choice of treatment depends largely on the severity of the condition and on the physical status of the patient.

Once a cerebrovascular accident, or other benign cause, has been eliminated treatment with corticosteroids (dexamethasone) is commenced at a dose of 16mg/day in divided doses. These act as anti-inflammatory agents, prevent increased capillary permeability and promote diuresis. It is also believed that they stabilise cerebral membranes and so help to prevent the development of cerebral oedema. Corticosteroids should always be given with food or milk; concurrent antacid therapy is also recommended to reduce the risk of gastrointestinal haemorrhage due to mucosal irritation.

In many cases, however, increased intracranial pressure is due to intracranial tumour or metastatic tumour spread; when a primary tumour is incompletely excised, radiotherapy is recommended. Radiotherapy may also be helpful when the patient's condition is such that it precludes surgical intervention. In most (40-60%) cases, however, metastatic brain lesions are multiple and whole brain irradiation is needed. For those who have received prior radiation, and in whom the tumour is known to be chemoresponsive, chemotherapy may be employed in an attempt to prevent further spread and to minimise

293

unpleasant symptoms. Although the average post-treatment survival averages only 5 months, neurological and major functional improvements are usually achieved in more than 40% of patients (Portlock and Goffinet, 1986).

When the condition is severe, osmotic diuretics, such as mannitol or urea, are given to achieve cerebral decompression. Their use is, however, controversial since mannitol removes fluid from normal brain tissue and not from the oedematous tissue; it is also associated with a number of secondary problems including:

1. A 'rebound' effect when, after an initial decrease, the intracranial pressure becomes high again.
2. The production of a hyperosmolar state.
3. Repeated use leads to decreased effectiveness.
4. Aggravation of cerebral oedema in some patients.

(Youmans, 1973).

Care

It is essential that the patient is constantly observed and monitored to identify whether he is improving or whether his condition has remained unchanged or is showing signs of deterioration. Physicians depend on nurses for accurate reporting so that appropriate care can be rapidly initiated as and when it is required.

Bedrest should be maintained; passive movement should be encouraged. Regular re-positioning should be encouraged to prevent the development of pressure sores. When the patient's level of consciousness is altered he should be nursed lying on his side to decrease the risk of aspiration. Affected patients require considerable reassurance and psychological support; this must be continued until his treatment ceases and neurological dysfunction is alleviated. Care must be symptomatic and designed to prevent further discomfort.

SPINAL CORD COMPRESSION

Most cases of rapidly evolving spinal cord compression (SCC) are due to neoplastic encroachment on the spinal cord; approximately 5% of those with systemic malignancies develop SCC (Portlock and Goffinet, 1986). SCC can develop from metastatic tumours, which account for about 95% of its total incidence; solid tumours account for some 50% of all affected patients (Bruckman and Bloomer, 1978). Tumours of the lung, breast and prostate carry the highest risk accounting for 16%, 12% and 7% respectively. SCC is a serious condition which causes permanent neurological damage unless prompt and effective emergency care is initiated.

Damage to the spinal cord may be due to compressive or invasive tumour growth; its severity depends on the location of the tumour. Extradural involvement most commonly accompanies invasive growth and tends to invade the vertebral body progressing to the epidural space. Symptoms are due to vertebral destruction, blockage of the cerebrospinal fluid and pressure on the spinal cord. Intradural tumours usually result from primary spinal tumours (eg. angioma or gliomas). On occasions vertebral metastases will extend directly into the intradural space (Figure 15.1).

Figure 15.1   Spinal cord compression

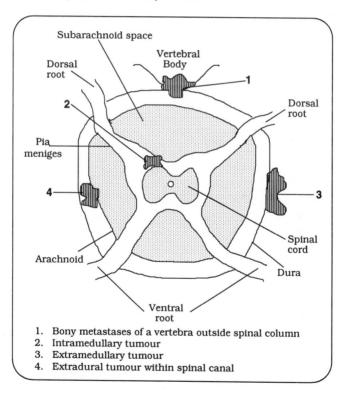

1. Bony metastases of a vertebra outside spinal column
2. Intramedullary tumour
3. Extramedullary tumour
4. Extradural tumour within spinal canal

As the spinal cord contains both motor and sensory fibres partial compression may result in unequal patterns of motor and sensory loss; total transection results in paralysis below the level of transection.

Typical History

Typically, the history is one of progressive back pain that occurs for perhaps 6 months before diagnosis is confirmed. This is described as the *Prodromal phase* during which the pain may be exacerbated by lying down, coughing or moving; it can often be alleviated by sitting upright. There may be an extended period during which the pain is diffuse or referred although, as the tumour increases in size causing chronic compression, the intensity, character and referral patterns may change. Alternatively, severe and agonising pain may indicate vertebral collapse and be accompanied by paralysis that develops over several hours. At this stage, spinal tenderness and local kyphosis are likely. The signs and symptoms vary depending on the location and degree of infiltration.

The emergency, *compressive phase* follows. The resultant severity and impairment depend entirely on the site of the tumour and the speed with which the diagnosis is made and treatment commenced.

Treatment

The diagnosis of SCC must be made early so that rapid treatment can be initiated before damage to both motor and sensory function becomes irreversible. The objective of treatment is to relieve the compression as rapidly as possible so as to prevent further damage to the spinal cord. This is most commonly achieved using radiotherapy, delivering 30-40Gy over a 2-4 week period. Dexamethasone is administered to decrease inflammation, reduce pain and improve neurological function. This approach can restore some, or all, function depending on the severity of the compression. Chemotherapy is not usually employed since it does not demonstrate the immediate effect necessary for emergency treatment. It may, however, be used after radiotherapy if the underlying tumour is known to be responsive to such therapy.

Surgical decompression may be indicated when, for example, there is an inadequate response to the treatment outlined above or when there is a need for stabilisation of the spinal column. Other indications for surgery include a complete compression with rapidly progressing neurological defects, high cervical lesions that may cause respiratory distress, an uncertain diagnosis or prior radio-therapy in which spinal tolerance has been reached. In the majority of cases surgery is followed by radiotherapy to destroy any remaining tumour cells.

SUPERIOR VENA CAVA SYNDROME

Compression of the superior vena cava (SVC) is caused by a mediastinal mass, which may be due to a primary tumour or to metastatic deposits, or by a contiguous pulmonary mass which invades the mediastinum and impairs venous drainage (Portlock and Goffinet, 1986); rarely this may arise as a result of obstruction of the lumen by a neoplastic thrombus. It is potentially life-threatening and constitutes a medical emergency. Recognition, assessment and prompt action are essential since the vena cava is the major channel returning blood to the heart. Obstruction will result in an increase in venous pressure and dilation of superficial veins and interferes with venous drainage.

Approximately 95% of all cases of SVC obstruction are due to malignancy when it results from compression by a tumour *per se* or from metastatic disease affecting the paratracheal or mediastinal lymph nodes. Alternatively the vessel walls may be infiltrated by the tumour causing the formation of a thrombus within the lumen. It arises in 3-8% of those with lung cancer and/or lymphoma; it is, rarely, seen in those with Hodgkin's disease.

Typical History

Although SVC compression is potentially life-threatening its onset may be insidious. The primary signs and symptoms result from obstruction of the blood flow in the venous system of the head, neck and upper trunk. The severity of the symptoms depends on the rate of onset and location of the obstruction. When the condition develops slowly, a collateral circulation may develop. When the compression is fully developed, patients commonly develop dyspnoea accompanied by swelling of the face and neck (cervicofacial oedema) and dilation of the veins of the neck and thorax. Occasionally, swelling of the trunk and upper extremities may be present. Dysphagia, coughing and chest pain are also common and disturbances of the central nervous system, such as headache, visual disturbances and an altered state of consciousness, may also occur although these are rare.

Thus the patient usually presents with distension of the thoracic and neck veins, facial oedema and a rapid respiratory rate accompanied by cyanosis and, on occasions, oedema of the upper extremities. Disruption of the cervical nerve supply may result in paralysis of the vocal cords so that the patient becomes hoarse and finds difficulty in talking.

297

Diagnosis is confirmed by X-ray; significant findings include evidence of a right superior mediastinal mass, paratracheal or mediastinal lymphadenopathy and right-sided effusion. SVC obstruction may, occasionally, occur before the histology of the lesion has been established; bronchoscopy and/or biopsy of the lesion will then be performed. However, when the patient is in acute distress, treatment may be undertaken even in the absence of a confirmed diagnosis. A diagnostic work-up is then carried out when the patient's condition has improved.

Treatment

The major goal of treatment is to relieve the obstruction and restore venous drainage. Treatment is usually by means of radiotherapy as the prime goal is an immediate reduction in the size of the tumour. Subjective improvement is usually noted within 72 hours of initiation of therapy (Portlock and Goffinet, 1986). Chemotherapy may be used in conjunction with radiotherapy but is rarely the sole method of treatment. The agents usually employed are cyclophosphamide, methotrexate and mechlorethamine (Chernecky and Ramsey, 1984). Appropriate supportive care will be necessary. For example, oxygen therapy will help to relieve dyspnoea and analgesia and/or tranquillisers to decrease chest pain and anxiety. When oedema is present diuretics may provide temporary relief.

Surgery is of only limited benefit in treating SVC obstruction and also carries a high morbidity. It is, therefore, rarely used as a method of treatment.

CARDIAC TAMPONADE

Cardiac tamponade affects approximately 10-20% of all patients with cancer although few will manifest clinical signs of cardiac disease prior to death (Portlock and Goffinet, 1986). It is most commonly due to secondary involvement arising from tumours of the lung or breast, lymphoma, leukaemia or melanoma; it may, rarely, arise from a primary tumour of the pericardium. Previous radiation therapy (total dose in the region of 20-30Gy) may cause radiation pericarditis and pericardial thickening that may, ultimately, cause cardiac tamponade.

Cardiac tamponade results in an increase in intrapericardial pressure; this may be due to an accumulation of fluid (pericardial effusion) or to constriction due to thickening (fibrosis). This, in turn, causes cardiac compression and decreased ventricular filling so that both stroke volume and cardiac output are decreased. At the same time, pericardial distension will compress the lungs and bronchi resulting in dyspnoea and orthopnoea.

The condition may, or may not, be accompanied by chest pain but is characterised by distension of the jugular veins, muffled heart sounds, cyanosis, oedema, râles, a rapid and irregular pulse of decreased pressure, decreased systolic blood pressure and raised central venous pressure; these, ultimately, lead to cardiac failure and shock and, if untreated, to death. Pain, when present, may vary in intensity ranging from mild to severe over the precordial or substernal area and may radiate to the shoulder and down the left arm; it may be aggravated by swallowing, coughing and lying flat and relieved by sitting up and leaning forward. Alternatively pain may be dull, diffuse and oppressive. The patient will be extremely anxious and apprehensive.

Clearly an affected patient is acutely ill and requires emergency care and treatment. Bedrest is initiated and vital signs and cardiac function are monitored. Oxygen therapy, analgesics and/or sedatives are given as required and the patient is prepared for emergency treatment. Initially, pericardiocentesis is undertaken to provide immediate relief. This is usually achieved by removal of 50-100ml of fluid and may necessitate incision through the chest wall. However, although pericardiocentesis will immediately relieve cardiac tamponade, a more permanent solution is sought. This may include radiotherapy or systemic chemotherapy. A total dose of radiation 20-30Gy is usually adequate to relieve the symptoms. A total pericardectomy may be indicated when the condition is due to radiation-induced constrictive pericarditis.

When the condition is recurrent and prolonged palliation is required, a surgical opening (pericardial window) may be made to drain fluid into the pleural space. Alternatively, an indwelling catheter may be inserted to provide continuous drainage. It is, however, often necessary to combine this with local therapy to achieve sclerosis. Common sclerosing agents include tetracycline, thiotepa, mechlorethamine and 5-FU which are instilled into the pericardial sac to induce fibrosis (Portlock and Goffinet, 1986). This is successful in about 50% of cases (Maush and Ullman, 1985) although it may cause transient chest pain, pyrexia and nausea. Intracavity therapy may also involve agents such as 5-FU, gold[198], mechlorethamine or triethylene thiophosphoramide. Portlock and Goffinet (1986) report that remission is common and usually lasts in excess of 4 months before further therapy is required.

Other malignant effusions (eg. pleural effusion) can also cause distressing symptoms, such as chest pain, dyspnoea, cough, tiredness and dysphagia. At times these can be successfully treated by means of local chemotherapy that is instilled into the affected cavity where it acts as a sclerosing agent.

LEUCOSTASIS

Leucostasis is associated with an absolute lymphocyte count in excess of 10×10^9/litre, composed primarily of blast cells (myeloblasts and lymphoblasts). This causes hyperviscosity of the blood and results in capillary plugging that, in turn, leads to the rupture of blood vessels. It arises in those with acute or chronic myelocytic leukaemia and may contribute to death in about 25% of cases. It rarely occurs in lymphocytic leukaemia. The difference between the effects of myelogenous and lymphocytic leukaemia has been attributed to the relatively larger size and rigidity of myeloblasts as compared to lymphoblasts (Portlock and Goffinet, 1986).

The mechanism(s) underlying the development of leucostasis is not fully understood. However, since blast cells are larger and more viscous than their mature equivalents (Passmore and Robson, 1974) they cause an increase in blood viscosity and stagnation of circulatory flow. Thus, when present in large numbers, blast cells may adhere to both the endothelial lining of the vessel walls and to each other causing mechanical obstruction; adherence also damages the endothelium and enhances aggregation. Damage to the vascular endothelium is exacerbated by hypoxia which is usually a secondary consequence of a variety of factors including anaemia, impaired pulmonary gas exchange, localised obstruction and the high oxygen consumption of blast cells (Passmore and Robson, 1974). These combined effects weaken the vessel wall that eventually ruptures leading to haemorrhage. Leucostatic aggregation most commonly affects the central nervous system (CNS) and the respiratory tract; it may be life-threatening. Emergency treatment is essential to prevent haemorrhage and/or serious organ dysfunction.

Regular assessment of both pulmonary and neurological function is required to establish a baseline and permit rapid identification of any changes. The abrupt and rapid onset of neurological dysfunction may indicate the development of intracranial haemorrhage whilst respiratory distress may be due to obstruction of the airflow and an inability to clear secretions; hypoxia and hypoventilation may also be contributory factors. When leucostasis occurs in the pleural space a pleural effusion may develop.

As previously stated, rapid treatment is essential to reduce the leucocyte count. This is usually achieved by means of chemotherapy which should both control the underlying disease and decrease circulating leucocytes. Drugs employed may include:

a. Hydroxyurea which inhibits synthesis of DNA producing a rapid decrease in circulating leucocytes. This is given orally using one of two schedules: $3g/m^2$ daily for 2 days or $50-100mg/m^2$ daily until the leucocyte count falls below 10×10^9/litre.

b. Cyclophosphamide (20-30mg/kg) which inhibits replication of DNA.

c. Daunorubicin and cytosine arabinoside both of which disrupt DNA and RNA synthesis and rapidly reduce the leucocyte count.

There is, however, some variation in treatment which differs with the physicians concerned. Chemotherapy may, at times, be combined with cranial irradiation, usually a single dose of approximately 6Gy, to destroy any leucostatic aggregations present in the brain. Similarly, leucophoresis or exchange transfusions can be used to achieve a rapid decrease in circulating leucocytes; these techniques will not, however, have any effect on pre-existing leucostatic foci.

Effective cytotoxic therapy will result in cellular destruction and, therefore, a release of uric acid which is normally excreted by the kidneys. The leukaemic patient often has abnormally high serum urea concentrations; a further increase may saturate renal clearance mechanisms so that urate precipitates in the renal tubules resulting in renal failure. Thus, oral allopurinol, which inhibits uric acid production, is often given concurrently. The usual adult dose is 300mg per day; when the risk of uric acid nephropathy is high this may be increased to doses in excess of 800mg daily.

Care

The 'at risk' patient must be closely monitored so as to ensure that changes in their condition are rapidly detected. As previously described, the major complications of leucostasis are respiratory distress and pulmonary or intracranial haemorrhage; it should, however, be noted that pulmonary complications are attributed to leucostasis only after other causes have been eliminated. However, when a pulmonary haemorrhage does occur, this will result in respiratory distress which may/may not be accompanied by haemoptysis.

The goals of care are to ease respiratory distress and to provide support and reassurance for affected patients who will be anxious and fearful. An explanation about the syndrome and its relationship to the disease is essential; understanding of the rationale underlying treatment will also be beneficial.

The dyspnoeic patient must be nursed in the position that he finds most comfortable and he is the best guide to the position that enables him to breathe with minimal difficulty; upright or sitting positions are usually preferred (Figures 14.2 and 14.3).

If a pulmonary haemorrhage has occurred it can be beneficial to turn the patient on to the affected side to reduce the risk of blood entering the unaffected lung. Similarly, when a pleural effusion is present, lying on the affected side will help expansion and aeration of the unaffected lung. A haemorrhagic effusion requires immediate medical treatment to aspirate blood from the pleural cavity; this may necessitate insertion of an underwater-seal chest drain. Transfusion of blood or blood products may be necessary depending on the extent of the blood loss. Similarly, mechanical ventilation may be necessary depending on the patient's prognosis, the goals of treatment and the wishes of both the patient and his family.

When respiratory distress is severe the patient is often apprehensive and withdrawn so that comprehensive supportive care is required. Hypoxia may cause changes in the level of consciousness. Similarly, the presence of an intracranial haemorrhage may result in changes in both neurological function and the level of consciousness. Its onset, however, is often insidious and the early signs vague and non-specific (eg. irritability, restlessness, headache and nausea). The care required is as previously described.

DISSEMINATED INTRAVASCULAR COAGULATION (DIC)

DIC is seen not as a primary disorder but as a secondary complication. It may be an acute or chronic condition which results in widespread formation of small thrombi throughout the microcirculation. DIC has been associated with intravascular haemolysis following a transfusion reaction, overwhelming infection, and the release of thrombin from malignant cells (eg. in acute myelocytic leukaemia, melanoma or cancers of the stomach, colon, lung, breast, prostate or ovary) (Yasko and Schafer, 1983).

In the acute phase, DIC is dramatic and easily recognised due to the development of generalised ischaemic damage or necrosis and, on occasions, widespread haemorrhage. When DIC is both acute and severe the patient may rapidly become shocked and comatose; the condition may prove fatal.

Chronic DIC is much less dramatic and microthrombi are much less numerous so that there is less ischaemic damage. The chronic stage may, however, culminate in acute active bleeding, perhaps because chronic DIC gradually depletes the available clotting factors (Bavier, 1985).

The mechanisms underlying DIC are complex and are not clearly understood (Figure 15.3).

Figure 15.3   Schematic representation of the development of DIC

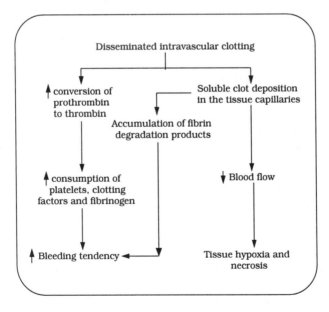

DIC basically represents an exaggerated haemostatic response within an otherwise normal vasculature. It can be described in terms of four phases:

1. Due to platelet and fibrin deposition in small vessels microthrombi develop and can cause multiple organ failure.

2. Secondary activation of kinin, combined with damage to the platelets, can lead to metabolic acidosis and/or hypotension.

3. When DIC is severe there may be marked consumption of platelets and clotting factors leading to thrombocytopeonia and haemorrhage.

4. Activation of the coagulation system results in activation of the plasma fibrinolytic system which may, in turn, contribute to the haemorrhagic tendency.

(Green et al, 1983)

In malignant disease, acute DIC is most commonly associated with promyelocytic leukaemia and prostatic carcinoma although it is believed to affect about 10% of all patients with cancer when it is thought to be due to the release of thromboplastin-like material from the tumour itself (Portlock and Goffinet, 1986). Chronic DIC is most common in patients with adenocarcinoma of the pancreas or other mucin-secreting tumours (Smith, 1988).

Any patient developing widespread bleeding, particularly in response to minor trauma, or who develops unexpected bleeding, must be carefully assessed (p155-156). The patient's condition may change gradually so that regular assessment may enable early diagnosis and intervention. Some patients may develop other conditions (eg. sepsis, hypovolaemia, transfusion reactions) which may be associated with DIC. Others may slowly become aware of a variety of changes that will cause them to seek advice and/or help from members of the health care team. Small changes, such as the development of petechiae or a gradual limitation of the ability to participate in normal activity, may arise; other, more dramatic, events, such as frank bleeding (commonly affecting the genito-urinary or GI tract), may cause significant distress and anxiety.

Diagnosis depends on a combination of haematological tests and careful clinical assessment. Thus, prothrombin time (PT), partial thromboplastin time, thrombin time, serum fibrinogen and platelet count should be monitored and, as clotting factors are depleted, PT and partial thromboplastin time will become increasingly prolonged; platelets are markedly decreased ($<20 \times 10^9$/litre). When blood loss is acute, the haematocrit will fall.

The primary treatment is removal of the precipitating cause. Since this can be difficult, treatment is directed at the underlying tumour and, where possible, elimination of the precipitating factor. It is, therefore, largely dependent on the cause of the condition. Thus, when DIC is due to the malignant process *per se*, chemotherapy may be administered; antibiotics are given in an attempt to control infection. Clotting factors, and other blood components, are replaced by infusion of fresh frozen plasma, cryoprecipitate, fresh whole blood or platelets. When haemolytic anaemia is present (due to fragmentation of erythrocytes), or when haemorrhage has occurred, packed red cells may be administered. Intravenous fluids are given to correct hypovolaemia.

Although controversial, heparin may be given to disrupt normal coagulation mechanisms (Smith, 1988). Heparin exerts an anti-thrombin effect and also prevents the formation of prothrombin activator so that it may be used in situations where there is evidence of severe bleeding whilst treatment of the underlying cause/tumour is initiated. 100iu/kg body weight is administered as a single dose followed by 10-15iu/kg/hour as a constant infusion (Green et al, 1983). The response to treatment must be closely monitored; a successful response is accompanied by a fall in fibrin degradation products and an increased fibrinogen level.

Care
The care of the patient centres on three main areas:
1. The risk of significant haemorrhage.
2. Alterations in fluid balance.
3. A decreased ability to transport oxygen.

Disruption of clotting mechanisms means that the patient is unable to form a stable clot and even minor procedures can cause major bleeding. Thus every effort should be made to prevent trauma and/or blood loss. Small gauge needles should be used for injection or withdrawal of blood samples and direct and prolonged pressure applied to any puncture site. Such procedures should, however, be kept to a minimum and, wherever possible, an existing infusion line should be used. Trauma to the gums should be minimised by using a soft toothbrush. An electric razor should be used to reduce stress to the skin on the neck and face. Blood loss should be closely monitored and any acute bleeding episode should be immediately reported to the attending physician.

Careful records of fluid balance must be maintained since this may fluctuate rapidly between hypovolaemia and fluid overload. Haemorrhage may result in significant fluid loss and lead to hypovolaemia whilst administration of blood/blood products and intra-venous fluids may lead to an overload.

Inadequate transport of oxygen is often manifested by tachycardia and dyspnoea which represent an attempt to increase circulatory flow and oxygen intake so as to increase the oxygenation of body tissues. Transfusion of red cells and supplemental oxygen therapy are then required. Important interventions include providing care designed to restrict unnecessary movement and ensuring that the patient has adequate rest [see care of the patient with anaemia (p157-158).

Affected patients require a considerable degree of support and reassurance and, at the same time, require information about the symptoms they are experiencing and the rationale underlying his treatment. The risk of changes in haemostatic mechanisms must be explained to the patient and his family so that they can recognise the need for professional help.

REFERENCES

Adams RD, Victor M, 1985, Principles of Neurology (Third edition), McGraw-Hill, New York.

Bavier AR, 1985, Alterations in hemostasis. In: Johnson BL, Gross J (Editors), Handbook of Oncology Nursing, John Wiley and Sons Inc., New York.

Bruckman JE, Bloomer WD, 1978, Management of spinal cord compression, Seminars in Oncology **5**, 135-40.

Carter SK, Bakowski MT, Hellmann K, 1987, The Chemotherapy of Cancer (Third edition), John Wiley and Sons Inc., New York.

Chernecky CC, Ramsey PW, 1984, Critical Nursing Care of the Client with Cancer, Appleton-Century-Crofts, Norwalk, CT.

Green JA, Macbeth FR, Williams CJ, Whitehouse JMA, 1983, Medical Oncology, Blackwell Scientific Publications, Oxford.

Maush PM, Ullman JE, 1985, Treatment of malignant pericardial effusions. In: DeVita VT, Hellman S, Rosenberg SA (Editors), Cancer Principles and Practice of Oncology, JB Lippincott Co., Philadelphia.

Passmore R, Robson JS (Editors), 1974, A companion to medical studies, Volume 3: Medicine, Surgery, Systemic Pathology, Obstetrics, Psychiatry, Paediatrics and Community Medicine, Blackwell Scientific Publications, Oxford.

Perez C, Presant C, Van Amburg A, 1978, Management of superior vena cava syndrome, Seminars in Oncology **5**, 123-34.

Portlock CS, Goffinet DR, 1986, Manual of Clinical Problems in Oncology (Second edition), Little, Brown and Company, Boston.

Salcman M, Kaplan RS, 1986, Intracranial tumours in adults. In: Moosa AR, Robson MC, Schimpf SC (Editors), Comprehensive Textbook of Oncology, Williams and Wilkins, Baltimore.

Smith I, 1988, Systemic manifestations of malignant disease. In: Pritchard P, Oncology for Nurses and Health Care Professionals (Second edition), Volume 1, Pathology, Diagnosis and Treatment, Harper and Row Publishers, London in co-publication with Beaconsfield Publishers, Beaconsfield.

Twycross RG, Lack SA, 1986, Therapeutics in Terminal Cancer, Churchill Livingstone, Edinburgh.

Yasko JM, Schafer SL, 1983, Disseminated intravascular coagulation. In: Yasko JM, Guidelines for Cancer Care: Symptom Management, Reston Publishing Co., Reston, Va..

Youmans J (Editor), 1973, Neurological Surgery, Volumes 1, 2 and 3, WB Saunders Co., Philadelphia.

CHAPTER 16   THE PATIENT AS AN INDIVIDUAL

An individual approach to the care of patients undergoing chemotherapy is essential since they must be recognised as *'individuals
experiencing a special and severe form of stress'* (Schneider, 1978)
related both to the disease itself and its treatment. No aspect of the
patient's life is unaffected. Indeed, it is widely acknowledged that
cancer is *'one of the most feared and stressful of all diseases'*
(Jalowiec and Dudas, 1991). The development of cancer, therefore,
poses a severe threat not only to the physical welfare of patients but
also to their psychological condition (Benner and Wrubel, 1989). As
nurses have the most consistent and continuing relationship with the
patient they are ideally placed to help him to come to terms with his
difficulties although all health care professionals have a role to play.
A thorough assessment, designed to provide information about both
actual and potential problems, is essential and will help to identify
appropriate interventions or the need for specialist help.

In carrying out such an assessment it must be recognised that
each patient is unique having his own personality traits and
personal circumstances (McGee, 1992). Thus the meaning of the
disease, and the person's interpretation of it, is also unique. An
individual assessment implies a willingness to listen to the patient
and his family to identify their needs, concerns and anxieties. It will
also enable these factors to be placed in the context of the patient's
understanding of his disease. Indeed, Maxwell (1982) emphasises the
importance of viewing the impact of cancer on the lifestyle of an
individual within the context of his home and social network. Thus, a
truly individual approach focuses on well-being helping to develop an
understanding of the patient and enhance his dignity and self-
esteem; it will also help to increase his confidence and trust in the
health care team.

The cancer patient is required to make numerous decisions many
of which relate either to treatment options or to adaptation to the
various changes in lifestyle that, almost inevitably, follow the
diagnosis of cancer and/or the start of treatment. Responses to the
diagnosis are often compounded by reactions to its treatment. It
must, therefore, be recognised that patients facing chemotherapy are
often very vulnerable, particularly when this commences within a

short time of diagnosis. Following diagnosis many patients suffer overwhelming feelings of loss of control which may, in turn, lead to feelings of both helplessness and hopelessness and a belief that they have no influence over what is happening to them. Alternatively, chemotherapy may be the last in a long line of debilitating treatments when the prevailing feelings may be despair and anger.

EFFECTS OF CHEMOTHERAPY

Patients often regard chemotherapy as an indication that their disease is unmanageable by any other means and so believe that their cancer is in the advanced stages. This may be exacerbated when chemotherapy is given as an adjunct to surgery or radiotherapy. For example, Maguire et al (1980) found that adjuvant chemotherapy after mastectomy significantly increased the incidence of depression, anxiety and sexual problems augmenting the effects of mastectomy *per se* [eg. depression (Maguire et al, 1978), curtailment of social life, and sexual problems (Silberfarb et al, 1980a)]; such effects were particularly marked in those experiencing toxic reactions to chemotherapy. Thus, in addition to the anticipated side-effects of cancer chemotherapy, the patient's perceptions and interpretation of his treatment must be assessed so that misconceptions can be clarified.

Many patients experience anxiety preceding treatment which at times can be so severe as to prevent them attending for that treatment (Moorey and Greer, 1989). In others, the thought of chemotherapy can provoke the onset of anticipated side-effects; for example, 10-15% of all patients receiving drugs that cause nausea and vomiting will develop symptoms on entering the hospital even before treatment has been given (p302-303). Prolonged nausea and vomiting not only interfere with food intake and, therefore, nutritional status, but also affect well-being by reinforcing withdrawal from many physical and social activities. This, in turn, may exacerbate depression and the associated physical and emotional symptoms adding to feelings of helplessness and a loss of hope.

Other potential threats include changes in body image, due to for example, alopecia, oral lesions or skin disorders; mood changes, repeated infection and an associated need for isolation, and changes in neurological function may all be interpreted as a further threat to life. Similarly, Silberfarb et al (1980b) have demonstrated that cognitive impairment is associated with a wide variety of chemotherapeutic agents; this may be very distressing for the patient.

Understanding can help the patient to maintain an element of control; many will seek information in an attempt to reduce the uncertainty surrounding both the diagnosis and the treatment. Cassileth et al (1980), however, suggested that, although patients frequently sought information, this was not always forthcoming. They also found that although most patients wanted the maximum amount of information those seeking detailed information were predominantly younger, better educated and more recently diagnosed than those who avoided information wanting others to make decisions for them.

However, although most patients want information, and find it helpful, some believe that giving information when this is not wanted may disrupt denial mechanisms leading to a loss of hope and even depression (eg. Kellerman et al, 1980). Those with advanced disease are likely to seek less information than those with more limited disease; this has been attributed to the self-protective use of denial and avoidance mechanisms (Gotay, 1984; Hopkins, 1986). This suggests that the provision of information is not always desirable and stresses the need to treat each patient as an individual assessing his need or desire for information (Ch. 17).

The kind of information wanted by patients has also been studied (eg. Cassileth et al, 1980; Derdiarian 1986, 1987) showing that most of those wanting information want this to be related to the disease it-self, the side-effects of treatment, treatment outcomes and the potential for cure. However, although many patients would welcome the opportunity to discuss their situation more fully, many felt it was not appropriate to do so with those staff with whom they most commonly come into contact (ie. medical, nursing and technical staff) believing they are 'too busy' to 'waste time' talking to them (eg. Holmes and Dickerson, 1987). This highlights the challenge to be faced in helping patients to reach understanding of their disease and treatment and may go some way towards explaining the burgeoning interest in self-help groups and complementary approaches to cancer treatment.

The most effective way of providing information is through carefully planned education that takes individual needs into account. It is probable that *'.. in no other illness is the need for continued and supportive education so necessary'* (Muntz and Zur, 1978) Thus health care professionals are important resources for the patient and his family; they must, therefore, develop their own level of knowledge and understanding so that simple but accurate explanations can be given. Appropriate education will help the patient to make the necessary decisions regarding his treatment.

Effective supportive care must be individualised and based on knowledge of the factors that make each patient unique. Thus psychosocial factors must be considered including details of his family background, awareness of his financial situation (illness may raise considerable difficulty), the usual coping strategies of both the patient and his family and identification of his usual source of emotional support. Supportive care provides time for the patient enabling him to build a relationship with members of the caring team and gives him 'permission' to voice his concerns and express his emotions.

A trusting relationship will enable identification of specific patient or family concerns so that the appropriate resources can be mobilised to deal with them. At the same time, an on-going relationship with members of the caring team will help to reduce the patient's isolation indicating that the staff involved care about him as an individual. Supportive care must also consider the family who provide continuing care and support for the patient and act as his primary resource.

Involving patients can help to decrease unnecessary morbidity and demonstrate the important role they can play in their care. Indeed, Cassileth et al (1980) have shown that the most hopeful patients are those who are actively involved in their care; the importance of patient participation cannot be overemphasised. It is this which forms the basis of many of the 'alternative' approaches to cancer care and, perhaps, accounts for at least some of the increasing interest in such approaches. Since Jacobs et al (1983) have shown that appropriate education decreases anxiety and reduces the incidence of treatment-related problems, depression and disruption of the lifestyle, education must be regarded as a vital component of total patient care.

ANXIETY AND LEARNING

As anxiety may limit both retention and understanding, and affect the amount of information that can be given, staff must be aware of the patient's level of anxiety. This will be affected by his previous knowledge, understanding and beliefs about both cancer and its treatment. These, combined with fear and anxiety, may lead to a failure to ask questions and seek clarification about what is to happen to them; this, in itself, may indicate stress or suggest denial of the significance of the disease (Moorey and Greer, 1989). The initial assessment will have identified some of the patient's beliefs; these can be taken into account when planning a teaching programme. Other factors that must be considered include the ability of the professional to teach what the patient needs to know and the recognition of that need by the patient. It must be remembered that an individual will only learn what he needs or wants to know; learning/teaching goals must be set with the patient. In addition, his priorities may change as treatment progresses so that continued reassessment and evaluation of the teaching plan are essential.

The patient's motivation provides the key to his willingness to learn; the first task is to motivate him whilst, at the same time, establishing his needs, wants and worries as these are central to the learning process. Teaching will not be successful unless it involves the patient and, if he is not convinced that he needs to learn, the amount of information retained will be significantly reduced. This enables the patient to play an active role in his learning and will help to build trust between the professional carer and the patient helping him to maintain his dignity and self-esteem. Such a relationship will encourage the patient to ask questions and seek the information that he needs. It should also be recognised that repetition strengthens learning; positive feedback and reinforcement are essential.

Thus, if our teaching is to be successful, we must first identify what is needed and help the patient to interpret the facts and identify possible courses of action based on them. The success of teaching can be evaluated by the role the patient is able to play in his care and the quality of his life when he returns to his usual environment. It is also indicative of the quality of care he receives.

Basic steps

Once the goals of teaching/learning have been established the basic steps outlined below will simplify the teaching process:

- Tell the patient what information is to be covered during each teaching session
- Organise the information into related categories; cover the most important first
- Keep the teaching sessions short
- Keep the information simple, use short words and sentences that are easily understood. Avoid the use of 'jargon'
- Summarise and review the material covered.

However, not all teaching need be formalised as the patient may ask direct questions that must be answered. Nurses, in particular, have many opportunities to talk to patients and can use these to exchange information. Such informal teaching is valuable and can signify motivation and interest on behalf of the patient. It also helps to demonstrate the nurse's interest in the patient as an individual.

The last, and most important, step is evaluation which is often forgotten. It cannot be assumed that information given is either retained or understood; teaching does not, in itself, equate with learning. Thus teaching must be evaluated to ensure that the patient understands the information and can relate or apply it to his situation. Evaluation allows care to be dynamic and so subject to continued change and reassessment. Each patient requires an individual approach as both the beneficial and the side-effects of therapy must be assessed and appropriate interventions planned and implemented. Concurrent evaluation will be carried out by the physician and appropriate adjustments made to the treatment plan.

It is important that consistent, long term follow-up is carried out after chemotherapeutic treatment of malignant disease. This enables monitoring of both individual progress and the incidence of late side-effects and/or complications. The patient should be encouraged to attend as instructed and be assured that follow-up care is planned not because a recurrence of the disease is expected (although this may be the case in palliative treatment) but simply to monitor his progress. However, if the disease should return, regular examination should enable early detection and an improved chance of control.

INFORMED CONSENT

A well-planned teaching programme will also help the patient to participate in decision making regarding the treatment he is to receive (Ch. 17). It must, however, be recognised that it is often necessary for surgery to be carried out immediately or treatment commenced rapidly once diagnosis is confirmed so that there may not be time to carry out a carefully planned teaching programme. It is, nonetheless, essential that the patient is given sufficient information to enable him to make an informed decision about his treatment based on a full understanding of the rationale of that treatment and the factors relevant to the proposed care. In other words, patients 'have the right to know and the right to say no' (Faulder, 1985) (ie. the right to decide whether to accept the proposed treatment) (p325-328). The principle of informed consent thus recognises the individual's right to self determination and also his autonomy (Gillon, 1986). It ensures that the patient is aware of the treatment(s) he is to receive and also helps to protect him from the dangers inherent in some forms of treatment.

Although, legally, it is the physician's responsibility to obtain informed consent it is the nurse's ethical responsibility to ensure that such consent has been obtained before treatment is given. Unfortunately, much attention is focused on obtaining signed consent rather than on ensuring that the purpose of treatment has been understood. Thus the nurse, in her role as patient advocate, must also ensure that the patient truly understands the procedure(s) he is to undergo since *'each nurse .... shall act at all times, in such a manner as to justify public trust and confidence, to uphold and enhance the good standing and reputation of the profession, to serve the interests of society, and above all to safeguard the interests of individual patients and clients'* (UKCC, 1992). She can, therefore, raise questions that the patient may have forgotten and can also reinforce or expand on the information he has been given. Since his level of anxiety may affect comprehension, considerable patience may be needed during the consent process. The guidelines given below may help to simplify the procedure and improve its effectiveness:

- Give the patient a copy of the consent form at least 24hrs before he is required to sign it; encourage him to read it carefully.
- Suggest that he identifies and writes down any questions he may have so that he can ensure that they are all answered during subsequent discussion.
- Set aside a time when the patient, and a family member or close friend, can meet privately with the physician and a nurse to discuss the proposed treatment. Ideally this should be in an informal setting where all members can sit in comfortable chairs or around a table so that the patient does not feel intimidated.
- Ensure the patient's understanding by asking questions related to the previous discussion.
- Ensure that the consent process is documented in both the medical and the nursing records.

NEEDS OF STAFF INVOLVED CARING FOR CHEMOTHERAPY PATIENTS

Since health care professionals are required to help patients to express their problems and fears, and to develop an environment conducive to communication and support, it is essential that they are, themselves, provided with the appropriate skills and training and also have access to appropriate methods of support. Without effective interpersonal skills staff may feel uncomfortable in communicating with patients and may experience marked difficulties in meeting patient needs with regard to information and emotional support.

Health care professionals, like any other individuals, may need help in sharing their feelings and their reactions to patients which will, in turn, help their approach to problem solving both on a personal level and with regard to the patients in their care. Communication among staff can, however, be as difficult as that between staff and patients. Nurses, in particular, have been shown to work in relative emotional isolation such that Vachon et al (1978) have shown that stress in nurses can be considerably higher than that of patients beginning treatment for breast cancer and only slightly lower than that of new widows. Yet, to disclose such feelings to peers would mean admitting to what may be thought to be an 'unprofessional attitude' so that there may be an understandable reluctance to share responses and to identify not only the need for help in resolving difficulties on an individual basis but also a failure to appreciate that there may be common difficulties to be faced and overcome (Bond, 1982). This is important not only in relation to the difficulties faced by staff but also to patients since Cassee (1975) has shown that open socio-emotional communication between staff and patient is less likely to occur when there is an absence of staff communication on an emotional level.

Thus a support network for staff can only be beneficial to patient care. Regular, multidisciplinary staff meetings can be helpful in providing a mutually supportive environment, particularly when this is facilitated by a psychologist who can both help the staff to cope with their own problems as well as those of the patients in their care.

REFERENCES

Benner P, Wrubel J, 1989, The Primacy of Caring, Addison-Wesley Publishing Co. Inc., Menlo Park, Ca..

Bond S, 1982, Communication in cancer nursing. In: Cahoon MC (Editor), Cancer Nursing, Recent Advances in Nursing 3, Churchill Livingstone, Edinburgh.

Cassee E, 1975, Therapeutic behaviour, hospital culture and communication. In: Cox C, Mead A (Editors), A Sociology of Medical Practice, Collier MacMillan, London.

Cassileth B, Zupkis R, Sutton-Smith K, 1980, Informed consent - why are its goals imperfectly realised? New England Journal of Medicine **302**, 896-900.

Derdiarian AK, 1986, Informational needs of recently diagnosed cancer patients, Nursing Research **35**, 276-81.

Derdiarian AK, 1987, Informational needs of recently diagnosed cancer patients, Part II, Method and description, Cancer Nursing **10**, 156-63.

Faulder C, 1985, Whose Body Is It? Virago Press, London.

Gillon R, 1986, Philosophical Medical Ethics, John Wiley and Sons Ltd., Chichester.

Gotay CC, 1984, The experience of cancer during early and advanced stages: the views of patients and their mates, Social Science and Medicine **18**, 605-3.

Holmes S, Dickerson JWT, 1987, The quality of life: design and evaluation of a self-assessment instrument for use with cancer patients, International Journal of Nursing Studies **24**, 15-24.

Hopkins MB, 1986, Information-seeking and adaptational outcomes in women receiving chemotherapy for breast cancer, Cancer Nursing **9**, 256-62.

Jacobs C, Ross R, Walker L, et al, 1983, Behaviour of cancer patients: a randomised study of the effects of education and peer support groups, American Journal of Clinical Oncology (June) 347-50.

Jalowiec A, Dudas S, 1991, Alterations in patient coping. In Baird SB, McCorkle R, Grant M, (Editors), Cancer Nursing: A Comprehensive Textbook, WB Saunders Co., London.

Kellerman J, Riglee D, Siegel SE, et al, 1980, Disease related communication and depression in pediatric patients, Journal of Pediatric Psychology **2**, 52-3.

Maguire GP, Lee EG, Bevington DJ, et al, 1978, Psychiatric problems in the first year after mastectomy, British Medical Journal **178**, 963-5.

Maguire GP, Tait A, Brooke M, et al, 1980, Pyschiatric morbidity and physical toxicity associated with adjuvant chemotherapy after mastectomy, British Medical Journal **281**, 1179-80.

Maxwell MB, 1982, The use of social networks to help cancer patients maximise support, Cancer Nursing **5**, 275-82.

McGee RF, 1992, Overview of psychosocial dimensions, In: Groenwald SL, Frogge MH, Goodman M, Yarbro CH (Editors), Part IV from Cancer Nursing. Principles and Practice (Second edition), Jones and Bartlett Publishers, Boston.

Moorey S, Greer S, 1989, Pyschological therapy for patients with cancer: a new approach, Heinneman Medical Books, Oxford.

Muntz ML, Zur BH 1978, The role of the nurse in patient education. In: Kellogg CJ, Sullivan P (Editors), Current Perspectives in Oncologic Nursing (Volume 2), CV Mosby, St Louis.

Schneider L 1978 Identification of human concerns by cancer patients. In: Kellogg

316

CJ, Sullivan BP (Editors), Current Perspectives in Oncologic Nursing (Volume 2), CV Mosby, St Louis.

Silberfarb PM, Maurer LH, Crouhamel CS 1980a, Psychosocial aspects of neoplastic disease. 1. Functional status of breast cancer patients during different treatment regimens, American Journal of Psychiatry **135**, 960-5.

Silberfarb PM, Philibert D, Levine P 1980b, Psychosocial aspects of neoplastic disease. II. Affective and cognitive effects of chemotherapy in cancer patients, American Journal of Psychiatry **137**, 597-601.

United Kingdom Central Council (UKCC), 1992, Code of Professional Conduct, United Kingdom Central Council for Nursing, Midwifery and Health Visiting, London.

Vachon MLS, Lyall WAL, Freeman SJJ, 1978, Measurement and management of stress in health professionals working with advanced cancer patients, Death Education **1**, 365-75.

CHAPTER 17   CLINICAL TRIALS OF NEW ANTI-CANCER DRUGS

As was shown in Chapter 1, many of the developments in anticancer therapy have arisen as a result of research directed towards rather different objectives (eg. chemical warfare (nitrogen mustard), the biological activity of sponges (cytosine arabinoside) or electric fields and bacteria (cisplatin)). Others have been discovered through a deliberate search for novel compounds exhibiting cytotoxic activity (eg. paclitaxel). Once such substances are identified, their anticancer activities are tested in appropriate animal or cell models. This may involve, for example, mouse tumours or cell lines derived from human tumours (eg. lung, breast and colon). Such preclinical studies are an essential prerequisite to clinical testing of potential anticancer agents (clinical trials).

However, although such *in vitro* testing of drugs can provide an indication of their cytotoxic activity it has a number of limitations that make it difficult to predict clinical activity (Phillips et al, 1990). Many drugs require metabolic activation to be effective (p36-37). Secondly, pharmacokinetic factors cannot easily be evaluated *in vitro*. Host factors related to, for example, the route of drug administration and the rate of distribution and clearance in the tissues will determine how a drug functions in the body (*in vivo*) (Pratt et al, 1994). Similarly, the architecture of a solid tumour is very different from that of cells growing in suspension or in a monolayer culture so that their effects may be very different when administered to man.

The chemical characteristics of a drug (eg. lipid solubility, ionic charge, molecular size) may influence its ability to penetrate a solid tumour. Such effects may mean that a drug that appears to be active against tumour cells in culture may or may not have equivalent activity *in vivo* (Phillips et al, 1990). Various methods have been developed in attempts to circumvent such problems including the transplantation of human tumours into mice (Bennett et al, 1985); a variety of other methods are under development (Pratt et al, 1994).

As developing a new agent takes some 10-12 years, and requires considerable financial investment and a significant amount of work, virtually all such activity occurs within the pharmaceutical industry. Apart from the basic chemistry and pharmacology required to develop

318

a new drug, a significant amount of toxicological data, derived from animal testing, is needed to satisfy the Committee on the Safety of Medicines (CSM) that it is unlikely to cause serious adverse effects in man. Thus, after its antitumour activity has been determined, and sufficient information has been gathered about the formulation, toxicology and dosage schedule, application is made to the CSM for a Clinical Trials Exemption or Clinical Trials Certificate (UK). If the CSM is satisfied that adequate preclinical testing has been carried out permission to test the drug in clinical trials with patients will be granted (Figure 17.1).

Figure 17.1 **Summary of the development and testing of a new anticancer agent**

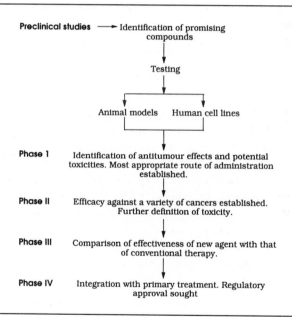

CLINICAL TRIALS

Although preclinical testing provides 'clues' about what can be expected, in terms of toxicity or efficacy, it is only through clinical trials that the effects on humans can be established (Reich, 1982). This involves several phases of study each designed to answer specific clinical questions at different stages in drug development. These are identified as phases I, II, III and IV, each of which has a different purpose and design. The ultimate goal is to improve both the survival and quality of life of cancer patients.

A clinical trial is a carefully and ethically designed study directed towards answering a specific scientific question (Gross, 1986) (eg. to identify toxicities or maximum dosage or enable comparison with existing therapies). Since it is important that the results of such studies are both reproducible and applicable, clinical trials must be carried out under controlled conditions that enable the results to be interpreted with confidence. Thus, a protocol is developed which clarifies the purpose of the study and the procedures to be followed (Table 17.1); in other words, it clearly defines the study and provides guidelines for its conduct. A clear and descriptive protocol that clarifies the research question and methods to be employed will, provided it is strictly followed, result in sound clinical trials (Hubbard and Donehower, 1980).

Table 17.1   Components of a study protocol

1.	Introduction and scientific background	Justifies the need for the study.
2.	Objectives	Outline the hypothesis/hypotheses to be tested and identify the related general observations.
3.	Criteria for patient selection	Type of population to be studied, prior therapy allowed, number of patients and age eligibility. Unsuitable patients also identified.
4.	Study design	Details of the way the sample will be selected and the methods to be followed.
5.	Treatment programme	Range of dosage to be given; route of administration specified.
6.	Procedures to be followed in event of response, no response or toxicity	Details of the way in which toxic effects are to be managed; drugs that may be used to control pain, etc..
7.	Pre-treatment evaluation criteria	May include, for example, detail of disease (extent, stage, etc.), performance status or quality of life.
8.	Evaluation criteria	Details of how the outcome will be evaluated.
9.	Statistical considerations	How data will be 'handled'.
10.	Ethical issues	Procedures for gaining informed consent and what should be done when the patient no longer wishes to participate in the trial.
11.	Record forms	
12.	References	

Phases of clinical trials (Table 17.2)

A *Phase I trial* is the first clinical testing of a new agent in humans. Its purpose is to determine schedules and toxicities. Such trials enable the maximum tolerated dose to be established and the response of tumours to be evaluated *in vivo*. Pharmacological studies may also be conducted to investigate how well the agent is absorbed, the blood levels that can be achieved and how the drug is metabolised or excreted. For this reason, the collection of timed blood samples is common and requires precision by all those involved.

Table 17.2   The phases of clinical trials

Phase I	Designed to:	Define toxicities of a new agent. Determine the maximum tolerated dose. Determine new treatment schedules. Determine appropriate route of administration.
Phase II	Designed to:	Determine extent of antitumour activity at given doses. Further define toxic effects.
Phase III	Designed to:	Enable comparisons with existing therapies and therapeutic regimens.
Phase IV	Designed to:	Provide more information about the drug and determine the principles under which it can be integrated with proven treatment plans.

Phase I studies are usually designed to start at a low dose that, based on toxicological reports, is not expected to produce serious side-effects (Simon, 1982). There are usually 5 dose escalations in a phase I study involving three to five patients at each dose level (Buyse et al, 1984; Gross, 1986). Dose escalation occurs in small increments because side-effects can be anticipated at higher levels (Gross, 1986).

The observation and evaluation of toxic responses is essential to this phase of the clinical trial process. In some studies, the potential toxicities are both unknown and life threatening; anticipated and unanticipated toxicity can occur. For this reason, such studies are carried out only in units where the full spectrum of clinical support is available to maintain the highest level of patient safety as well as to ensure continuity of the data obtained.

Only patients whose disease is unresponsive to current therapies are eligible for entry into a phase I trial; patients for whom other treatment options exist are not eligible. Thus there is often little or no direct benefit to the participants although they may feel satisfied at having contributed to the development of treatment for others. In addition, they are often hopeful that this may lead to prolongation of life for themselves or for others (Grant and Padilla, 1992).

Phase II studies. The focus of phase I studies is the evaluation of drug toxicities and the determination of safe drug dosages that can be tested further in a phase II trial. The purpose here is to determine the effectiveness of the agent against a variety of cancers (Hubbard, 1985). Toxicity data may be augmented and further pharmacological studies may provide additional information.

Specific tumours that have shown some degree of positive response during preclinical or phase I studies are selected for study. Many of the patients will have received prior cancer therapy; their disease may be refractory to such therapy or have progressed. Pre-treatment organ function must be normal and life expectancy must be such that it allows a significant period of observation. If the response to the therapy is to be established, the tumour must be measurable; responses can then be graded as shown in Table 17.3.

Table 17.3   Grading of the response to investigational agents

Complete response	All tumour regresses
Partial response	> 50% regression
Minimal response	< 50% regression

Toxicities may be significant during phase II trials so that close monitoring and observation are needed; responses must be carefully documented. Such studies usually involve 18-30 patients as this number is needed to enable statistical determination of the effectiveness of the agent in specific human tumours (Simon et al, 1985). Similar numbers will be required for each tumour type investigated. On completion of a phase II study, adequate information should be available to justify further study.

The goal of *Phase III trials* is to compare the effectiveness of an experimental drug with conventional treatments of individual diseases (Gross, 1986). This requires a more complex design than either a phase I or phase II study. To prevent bias, patients are randomly assigned to two or more therapeutic regimens so as to compare established therapy with a new agent in terms of its impact on overall survival, disease-free survival and quality of life. In addition, patients are stratified according to a number of variables that may affect the outcome of the study (eg. age, performance status, tumour stage) thus helping to make the study groups comparable so that valid conclusions can be drawn from the findings.

The drug may be given in a number of ways: it may be given alone, combined with standard therapy or substituted for drugs in a combination therapy regime; it may be compared to single or combined drugs that are already known to be effective (Gross 1986). The end-point is to determine whether the new drug demonstrates:

- Greater effectiveness than conventional therapy
- Equivalent or lower toxicity
- Greater potential in combination
- An improvement in survival and/or quality of life.

(Knobf et al, 1984)

As phase III studies require large numbers of patients (to enable comparisons to be made) they are usually multi-centre to enable an adequate sample to be entered into the study in a timely manner. They are, therefore, difficult to plan and to implement; they are also expensive to run. Phase III studies are, however, vital if improvements in cancer therapy are to be achieved. The demands on participants are high; they are required to make frequent visits to the treatment centre so that the effects of therapy can be monitored. Such patients may require considerable support and reassurance. Assuming the findings are satisfactory an application is then made for a Product Licence so that marketing and promotion of the new drug can begin.

Finally, post-marketing, *Phase IV,* studies are used to examine the effects on a much larger sample of patients and to enable a new drug to be integrated into a proven or primary treatment plan; it may be combined with other treatment modalities. Such studies are designed to identify the optimum use of the new treatment. Its value as an adjuvant agent may be explored together with its potential to produce long-term survival or cure. Long-term follow up is necessary to monitor long-term efficacy and the development of late toxicities.

Patients eligible for phase IV studies are usually those with localised disease with significant recurrence after surgery or radiation therapy (Hubbard, 1985).

DRUG REGULATION AND LICENSING

The thalidomide tragedy of the late 1950s led to an epidemic of limb abnormalities (phocomelia) amongst babies born to mothers treated with the drug. Once the nature of the relationship between thalidomide and phocomelia was identified it was withdrawn. The recognition of this reaction, and the ensuing public pressure, was directly responsible for the formation of the UK Committee on the Safety of Drugs (1965) and the resultant legislation concerning all aspects of drug manufacture, testing and marketing. This legislation is enshrined in the UK Medicines Act (1968); most countries now have comparable systems of vetting and legislation.

The Medicines Act is administered by the Medicines Control Agency which, together with Health Ministers, acts as the Licensing Authority. A Product Licence is granted only when the Authority is satisfied as to the safety, quality and efficacy of a new drug. No medicinal products may be sold in the absence of a Product Licence. The Licensing Authority is, in turn, advised by a number of committees, usually referred to as Section 4 committees, the best known of which is the Committee on Safety of Medicines (CSM) that scrutinises all applications for Clinical Trial Certificates and Product Licences for new products (ie. a new drug or a new formulation of an existing drug). It also reviews data related to adverse drug reactions and may, when required, revoke the Product Licence.

The monitoring of drugs for adverse reactions is carried out by the Safety, Efficacy and Adverse Reactions (SEAR) subcommittee which collects and evaluates data through the 'Yellow Card' system. Doctors or dentists observing unusual or serious responses to either an existing (old) drug or any suspected reaction to a new drug are encouraged to complete a card (yellow) and return it to the Medicines Division or one of the Regional Monitoring Centres for evaluation. This enables substantial data to be accumulated; this is regularly analysed to identify associations between adverse events and individual drugs.

Several other monitoring systems have also been suggested and a number are under investigation. Many pharmaceutical companies have established systems of post-marketing surveillance to monitor individual patients receiving new drugs. However, regardless of the system employed, large numbers of patients will need to be given a drug before rare adverse reactions can be detected by any system.

ETHICAL CONCERNS IN CLINICAL TRIALS

Clinical trials have become, and will remain, integral to cancer care; they are central to improvements and/or advances in care and treatment. Consideration must be given to the ethics underpinning research involving human subjects; it is also both morally and legally imperative.

Clearly basic ethical principles should underpin any sound clinical trial and the benefits of that trial should outweigh the potential harm or risk to the patient (Hubbard, 1985). Such principles are based on respect for human dignity, autonomy (self-determination) and truth (veracity). Justice is also important; the researcher must demonstrate fairness in the selection of subjects. There should be no preference in selecting subjects (eg. older versus younger patients) and there should be no implied benefit from being involved in particular studies (for example, prisoners should receive no remission on their sentence for participating in a drug trial). Care must be taken to ensure that there is no preferential advantage to potential subjects.

The general relationship between health care professionals and patients is that the actions of the former should benefit the latter, to *'help, or at least, do no harm'* (Jones, 1923). This is not always the case in clinical trials since, although it is believed that investigational agents will be effective against cancer, it is not until they have been studied in man that this can be confirmed or their toxicities identified. Thus the role of researcher may conflict with that of clinical practitioner. While both roles may 'benefit the sick' the scientific role may project that benefit to some future date while the clinical role seeks to benefit patients now.

The purpose of a clinical trial is to generate knowledge that will ultimately benefit patients but, in the short-term at least, may have, at best, no effect and, at worst, be clearly deleterious to those concerned. Thus involving patients in such studies places great emphasis on the principles of autonomy and informed consent and stresses the need for truth and disclosure of relevant information.

Autonomy
Respect for individuals as persons is expressed by recognition of their autonomy and the right to self-determination which underpin the abilities of individuals to make judgements and decisions for them-selves. This underlies the need for informed consent, the primary goal of which should be to enable individuals to make truly auto-nomous decisions about whether to authorise medical or research interventions (Beauchamp and Childress, 1989).

Informed consent is mandatory in clinical trials; it is both a legal and an ethical requirement. Informed consent comprises three major elements:

- Information
- Voluntariness
- Comprehension

Providing information ensures that the patient is given sufficient detail regarding the nature of the research and the procedures involved. The potential risks and benefits, the objectives of the study and the alternative treatments must be made clear. Comprehension refers to the ability of the individual to understand the information he has been given (see below).

Professionals must take care to ensure that the patient makes his decision voluntarily since the sick are very vulnerable and it is not difficult to 'persuade' them to undergo a particular procedure or treatment. In seeking to obtain consent, the practitioner should consider the principle of non-maleficence (to do no harm) and acknowledge, where appropriate, that the benefits and/or effects of such treatment are not known.

The concept of informed consent is not, however, as straight-forward as it might appear. For example, there is considerable debate as to the meaning of 'informed' and Downie and Calman (1987) have questioned whether it is possible for a lay person to be fully informed and to fully comprehend the information he is given, particularly when he is also ill. A person who suspects, or who knows, that his prognosis is poor may agree to anything and the distinctions between treatment and research may mean little; he may simply feel too vulnerable to refuse. The question then becomes that of whether voluntary consent is truly possible under such circumstances.

However, since the primary function of informed consent is to protect and promote individual autonomy, effective communication between health care professionals and patients should be designed to prevent ignorance from constraining individual choice whether that ignorance is due to lack of information or lack of understanding (comprehension) (Beauchamp and Childress, 1989).

In practical terms, this necessitates that clear and unambiguous information is given and reinforced by written material (Table 17.4). Sufficient time should be allowed for the patient to consider his options and to seek clarification of the information he has been given; he should not be pressurised or coerced into making his decision.

Table 17.4 Information which must be included when gaining informed consent to clinical trials

1.	**Experimental nature of the trial**	A statement making it clear that the study involves research and the purposes of that research.
2.	**Clarification of the nature of participation**	Detail of what is involved (duration, procedures, monitoring, etc.). Circumstances under which participation may be terminated.
3.	**Identification of predictable risks to individuals**	Detail of any anticipated toxicities or clear statement of the uncertainty of deleterious effects. Where appropriate, this should make it clear that the therapy may involve risks to that cannot, at present, be foreseen.
4.	**Identification of any potential benefits of the study**	Detail of any expected benefits to the individual patient or to other patients.
5.	**Disclosure of any appropriate alternative therapies**	A statement of the options available and consideration of their advantages and disadvantages where these are known.
6.	**Assurance of the confidentiality of information related to individual subjects**	Explanation that the data will be aggregated, and individual patients will not be identified.
7.	**Detail of who to contact should problems arise**	The contact should be able to provide support and/or further information when this is required.
8.	**Right to refuse to participate**	The rights of individuals should be stressed. Includes a statement that participation is voluntary and that refusal involves no penalty; the patient will continue to receive care and support from the institution concerned.
9.	**Right to withdraw as study proceeds**	Clarification of the right to withdraw from the trial without penalty to the individual.

Whether an individual patient is capable of making an autonomous decision must also be considered (ie. is he competent to consent?). In this context, competence refers to the ability to comprehend the information that has been given.

In considering the concept of autonomy it is assumed that all patients are mature and rational adults; this is not always the case in health care. For example, the patient may be a dementing older person, a mentally handicapped adult or, perhaps, someone in a coma. Incompetent patients such as these would be unable to give valid informed consent to any medical or nursing procedure.

The process of determining competence is, however, complex and the judgements involved are often difficult. It is necessary to evaluate the ability of the individual not only to 'receive' information but also to remember and to understand it and to use that information in making his decision. This is difficult to achieve. Provision must be made to adapt the way in which information is presented to ensure individual understanding.

The issue of veracity is also important. Beauchamp and Childress (1989) suggest that, in health care, telling the truth is central to enabling a patient to exercise his right to choose whether to accept a particular treatment. In the past it was believed that being truthful with patients may be harmful and that they do not want to hear 'bad news' (Bok, 1978). Beauchamp and Childress (1989), however, point out that such claims set dangerous precedents for paternalistic actions under the guise of respect for autonomy (ie. doctor knows best!). In practice, however, health professionals have both an ethical (moral) and a legal obligation to disclose the information necessary for consent or refusal. This includes two major types of information: that related to the diagnosis and prognosis and that about diagnostic and therapeutic alternatives (including the risks and benefits) (Schoene-Seifert and Childress, 1986) (Table 17.4).

It is generally agreed that competent patients should be given complete information unless they specifically ask not to be informed (Beauchamp and Childress, 1989), whether or not they are included in a clinical trial.

CONCLUSION

It is clear that clinical trials are essential to the continuing development of anticancer therapy. It is equally clear that the development of new drugs and other approaches to treatment is both long and expensive.

The difficulties associated with drug development include many 'unknowns' necessitating consideration of its effects on patients involved in such work and raising many challenges for those involved in their care. Some of these have been highlighted in this chapter emphasising, in particular the ethical principles which are essential components of any research involving human subjects. Every clinician involved must consider both the scientific and human questions raised by such research. It is only by maintaining ethical principles that we can ensure that individual rights are protected.

REFERENCES

Beauchamp TL, Childress JF, 1989, Principles of Biomedical Ethics (Third edition), Oxford University Press, New York.

Bennett JA, Pilon VA, MacDowell RT, 1985, Evaluation of growth and histology of human tumor xenografts implanted under the renal capsule of immuno-competent and immunodeficient mice, Cancer Research **45**, 4963-9.

Bok S, 1978, Lying: Moral Choices in Public and Private Life, Pantheon Books, New York.

Buyse M, Staquet M, Sylvester R, 1984, Cancer Clinical Trial Methods and Practice, Oxford University Press, New York.

Downie RS, Calman KC, 1987, Healthy Respect: Ethics in Health Care, Faber and Faber, London.

Grant M, Padilla GV, 1992, Cancer nursing research. In: Groenwald SL, Frogge MH, Goodman M, Yarbro CH (Editors), Issues and Resources for the Cancer Nurse. Parts VIII and IX from Cancer Nursing: Principles and Practice (Second edition), Jones and Bartlett Publishers, Boston.

Gross J, 1986, Clinical research in cancer chemotherapy, Oncology Nursing Forum **13**(1), 59-65.

Hubbard SM, Donehower MG, 1980, The nurse in a cancer research centre, Seminars in Oncology **7**(1), 9-17.

Hubbard SM, 1985, Principles of Clinical Research In: Johnson BL, Gross J (Editors), Handbook of Oncology Nursing, John Wiley and Sons, New York.

Jones WHS, 1923, Epidemics. In: Jones WHS (Editor), Hippocrates, Harvard University Press, Cambridge, Mass.

Knobf MK, Fisher DS, Welch-McCaffery D, 1984, Cancer Chemotherapy - Treatment and Care (Second edition) GK Hall Medical Publisher, Boston.

Phillips RM, Bibby MC, Double JAI, 1990, A critical appraisal of the predictive value of in vitro chemosensitivity assays, Journal of the National Cancer Institute **82**, 1457-68.

Pratt WB, Ruddon RW, Ensminger WD, Maybaum J, 1994, The Anticancer Drugs (Second edition), Oxford University Press, New York.

Reich SD, 1982, Clinical trials - a review of terms and principles: Part 1, Cancer Nursing **3**(5), 232-3.

Schoene-Seifert B, Childress JF, 1986, How much should the cancer patient know and decide? Ca: A Cancer Journal for Clinicians **36**, 85-94.

Simon RM, 1982, Design and content of clinical trials In: DeVita VT, Hellman S, Rosenberg SA (Editors), Cancer Principles and Practice of Oncology, JB Lippincott Co., Philadelphia.

Simon R, Wittes R, Ellenberg S, 1985, Randomised phase II clinical trials, Cancer Treatment Reports **69**, 1375-81.

GLOSSARY OF TERMS

Acute side-effects: Side-effects occurring during or shortly after administration of anticancer drugs.

Adjuvant therapy: The use of cytotoxic drugs following surgery or radiotherapy to eliminate remaining metastatic cells and reduce the chance of relapse.

Alkaloids: Group of organic substances found in plants that exert pharmacological activity (see vinca alkaloids).

Alkylating agents: Substances that enable substitution of an alkyl group for an active hydrogen atom in an organic compound (eg. DNA).

Alopecia: The absence of hair from skin areas where it is normally present; baldness.

Anaemia: Reduction of the numbers of erythrocytes, quantity of haemoglobin or volume of packed cells in the blood.

Anaphylaxis: Type I hypersensitivity reaction: An exaggerated systemic reaction to a foreign protein or other substance to which an individual has previously been sensitised. Reaction requires immediate treatment to prevent death through respiratory obstruction.

Anorexia: Reduction in or loss of appetite for food.

Anthropometry: The science dealing with measurement of size, weight or proportions of the body.

Antibodies: Proteins produced by the body in response to the introduction of a substance recognised as 'foreign'.

Antiemetic: Pharmacological agent that prevents or alleviates nausea and vomiting.

Antigen: A substance that stimulates the production of antibodies; may be soluble, such as a 'foreign' protein, toxin or drug; or particulate (eg. blood cells, bacteria).

Antihistamine: A drug counteracting the effects of histamine.

Antimetabolite: A substance which, due to its close structural similarity to a normal metabolite, can compete with or substitute for that metabolite disrupting normal physiological or metabolic processes.

Ascites: The effusion and accumulation of serous fluid in the abdominal cavity.

Biological response modifiers: Agents which modify the host's biological response to the presence of tumour cells (eg. lymphokines (such as interleukins) tumour necrosis factor and interferon)

Biotransformation: The series of chemical or biochemical changes that occur to a compound (eg. drug) taken into the body.

Blast cell: Cell at an immature stage of development before the definitive characteristics of that cell have developed.

Blood-brain barrier: Selective barrier between the circulation and the parenchyma of the central nervous system.

Carcinogenic: Capable of causing cancer or contributing to its cause.

Carcinogenesis: The production of cancer.

Cardiac tamponade: Cardiac compression due to the collection of fluid (eg. blood) in the pericardium.

Cardiotoxic: Having a toxic or other deleterious effect on the heart.

Cell cycle: Term used to describe the phases of cell division.

Chemotherapy: The treatment of disease with chemical agents (usually drugs); in the case of cancer therapy refers to cytotoxic drugs.

Colony stimulating factors: Haemopoietic growth factors that, under normal circumstances, act to regulate the proliferation, maturation, regulation and activation of blood cells.

Combination therapy: The administration of a combination of cytotoxic drugs; may be superior to single drug therapy in treating some tumours, optimise tumour destruction and minimise toxic effects. May also circumvent the problem of drug resistance

Cystitis: Condition causing inflammation of the bladder. Characterised by dysuria, frequency/urgency of micturition, often accompanied by stress incontinence and, occasionally, haematuria.

Cytotoxic: Exerting toxic effects upon cells.

Dental caries: Destructive process resulting in decalcification of the tooth enamel; leads to continued destruction of both enamel and dentine and cavitation of the tooth.

Desquamation: Shedding of the epithelial elements, chiefly of the skin, in scales or sheets.

DNA: Deoxyribonucleic acid; genetic material present in the nucleus of all cells; essential for cell replication.

331

Disseminated intravascular coagulation: An acute or chronic condition resulting in widespread formation of small thrombi throughout the microcirculation.

Drug resistance: A reduction in the effectiveness of therapy with successive doses until, eventually, no effect is observed; such effects may severely limit the success of therapy. May be primary (natural or intrinsic) or acquired; represents the combined characteristics of a specific drug, a particular tumour, and a specific host whereby the drug is ineffective in controlling the tumour without excessive toxicity.

Dumping syndrome: Nausea, weakness, sweating, palpitations, syncope often accompanied by a sensation of warmth and, sometimes, diarrhoea occurring after food ingestion when food 'dumped' into duodenum in uncontrolled fashion (eg. after partial gastrectomy).

Dysgeusia: Impaired sense of taste.

Dysphagia: Difficulty in swallowing.

Dyspnoea: Laboured or difficult breathing.

Dysuria: Painful or difficult urination.

Erythema: Redness/flushing of skin due to capillary congestion.

Erythropoeisis: The production of erythrocytes (red blood cells).

Extravasation: A discharge or escape of blood/fluid from a vessel into the surrounding tissue.

Fibrosis: The formation of fibrous tissue.

First-line therapy: Therapy used during the initial treatment of malignant disease and involves use of those drugs known to be effective against a given tumour.

Gastritis: Inflammation of the stomach. Mucosal permeability greatly increased. Characterised by significant burning and discomfort.

Gene amplification: An increase in the synthesis of the gene coding for a particular protein. Affected cells can then synthesise more of that protein

Gene therapy: Insertion of new genetic material into cells; designed to alter their biological behaviour for therapeutic ends.

Granulocytes: Any cell with granules (eg. granular leucocytes).

Growth fraction: The fraction of cells in any tissue that are in the state of active division.

Haematemesis: Vomiting of blood.

High-dose chemotherapy: High doses of chemotherapeutic agents given in attempts to destroy a correspondingly high proportion of the tumour.

Haematocrit: The volume percentage of erythrocytes in whole blood. Also used to describe the procedure or equipment used in its determination.

Haemopoietic tissue: Tissue, such as the bone marrow, in which the formation and development of blood cells takes place.

Haemostasis: The arrest of bleeding either by the physiological processes of vasoconstriction and coagulation or by surgical means. May also describe the interruption of blood flow through any vessel or any anatomical area.

Hepatotoxic: Toxic to the liver.

Hormone: A chemical substance produced in the body which has specific regulatory effects on the activity of certain cells/tissues/organs within the body.

Hormone antagonist: Substance used to oppose (overcome) the effects of a hormone. Used to alter the hormonal environment surrounding a tumour.

Hypercapnia: Abnormal retention of CO_2, with pH <7.35 which produces respiratory acidosis.

Hyperemia: An excess of blood in a part of the body.

Hypersensitivity: Exaggerated response to a foreign agent (eg. protein, drug). Usually involves immunological mechanisms.

Hyperventilation: Abnormally increased pulmonary ventilation resulting in reduced concentration of CO_2 in the bloodstream. If prolonged, leads to respiratory alkalosis. Blood gases will show decreased pCO_2, increased pO_2 and elevated pH (>7.45).

Hypoguesia: Decreased taste sensation.

Hypoventilation: Reduction in amount of air entering the pulmonary alveoli. Blood gases will show elevated pCO_2, decreased pH (<7.35) and decreased pO_2 unless the patient is receiving supplemental O_2 when pO_2 may be satisfactory but CO_2 retention will continue.

Immunocompetence: The ability to mount an immune response following exposure to an antigen or infectious agent.

Immunodeficiency: A deficiency of the immune response due to hypo-activity or decreased numbers of lymphoid cells.

Glossary

Intra-arterial: Into an artery.

Intrathecal therapy: Injection of a drug through the theca of the spinal cord into the subarachnoid space.

Irritant: An agent capable of causing irritation or sensitivity.

Leucocyte: White blood cell.

Leucopoenia: A reduced number of leucocytes in the blood.

Long term side-effects: Side-effects that are manifested at least 7 days after treatment; many are cumulative and may lead to a discontinuation/postponement of therapy or a change in the planned treatment regime.

Mitosis: Cell division.

Monoclonal antibodies: Highly-specific antibodies to selected antigens produced from a single immortalised cell of the immune system.

Mucositis: Generalised inflammation of the mucous membranes.

Multimodal therapy: The integration of more than one antineoplastic therapy into a treatment regime for individual patients is described as multimodal therapy.

Myelosuppression: Inhibition of bone marrow activity resulting in a decreased production of blood cells and platelets.

Myelotoxicity: Cytotoxic destruction of blood cells/bone marrow.

Necrosis: Morphological changes indicative of cell death due to progressive enzymatic degradation. May affect groups of cells or part of an organ.

Neo-adjuvant therapy: Use of chemotherapy to reduce tumour size prior to surgery or radiotherapy when it may lessen the need for mutilative surgery or increase the likelihood of a favourable response to radiotherapy.

Nephritis: Inflammation of kidney; may affect the glomerulus, tubules or interstitial tissues resulting in a focal or diffuse and proliferative disease.

Nephrotoxic: Destructive to kidney cells.

Nutritional assessment: Means of assessing nutritional status by collecting and interpreting data related to nutritional status.

Nutritional status: Extent to which an individual's physiological need for nutrients is met by the food he is (or has been) eating.

Oestrogens: Generic term describing the oestrus-producing hormones (female sex hormones) that, with progesterone, stimulate development of secondary sexual characteristics and repair the endometrium after menstruation. Also important in maintaining nitrogen balance; metabolism of calcium and phosphate; retention of sodium chloride and so sodium and water balance; control of blood proteins and lipids; the vascular and skeletal system, and insulin production and thyroid and adrenal function.

Oocytes: Immature ovum (female reproductive or germ cells).

Palliate: Relieve symptoms.

Palliative care: Care directed towards the relief of distressing symptoms and maintaining the quality of life,

Parasthesiae: Unpleasant sensations of numbness or heaviness; usually affects a limb or limbs.

Petechiae: Tiny haemorrhagic spots due to intradermal or submucosal bleeding.

Pharmacodynamics: The study of the biochemical and physiological effects of drugs and their mechanisms of actions.

Pharmacokinetics: The study of drug action over a period of time, including absorption, distribution, localisation in tissues, biotransformation and excretion.

Photodynamic therapy: Involves the administration of drugs which, once given, require activation by light (usually from a laser). By directing light specifically at the tumour, some degree of selectivity in treatment can be obtained.

Pneumonitis: Inflammation of pulmonary tissue accompanied by a dry, persistent cough, dyspnoea on exertion, weakness and fatigue and, occasionally, pyrexia.

Progesterone: With oestrogen, progesterone is involved in development of secondary female sexual characteristics and in menstruation when its role is to prepare the endometrium to receive the fertilised ovum and enhance its development. Secreted by the corpus luteum, adrenal cortex and placenta it also plays a minor role in sodium and water balance, influences nitrogen balance, breast function and the regulation of body temperature during the menstrual cycle.

Progestational agents: A class of pharmaceutical compounds with effects similar to those of progesterone.

Purpura: Purplish/brownish red discoloration of the skin easily visible through the epidermis due to haemorrhage into the tissues.

Radiotherapy: Treatment of disease by means of ionising radiation.

Recall phenomena: Recall or reactivation of radiation-induced skin reactions following administration of certain cancer chemotherapeutic agents.

RNA: Ribonucleic acid found in the nucleus of all cells. Essential for protein synthesis.

Second-line therapy: Used when a tumour recurs, probably as a result of drug resistance. Employs drugs known to have less activity against the tumour but a response or second remission may still be possible In some cases, third- and even fourth-line therapy may be available.

Selectivity: In pharmacology, refers to the degree to which a dose of a drug produces the desired effect in relation to any adverse effect(s).

Selective toxicity: The ability of a drug to affect only specific cells (eg. tumour cells).

Spermatogonia: Undifferentiated male germ cell; originates in the seminal tubules; each spermatogonium divides to form two spermatocytes.

Staging procedures: Diagnostic tests designed to evaluate the spread of the disease; attempts to define the size of the tumour and the sites of metastases.

Stomatitis: Generalised inflammation of the mucosal lining of the oral mucosa.

Subacute side-effects: Side-effects arising within 3-7 days of therapy.

Superior vena cava syndrome: Compression of the superior vena cava by a mediastinal mass; may be due to a primary tumour or to metastatic deposits, or by a contiguous pulmonary mass which invades the mediastinum and impairs venous drainage

Testosterone: The major androgenic hormone produced by the interstitial cells of the testes. Responsible for the development of secondary sexual characteristics in the male. Also believed to act in protein anabolism; important in maintaining muscle mass and bone tissue.

Thrombocytopoenia: Decrease in the number of circulating platelets.

Teratogenic effects: Effects of agents (eg. drugs) producing malformations in the developing embryo or foetus. Most commonly occur during the first trimester of pregnancy.

Toxin:	Any chemical that can damage the living body.
Toxicity:	Damaging effects exerted by a toxin.
Toxicity testing:	Tests carried out on new drugs, cosmetics, pesticides, etc. to investigate their safety for use in humans. The purpose is to identify potential toxins, carcinogens, teratogens or mutagens. Usually involve tests on animals but may also use human cells grown in culture or live bacteria.
Vesicant:	Agent that produces blistering/ulceration when extravasated into the tissues.
Vinca alkaloids:	Antineoplastic agents derived from vinca rosea (periwinkle).
Xerostomia:	Dryness of the oral cavity due to lack of normal secretions (saliva).

INDEX

Index